The Assassination of Michael Collins

What happened at Béal na mBláth?

by
S M Sigerson

The Assassination of Michael Collins:
What happened at Béal na mBláth?

© 2009, 2013 S M Sigerson
The right of S M Sigerson to be identified as the author
of this work has been asserted.
All rights reserved.

First published October 2013 KDP

July 2015 edition

Cataloguing data
Sigerson, S M
"The Assassination of Michael Collins :
What Happened at Béal na mBláth?"
1. Collins, Michael; 2. Ireland – History - Civil War
3. Ireland – History - War of Independence
4. Criminology – Assassination 5. Title

Cover graphic by C Leighton

Table of Contents

Forward 11
    Why do we need to know? 14
    My distinguished predecessors 17
Part 1: What do we really know? 29
    Chapter 1: Michael Collins 31
        The War of Independence 34
        The Treaty 38
    Chapter 2: The assassination of Michael Collins 45
    Chapter 3 50
        The Free State men's accounts 52
        The anti-Treaty men's accounts 61
        Medical testimony 70
        Witness fragments 71
        Conclusions 80
        Unanswered questions 83
Part 2: A new analysis 85
    Chapter 4: Cabinet counter-revolution? 88
    Chapter 5: The authors of the Civil War and their purposes 94
    Chapter 6 98
    Chapter 7: Why and How did the Civil War start? 107
    Chapter 9: Collins, Griffith and Boland 139
    Chapter 10: The peace negotiations 153
    Chapter 11: The escort 163
    Chapter 12: Dalton 172
    Chapter 13 Lady Lavery & the Churchills 182
    Chapter 14: What did Michael know and when did he know it? 192
    Chapter 15: The usual suspects 203
        Summary: Let us count the ways 209
    Chapter 16: Unanswered questions revisited 212
    Chapter 17: What happened at Béal na mBláth? 225
Part 3: Aftermath, legacies and ramifications 241
    Chapter 18: Aftermath 243
    Chapter 19: What if Collins had lived? 261
    Chapter 20: Revolution: Don't try this at home 279
Epilogue 285
    Afterword: Republicanism and Michael Collins today 288
Appendices 295
    Appendix 1: The Escort 296

Appendix 2:   The Accounts by eye-witnesses...................................298
Appendix 3:   Contradictions and corroborations catalogued 313
Appendix 4:   Peace terms connected to the C-in-C's journey 379
Appendix 5:   People's Rights Association mediation......................381
Appendix 6:   The Myths...384
Appendix 7: 403
  Bibliography 409

To Una and Sinead

Couldn't have done it without you!

The Minister for Finance at his desk during the War of Independence

FORWARD

Why is another book about Michael Collins needed? Why should this one particular aspect of his story form the focus of such a book? In this the author defers to some of her most distinguished predecessors, to let them speak for themselves:

"Undoubtedly Michael Collins has been air-brushed out of the national psyche for seventy-five years. I grew up with a rich lore of family history and virtually total silence outside the family. Certainly there was no mention of him in the history books. There was never a mention of his name in the discussion of national life, except on the occasion of a visit to Béal na mBláth in August. All of that changed in 1996-7."

— Mary Banotti (grand-niece of Michael Collins)

" ... The 1919-1932 period remains relatively neglected and understudied. ... Neglect, denial of access to archives and the slowness of historical scholarship therefore may explain the silences and the relative ignorance about most prominent members of that generation.

"Michael Collins at first sight appears to be the exception. Biographies by Pearas Béaslaí, Frank O'Connor, Rex Taylor, Margery Forester, L O'Bróin, D Ryan and T R Dwyer, among others, point to his attractions as a subject. But the task of the historian is far from over.

... There has been a tendency among writers on the subject of Michael Collins to accept without real question the provenance of certain quotations ... [there has been] over-reliance upon the blind use of secondary texts.

"The events of the War of Independence and the Civil War ... have only recently been deemed suitable for historical study in Irish schools and universities. Popular and professional historians alike were refused access to personal papers and the official State archives until the 1970s and 1980s. The study of 20th century Ireland has really only become academically possible in the 1990s with the introduction of a 30-year rule under which both the National Archives, Bishop Street, and the Military Archives, Cathal

Brugha Barracks, Dublin, now splendidly operate. However, despite [this] there continues to remain great sensitivity about release of certain Civil War records such as those contained in the files of the Military History Bureau. There is no justification for the continuation of this policy of restrictiveness."

- Gabriel Doherty and Dermot Keogh "Michael Collins & Making of the Irish State"

"There is not a shred of evidence that Lloyd George's Troy-dominated government would have moved from the 1914-style Government of Ireland Act of 1920 to the imperfect generosity of the Treaty if they had not been impelled to do so by Michael Collins and his assassins."

- Ronan Fanning "Michael Collins: An Overview"

"It cannot be credibly claimed that Michael Collins has been neglected by ... biographers. ... He has attracted intense biographical attention by Irish standards. More words have probably been written about him than about Eamonn DeValera, more ... than Arthur Griffith. "[Other key figures of the War of Independence have had at best one or two biographies, many none at all.] Nevertheless ... we are in many respects still scratching the surface ... [All this explains why] so much remains to be explained about Collins, despite the number of words lavished on him."

- J J Lee "The Challenge of a Collins Biography

INTRODUCTION

Michael Collins is a man capable of inspiring people all over the world. His struggles, triumphs and tragedies, and those of Ireland, hold unique, invaluable and particularly vivid lessons for every nation.

His mysterious death is a subject which has earned more than one book of its own before this. Yet many questions are still unanswered; or without satisfactory answers. Such investigation as has been made, is greatly flawed. The debate, as it stands, merits more attention. Decades have now passed since the last major publication devoted to it; since the one hundredth anniversary of his birth, in 1990, inaugurated a renaissance in the study of his life. This renaissance has since uncovered a treasure trove of new research and analysis.

Still there are those who disparage such inquiry. Some characterize this as raising bygone ghosts of a past era, needlessly re-hashing dead issues, etc. But the issues surrounding Michael Collins' end are very far from closed.

The 26-county Republic of Ireland, and the 6-county Northern Ireland statelet, directly owe their existence, their institutional structures, and much of their history, to Michael Collins' life and times; to the controversies which culminated in his death; and to the travesties which his death enabled.

It is not true to say that Collins alone won the fight for freedom, but it is true to say that were there no Collins, Ireland would have lost the war. [1]

The inherited power structures of Irish society today, come down to us from that pivotal turning point. As may be seen in the "Forward" to this volume, elements entrenched in national institutions have inhibited the discussion of that era, ever since.

What can we gather from all this, but that something there remains yet to be revealed? Something which is bound to have an impact, even today, if scrutinized. Some hidden truth so potent, that, after ninety years, it has still not reached its "sell-by date." Some powerful incentive for suppressing this discussion remains highly active; so as not to say potentially explosive.

---

1   J Feehan

His surviving family must be admired, for their determination to extinguish old vendettas, in favor of the kind of national unity which was always Collins' own top priority. Still, the fact that his end is considered, in some quarters, too hot to hold, proves that the question is not merely academic, nor who-dunnit entertainment (although it can deteriorate into that.)

A nation which fails to adequately remember salient points of its own history, is like a person with Alzheimer's. And that can be a social disease of a most destructive nature. However important, in pragmatic, political or emotional terms, for countrymen to cease fighting each other over the past, Collins' demise remains an unresolved historical question of paramount importance. One which has by no means yet enjoyed the kind of exhaustive scrutiny which it requires.

> *How long shall they kill our prophets, while we stand aside and look?*
> *- Bob Marley*

Of all the sore subjects which make that history so sensitive, this one remains most tender, at this writing: in an Ireland not so far removed from that generation, as to consider its actions with dispassionate impartiality. [2] At bottom of this there remains a social inhibition, that it is indelicate to praise Collins' role, because to do so might seem to condemn DeValera's. [3] It is considered more polite to avoid observations which may cause pain or resentment; perhaps among those whose relatives lost their lives, for the sake of arguments which may have proved chimerical.

WHY DO WE NEED TO KNOW?

> *Those who cannot remember the past are doomed*
> *to repeat it.*

---

[2] On her accession, President Mary Robinson claimed her electoral success as a national emergence from the post-Civil War period and its legacy.

[3] Eamonn DeValera was a contemporary of Collins: like him, an officer of the 1916 Rising, and a fellow member of the First Dáil. His later conflict with Collins is inextricably connected with the subject of this study: as will be discussed in detail below.

History repeats itself. As do the methods used by those specializing in the elimination of leaders who unite people into a strong force for dignity, justice and self-determination.

> *By means of an old police trick: pretending that his comrades had betrayed him ...* [4]

That "old police trick" has been re-run by British imperialism in Ireland, ever since the Nine Years' War of the 1500s.

There are those who are fond of punctuating speeches with "*If Michael Collins were here today, he would say ...* " Wouldn't it be grand if we had a leader capable of stealing a march on Collins? If we had an army commander whose accomplishments qualified him to pooh-pooh the military skill of the man who engineered Britain's final surrender in the 26 counties? This writer feels secure both that no one has a clue what Michael Collins would say today; and that, whatever he would say, it would be sure to surprise most statesmen and officers right out of their chairs.

It is a national travesty that leading public figures customarily speak of Michael Collins' death by quoting unsubstantiated myths. In the absence of an authoritative inquiry into his demise, such irresponsible comments are passed off as "the official story". It is a grave injustice to the public, indeed to the nation, that negligent misstatements are allowed to stand in the place of scholarship; particularly in questions at the crux of the Republic's very foundation: its early development, national and international issues, which stand unresolved to this day.

We ourselves may not always be the best curators of our own culture. There are many examples in history. The priceless classics of ancient Greece would have been lost to us forever; had not the "infidel" Muslim regime of mediaeval Spain alone preserved them. The book-burning times wiped them out, everywhere else in Europe. The originals of Britain's revered Arthurian cycle likewise succumbed to some ancient regime change: all our earliest versions must be taken from the French. The famous Zapruder footage [5] was never available to the American public in its entirety; until a Middle Eastern entrepreneur published it stateside, in the 1990s: thirty years after President Kennedy's death. When asked to explain how the rock

---

4   D Neligan

5   A private home movie, which is the only film of President Kennedy's assassination.

band Cream outdid American groups, taking the USA by storm, Eric Clapton answered, *"Why, they hadn't listened to any of the proper records!"*

Sometimes it's possible to be "too close" to a conundrum to get a clear view. A key obstruction for his countrymen, when examining Collins' death, is a sense of guilt and shame: entailed in the assumption that his own people were responsible. Whether struggling for or against that belief, it remains a perceptual obstacle.

Remove that assumption; and look at Béal na mBláth in the larger context of similar cases: involving similar types of leaders, at a similar moment in a similar struggle with a similar (if not the very same) foe ... And Collins' death will look very different; with a lot more to say to people about who we are, where we've been and where we could go from here. Because a story like his is for all people, everywhere, in all times.

*   *   *

Tim Pat Coogan introduces his discussion of Béal na mBláth with a lament that "*It is a perversion of Collins' significance to Irish history that the circumstances of his death ... should have come almost to overshadow the significance of his life.*" Yet it is the special importance of his life, which makes it necessary to answer the questions surrounding his death.

That one man's life should change history, is a great thing. That one man's death could change the future is astounding. How and why we lost such a man, is as important as any other question. If there is any perversion, it is the failure to fully account for the nation's terrible loss, of the man they needed most, at the moment he was most needed. It may not be in our power to make another like him. What we might learn from this story, should we ever get such a one again, is how we could better manage to keep him. Certainly that is a lesson worth studying.

It is safe to say that the Director of Intelligence thrived on information, not ignorance. And that this was the key to his success. No one can deny that he was characterized above all by his inquiring mind. Nor was he content to let skeletons in the closet lie unexamined. In serving his country, Collins left no stone unturned.

Has his memory been treated in kind? Has all his sacrifice won him the most basic, common consideration of his demise? If one received news of a near relative's sudden passing, and never inquired what had happened to them, we would consider that shocking.

Anthropologists agree that one of the most basic, universal characteristics of human behavior, is ceremonial disposal of the dead.

Graves or pyres, which bear the signs of such symbolic gestures as flowers, beads or other offerings: this is what distinguishes us from the animal world. This is the point at which we can identify the earliest remains, as belonging to people who were fully human, who had acquired the first rudiments of culture.

Has Collins' demise ever been treated with the kind of ceremonial appropriate to his place in society? Well of course, there was the lying in state, the multitudes who filed by for days, and lined the streets for miles as his cortège passed. In the common people's spontaneous outpouring of grief, nothing was omitted.

Still there was something distinctly lacking in his treatment. Something universally required in the death of any national leader of his stature: an autopsy. [6] A detailed, public inquiry into the circumstances of his death. The continued failure to complete a thorough, scientific and disinterested inquest into his fate is a shameful disservice to his memory, to Ireland and to future generations.

Has the Republic then, in some sense, behaved less than entirely human, entirely civilized, where he is concerned? How did *"the greatest Irishman in a thousand years"* ever come to this?

My distinguished predecessors

Of course this present examination would be impossible without the work of all those accomplished authors who have previously devoted some of their finest efforts to unravelling Michael Collins' fascinating and enigmatic story.

My father used to say, *"No matter what you do, there'll always be someone to stand over your shoulder and say, 'You missed a spot.'"* (Needless to say, this remark was directed at myself: a born critic, even as a child.)

Those very fine biographies can hardly be improved upon, by myself or anyone else; except in navigating the unsolved conundrum of Collins' end: the treacherous shoals on which they have invariably foundered, one and all.

Deep, searing emotional issues have inhibited some of the best Irish writers' discussion of this subject; to say nothing of the suppression of discussion by government, educational and journalistic institutions for decades.

---

[6] The question of whether an autopsy was performed in Collins' case will be discussed herein.

The present author may not be more clever, more experienced nor a better writer than any of those auspicious predecessors; but only enabled by all their hard work, and by the passage of time, which lends greater perspective; so sorely needed in this, and so impossible for those closer to his era.

It might also be considered whether Collins' story has not suffered from the fact that it has been told chiefly by writers armed with either delicate Irish tact or profound English diplomacy: with marvellous sensitivity to the objections which may be raised by a too explicit discussion of some issues.

It could therefore be advantageous at this juncture, that the tale be taken up by an Irish-American: whose native, tactless tendency to blurt out uncomfortable truths, could in this case be an asset. It is hoped that Collins himself, who acknowledged his own difficulty calling a spade anything other than a spade, might not disapprove.

We all know that men are prone to sometimes kill each other over the political domination of their governments. It is the stuff of history. Anyone with sufficient interest to have read thus far, could probably quote a number of cases, from various lands and eras. Yet, understandably, we do not like to think of it being done by our *own* leaders, in our *own* country. This kind of discomfort has hampered American eyesight in the Kennedy assassinations, for the same reasons that Collins' end has remained understudied, for so long.

There are so many loose ends, unanswerable questions, details that don't add up around Béal na mBláth. This is what has reduced otherwise competent biographers to lame conjectures like "carelessness", "drink", even "death wish", entirely unsupported by evidence, and contradicted by everything we know of him up to that fateful day.

Because Béal na mBláth remains an unsolved mystery, because its enigmas have stumped us (and/or been covered up) for so long, we are assailed by the disturbing sensation of reaching an impasse where reason fails us. It is a terrible thing to feel our reason inadequate. Especially in any matter where both our need to know and our emotional investment are so great: such as in the tragic fate of a "founding father." It is in many ways like the loss of a parent. At Béal na mBláth, the failure of reason, and of the social institutions every adult must depend on with all but childlike helplessness, ... throws us back on ... whatever other means we have. We feel reduced to respond with something other than logic.

Biography is considered a scholarly calling. Yet it is not an exact science. This has rendered its practitioners deeply reluctant to concede "*we just have no idea why he was there at that moment, what he was doing there, or exactly what happened."* This is an admission which such authors understandably prefer to avoid at all cost.

> *The necessity of saying something, the perplexity of having nothing to say, and a desire of being witty, are three circumstances which alone are capable of making even the greatest writer ridiculous.*
> - Voltaire

This is another of those great stumbling blocks in the volatile emotional landscape around Béal na mBláth. We must be forgiven for not knowing the answers to those questions. It is not a failing on our part: all of us who examine history are also "in" history, and part of history ourselves. The larger picture of republican revolutions in world history is very much a work in progress. We, the natives of modern Western democracies are the living products of that political maelstrom: the ending of which has yet to be written. What John Stuart Mill called *the great modern social and spiritual transition.*[7] In this greater ongoing process, Ireland is indubitably a success story, not a failure.

> *I may not get there with you. But we, as a people, are going to make it to the Promised Land.*
> - Martin Luther King (on the eve of his assassination)

The leaders of great revolutionary struggles often do not live to see the fulfilment of their own handiwork. That is an occupational hazard. One which they all accept at the very outset. One which Collins, judging from his own words on the subject, was thoroughly prepared for every day.

All great leaders of this kind take on a very old system: an ancient imperialist war and political machine, oiled by centuries' experience in putting down popular revolutions. And in eliminating great popular leaders.

Collective guilt complex in his demise has distorted our view of it. It is because we blame ourselves, that we have been willing to blame *him*: even when to do so defies logic, and contradicts everything we know of the man.

---

[7] The debate is over: Statistics show that modern democracies, governed on principles of universal human / civil rights, the rule of law and separation of powers, are the most successful form of government. Such republics tend to be more prosperous and more stable than autocracies. Countries where the public has a powerful voice in decision-making are dramatically less likely to go to war, or to deteriorate into anarchy. Such stability fosters more flourishing trade, health, industry, learning and generally enhanced cultural and economic development, over longer sustained periods.

In this also, the public is more sinned against than sinning. In every crime, disinformation about what really happened is a key agenda of the perpetrators. In Collins' case, the nature and source of disinformation is one of our best leads out of the labyrinth.

Yet, in scholarly research, questions are frequently more important than answers. We must have the former before any of the latter are possible. In that context, simply identifying the question can be a "discovery" of great moment. When we can set aside the exigencies of personal prestige, to admit how little we know, it may become instantly clear that the conundrum in question is ... quintessentially Michael Collins himself all over.

The reason we don't know why he was in that particular spot and what he was doing there is perfectly logical, and staring us in the face all along (as answers do.) It is simply because, at the time, *he did not intend for anyone to know*. And so they don't. To this day.

"*The Shooting of Michael Collins: Murder or Accident?*"

> *At the outset I would like to make it clear that this chapter does not set out to prove that Collins was murdered, but it does show that he could have been murdered, and it raises a few important, embarrassing and unanswered questions.*
>
> *- J Feehan*

It speaks volumes (so to speak), that the depths of this mystery have never been penetrated in the course of any major full-length biography: because it really requires a separate book of its own. Among all previous studies, John Feehan's [8] is of course in a class by itself. It has made the greatest contribution to posterity, on the particular subject of the great man's end.

Feehan for the first, and heretofore only time, placed before the public a complete compendium of all the existing evidence to date. His work is not a stew of selected ingredients; not merely his own redaction of stories based on anecdotes based on rumours. He re-printed the original statements of each and every eye-witness, for readers to examine for

---

[8] Those familiar with M. Ryan's "*The Day Michael Collins Was Shot*" are aware that, unlike Feehan's book, it is less a catalogue of all known facts and their origin, than the presentation of that author's own summary. While recognizant of Ms Ryan's valuable original research therein, this present work will also be regrettably obliged to refute some of her conclusions.

themselves. He dissected the folk tale and conventional wisdom, tracing every element to its original source; and laid it out for the public's scrutiny.

He was also able to publish, for the first time, statements from some of the last surviving witnesses, whose testimony had never before been recorded. Working as he did in the 1970s and 80s, we are very fortunate indeed to have much which he alone salvaged from permanent oblivion.

Organizing the existing evidence according to the various theories which it supports, Feehan gave the public its first opportunity for a clear idea of exactly what information we have about Collins' death, where it comes from, and how reliable it is. Which, in the final analysis, was found to be precious little indeed; its sources frequently conflicting and highly questionable.

It would be impossible for anyone approaching the subject after Feehan not to quote him frequently; unless they were to entirely duplicate his work themselves. No one would be in a position to do that, because he was the last one to interview many participants who are now gone forever.

Thankfully, we can draw on his work with confidence in his own highly critical treatment of the material. His sources are largely drawn from existing records which are public; as well as records which should be public, soon will be public, etc. At the same time, as he observed in his Introduction,

> *In the grey misty area of possible political murder, ... killers do not write memos to be put on file for the benefit of scholars, nor do secret service men carry placards announcing their profession ... Quite a few spoke more freely and more openly than normal because they knew that I would not reveal any of my sources without permission.*

In a case of this kind, it is understandable that some who were willing to speak to Feehan would not allow their names to be published. Yet despite such inherently mysterious elements of this murder mystery, he maintained strict standards of reportage. He consistently disclosed as much about his informants as he was at liberty to. When something was hearsay, he said so. When there is quotable evidence on a certain point, but he found cause to doubt that evidence, he explained why. Wherever witnesses contradicted themselves, exaggerated, or spoke to events of which they had no direct knowledge, he pointed this out. Although not without his own opinions, he was as far from having "an axe to grind" as anyone could be; who also cares enough to approach this difficult subject at all.

In this way he was able to air, in a responsible manner, important allegations which have never been proved, but which need to be considered and discussed. For the same reason, in those passages where we are dependent on his summary of interviews, with witnesses who are not named and may never be, readers feel confidence in his fidelity to detail and abhorrence for inaccuracy, which he demonstrates throughout.

Therefore, it is reasonable to rely on him, where we have only his own record of important testimony, which he took in person, and which exists nowhere else. His summary of statements from a majority of the five ambushers is one such example, which is extremely valuable.

Feehan's timing was flawless, in that he captured so much important testimony, just before many protagonists took their secrets to the cemetery. However, in 1981 he was largely a voice crying in the wilderness: a pre-cursor to the great re-opening of Collins' story which the 1990s would bring.

TP Coogan (a later biographer, discussed below) often relied on Feehan, and drew upon his work. Yet in the same breath he could be dismissive of Feehan's most grave observations, labelling them in a pejorative way as "conspiracy theories." A number of crucial questions, raised by Feehan, were merely waved aside by Coogan, without satisfactory answers.

In a case of this kind, it is not acceptable to trivialize serious unresolved issues, simply because you can't answer them, or because they don't fit into your favored hypothesis. Generally, this writer has found Feehan to be more even-handed than Coogan; and also more critical, both of the evidence, and of his own perceptions.

This present volume is intended neither to take the place of Feehan's work, nor to stand entirely in its shadow: but hoping to carry on what he began, with the benefit of all that's been published, researched and revealed in the decades since his landmark study first appeared.

> *Having finished the work I now freely admit I have only touched the tip of the iceberg. I know there is far more to be said but I could not say it because I failed to find sufficient proof ... So this book then is no more than an opening of windows, a letting in of some fresh air ... I hope it may help to inspire those who have useful and informative documents in their possession to make them available. Michael Collins deserves better than that his memory should be left clouded in shabby mystery.*

He closed his volume with a persuasive demand for an official inquest at last: with the full benefit of all that modern forensic science could now glean from an examination of Collins' remains. This author whole-heartedly seconds that motion.

Tim Pat Coogan's "Michael Collins"

Tim Pat Coogan's landmark 1990 biography remains, at this writing, head and shoulders above the others. It stands alone in being an authoritative compendium of all previous work on Collins' life. Coogan was uniquely qualified indeed to undertake such a project. In his capacity as a journalist, he had interviewed, over decades, practically every surviving major participant from the War of Independence and Civil War. His biography is the product of vast, minute original research, combined with numerous personal contacts, through that writer's own family members, who had themselves taken part in these conflicts.

Yet Coogan is living proof that even the best efforts of the best writers on Michael Collins stumble when they reach Béal na mBláth. And that this loss of footing is directly connected to their Irishness, and to inescapable personal connection with the tragedy.

Well-known journalists like Mr. Coogan sometimes have the happiness to become successful in other genres as well. Indeed, most of the greatest authors in recent centuries, got their start in periodicals. And / but ... a career in journalism requires a certain combination of both intrepidity and circumspection. Whatever else it takes, survival in that field calls for a kind of congeniality to the conventional wisdom and the status quo. As discussed above, these assets may actually become liabilities, in exploring this particular territory.

It must be allowed that Mr. Coogan left something out which his readers would require, in order to judge his work accurately. He makes only a few enigmatic references to the deep impression made on him by his father Eamonn Coogan, who was active in the War of Independence. What he fails to mention is that the senior Mr. Coogan served as a deputy commissioner in the post-Civil War government headed by WT Cosgrave (a statesman not entirely unconnected with this inquiry; who will be discussed later.) [9]

---

9   Coogan cannot be absolved of an agenda to "wash the corpse" of the Cosgrave government. Albeit this may be more discernible to Collins aficionados than to the general reader; it no less impacts his perspective. It should also not be overlooked that

Coogan himself got his start as a protégé of the Irish Press, the organ of the DeValera family, [10] with whom he has had a particular personal relationship. This in itself must necessarily heighten his sensitivity to considerations about discomfort in that quarter, which public comment about Collins' end may cause.

In perusing his brilliant study of Collins' life, this writer senses that Coogan unconsciously strove to convince himself that he was objective; to convince himself that he was even capable of being truly objective. In doing so, he unconsciously persuades his readers that he is objective. When actually he is in every way subject to precisely the type of emotional burden described above, in dealing with the life, and particularly with the death of Collins.

Still his treatment of the Collins-DeValera conflict demonstrates the best intent to record it with detail and fairness. Subsequent writers are deeply indebted to him for his sterling research, and painstaking examination of that controversy. He may indeed have accomplished all the traffic would bear, at that writing. And, as stated in his own preface, he was addressing his book to the two relatively small islands of Ireland and England, where he himself lives.

In his chapter on Béal na mBláth ("*The Mouth of Flowers*") Coogan promises to "*make it clear once and for all how he came to be killed.*" He follows this with a scoffing reference to "*theorists*" who are dissatisfied about certain unanswered questions. However, we are not much more enlightened at the end of Coogan's chapter, than by any other biographers' version.

Coogan is an accomplished researcher, and brought to light a wealth of information about Collins, not previously available to the public. However, his fine scholarship is occasionally marred by his own eagerness to draw lines where there are none, if it supports his own "theory." If a particular piece of information was unearthed by himself personally, he

---

Eamonn Coogan, as a Fine Gael TD, reportedly favoured Ireland's remaining a part of the British Commonwealth.

[10] Considerable controversy has been raised in recent years concerning allegations that Eamonn DeValera absconded with millions in donations, gathered during his American fund-raising tours for the Irish independence movement; and that this was the bankroll which started his successful career in newspaper publishing. The Irish Press' formidable, direct influence over public discussion and publishing in general, certainly went far to support proliferation of the DeValera version of Irish history. Of that publishing empire, Mr. Coogan was a product.

sometimes seems keen to vaunt that bit as the end-all, be-all answer to the mystery. [11] Yet, especially in his chapter on Collins' death, he shows a shocking refusal to "connect the dots" in more obvious ways.

This also may be a symptom of the field of professional journalism. Perhaps a strategy for survival in that sphere may read like: "Do great research; give detailed reports; but, upon your life, do not connect the dots!" I'm afraid we will at times be obliged to take Mr. Coogan to task on some points.

At the same time, the mighty labour of such a detailed, full-scale biography, necessarily precludes the possibility of an exhaustive examination of any one particular day, however important. For all these reasons, despite the awe-inspiring stature of Coogan's work, this author feels confident of adding something to his treatment, on that particular subject.

Neil Jordan's feature film "Michael Collins"

Another tendency of biographers is simply to say *"There are questions [about Béal na mBláth] which are still not cleared up"* and leave it at that. This was in a sense repeated by Neil Jordan's brilliant 1996 feature film. That work is a compact jewel of film-making: which, all filmmakers know, is not exactly the same as telling the whole story in literal detail. Yet while getting this bio-pic so far right, he seemed strangely to make no effort to accurately portray either the topography of Béal na mBláth, the location of the ambushers, their numbers, etc: information which was readily available. Being a native of Ireland himself, wasn't he well aware that this scene would be picked to pieces by every Collins aficionado in the land?

Did he make a decision to include enough suggestions, from all the different hypotheses combined, to let each viewer decide, or fail to decide, what happened, according to their own lights? This is a technique popular among contemporary dramatists. Shortly after its release, this author had a chance to discuss the film at a meeting of Irish language students. Each one in the room had come away from Jordan's movie with a different idea of what they *thought* the film *said* had happened. In this sense, Jordan perfectly reproduced the controversy which surrounds Collins' death. Was it the director's intention to leave viewers as confused as the world remains to this day? If so, his film was a complete success.

* * *

---

11   See footnote in section below "*The assassination of Sir Henry Wilson*" re: Coogan's unusual analysis.

Had he survived to write his memoirs, Michael Collins may have explained much about this period, from the safe distance of say, the 1970s; as did a number of his contemporaries. That chance to tell his own story is one of the great national treasures, lost to posterity; targeted by his assassins, and sacrificed by him in the service of his country.

This places us under an obligation to exert all our resources to tell it for him, with all the justice and detail which we can muster, at this writing.

What I here make public has, after a long and scrupulous inquiry, seemed to me evidently true, and not unuseful to be known ... Whether it be so or no, I am content the reader should impartially examine.

- George Berkeley

PART 1

WHAT DO WE REALLY KNOW?

Chapter 1

Michael Collins

The following is a minimalist sketch, intended to make this volume accessible both to Collins enthusiasts and to readers who are hearing his story for the first time. The author heartily recommends those with interest to enjoy one of the fine complete biographies, by such authors as T P Coogan, P Béaslaí, Frank O'Connor, R Taylor or Margery Forester.

> *He believed and hoped and ardently loved his hope and belief. He was selfless and had a nobility of mind. A simplicity of aim and a genius for method, allied with whole-hearted and indeed joyous enthusiasm, were the distinguishing qualities of the dead Commander-in-Chief; a brilliant quality of thought and action ... He loved Ireland not in theory but in practice. He was a man of the people and for the people, yet a born governor and wise leader of men ...* [12]

Michael Collins was the youngest son of a farmer, born in the west of the County of Cork, Ireland, in 1890. The Collins were relatively prosperous, as poor farmers go: his father held 90 acres, which his grandfather had in turn also cultivated. Some say that the farm (known as "Woodfield") had been held by them for seven generations. His family had a long background of staunch republican sympathies, and connections stretching back to the Fenian movement, to Wolfe Tone and to the 1798 Rebellion. His maternal grandmother was born a McCarthy: a clan of great prominence in the ancient annals of Ireland. She had vivid memories of the Great Famine of the 1840s. [13] Arthur Griffith's pioneering periodical, *The*

---

[12] M F McHugh, "*The Free State*" (periodical) 30 August 1922

[13] It was a McCarthy who was responsible for adding a famous Irish-derived word to the English language. During the 16th century, Queen Elizabeth I pursued a war-like campaign to force Ireland's indigenous rulers into vassalage to the British crown. In this context, she corresponded with the McCarthy of Blarney Castle, with numerous demands for his submission. However, he persisted in neither explicitly submitting nor refusing. As she listened to the reading out of yet another of his equivocating replies, she exclaimed in exasperation, "*This is all Blarney!*" (according to the English custom of calling a nobleman by the name of his domain, rather than by his surname.) Hence the name came to mean "*charming and flattering speech, which is intended to deceive without offending.*"

United Irishman, was received at home; and always perused with great interest by young Michael, who was an avid reader.

His family was also well-educated. Both his parents had mastered more than two languages, such as French, in addition to Irish and English. They were familiar with Greek and Latin. His father, who got his learning at a "hedge-school", when teaching Irish Catholics was still outlawed, was very keen on mathematics. Although his mother Mary Anne (who was much younger) did attend school, much of their study was pursued independently at home.

Their children attended the National Schools (which the later 19th century saw widely established); but had little opportunity for formal third level education. Most of Michael's seven siblings, like himself, were groomed for careers away from the farm, which only the eldest son would retain. Several of his brothers and sisters ultimately followed callings in the civil service, the church, journalism or policing.

As a child, Michael's patriotism attracted the notice of his elders. A teacher at school reported the boy's vivid interest in "*anything pertaining to the welfare of his country.*" In a dramatic deathbed statement, his father admonished the family to "*Mind that boy: he will do great things for Ireland.*"

While still quite young, he won a local wrestling championship; and often challenged wrestlers older and larger than himself, as a pastime. In his teens, Michael distinguished himself as a contributing sports writer for a local newspaper operated by a brother-in-law. In 1906, shortly before his sixteenth birthday, he took a job as a clerk in London, where an elder sister was already established.

Michael assuaged a keen homesickness for Ireland, by way of enthusiastic participation in clubs and sports of London's Irish community. In the Gaelic Athletics League there, he began to take a leadership role among his young peers, playing for the local Geraldines Hurling Club and acting as their secretary

He took advantage of opportunities for study offered by access to fine metropolitan libraries; and undertook to develop a knowledge of the world and a political philosophy. For the civil service examination, he took night classes at King's College in accountancy, taxation, commercial law and economics.

He pursued a successful career in banking there for nine years. Yet he found that "a glass ceiling" for the Irish frustrated his hopes for advancement. In the meantime, he and his friends frequented the London theatre, where compatriot George Bernard Shaw was all the rage. To improve his public speaking, he is said to have studied elocution and voice projection with theatrical professionals. His later career strongly suggests that these were not the only dramatic skills which he acquired. It is clear from his correspondence that in time he fancied himself a qualified critic and armchair casting director.

Continuing to write, he presented papers at political societies which supported Irish independence. He became known as "*a Wolfe Tone republican*" in his political outlook. In 1909, sponsored by the famous athlete Sam McGuire, he joined the Irish Republican Brotherhood (IRB), a clandestine body organizing the struggle for independence. By 1914 he was secretary to the London and Southeastern district. In April 1914 he, along with his cousin and close friend Sean Hurley, enlisted with the London Brigade of the Irish Volunteers. When the Easter Rebellion of 1916 was in its planning stages, he and a number of his boyhood friends from home all volunteered together.

This brought him to Dublin, where he worked for an accounting firm and acted as financial advisor to Count Plunkett. His spare time was devoted to drilling with the Volunteers and preparing armaments for the Rising. So began his twin specialties in finance and the military.

During the Easter Rising, he served as staff Captain and aide-de-camp to Joseph Plunkett, at the Rising's headquarters in the General Post Office building (the "GPO".) There he and his comrades underwent a crucible of fire. Hundreds of vastly outnumbered and out-gunned republicans held out against thousands of British troops, under brutal artillery bombardment, for a week. There, and in the Rising's aftermath, he saw many of his mentors and closest friends lose their lives.

Following the Rising he was imprisoned with over a thousand others. The execution of the Rising's leaders thrust young men like himself to the fore. As he boarded the boat with his fellow prisoners, he was already discussing plans for "*next time.*" While still interned at the prison camp, he was instrumental in re-organizing the survivors: first in a campaign of non-cooperation with prison authorities. [14] Later planning the underground campaign, which would lead ultimately to Britain's capitulation in 1921.

> *[Collins] had a mobile, expressive face, quick wit and a quick temper. He was gay, boisterous, optimistic, bubbling with dynamic energy.*

---

14   The Frongach internees' protests included refusal to answer roll call, to wear prison clothes, to do demeaning menial service for British soldiers, etc.; not unlike republican prisoners in Northern Ireland of the late 20th century.

That would not have made a man of him of course, but behind the dashing exterior there was a keen intelligence, great strength of character, steadiness, determination, and vision. He had the qualities I thought we needed most in our leaders. [15]

Released in December 1916, Michael was employed first by Count Plunkett as private secretary, then as executive for the Irish National Aid Fund, a charitable organization which provided support for the families of republican prisoners. He carried on as an active campaigner for independence, speaking at public meetings, opposing the Irish Parliamentary Party and advocating an open break with Westminster.

THE WAR OF INDEPENDENCE

The War of Independence was a life-and-death struggle. For three hundred years, the British [16] *had sent fire, sword and famine through Ireland, in a never-ending campaign to reduce it to the status of an English colony. Massacres and pogroms were a frequent feature of this policy, and starvation a genocidal tactic, visited on the Gaelic-speaking majority. In the 1840s, half the population perished or emigrated. But still, Ireland tenaciously held to its cultural identity (one of the oldest in Europe.) Each generation asserted in arms their claim to national independence. By the dawn of the 20th century, Britain found it politic to claim that they ruled with the consent of the silenced Irish public; but continued to depend on violent suppression. In 1890, the year of Michael's birth, there was famine. Those who took a public stand for independence still took their life in their hands.*

In 1918, the republican Sinn Fein party swept the polls. Michael stood as a candidate and was elected, along with many of his associates.

---

15   F O'Donoghue

16   In the course of this study, it is necessary to refer frequently to Collins' opponent in the War of Independence: this was the British Empire. The term "British" is used herein virtually exclusively to denote that imperialist establishment of the early 20th century: including its formidable arsenal of military and political institutions; as well as the interest groups and strategists who decided and oversaw the Empire's agenda in Ireland

The term "British", as used herein, and discussions about "British agenda, policy," etc., therefore refers strictly to those institutions. *It is not intended as a generalization regarding people who populate the United Kingdom, then or now (whose political outlook and views regarding Ireland may differ widely.)*

These new deputies abstained from the London parliament and formed the First Dáil: Ireland's national legislature. [17]

> *We should get justice for Ireland today ... That is, we'll get nothing but what we take from them by hard fighting.*
> — A Trollope [18]

On the day of the Dáil's first meeting, a guerrilla military campaign commenced. A bold ambush led by Dan Breen at Solohedbeg seized a shipment of gelignite (an explosive for military use.) This marked the start of the War of Independence 1919 - 1921.

Although this military action was not approved in advance by the Dáil (which had not convened before it took place) Michael implicitly accepted responsibility on behalf of the IRB, of which he was now a member of the Supreme Council. Following some debate, he won the cooperation of Arthur Griffith. Soon after, Dáil support for the military campaign became official.

Griffith was the ideological founder of Ireland's 20th century independence movement. He had founded Cumann na hGaedheal in 1900 and in 1905, he authored the first Sinn Fein Manifesto. After centuries of continual battle against British imperialism, it was his political strategies which brought nationalism into a new, ultimately victorious phase.

---

[17] "TD" is the abbreviation for the Irish term "*Teachta Dála*", which means deputy to the Dáil, a member of the Irish national legislature: equivalent to a Member of Parliament (MP) in Britain, or Congressman in the USA.

[18] The famous English novelist, after many discouraging early failures, found his first success in Ireland: as a civil servant for the Post Office. He lived and worked there through the years of the Great Famine. Later a candidate for Parliament, he was keen on Irish issues and sympathetic to reform. Several of his novels were set in Ireland. This quotation is from *The Kellys and the O'Kellys,* which opens with a vivid description of the trial of Daniel O'Connell at Four Courts. In *Phineas Finn*, his titular hero ruins his Parliamentary career by voting for political change in Ireland. Trollope's last, unfinished novel, entitled *The Landleaguers*, was also on Irish themes.

When Arthur Griffith first put forward his programme for the overthrow of British rule in Ireland, the Sinn Fein organisation, of which he was the founder and inspirer, consisted of a handful of young teachers, poets and journalists, scarce known outside their own circle and utterly without political influence; and so they remained for twelve years longer. In 1921 these same men had made themselves the de facto rulers of the greater part of Ireland, and were in a position to dictate terms to the ministers of a power which had just been victorious in a great war. History records no more amazing overturn. [19]

Griffith had a great genius for uniting Ireland's internal divisions, toward the common goal of independence. Key to that ultimate victory was the cooperation of various factions, who favored different means to that end. The fulcrum of this movement was an understanding between the "physical force" strategists of the IRB, and "non-violent" Sinn Fein; the latter serving as an umbrella group, bringing together all the differing approaches and concerns among Ireland's nationalists (i.e. those who favored independence from Britain.)

"Never before had the country been so ... determined to bring the struggle to final victory."[20]

All that was needed now was leadership equal to the military campaign required. Which Michael, more than any other single individual, provided. Throughout the War of Independence, Michael's was the military genius which made this conflict different from the many rebellions which had gone before. He was the leading organizer who galvanized the nation into an efficient underground revolutionary force, capable of carrying on a sustained campaign, which hit the British establishment where it hurt: with the cooperation of thousands of men, women and youth, in all walks of life, throughout the country; as well as in the Irish diaspora overseas.

From his experience in the Rebellion, Collins correctly concluded that an open fight against the superior British forces did not have a

---

19   A Phillips

20   L Deasy

> *chance, so he prepared for an underground war. A man of daemonic energy and ability, he first decided on wiping out the British intelligence system, which many times in the past had beaten the Irish.*[21]

As president of the IRB he was, according to that organization's by-laws, *de facto* president of Ireland in their eyes. It was the IRB which constituted the bulk of fighting men, including many veterans of 1916. With Michael as chief strategist, these became the "flying columns," brigades and squads who fought the war (also known later as the Irish Republican Army or IRA.) Michael frequently took part in such raids personally.

> *It was guerrilla warfare characterised by attacks on British convoys, ambushes and the capturing of police barracks. The police, who were the eyes and ears of Dublin Castle, were forced to live in the larger towns, thus leaving the countryside virtually in the hands of the IRA. He struck a severe blow also at the British administration by ordering the burning of more than one hundred Income Tax Offices.*[22]

Combined with his cabinet portfolios as Minister for Finance and Director of Intelligence, he planned, organized and oversaw a mind-boggling array of day-to-day operations, from the importation of arms and ammunition, to the financing of the provisional government [23] through a national loan scheme, to arranging support for Volunteers on the run and their families. Most crucially, he orchestrated a complex network of intelligence, which went to the heart of the British administration in Ireland, and crippled its system of violent domination.

---

21 D Neligan

22 J Feehan

23 From the time of the formation of the First Dáil in 1919, a cabinet of its ministers functioned in the capacity of a "provisional government". The Dáil government-in-hiding is generally referred to herein as the provisional government (small case.) The Provisional Government (of 1922) is capitalized for identification. Likewise, "Cabinet", when capitalized herein, refers specifically to the Cabinet of the Free State government of 1922.

> *The outstanding figure in all GHQ [24] was Michael Collins, Director of Intelligence. This man was, without a shadow of a doubt, the effective driving force and backbone at GHQ of all armed action of the nation. A tireless, ruthless, dominating man of great capacities, he worked like a Trojan in innumerable capacities to defeat the enemy. ... No man, inside Ireland or outside it, contributed more than Michael Collins to the fight for Irish independence.* [25]

Swiftly following announcements by the British government that they had the Irish rebels beaten and "*by the throat,*" Collins pulled a startling coup. On "Bloody Sunday," November 1920, his men wiped out most of Britain's top secret service men in Dublin in a single day. A week later there was an equally devastating defeat to British troops by the Third Cork Brigade at Kilmichael. The London government began to seek talks. In the summer of 1921, a truce was declared.

THE TREATY

> *All the streams - economic, political, spiritual, cultural and militant, - met together in the struggle of 1916 - 1921, which has ended in a peace in which the Treaty of Limerick is wiped out by the departure of the British armed forces, and the establishment of an Irish Army in its place ... The Union is wiped out by the establishment of a free native parliament, which will be erected on a Constitution expressing the will of the Irish people ... With the termination of the Union goes national enslavement if we will it. Complete national freedom is ours and nobody but ourselves can prevent us achieving it.*
>
> *- Michael Collins 1922*

The peace negotiations, and the Treaty which they produced, are the events which led directly to Michael Collins' death.

They cannot be described in any nutshell summary. The individuals and meetings involved were manifold, and constitute a tangled skein of

---

24 "GHQ": in the War of Independence this was the national General Headquarters of the Irish Volunteers / independence movement. Located in Dublin.

25 Tom Barry, 3rd Cork Brigade, memoirs "*Guerilla Days in Ireland*"; and Barry's speech at the 1965 unveiling of the Michael Collins monument at Sam's Cross.

events. Some aspects of the negotiations were shrouded in secrecy, which has never been penetrated to this day. What can be said with certainty, is that the Treaty process remains an unsolved conundrum of history, which has never yet been entirely unravelled; and will not be resolved here.

A number of meetings took place, involving a cast of players on both sides, between late 1920, when the first efforts at negotiation began, and the signing of the Treaty in London in December 1921. First-hand accounts exist as to what took place in some of the meetings. In others, what passed was never recorded or discussed outside closed doors, and will never be known to posterity, the participants having taken the story to their graves long ago.

What is necessary to understand for the purposes of this study is: It has been a pattern in Irish history that British diplomats, notorious for Machiavellian cunning, have repeatedly snatched victory in the eleventh hour from victorious Irish armies. *"England, would again, we feared, win the war having lost the battle."* [26] Notorious examples include the Treaty of Limerick of 1688, the dissolution of the Irish parliament and 1803 Act of Union; more recently the Home Rule Bill whose provisions for increased Irish autonomy, though passed into law before 1914, were never implemented.

The general public in Ireland had a high consciousness of this. Such searing lessons of history were burned into the mind of the average Irish child, at their mother's knee. Those most active in the War of Independence were particularly well versed in these issues. Betrayal by Irish leaders, who sold out for British perks, had been part of these patterns of the past. *"Naturally [the Truce] was received with enthusiasm, particularly by the civil population who had suffered so much in the years of strain and terror. Yet, for us who were fighting in the field, it was viewed with some suspicion."* [27]

The first negotiations, which secured the Truce and set the stage for peace talks, were held in secret. These were largely handled by Eamonn DeValera. In correspondence between DeValera and Lloyd George, preliminary language was thrashed out, and a basis for talks agreed. During one of the first trips to London by Irish negotiators, these two met privately for a lengthy discussion, one-on-one. No details of that conversation have ever been revealed.

---

26   L Deasy

27   Ibid.

The Truce was then announced in the newspapers. That is when it was first heard of by the Volunteers and fighting men, whose efforts, at the risk of their lives, had brought all this about. They were not consulted in any way regarding the preliminary terms agreed. This in itself first gave rise to bad feelings and suspicions, which would prove disastrous later on.

DeValera had been a commander in the 1916 rising. He held the title of President of the Republic. However, he spent most of the 1919 - 1921 conflict touring the United States as a fundraiser. His return to Ireland coincided with the commencement of peace feelers from the British. On his arrival, he had expressed considerable pique at Michael Collins' now prominent position, and explicitly expressed an intention to eclipse him. Soon after, he became embroiled in differences with Collins as to how the military campaign should proceed. [28]

"It must be emphasized that at no time had the Dáil or the IRA asked for a conference or a truce." [29] Until 1921, Michael Collins was characterized by his open hostility to compromise with the British. Up to then, he consistently argued against any settlement which fell short of absolute independence. During the first overtures from the British, Michael's own stated position was:

> *There will be no compromise and no negotiations with any British Government until Ireland is recognized as an independent republic ... The same effort that would get us Dominion Home Rule will get us a republic.*[30]

However, being in government is different from being a revolutionary. The Dáil, of which he was only one member, decided to accept the truce and commence negotiations with London, *although a 32-county republic was not among the terms on offer*. [31]

---

[28] It was on DeValera's insistence that the Dublin Brigade abandoned their guerilla tactics for an open battle with superior British forces at the Customs House. The Brigade was decimated. (This was Collins' flagship unit.)

[29] L Deasy

[30] Collins to syndicated columnist CW Ackerman, August 1920

[31] The Truce came into effect only after the King's official opening of the new mini-parliament in Belfast, created to govern a northern statelet in Ulster (as set out in Westminster's Government of Ireland Act 1920.)

Then came the question of choosing a delegation to travel to London and officially negotiate and sign an actual treaty. DeValera was indisputably Ireland's most able negotiator. Lloyd George's own sincerest form of flattery was his comment to the press that negotiating with DeValera was *"like trying to lift mercury with a fork."*

It was therefore extraordinary that DeValera himself (along with Cathal Brugha and Austin Stack) refused to form part of this delegation; but insisted that Michael Collins must go instead. (All three had been recently distinguished by their hostility to Collins.)[32] Collins himself was vehemently opposed to this plan. *"I'm a soldier, not a politician,"* he declared, pointing out that others, such as DeValera or Arthur Griffith, had far more suitable background and experience.

> *Having left Collins at home while he teased out from Lloyd George what was on offer, he now, having found out, began to steer Collins towards the negotiating table in Downing Street. The man who had felt his place was in America during most of the Tan war felt he must stay in Dublin during the coming diplomatic offensive in London.*[33] ... *He knew that any agreement brought back would be a compromise. He admitted to the Dáil when announcing his decision to stay in Dublin that "he knew fairly well from his experience over in London how far it was possible to get the British Government to go."* [34]

The cabinet split on this issue. Collins, Griffith and Cosgrave voted against DeValera's plan to remain in Dublin while Collins took off his soldier hat, to play diplomat in London. Brugha, Stack and Robert Barton [35] supported the plan and DeValera's was the deciding vote.

---

32 Cathal Brugha was a hero of the 1916 Rising, and titular Minister of Defense. He acted chiefly in an executive role 1919-1921, Collins running the struggle on the ground. While Collins had great affection and respect for Brugha, their clashes over methods and practices were not infrequent. Stack had initially been sponsored by Collins, who once organized the former's escape from prison. However, Collins was later frustrated by Stack's inefficiency. Stack often suffered from Collins' famous plain-speaking on this account; such as *"Austin, your department is a **'ing joke."*

33 T P Coogan

34 Dáil Eireann, private sessions 14 Sept 1921

35 Robert Barton was a Sinn Fein TD who came from a family of the "Anglo Ascendancy"

Another point DeValera particularly demanded was that the members of the delegation must be officially designated as "plenipotentiaries," and no other title. He demanded that they must be entirely authorized in advance to negotiate and conclude a binding agreement on behalf of the Irish nation. During Dáil discussion, DeValera threatened to resign over this. "Plenipotentiaries" they were duly designated.

After much soul-searching and all-night discussions with his closest advisors, Collins bowed to the Dáil's decision. Under vigorous protest, he accepted his nomination in the spirit of "*a soldier following orders.*" In his personal correspondence, he expressed grave misgivings about the mission. Yet at the same time, he defended this decision to his own friends, who counselled him not to go: "*Let them make a scapegoat or whatever they like of me. Someone must go.*"

The delegation of which he was the head left Collins with the undisputed lion's share of responsibility. Arthur Griffith was the only other member with comparable experience and credibility.

During the negotiations, the Irish delegates found communication with the provisional government (that is to say, with DeValera) difficult and strained. On one weekend journey for conferral with Dáil colleagues, an exasperated Collins wrote, "*I don't know whether we're being instructed or confused.*" At the moment of truth, DeValera and associates in Dublin were presented with details of the negotiations, and asked point blank by Collins, whether to sign it or not. He could not get a straight answer. (" ... *like lifting mercury with a fork.*")

After lengthy sessions over several weeks, progress came to an impasse. Following exhaustive wrangling, the Treaty was signed. [36] Ireland would be governed by the Dáil in Dublin. Britain would withdraw its army and government personnel entirely from Irish soil in most of Ireland's thirty-two counties. Ireland would be constituted "The Irish Free State", but would remain part of the "British Commonwealth", on a basis similar to Canada. TDs would be required to take an oath of allegiance to the Crown. Between two and four counties in Ulster would remain separate: with a

---

landlord class. He was cousin to Erskine Childers, another TD from the same background. Childers and WT Cosgrave are discussed in detail in Part 3.

36 Historians have repeated the assertion that the Treaty was signed in response to British threats of all-out military invasion. However, during the Dáil debates on the Treaty, Collins refuted this: "*It has been said we signed under the threat of 'immediate and terrible war.' That is untrue. It was Barton who first made that charge ... But [when] challenged to quote the exact words used ... admitted that it had never been voiced in words.*"

border to be drawn up later by a Border Commission, according to the wishes of a majority in each northeastern county. Collins wrote to a friend,

> When you have sweated, toiled, had mad dreams, hopeless nightmares, you find yourself in London's streets, cold and dank in the night air. Think - what have I got for Ireland? Something which she has wanted these past seven hundred years. Will anyone be satisfied with the bargain? Will anyone? I tell you this - early this morning I signed my own death warrant. I thought at the time how odd, how ridiculous, - a bullet might just as well have done the job five years ago.

On arrival back in Ireland, the delegates found that controversy about the Treaty already raged. DeValera, the original author of most of the compromises in it, immediately led the charge to denounce Collins and other delegates as turncoats who had betrayed the Republic. Partition, and the oath of allegiance to the Crown, were key objections.

The Dáil debated whether to ratify the Treaty. In one of our greatest losses to this history, our record of those debates is but imperfect. [37] Accounts are of a fragmentary or anecdotal nature. However, the Dáil did vote to ratify, by a narrow margin. DeValera then split the provisional government in two by walking out of the Dáil, calling on those who had voted against the Treaty to follow him. A large number did so.

In the subsequent months, painstaking efforts were made to restore unity. The Dáil, the IRB, and Army representatives met continually, striving to find some means to proceed without armed conflict. [38]

Following such negotiations, the Collins-DeValera Pact was formed: agreeing to place the issues before the public, in the form of elections for a new Dáil. This is referred to as the Pact Elections. Candidates declared themselves as either pro-Treaty or anti-Treaty. According to the Pact, no matter who won a majority, both sides would cooperate in this new (Third) Dáil.

---

37 "*The Treaty Debates*", published by Dáil Eireann, is an important compilation of all known records. "*Michael Collins: In His Own Words*" edited by F Costello, provides rich details of Collins' viewpoint in that discussion.

38 In his biography of Liam Lynch "*No Other Law*", Florrie O'Donoghue provides one of the most authoritative chronicles of this process: detailing meetings which took place between January and June 1922, those who attended, and the outcome of each discussion.

Meanwhile, a small garrison of anti-Treaty fighters, including Cathal Brugha, Rory O'Connor and other prominent heroes of 1916 and the War of Independence, occupied the Four Courts (the center of the island's courts system, and national archives); as well as a number of public buildings. Collins, ordered by his colleagues in the Free State government to dislodge the rebels, promised to do so; but for weeks, he avoided firing on comrades. He ordered that the anti-Treaty occupants be forced out by cutting off food and water to the buildings.

As electioneering got under way, anti-Treaty units engaged in a violent disruption campaign. At outdoor speeches given by pro-Treaty candidates, shots were fired over the audience' heads, in apparent attempts to incite dangerous stampedes. It was in the context of this campaign that DeValera made his infamous tirades, calling on his hearers to "*wade through rivers of Irish blood, and the blood of members of the Irish government.*"

Voters elected a majority of pro-Treaty candidates. DeValera remained recalcitrant, and continued to incite those opposed to the Treaty to take up arms against the new Dublin government.

While insisting that they were loyal to the Dáil, anti-Treaty leaders protested against the formation of the new Cabinet (the Free State Provisional Government.) The Dáil could not meet, due to threats to assassinate its members. Travel was rendered dangerous by civil violence, destruction of bridges, street battles, etc. Some anti-Treaty propaganda published vicious personal smears against Collins, portraying him as a cynical, bloodthirsty traitor, obsessed with self-aggrandizement at any cost, who was planning a military dictatorship.

Meanwhile Collins, although notoriously plain-speaking in private, avoided extreme language against former comrades in public. (For a sample of his arguments, see Appendix 7 below, "*Free State or Chaos*" a tract published for the Pact Elections.)

In the midst of all this turmoil, Collins, with the assistance of a legal team, set to work writing a constitution for the new Free State government. This he completed and saw ratified by the Dail. Although a new version was revised in the 1930s, the Republic of Ireland's Constitution today remains largely his work.

Collins sought to make provisions in the new constitution which would overcome republican objections, allowing them to lay down their arms in good conscience. However, under the Treaty, London had to approve the Free State's new constitution. In the teeth of compelling arguments that compromises were necessary to avoid civil war, Downing Street stubbornly blocked such provisions.

At this juncture came the assassination of Sir Henry Wilson.[39] An ultimatum was then issued by Winston Churchill, the British Cabinet's Colonial Secretary, threatening that the British would consider the Treaty broken, and re-invade the country, unless Four Courts were wrested from the rebels without further delay. The building was bombarded by Free State troops, using British-supplied artillery. This marked the official beginning of the Civil War.

---

[39] Precisely who was responsible for the inopportune slaying of Wilson has never quite been established. See chapter below.

CHAPTER 2

THE ASSASSINATION OF MICHAEL COLLINS

Collins, following the Dáil walk-out, for months carried the burden of several additional ministerial portfolios, abandoned by colleagues who'd left the fledgling government. But with the onset of civil war, he set these aside to assume direction of the armed forces as Commander in Chief ("C-in-C".) [40] Collins' generalship was proved once again. In a series of brilliant, decisive manoeuvres, the Free State troops made swift progress against the anti-Treaty insurgents. Within weeks, only a few pockets of resistance remained.

In August, Collins was criss-crossing the country, inspecting Free State garrisons, especially in areas recently recovered from anti-Treaty units. On Sunday August 20, he set out from his quarters at Portobello Barracks in Dublin, officially on such an inspection of County Cork.

Several of his associates advised him not to go. Some pleaded with him outright, (one so strenuously as to nearly come to blows with him over it.[41]) They feared that the danger to him was too great, in the unsettled state of the country. However, despite a head cold and feeling rather under the weather, he proved determined to make this trip at all cost.

There are many unanswered questions surrounding this journey from its beginning. Enigmatic and contradictory factors suggest that there was more to this trip than met the eye. His reasons for going, conditions in Cork at the time, what he was doing there, whether he was involved in secret peace negotiations, and a number of other issues have never been completely elucidated. There were several anomalies concerning the crew who formed his escort, questions as to why they were chosen, and by whom.

To commence our examination of events at Béal na mBláth, let us look at the few basic facts which are undisputed:

---

40 In correspondence around the time of his death, Michael Collins was frequently referred to as "the C-in-C": an abbreviation of his official title. In an effort to minimize redundancy (so difficult in a book of this kind) he is referred to below alternately as "Collins" or "the C-in-C."

41 Joe Sweeny

HIS LAST JOURNEY

At about 6AM on the morning of 22 August, Collins and his convoy set out from Cork City. The itinerary was to lead through Macroom, from there south to Bandon, and then west to Clonakilty and Skibbereen. They made several stops on a circuitous route before turning back toward the city.

He travelled in the back of a straight-eight Leyland touring car, with canvas roof folded back. With him in the touring car were two drivers in the front and one officer next to him in the back.

He was escorted by a full military convoy, consisting of a Crossley tender lorry commanded by an officer with eight soldiers, a driver and two machine gun operators (for one Lewis machine gun); an armoured car with one driver, one co-driver and one machine gunner (for one Vickers machine gun on the turret); and one motorcycle scout. (See "The Escort", Appendix 1) There is some question as to whether one or more additional officers rode in or outside the armoured car, and when they may have joined the convoy.

They first stopped at the Free State Army barracks in Macroom (which they had visited the previous evening as well.) They are said to have picked up a guide in Macroom, leaving there at about 8AM. The rural area they travelled through was served only by winding, narrow country roads. The one they took passed through Béal na mBláth, a small village, which today is marked by one shop and a pub. There they stopped "*to ask directions.*" The man they spoke to was an anti-Treaty sentry.

From there they proceeded to Bandon, a medium-sized town, where Collins had a long, private meeting with General Sean Hales. He and Hales had been friends since their youth in West Cork. Immediately after this meeting with Collins, Hales left for Cork City, regarding the organization of an important meeting of neutral representatives, on the subject of ending the war, to take place later that same night.

The convoy went on to Clonakilty, where they lunched. Collins' boyhood home was not far from the Clonakilty / Skibbereen road. His party made the detour to Sam's Cross, the village near Woodfield, where a family reunion was awaiting him. While the convoy took a break there, he absented himself for about half an hour, for a private meeting with persons unknown, who may have been contacts to anti-Treaty units. His next stops were Rosscarbery and then Skibbereen.

At Rosscarbery a rather strange thing happened. The officer in command of the Free State troops there, Captain Sean McCarthy, told Collins that there were a number of ex-British army soldiers in his unit and he had reason to believe that they planned to shoot him (Collins). He had, however, no proof, but as a precaution he took their rifles from them and confined them to barracks. He warned Collins to be careful as some of the ex-British army men were not to be trusted. Collins listened to all this in silence and made no comment on it. [42]

Collins' parting words to Capt McCarthy were, "*I'm going to end this bloody war as quickly as possible.*"

At Skibbereen, he carried out his official inspection and discussed matters with the commanding officers there. At about 5PM they left and headed for Bandon, where the convoy had tea, and there was another meeting with Free State officers at that town.

The convoy left Bandon, ostensibly to return to Cork City. They took the same route they had come by that morning, via Crookstown, a village near the main Cork City road. This was Collins' third trip toward Macroom in twenty-four hours. Around 7PM, for the second time in twelve hours, they approached Béal na mBláth Cross: an isolated junction where a major meeting of anti-Treaty leaders was planned for that evening.

About a half mile before this village, the convoy came into a stretch of road which was flanked by steep hills on both sides. There were five anti-Treaty men on a hill overlooking the road. They were all that remained of an ambush party that was now dismantling their equipment and preparing to leave. A dray cart blocked the road, impeding the convoy's progress. It came to a stop. Shots were exchanged: how many, by whom, is open to debate. Michael Collins was the only casualty: he died almost instantly from a massive head wound.

The anti-Treaty men retreated and were not pursued. The convoy proceeded into Crookstown and returned to Cork City. This journey of about 20 miles took them an inordinately long time. They arrived at the Imperial Hotel [43] in Cork City about 1:30AM.

---

42   J Feehan

43   The Imperial Hotel was serving as temporary headquarters of the Free State Army, since Victoria Barracks (now Michael Collins Barracks) had been burned by the retreating anti-Treaty troops.

THE AMBUSH SITE

The ambush began as the convoy proceeded north, returning from southwest County Cork (Skiberreen and Bandon), to connect with the main Killarney - Cork City road, near Crookstown (about three miles past Béal na mBláth.)

The forward end of the convoy (the motorcycle and Crossley tender) was northern-most, toward the village of Béal na mBláth Cross. The rear vehicles (the armoured car and touring car) were at the southern end, toward Bandon.

To the west of the road can be seen the lane which runs parallel to it. The ambushers were positioned along this lane. It lets into the road, at the northern end of a long "S" curve. This is where members of the ambush party ran to get off the road, and up onto the parallel lane, when they learned that the convoy was coming.

Most witnesses from the convoy tend to speak of the directions as follows:

- "ahead," meaning to the north, further along the road before them;

- "to the left" meaning to the west, which was on the left hand of those standing in the road and facing north toward Béal na mBláth cross;

- "up the road" or "back" meaning to the south, back on the road in the direction they had come from.

- The touring car driver, Private Corry, is the exception: he describes events in relation to his own position, after he got out of the car and *faced* the western hillside where the ambushers were. Thus, he describes the tender and cyclist (on the road to the north) as being on *his right*; the hill and ambushers as being in front of him, and the armoured car (on the road to the south) as being on *his left*.

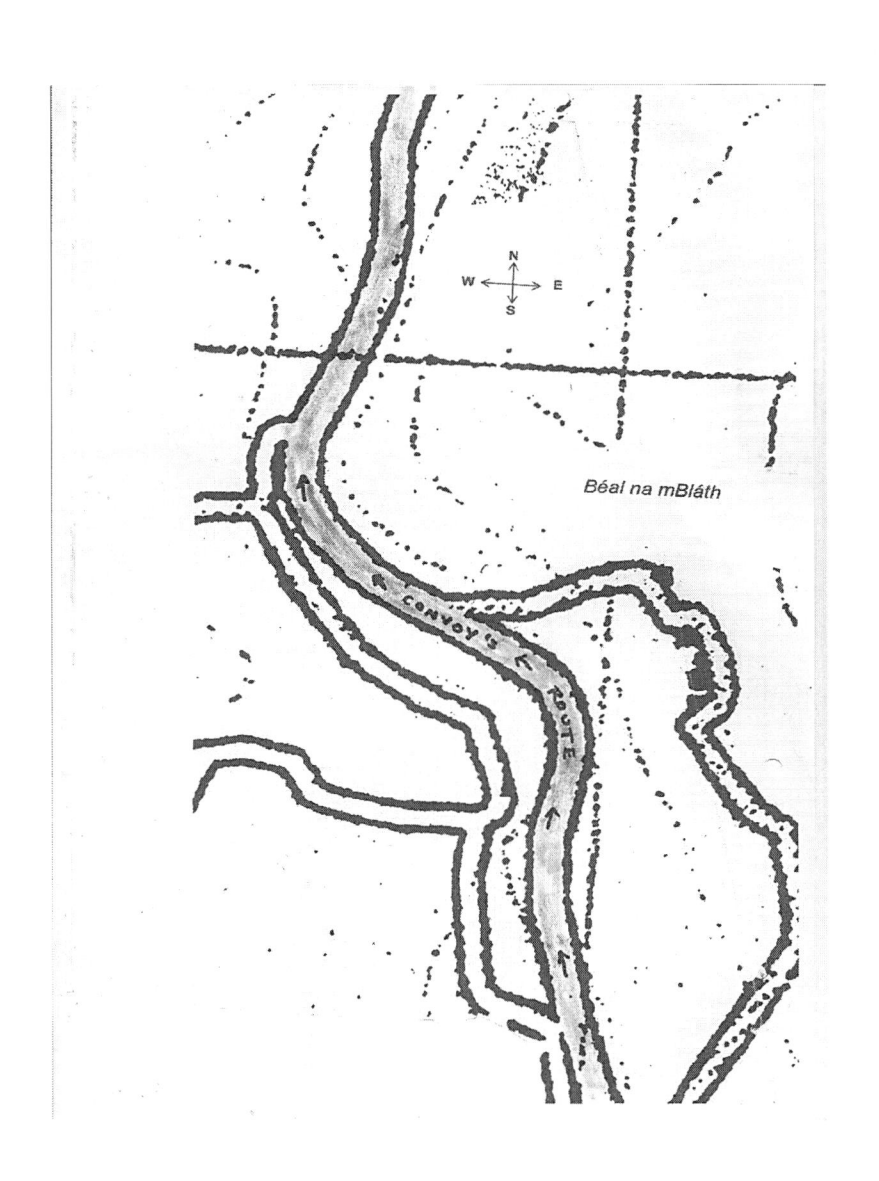

Béal na mBláth

CHAPTER 3

WHAT DOES THE EYE WITNESS TESTIMONY TELL US?

Well, here you have a fair collection of statements from eyewitnesses, each contradicting the other on vital and significant points, and none of which can be accepted as a completely reliable version. [44]

There are a number of reasons why Collins' death continues to be viewed by many as suspicious and unsolved. The most obvious is the eye-witness testimony: no two witnesses' statements are alike. Each and every one contradicts the other.

The witnesses disagree about how the shooting started; about whether the convoy came under heavy, prolonged attack by a large body of men with machine guns, or by only a few ambushers, with hand guns and rifles, who quickly dispersed and withdrew. They contradict each other about where they were, where were the vehicles, where was Collins. According to his bodyguards, while under fire, they rather lost track of where was the invaluable C-in-C, whose preservation was their whole purpose for being there. Yet these accounts are all we have to go on, as to how the great man came to be shot.

THE DEVIL IS IN THE DETAIL

Each witness describes roughly the same events set out in the previous section. At a glance, they seem straightforward enough. Each one is told from a different perspective: and it is the conflicting small points, some seemingly insignificant, which speak volumes about the men who made these statements, and about the events they witnessed. Upon close scrutiny, and careful comparison one with the other, their stories go awry. Let us examine these comparisons, telling details, and their meaning

WHERE DO THE WITNESS ACCOUNTS COME FROM?

What's worse than the testimony, is that we can't even be sure that the accounts we have are an accurate record of what the witnesses said. Because, contrary to government policy at the time, there was never any official inquest. None of the members of the escort were every formally questioned by authorities.

---

44   J Feehan

We have a few newsclippings, written by reporters who were not there (ostensibly the motorcyclist, Smith's account.) We have a somewhat romanticized re-telling published a year after the fact: attributed to the one person whose own actions are most seriously to be questioned (Dalton). Predictably, according to this version, its author, the effective head bodyguard, was in no way at fault. Then we have several reports which might be placed in a minor-characters-have-their-say category; published by biographers, years or even decades later. [45]

This does not seem like very much to have to show on the demise of "the most important man in Ireland" at the time. Why are our sources so beggarly?

The first and most significant clue which the eye-witness testimony gives us, is that this was a situation requiring a thorough, public, official examination. The very next, is the complete absence of the kind of records which such investigation would have bequeathed to posterity. The lack thereof speaks volumes; and raises the key question: why?

As shall be seen repeatedly throughout, the obscurity which continues to surround events at Béal na mBláth is chiefly due to the contemporary Dublin government's conspicuous and inexcusable failure, neglect and refusal to scrutinize the suspicious death of its own leading member, with the same official care accorded at the time to common foot soldiers.

Still it is not that alone which has kept Collins' death an unsolved mystery to this day. The next most obvious problem is that the witness statements are by no means of a nature to be taken as irreproachable gospel. To begin with, those present at his death fall into two categories: members of the Free State convoy, and the anti-Treaty ambushers. No one else was there.

These are the participants, whose actions are in question. Therefore, none of them can be called either entirely impartial nor disinterested. This is one of the first factors which any competent investigator would naturally have descried.

Some observations we can make with confidence at this point:

1) Not all these inconsistencies can be attributed to the lapse of time, differences of perspective, or even carelessness. That is to say:

---

[45] The full original account of each witness, where available, may be found in Appendix 2; while Appendix 3 provides an itemized break-down of what each witness said, cross-referencing contradictions, corroborations, and inconsistencies, between them.

2) They cannot all be telling the truth, Which is to say:

3) Some of them were *lying*.

These answers, as answers often do, raise questions:

4) Which one(s) lied?

5) Why did they lie?

6) Did some have more reason to lie than others?

7) If two mutually negating points are both corroborated by more than one witness, how can we tell which is correct? (i.e. The convoy came under machine gun fire; the convoy did not come under machine gun fire.)

8) Can we decipher the answers to these questions from the information before us?

If we compare all the testimony's various contradictions and corroborations, in light of the possible interests and pressures at work in each case, we may separate out some chaff: Which witnesses have adhered only to facts which were within their own knowledge? Which ones report events which happened when they were not present? Does the statement demonstrate that they were "coached" as to what to say? Did some deponents have reason to lie? Did some others have less reason? Do they stray so far from verifiable facts as to invalidate their testimony altogether?

In this way we may begin to sort out a few points as probably true; and others as much less so.

THE FREE STATE MEN'S ACCOUNTS

The first two Free State accounts were issued to the press, from army sources: that is, from Lieut. Smith and Major General Dalton. Soldiers in time of war would not normally talk to the press about details of their engagements or other military business, unless with the express permission of their commanders. Such permission was therefore implicit in the appearance of these accounts, and no others, following the ambush.

It is alleged that Dalton submitted an official report to the Free State Government; which largely follows the lines of that attributed to him in the press. (Ostensibly this was Pearas Beaslal's source.)

Neither the army nor any other official source ever contradicted, expanded, added to or subtracted from Smith's or Dalton's published accounts. Thus silently allowing them to stand has sent a further powerful message of approval. *Qui tacit consenti*: who remains
 silent, consents.

Some key inconsistencies in statements from members of the C-in-C's failed bodyguard, concern the number of their assailants and the amount of fire they came under. In some instances their statements on these points seem to have been then inflated by contemporary press. Put together, these important official sources presented the public with a version of events at Béal na mBláth which was patently false. What was the nature of that misrepresentation? What can it tell us about its possible motive?

Everyone in the Free State bodyguard accompanying the C-in-C was there under orders to secure his personal safety. Their entire failure to successfully fulfil those orders, places a grave onus on them to explain what happened.

If a company of twenty-five professional soldiers is sent out to escort an important dignitary, and they bring that dignitary back dead, it would not behove them to report that they had been assailed by a force of five men, with vastly inferior arms.

Had these facts been widely known at the time, there is no telling what the consequences might have been. Physical danger to those who had been present, the possibility of revenge attacks on their persons, might have been only the beginning. Such considerations were particularly compelling, in the extremely volatile situation of the Civil War. Under these circumstances, they would have a personal interest in presenting a version of events which is self-exonerating.

There was, then, in Collins' own party, a natural motive for exaggerating the number of the ambushers; as well as the amount, intensity, and duration of the fire they came under. A careful comparison of the corroborations and contradictions among the various accounts suggests that such exaggerations were made by Dalton, his alleged appointees Smith, Corry, McPeak and by J O'Connell.

Lieut. Smith (motorcyclist) account

This was the first published version of the ambush. It appeared in newspapers two days after Collins' death. It had wide circulation and currency at the time; and, along with Dalton's statement, came to be accepted as a kind of "official story".

It is particularly significant, therefore, that Lieut. Smith's report deviates in many points, so widely from practically all other eye-witness testimony.

Lieut. Smith was ostensibly the only person on either side, other than the C-in-C, to be injured. This is significant, because the fact of Collins' being the one and only casualty is in itself highly suspicious. The existence of such wounds to Smith is supported by Dalton, but contradicted by other relevant statements. Several give evidence about Collins' body being taken to hospital; but no one says Lieut Smith went to hospital.

Smith asserts that the C-in-C ordered the touring car to stop: something which he was not, by his own account, near enough to have heard himself. This means he was not speaking directly from his own experience, but, at best, was influenced by others with whom he discussed it, prior to giving his story. At worst, that he was "coached": told what to say. In either case, it impairs the value of his evidence.

The missing vehicles

Smith says that his handlebar was struck by the same fire which injured his hand. Dalton said that the touring car's windscreen was shattered by a *"fierce fusillade of machine gun fire."* McPeak said that the armoured car showed visible damage where it was struck by bullets. Smith says that both the motorcycle and the touring car were abandoned on the way back to Cork City. McPeak himself shortly afterward was responsible for the theft, disappearance and dismantling of the armoured car.

These vehicles were evidence. What happened to them? Their condition on arrival in Cork would have been worth a thousand words from witnesses. The Free State Army in 1922 was hardly in a position to carelessly discard expensive major equipment of this kind.

Maj Genl Dalton's account

Published exactly one year after the ambush, this was the second version of events from a Free State official to appear after Collins' death. This account also has tended to be accepted as unexamined gospel.[46] It has

---

46 Accepted everywhere, that is, except among those who were personally close enough to the events, to find these statements doubtful through their own direct knowledge; or to know of the existence of other versions.

been reproduced in many books about Collins, and continues to be quoted by prominent commentators today.

In an incident resulting in fatality, any prolonged delay in making a report, calls for explanation. There are several such unexplained delays in connection with Collins' death. One of the most glaring is the date of this statement: why was it not published until a full year after the fact?

It is a fine piece of dramatic narrative. It may be appropriate to ask whether it is not a little too fine. It's positively poetic: certainly hitting all the right notes to touch the heartstrings of the Irish reading public of the time. However, it bears little resemblance to any other example of Dalton's usually terse, unsentimental communication style. All in all, it strongly suggests the hand of a professional "ghost writer".

It cannot be over-emphasized that, as the officer most responsible for Collins' safety on his journey through West Cork, Dalton is a person very much to be scrutinized. It would be entirely unacceptable to any military investigative body, and should be to the public and to all thoughtful commentators, to merely accept the account given by himself and his picked men. Feehan, a retired officer himself, assessed Dalton's version as "*incomplete*" and observed that "*any self-respecting commanding officer would have sent it back to him.*"

This narrative which describes Dalton, kneeling beside the wounded C-in-C, shedding tears and saying prayers, struggling to bandage his head, as bullets "*ripped the ground*" around him, is certainly touching indeed. Just imagine, that Dalton's own name was among the last words on Collins' lips. Picture the mighty fallen hero, feebly calling out, among all the people in Ireland, to Dalton alone, in his hour of death. If Collins himself placed that kind of trust in him, certainly there can be no reason for us to question Dalton's performance.

There is nothing unbelievable in the action described: it all sounds entirely natural and human. However, *other witnesses do not support all this*. Not even those who corroborate Dalton on the largest number of his most dubious other points.

Dalton and his account require special attention; which will be continued in his own section, in Part 2 below.

Private Corry's (touring car driver) account

Corry's account was said by Rex Taylor to have come to him as a "*detailed and signed*" document. J Feehan says that this written statement had "*circulated privately*" for a number of years before Taylor published it.

This is to say that neither of these chroniclers interviewed Corry in person, nor could they absolutely vouch for the statement's provenance.

Corry's is the only account we have, other than Dalton's, as to what happened around the outside of the armoured car, before the end of the ambush. As Feehan pointed out, it's interesting that it differs so widely from Dalton's: they were sitting in the same car, just inches away from each other.

As opposed to Dalton's *"fierce fusillade,"* Corry reports the first fire on the convoy as a single, isolated shot (tallying closer to anti-Treaty accounts.) While supporting Dalton that the convoy came under "*heavy fire*", he does not report any machine gun fire from the ambushers.

Corry's description of Dalton's actions and demeanor forms a highly interesting counterpoint to the "*moving narrative*" attributed to Dalton. The cool and laconic words reported by Corry ("*The General's finished.*") ring more true with Dalton's usual communication style in every other available example. It includes nothing about tears, prayers or bandages.

Private John O'Connell's account

Rex Taylor, in his 1958 biography of Collins, explains how J O'Connell wrote to him and met with him, in response to Taylor's articles about Béal na mBláth, which had appeared in a newspaper. Taylor double-checked documentation which O'Connell showed him (army papers, birth certificate, and other documents) and was convinced
that O'Connell had formed part of the convoy.

O'Connell's statements fall into three categories. First, a few are supported by either Dalton or Corry: Only Corry corroborates that Collins was firing from a standing position and then fell. Only Dalton corroborates that there was machine gun fire from the ambushers.

Then there are the usual three items corroborated by all relevant accounts: the dray cart barricade, Collins' head wound, and dusk falling as the ambush ended.

All the rest of J O'Connell's statements are unanimously contradicted by all other relevant accounts. Several of these are truly unique: he is the only one who says that the touring car was at the head of the convoy, when all others agree it was at the rear (as would be natural, in a bodyguard escort, for the party under protection.) His assertion that they travelled from Cork to Bandon "*via Skiberreen*" demonstrates shocking ignorance of the location of these towns: and he claims to have served the convoy as a *guide*!

He claims to have joined the convoy to guide it from Mallow to Cork City: but the road between these towns is a direct, main route, requiring no guidance. In addition, Mallow anti-Treaty forces contend that they cleared the Mallow-Cork road of all mines to assure Collins' safe passage. If he joined the convoy for the reason he said, why would he have remained with them after they reached Cork City? Generally speaking, his explanation on this point seems highly questionable. As will be seen in Part 2, there may be further reasons to scrutinize changes in the convoy's personnel, which took place in County Cork.

J O'Connell represents himself as riding in the Crossley tender. According to all other relevant accounts, the soldiers in the tender were nowhere near Collins until after the ambush was over. *J O'Connell never contradicts that*. This means that his statements about what happened near the touring car were, at best, hearsay; at worst, he was coached / told what to say on that subject. This, especially in combination with the other glaring inaccuracies described above, further weakens the value of his already dubious evidence.

Private Jock McPeak

This enigmatic figure has been a subject for considerable speculation; for his central position at the much-disputed Vickers machine gun, as well as for extraordinary turncoat adventures and criminal convictions, in the wake of Béal na mBláth.

McPeak was a native of Scotland, reputedly of Irish parents, and an ex-British Army soldier. Feehan says that he was "*devoted to Collins*," and worked for him "*before the Treaty*." He does not say "before the Truce." M Ryan writes that he was recruited in Scotland for the "Irish army", ignorant that there had been any split; and was shocked on arrival to find a civil war in progress. Another account says that he was simply one of the British soldiers stationed in Ireland before the Truce, who was taken into the Free State army.

All told, McPeak's service seems of a late date indeed. At best, a "Trucileer". [47] That is to say, like several others in this *dramatis personae*, he appears on the scene, just in that period which led up to Collins' death; and also like others, made a sudden exit soon after. (Lest we forget that nothing is so often, so successfully counterfeited as "devotion.")

---

47 "Trucileer" was a pejorative term applied at the time to those soldiers who joined the Irish armed forces only after the Truce.

McPeak's interviewers

As noted in the Appendix, the account attributed to him herein is gleaned from 1971 newspaper articles, quoting interviews with McPeak. While this is very much of interest, newspaper versions have their flaws. Anyone who reads the papers regularly is probably aware that journalists are notorious for misquoting people; and that not infrequently, those interviewed by the media stridently protest that they never said some of the things imputed to them.

Certainly journalists are usually allowed some degree of poetic license in translating the words of those whom public curiosity have rendered newsworthy. In the case of Collins' demise, we have already seen different newspapers' conflicting versions of Lieut Smith's estimate about the ambushers' numbers: one such paper inflating it to two hundred men. Such discrepancies strongly indicate that some changes may have been made by news editors, for dramatic effect.

Articles of this kind therefore are not to be read in the same way as testimony taken down by a court reporter, transcribed from audio recording, or otherwise scrupulously authenticated.

As for the McPeak articles in particular, they are not entirely even-handed; nor can their authors be absolved of having any agenda. On the contrary, they hammer rather heavily on the ricochet theory. [48]

This in itself casts come doubt upon the reporters who took down McPeak's words, then "*compiled*," quoted and paraphrased them for public consumption. It raises the suspicion that, in that process, their discretionary journalistic license may have been exercised in a similarly uneven manner.

McPeak's statements

All of that said, what then do the statements thus credited to McPeak have to say for themselves? As may be seen in Appendix 3, he has a number of entries under "*points which were not within the witness' direct personal knowledge*" and also some under "*self-contradiction*". He states that no second gunner left Portobello Barracks with him. Later he says that his second gunner was left behind in Cork City. While Feehan quotes him as saying that his second gunner was changed at Cork City, and replaced with one whom he'd never met before.

He contradicts Dalton, Corry and Smith as to the intensity of fire coming at the convoy: specifying that he experienced only "*a few odd shots*"; and explicitly estimating they were faced with no more than a small

---

48 The theory that Collins was killed by a ricochet.

band, armed only with rifles. In this he corroborates the ambushers, as well as McKenna.

It hardly seems credible that a private would ask a captain to get out of the armoured car, under fire. Either this reported exchange may be inaccurate, *or they weren't under much fire to speak of.* If he felt safe enough to open the hatch for some air, that also indicates that the threat was perceived to have been minimal. While his remarking that a shot then struck the hatch seems to indicate that this was one of the *"odd shots"* described earlier: that it was an unexpected, single shot, which occurred at a time when fire from the ambushers was otherwise quiet.

It's difficult to understand how he could have taken time out to train someone to refill ammunition belts, while under fire, and covering the C-in-C. Certainly this in itself would have caused a cessation of fire for some minutes. This general failure to adequately provide for ready ammunition seems a shocking oversight; for which the gunner himself must take some responsibility.

His words about visible exterior damage to the armoured car seem a bit belaboured and unnatural. (His own actions, soon after the ambush, assured that history would have to take his word on this, as no one could ever "see" that vehicle again.)

His flippant comment as to how he "*walked out*" with the armoured car shortly afterward, [49] does not produce an impression of his having a high moral sense toward whatever he may do. His tone seems that of a devil-may-care fellow with little regard for right or wrong actions.

Questions of his character are highly significant, and shall be discussed further below, along with the rest of McPeak's remarkable story.

William McKenna

In his Preface to the Fourth Edition, Feehan acknowledges that this was "*one of the last surviving*" soldiers from the Crossley tender, who provided him with an account of the ambush. (McKenna having since passed away, his "personal reasons" for remaining nameless in earlier editions were apparently rendered moot.)

We cannot be absolutely sure at this juncture that the version attributed to Dalton, Corry, or Smith, accurately recorded their own words. We are fortunate in having McKenna's testimony with clear, direct provenance. It was not re-stated by an unknown number of editors before reaching us. It was not passed hand to hand by journalists or dressed up for

---

49 See Part 3, Aftermath, regarding McPeak's further adventures.

popular consumption. He was living when it first appeared, and in a position to protest inaccuracies or to publish corrections. Therefore it seems to have had his sanction in its present form.

It has been noted above that imminent pressures and dangers gave members of the convoy a natural interest in presenting events in a certain light. Such pressures tended to be of greatest concern immediately following the tragedy, in the violent atmosphere of the Civil War. Those concerns would tend to diminish intensity with the passage of time.

Delay is usually a disadvantage in witnesses. Yet in this sense, it may also bring some benefits: in statements from members of the convoy, who spoke after the passions of that period had substantially faded. This witness having reached retirement age, and the question of government investigation being long subsided, there was little danger of any repercussions for him (either official or unofficial.)

It is also interesting that, while differing substantially from Dalton and his alleged appointees Smith and Corry, McKenna does *not* contradict testimony from the anti-Treaty side. Unlike some Free State accounts, it is possible to read it alongside the ambushers' statements, and recognize it as describing the same events.

Most significantly, his estimate of the time intervals, as well as the intensity of fire, syncs more closely with anti-Treaty reports than with those of Dalton, Smith, Corry and J O'Connell.

"He was not shot by the ambushers."

Feehan was impressed with this deponent's particular care in speaking only to his personal experience, and his unwillingness to speculate. Immediately after saying so, he recorded verbatim McKenna's reply to the question "*Who killed Collins?*"

McKenna reported, in the most positive manner, his own conviction that Collins "*was not shot by the ambushers*"; and that this was shared by "*most*" of his fellow soldiers in the tender. In the breakdown of his statement, [50] this is *not* placed under the heading of "*not within the witness' direct personal knowledge";* albeit he was visually separated when the C-in-C fell.

It is within his personal knowledge to know what are his own convictions. He may also reasonably be in a position to report that comrades shared them. He did not conjecture as to who was the

---

50   See Appendix

perpetrator. He did not pretend to any knowledge about that, stating clearly that he didn't know. But he was "*sure*" who it was *not*.

This indicates a process of elimination. In a soldier with combat experience, it suggests a *technical judgement call based on evidence*. Such a judgement could be based on knowledgeable interpretation: of the sound of gunfire, its apparent direction; whether it sounded like rifle, machine gun or Mauser pistol. Knowledge about who had what sort of weapons there that day. Whether the fire they came under from the ambushers and the fire they heard near the touring car were the same, or different. The types of wounds inflicted, in view of such observations. The demeanor of persons present, etc. All this considered, it seems fair to allow that this statement by McKenna may be within his own experience.

It is regrettable indeed that Feehan did not publish more questions and answers on this point; which he must certainly have asked. At these words from McKenna, one can well imagine the interviewer starting from his seat, bristling with "why's" and "wherefore's". This was the titular question of his whole book.

However, both that writer and the interviewee were army men. All of the above would seem to suggest that McKenna had reason for not wishing to publish further details, which were respected by Feehan.

THE ANTI-TREATY MEN'S ACCOUNTS

These insurgents, referred to as "the ambushers" or "the anti-Treaty men" may be alternately called the Irish Republican Army (IRA); and may be identified with the same organization known later, in connection with "the Troubles" of the late 20th century. [51] The Irish Republican Brotherhood (IRB) had begun referring to its volunteers as the IRA, as far back as their internment in Frongach prison camp, following the 1916 Rising.

To live outside the law, you must be honest. - Dylan

As a guerrilla force, the IRA is one of the longest lived and most successful in the modern world. This success has owed a great deal to very particular by-laws, policies or rules of operation; and their consistent, predictable adherence thereto. One of these is that, if responsible for an

---

51 Northern Ireland's "Troubles" were the direct offspring of unfinished business from the War of Independence and Civil War.

action, they publicly claim responsibility: whether the action was good, bad or indifferent. Whether cause for pride or apologies.

This places the anti-Treaty accounts in a certain light. It should be noted that they seem to match up better than those of Dalton, Smith, Corry and J O'Connell. Some of those earlier Free State accounts confirm each other on points which all other witnesses refute. Some of them back each other on points which now seem to be patently false. They do seem to support the ambushers' contention that the Free State accounts (published before 1981) were *"teeming with inaccuracies and thoroughly unreliable"*

Provenance and reliability of their accounts

Appendix 2 includes two statements from the ambushers collectively. The first, "Ambushers 1964" was produced by a meeting in 1964 of six anti-Treaty veterans of Béal na mBláth, as recorded by Florence O'Donoghue.

Deasy, Crofts, and the ambushers themselves were interviewed again in preparing the publications of 1981.

The events concerned having taken place in 1922, all these men had to be in or nearing their eighties by that time.

Deasy and Crofts made a statement together, and so probably discussed it in advance. No doubt they must have talked together about these events more than once before. Feehan says that his summary of the ambushers' statements was the result of not one, but many conversations; and, with some of these survivors, was in the context of an intimate personal acquaintance with them.

Normally, one would prefer reports taken down within days of the event. Weeks, months, or years can naturally diminish the clarity and detail of one's memory. *Therefore the consistency of detail in these reports is remarkable.*

As for fear of consequences, the passions and dangers of the Civil War had long since subsided to a smoulder when they came forward. They had little if anything left to lose in the discussion. They were also speaking, effectively, at the end of their lives. Therefore, these were all but *deathbed confessions*.

Certainly, this was an incident which the participants would naturally think and talk about, for as long as they lived. A person who is present at an historical event of national / international importance, may have cause to recall, discuss, and repeat the story many times. Those who spend their youth involved in daring struggles like the War of Independence and Civil

War often observe that their subsequent lives may be paled and overshadowed by the excitement of such early adventures; which retain a freshness and immediacy in the mind, beyond anything known thereafter. For anyone accused of a murder which they didn't commit, and/or which took place under extenuating, suspicious or confusing circumstances, the details would naturally be burned into their consciousness more vividly than those of any normal occurrence.

All of these factors were present in this case. Experiences of this kind are in quite a different class from questions like, what color was the barman's tie at the pub last Tuesday. Certainly any long interval between the event and its report must be seen as a disadvantage; yet it is also reasonable that, in a case like this, the protagonists' memories might be clear enough, even after the lapse of decades.

Of course, discussion with others is also a factor which can impair accuracy. Therefore it is particularly valuable that McKenna so nearly corroborates the statements from the anti-Treaty side. While there is the possibility that the latter may have influenced each other or even coordinated details, McKenna would not have been included in that. He was interviewed by Feehan separately, on condition of anonymity.

McKenna was Feehan's own personal find; and that interview seems to have been kept quite private indeed. The anti-Treaty men were unlikely to have had any knowledge or contact with this member of the convoy, unless through Feehan. And Feehan would hardly have contaminated his process by inviting the surviving ambushers down to compare notes with this witness, who clearly did not wish his identity to be shared with others.

Who were they?

J Feehan's list	*TP Coogan's list*	*Ambushers' 1964 list*
"These included amoung others"	Dan Holland	Dan Holland
	Jim Hurley	Jim Hurley
Dan Holland	Tom Kelleher	Tom Kelleher
Jim Hurley	John O'Callaghan	John O'Callaghan
Tom Kelleher	Sonny O'Neill	Paddy Walsh
John Callaghan	Tom Hales	Sonny Donovan
Liam Deasy		Bill Desmond
Pat Buttimer		Dan Corcoran

    Feehan did not name the ambushers (apparently on their request,) whom he interviewed, until his 6th Edition of 1991. To that volume he added a new Epilogue, including some names. In it he specified that he had "*interviewed all known survivors*" from the anti-Treaty ambush party, except for John Callaghan. "*These included amoungst others*" Dan Holland, Jim Hurley, Tom Kelleher and Pat Buttimer. During his army service he had shared quarters with Buttimer and with Liam Deasy. These were apparently the two with whom he discussed Béal na mBláth many times, in the course of on-going friendly acquaintance.

    The ambushers' statement of 1964 confirms the names given by Feehan and Coogan. It adds four more, left behind to clean up the site, who may have taken part in the action: Paddy Walsh, Sonny Donovan, Bill Desmond, and Dan Corcoran.

    M Ryan concurs that there were about five anti-Treaty shooters. Yet, confirming all listed by Coogan, adds six who do not appear in either Feehan, Coogan, or the 1964 affidavit: Bill Powell, Danny Brien, Jim Kearney, John Lordan, Pete Kearney, and Timmy Sullivan.

    It seems that some would have left when the engineers (Callaghan and Holland) set about defusing the mine. (It was reportedly brigade policy to clear the area of non-essential personnel before working with explosives.)

    Camparison of accounts suggests that men left before the ambush in groups, at different times. Some perhaps as soon as the ambush was called off. Reportedly, others, like T Hales, listed among the initial clean-up crew of ten, were walking away, when met by Deasy and Crofts; and had been at the pub fifteen or twenty minutes, when the shooting began.

Most anti-Treaty accounts place the number of actual participants at around five men. (See "Witness Fragments" below, regarding others who may have been nearby.)

Testimony below states that S O'Neill was not present. If neither T Hales nor S O'Neill remained when the convoy arrived, that leaves four well-corroborated names, out of five.

Feehan rather exhaustively investigated claims made that Jim Kearney had been present. Apparently, no one who took part says that Kearney was there: except Jim Kearney (as pointed out by the family of Tom Kelleher. [52]) Pete Kearney was identified by participants as being at Béal na mBláth, but not taking part in the action.

Feehan referred to Tom Foley as "*the most important man at Béal na mBláth from the point of view of a writer*" because his job as errand boy to the ambushers meant that "*he knew the exact location of every participant and who they were.*"

Foley's name is not shown in any of these lists. Yet his testimony (which appears later in this chapter) gives a strong impression of direct personal knowledge of the ambush. As a "runner" who dealt with miscellaneous menial tasks, would he have been one left behind to remove the barricade? Was he not named, because he was under age and unarmed?

These uncertainties are the legacy of two key factors: the absence of a full, official, public inquiry; and the extra-legal nature of the anti-Treaty men's actions. They were "*outside the law*": men on the run, at war with government, in a bloody civil conflict, whose bitterness has still not entirely faded away. Therefore it is not surprising if they tried to preserve some anonymity: especially in connection with such a national disaster as Collins' end. Some report that the participants took an oath immediately afterward, not to discuss the action, nor to name anyone who was present. Yet apparently these concerns abated, sufficiently for them to come forward in later decades.

In view of these ambiguities, the anti-Treaty ambush party will be referred to herein simply as "the ambushers."

Liam Deasy's and Tom Crofts' account

Deasy and Crofts authorized Feehan to publish in their name the account attributed to them in his book. This was confirmed by Deasy's own publication, which agreed with the one in Feehan. This account includes nothing not within their own direct personal knowledge.

Deasy, in his expanded version, did fill out his chapter with hearsay from other sources. (He, also, quotes Dalton.) Yet when speaking from his own experience, his unique perspective offers valuable insights. (Some points from his book are included in Appendix 2 & 3; but only those which were within his own experience.)

Liam Deasy in "Brother Against Brother" [52]

Deasy's memoire of his Civil War experiences makes fascinating reading. He often includes the kind of detail to be expected in a military report, and slips into that style of narrative. His inventory of the republican arsenal in his area (Third Cork Brigade) is also of special interest. By the time of the Truce: "*Our armaments had increased from 18 rifles in 1918 and 30 in 1919 to a total of 130, together with <u>one</u>* [53] *Lewis machine gun.*" Divided among 5600 active Volunteers in the area, that would mean roughly 1 in 43 Volunteers had a rifle; one 1 in 5600 had a machine gun.

He does sometimes speak of events at which he was not present, quoting the words of others without credit (or criticism.) In this way, he repeats Dalton's version of what was said in Collins' car, sandwiched in with his own first-hand experiences.

However, there are unexpected clues to be gleaned even from errors of this kind. He says that the convoy "*screamed to a halt ...* " On this, Deasy was not speaking from direct observation. Earlier in that chapter, he states that he was a half-mile away in Béal na mBláth village, when the convoy stopped.

Yet he directly contradicts the ambushers' account, which specifies that the convoy was moving slowly, no more than 15 or 20 miles per hour. That means *Deasy did <u>not</u> coordinate his story with members of the ambush party*.

This increases the value of the points on which these different witnesses from the anti-Treaty side do agree.

With respect to his first hearing, from Long's pub, shots coming from the direction of the ambush site, Deasy quite specifically identified what he heard as "*rifle and machine gun fire.*"

---

52 It should be noted that Deasy's very valuable foray into authorship late in life, and the cooperation of Crofts, the Hales family and others with Feehan, seem to have been in direct response to M Ryan. They consistently contradict her version: especially her allegation that Deasy himself ordered Collins' death.

53 Emphasis is this author's.

An officer with considerable combat experience, like Deasy, might well be able to identify different types of arms by the sound, from that distance. What he reports is commensurate with the known weaponry of the two parties, as well as the timing. This could have been the first rifle shots of the ambushers, answered by the Lewis gun in the tender; and/or by the Vickers gun in the armoured car. Supported by other accounts, such details give us a foothold in the shifting sands of Béal na mBláth.

Deasy specified that, from the hill which he and Crofts clambered up to view the action, they "*could see very little - just a lorry and the turret of the armoured car, with a few soldiers darting from one position to another.*" The entire convoy was not visible to them. And if, as they say, the convoy "*moved off*" within a minute or two of their coming in sight of it, the ambush was essentially over when they reached the scene. (The Free State accounts appear to be unanimous that they remained on the road, dealing with the C-in-C's remains, for at least some minutes after the shooting had stopped, and all the ambushers had retreated.)

Nowhere in the accounts from Deasy and/or Crofts is there any observation of gunfire at the time when they reached the ambush site. For the few moments that they were at the ambush site at the same time as the convoy, the *only* gunfire they reported was "*a few shots*" fired by themselves, just before "*the whole convoy moved off.*" [54]

The ambushers' accounts

There are a number of important details which only the ambushers themselves can tell us.

Only this account can say anything first hand about the state of mind of the ambushers (which no other source can speak to.) It is certainly significant, if indeed they had spent the hot summer afternoon, discussing in the sunshine chances that "*the war would soon be over.*"

That is to say, their outlook was that of a soldier on the last day of the war. Not a day when anyone wants to get shot. By their own account, neither were they anxious to shoot anyone else. For, as is often the case in civil war, many combatants had friends and relations who were on the opposing side: a factor which makes orders to cease fire especially welcome.

---

54   These shots from Deasy and Crofts could be made to account for Smith's fire "*from both sides of the road,*" for his alleged wound, and for Dalton's allegations of "sniping" after the ambushers had retreated from the hill on the west. However, the timing of Deasy and Crofts presence, only moments before the convoy moved on, would rule all this out.

Their precise description of their positions corroborates Smith's statement, that the site was spread out over about a quarter mile. These positions and distances can be confirmed, by anyone who visits the site today, armed with these narratives.

The ambushers emphasized that "*they had the convoy at their mercy*" and "*could have picked them off.*" In this, they seem to wish to demonstrate that, *if* they had been shooting to kill, there *would certainly have been more than one fatality*.

All in all, their description does not sound like a team of hardened of assassins, panting for Collins' blood. Is that mere self-exoneration? Or are there reasons to consider its validity?

WHO STARTED THE SHOOTING?

Both Deasy and Feehan brought up the question as to whether it was the ambushers who attacked first. They both seem to be relating this contention as coming from a third party. Since neither of them were present at the time, this version of events can only have come from someone amoung the ambushers. (It was certainly not the position of any of the Free State witnesses.)

Contradicting the 1964 statement, the ambushers' 1981 version says that they fired off "*a couple of warning shots*"; and that "*members of the convoy*" then took cover and began firing *on them*: as if to say that the convoy gunners *started the fire fight*.

McKenna says that the Crossley tender came under fire, after they had stopped and begun to dismount; before they fired a shot. This would seem to contradict the ambushers. However, it does not entirely negate the value of the correspondences.

It must be remembered that Feehan did not interview all the ambushers. The ambush site was a quarter of a mile in length, and the five men thinly spread over it. Although the account specifies the anti-Treaty men's positions, it does not say which of them testified.

The two sentries to the south would have been the first to see the convoy come into sight. It follows that they were also the ones who fired the warning shots. Indeed they specified that they did so to warn their comrades, who were clearing the barricade, a quarter mile north. This suggests that at least one of these two at the southern end of the site were the ones Feehan spoke with.

McKenna was at the forward (north) end of the convoy. There was some hesitation before the warning shots were fired. He does not mention hearing separate warning shots. However, the ambushers' description of the escorts' actions sounds more like what happened at the rear (south) of the convoy, by the touring car. It is Dalton, Corry and Smith who recounted taking cover behind a small bank or ditch. They are corroborated by the ambushers. Corry also agrees with the ambushers, and contradicts Dalton, in saying that "*a single shot rang out*" first.

McKenna never mentions the men from the Crossley tender taking cover behind a ditch. Indeed, it seems an odd place to seek cover, from gunfire coming down from above, when you have a large vehicle handy, which would provide much better protection.

It's possible that they are both correct: the Crossley tender reached the barricade, stopped, and its occupants began to dismount. There was a warning shot. A quarter mile to the south, the men from the touring car got out, took cover behind a ditch, and started firing. If the tender was fired upon about the same time, McKenna may not have clearly distinguished the sound of a warning shot. Indeed, by his account, he first became aware of gunfire at the touring car's end, only after shooting near the Crossley tender had ceased.

Who ran?

Dalton says that Commandant O'Connell "*came running . . . round the bend.*" He also says that Collins "*ran 15 yards back up the road.*" Corry says that he, Collins and Dalton all "*walked*" together back up the road "*about 50 yards*." While Joe Dolan reported that "*Collins and Dalton ran back past the armoured car.*"

Ambushers characterized convoy members as "*running up and down the road.*" This seems to conflict with McKenna's version that his section "*moved cautiously*" up the road. However, McKenna is clear that they did so only after all shooting had ceased. By that time, it seems the ambushers had all retreated over the hill. So their account must refer to the movements of someone else.

The third man
Dalton says that Cmmdt O'Connell helped him carry Collins' body. Dalton and Smith say that Smith was wounded in the neck while trying to help move the body. But Corry says only he and Dalton carried the body, placing neither Smith nor Cmmdt O'Connell at that end of the ambush site at all.

MEDICAL TESTIMONY
Medical records also are suspiciously incomplete and contradictory. We have no authoritative record of precisely what happened to Collins' remains, in the critical hours immediately following his shooting. Controversy continues as to who examined him, the exact nature and location of his wounds, the identity of other doctors, observers, or handlers who may have been present (nurses, transport, etc.) and other routine details. Several doctors are alleged, in conflicting accounts, to have performed an autopsy. 55 But none has ever surfaced. In place of such reports, we are obliged to refer to interviews by historians, taken decades after the fact, and fraught with conflicting claims.

Dr. Patrick Cagney seems to be most widely identified as having examined Collins' remains at Shanakiel Hospital. His interview by Sean McGarry of the IRB was tape recorded in 1966. Dr. Leo Aherne was a medical officer for the Free State Army, under Dalton's direct command. There is debate as to the extent of Dr Aherne's role. While he did not take the body to Bon Secours as Dalton claimed, yet he does seem to have at least examined it briefly "outside the Imperial Hotel," sufficiently to confirm that the C-in-C was beyond medical help. It is alleged that he also took part in an autopsy, and assisted Dr Gogarty at the embalming. However, like other witness statements, no two entirely separate sources on this agree.

According to Feehan, Frank Friel and Matron Gordon confirmed each other's testimony; in this they may be unique in the medical evidence. Dalton, even while denying Friel's confirmation that the body went to Shanakiel, concurs that Friel was present and took part in its transport.

There is conflict between Dr Oliver St John Gogarty in his autobiography, and comments he allegedly made, literally over the C-in-C's body, which come to us only as hearsay. Yet it seems important to include

---

55   The possible fate of the alleged autopsy report, which has never yet surfaced, will be touched upon in Part 3.

them here; because of the flawed state of the record, and also due to indications that he may have had more to say in 1922, in private, than he was willing to commit to print in 1954. The issue of close range wounds is vital, and Dr Gogarty was not only a prominent physician, among those who may have performed an autopsy, but was a personal friend of Collins, as well. McKenna, who reported Dr Gogarty's words, has proved sober and well corroborated. Wherever his details can be checked, he has never been found to exaggerate or speculate outside his own first-hand knowledge.

Considerable testimony that there was at least one entry wound, as well as an exit wound, casts an interesting light on those who have been recalcitrant in their insistence that Collins had only one wound. [56]

The similarity between Collins' fatal wound(s) and that of President John F. Kennedy is also striking (i.e. a gaping wound out the back of the head.) Nor is it unreasonable to draw a line between similar circumstances in two famous political assassinations, albeit separated by a continent, an ocean and forty years. The types of elements capable of carrying out such crimes may be highly trained and organized. Those who are so organized and trained, like professionals of every kind everywhere, frequently draw from common sources and share standard techniques. Such "*modus operandi*" ("*m.o.*": 'way of operating') can be a kind of technical fingerprint or profile. Thus "*m.o.*" is one means of identifying perpetrators and their associates.

Witness fragments

There remain, in addition to the accounts listed here, bits of incomplete testimony which we may or may not ever be able to fill out.

Tom Hales, anti-Treaty Brigade Commandant:
Was the ambush not planned to kill Collins?

> *I would prefer to have one Tom Hales with me than twelve other men.*
>
> *- Michael Collins*

One of the bewildering anomalies of this battle is Tom Hales' direct, leading role in the action which took the life of Collins: a close personal friend of his family, since their childhood together in West Cork.

---

56   Such as Dalton and M Ryan.

The Hales family were particularly close to Collins and all brothers played a leading role in the War of Independence. [57]

During the Civil War, this remarkable clan was split: some siding with the Free State, and others going anti-Treaty. Notably, Tom's brother Sean Hales was a Free State general, and in close contact with Collins on this same journey (as mentioned above.)

Tom Hales was the anti-Treaty Brigade officer in charge of the twenty or more men who made up the planned ambush party (most of whom dispersed before Collins arrived.) [58] Many of these were local Volunteers who gathered in Béal na mBláth as bodyguard[59] for the anti-Treaty officers' meeting scheduled there for 22 August. A number of these would have been ordinary local men, rather than professional soldiers.

Feehan says that Deasy had called a meeting of anti-Treaty officers to take place at Béal na mBláth on 22 August. "*Since most of these officers were on the run and their time of arrival could not be forecast, the meeting was scheduled for a date rather than for a precise hour.*" The meeting would convene in the morning if all were present; if not, it would be postponed until the evening. That morning, all participants were not yet arrived. So the meeting was postponed. This is ostensibly the reason why there was an anti-Treaty column in the area; and, indirectly, the reason the ambush took place.

According to one report, "*Hales decided*" to organize the ambush party, as a kind of "busy work." It was a hot August day, there was a pub in the village, and he thought it would be best to give them something to do well away from it.

This was considered sound practice among the military of that time and place. It is important to note Deasy's observation: " *... that the convoy did return by the same route ... for Collins ... was inexplicable and in military terms baffling.*" To do so would be entirely uncharacteristic, and a violation of his usual practice.

---

57 J Feehan
58 Details of Tom Hales' role in the ambush seems to have been reported to Feehan, either by Hales, or by someone very close to him, very likely a family member, as coming from Hales himself.
59 Interestingly, there seems to have been an unusual abundance of leaders and their bodyguards in the area that day.

According to this account, Hales planned the ambush *because* he felt confident that Collins would *not* return by the same road he had passed through that morning.

Tom Foley interview

In response to the analysis presented by Colm Connolly's documentary "*The Shadow of Béal na mBláth*", the family of Sonny O'Neill sent to TP Coogan the following interview with Tom Foley, (mentioned earlier in this chapter, under "*Who were they?*") He testifies that O'Neill was *not* present when the ambush took place:

> *Fr Aidan O'Driscoll: ... this statement that Sonny O'Neill fired the fatal shot ... You were there as a seventeen-year-old ... what were you doing exactly on the day? What was your job?*
>
> *Foley: I went for the mines and I went down for the cigarettes. And any fellow wanted anything, I'd get it for him.*
>
> *Fr O'Driscoll: As to the claim that Sonny O'Neill shot Michael Collins, what do you think of that?*
>
> *Foley: ... It was raining in the evening ... Before the ambush started it got wet and that's why the lads were going away. [Sonny O'Neill] ... had left the ambush position an hour before it.*
>
> *Fr O'Driscoll: Is it possible to know who fired that shot?*
>
> *Foley: Not possible! Not possible ... you weren't going to keep your head up while they shot were you? And McPeak cleaning the briars off the top up while they shot, were you? Not a very safe place to put your head up at all, to see or otherwise. They were firing them shots now without ever seeing where they were going to, you can be sure of that. Oh life is sweet, but in an ambush like that, it's still sweeter.* [60]

---

60   This was provided to Coogan in the form of a transcript made from an audio recording of the interview. In his reproduction, two particles in this last sentence are given slightly differently than here: resulting in a statement which does not seem to make perfect sense. This author, having considerable experience in transcribing text from audio recordings, strongly suspects that the speaker's actual words were as shown

There is much to be gleaned in Foley's brief but pithy language. His colloquial mixing of pronouns ("*you weren't going to keep your head up while they shot were you?*") suggests he was speaking somewhat excitedly, at the memory of the gun battle. Saying, "*They were firing them shots now without ever seeing where they were going to,*" he makes it clear that his "*while they shot*" referred to the withering machine gun fusillade from the armoured car, which reduced the ambushers on the hill to firing blind, without lifting their heads to aim at anything.

This clearly corroborates the ambushers interviewed by Feehan, who asserted that they weren't aiming at anything in particular, and called it one chance in a million that they could have hit Collins. He also seems to refute O'Neill's claim to have felled Collins, and seen him fall. Fr O'Driscoll explicitly asks him, not who fired that particular shot, but whether it was "*possible to know*" who did. Foley responds most emphatically, in his vernacular style, that *no one* on that hill *could have had any idea* where his shots were landing, or what was taking place down on the road: because under the bombardment from the armoured car, it would have been suicide to even lift your head to look out.

Other parties of ambushers?

Some accounts exist from members of the main ambush party, who had left the site, but may have been nearby, in or around Béal na mBláth.

Some allege a second party, of ten or twelve ambushers, were crossing a field when they heard the convoy coming; and that they took a position near the Ahalarick Bridge (about a quarter mile south of the ambush site.) Some accounts say that this group fired on the convoy, others that they did not.

The evidence on this is incomplete. It is not supported by the witnesses whose definite presence and participation in the main action is most well-corroborated.

The Sonny O'Neill theory

Coogan argues, but not very persuasively, that Sonny O'Neill was the shooter. He neglects to share with us just why he felt so convinced. [61] He

---

above: saying, that one may perceive life's value to seem greatly increased, when one finds oneself under heavy fire. This emphasizes his previous sentence, about the unlikelihood of lifting their heads, under the armoured car's bombardment.

seems to attribute this explanation to Tom Hales. (Without, however actually claiming that Hales ever said so. Only that Hales recounted a conversation with O'Neill in which the latter inquired what was Johnny Collins' attitude about the shooting.) Yet Feehan had at least equal access to the Hales family, and found no support there for this view.

One most telling point is the ambushers' report to Deasy of no casualties on either side. If anyone in the party was sure that they hit anyone, let alone that they killed an officer, let alone that it was Michael Collins, this would hardly have been omitted from that report. The entire ambush party seems to have presented themselves to Deasy that evening. Yet even if not all of them were present, they certainly would have rendezvoused among themselves, following the action, to count heads and confirm whether they'd lost anyone. They could hardly have made said report without having first done so.

Coogan claims that O'Neill "*confided to his Commanding Officer*" his belief that his bullet felled Collins. Yet that officer is not identified. Deasy was the commanding officer of that Southern Division; the ranking man in charge, present on the day. Yet Deasy never mentions receiving any such report. Why, where and when would O'Neill have made it?

Feehan devotes his 6th Edition Epilogue to the question of Sonny O'Neill. He secured the full cooperation of O'Neill's surviving family; despite his assurances that, if he found "*the slightest ... solid evidence implicating him,*" it would be published.

Characteristically, his treatment catalogues and tracks each testimony to its source. Suffice to say here that he could find nothing but the flimsiest hearsay to implicate O'Neill. As for allegations that O'Neill was plagued by shame and remorse, Feehan himself attended a funeral at the O'Neill family home in 1944. There he saw Sonny O'Neill and Johnny Collins (Michael's elder brother) happily sitting together and chatting away for almost two hours.

There is the elusive Jim Kearney, who was quoted in the Cork Examiner 28 September 1989 as claiming that he had taken part in the ambush, and that O'Neill had shot the C-in-C. Rebuttals were immediately thereafter published by both Feehan and by the family of Tom Kelleher, all of whom had abundant testimony that no Kearney had taken part. Kearney was invited to substantiate his claims. Nothing further was ever heard from him.

---

61   At the same time, Coogan played fair by including Tom Foley's testimony, which seems to scrap the theory.

This strange anomaly was accompanied by others. Feehan mentions that Tom Foley recorded his taped interview, (declaring O'Neill had left an hour before the ambush,) just "*a few months before his accidental death.*" In the same paragraph, Cormac MacCarthaigh "*one of the greatest experts on the death of Collins*" is said to have had evidence that O'Neill was eating supper with other IRA men at a safe house when the ambush took place. Feehan made an appointment to get these details for his book, but MacCarthaigh "*died unexpectedly two days before I was to see him.*"

In any case of this kind, it is worth noting, when people who possess important evidence suddenly drop dead, unexpectedly, at a rate which defies statistics; and/or at a particularly important stage in an investigation.

That O'Neill was at a safe house eating dinner would tally with where other members of the main ambush party were; when the convoy unexpectedly returned, surprising the skeleton crew of five or six men left behind.

Why would anyone say he shot Collins?

There may be nothing so mysterious, in miscellaneous claims to have been the shooter. No less than seven men have been listed as having said, at one time or another, that they were the one who shot Collins. Several of these are not included in anyone's tally of the anti-Treaty men there that day. Few of these claims could stand up to the most cursory investigation. Most have been thoroughly discredited by my predecessors.

One must bear in mind that Collins was a legend in his own time: the man the British couldn't kill. Obviously, as his case remained unsolved, it would be inviting to tall-tale-tellers everywhere: "*Yes, I'm the one who did it.*" These sort of fellows, according to themselves, probably also shot Billy the Kid and "*gave a speech at Gettysburg for Lincoln that day.*"

There are also the factors of collective guilt combined with battlefield confusion. Experts have spent centuries arguing over precisely what happened at uncounted battles. During the shooting, hardly anyone in it can keep track of what's going on. The men who fought it have to read history books to figure out what they were in. It is not impossible that there were participants who really doubted whether they might have been the one who fired the fatal shot.

Of course, Collins' story has taken on a life of its own as folklore; including many versions which may have little to do with fact. After listing a few of the more outlandish reports (including one from a man who was sure that, as a little boy, he saw the C-in-C shot to death in the town of Bandon) Feehan observed:

> The "So-and-So told me " school of history, while amusing at times, is notoriously unreliable. Interviews ... to be of any value need to be backed up by corroborative evidence.

The armoured car's machine gun worked fine ... ?

Foley's testimony adds to others who belie the controversial assertion that there was any malfunction in the armoured car's Vickers machine gun. Considerable disagreement among the witnesses on this point begs the questions identified above: Can they all be telling the truth? If some lied on this subject, why did they lie?

Foley's account fragment is the most vivid description from those on the receiving end of the Vickers' gun. It colorfully demonstrates the inequality of firepower, between a few West Cork snipers and an armoured car. This in itself casts considerable doubt on some Free State men's accounts. *Because* the *possibility* of the anti-Treaty column getting off a clear shot at the C-in-C is hardly feasible, with the armoured car to cover him: *unless the Vickers gun is postulated to have malfunctioned*.

This seems to indicate that the existence of a malfunction in the armoured car's machine gun was necessary to support Dalton's version of events. *Yet Dalton never said that there was any problem with the machine gun*. On the contrary, he explicitly mentions that the Vickers gun kept up its bombardment of the ambushers' positions, right up to the end.

This could explain why witnesses contradict each other about the Vickers gun's performance; why the question of whether or not that machine gun failed is so important; and who had reason to lie.

Daily Express 25 August 1922

An article appearing in this newspaper on the date shown purported to be an interview with a member of Collins' convoy. In it, the escort member was quoted as saying that he was near to Collins, and had seen a sniper creeping up on hands and knees behind the C-in-C; who then fell in a subsequent "*burst of firing*."

We will not revisit this report, for the following reasons: Collins appears to have been struck with an entry wound at the hairline of his forehead, with an exit wound at the base of his skull.

Therefore, a sniper on his knees, firing at a man standing up (as Collins would have had to be, in order to "fall",) could not possibly be responsible.

22 August: Hold the front page.
Also coming from the Daily Express, is a story from its editor Max Aitken (Lord Beaverbrook.) Following the Treaty talks in London, he had assigned a journalist to cover Collins on a constant basis, as a sure source for breaking news. As a result, the paper did publish *"many interesting stories about Collins"* from that reporter. *"On 22 August, time unknown"* that same correspondent telephoned his editors to *"hold the main page"* for a headline story; although *"his contacts could not tell him what the news was."* The editors followed these instructions and held the space; until the writer rang them *"in the early hours of 23 August"* with the news of Collins' death.

"THE DAY MICHAEL COLLINS WAS SHOT"
We are at this stage obliged to point out that *all these eye-witnesses utterly refute* M. Ryan, in the well-known book of this title. As we have already seen, unanimous corroboration among these accounts, on any one point, can be difficult to find. Therefore, in belying Ryan, *their complete agreement must be regarded as conclusive.*

Ms Ryan places the action at an entirely different part of the road, re-arranges the order of the vehicles in the convoy, vastly increases the number of ambushers and their weaponry.

All those present who commented on the typography agree: the road was flanked by steep hills on both sides at the place where the ambush occurred. The ambushers confirm that the southernmost of their party were opposite where the monument stands today.

However, in the map accompanying her book, Ryan places the action at another location altogether, a further quarter mile to the south, near the intersection of the Ahalarick Bridge. At that spot, the ground is flat and level with the road on both sides. The parallel laneway, from which the ambushers fired, at that point swerves to within only about 10 meters of the main road.

If firing from that position, a well-aimed shot would be much more believable. However, they would have had practically no cover, and could hardly have escaped injury from the armoured car's machine gun onslaught.

The ambushers specified that the barricade they placed across the road was *"at the Béal na mBláth end of the position"* (that is, the northern end) and that the mine was "*a short distance*" from that, to be detonated from "*up a laneway which ran off the main road west, and then south, parallel to the main road*." This, they say, is where they ran, from the main road, onto the laneway.

There is no such laneway in the ambush site as Ms Ryan draws it. The laneway dead ends at the Ahalarick Bridge (the only way open west from the road, in her site map): from there the parallel lane runs only north. At that point, there *is no* parallel lane running south, nor any way running "*west, and then south*."

Ms Ryan's work is lamentably plagued with similarly outlandish inaccuracies. It is difficult to understand, for instance, her footnote explaining Arthur Griffith's identity as merely "*a volunteer who joined in 1913*"! It suffers as well from a tendency to present conjectures as certainties; and to generally overlook the complex nature of the record. The fact that conflicting accounts exist is frequently passed over. Readers are simply presented with the version Ryan favours, without acknowledgement that other witnesses may contradict it.

It should not be overlooked that Ryan sometimes indulges in Collins-bashing rhetoric, and relies heavily on witnesses known to have been particularly hostile to him, such as Ernest Blythe (an Anglo Protestant from Ulster.) The usually press-shy Dalton seems to have been uncharacteristically forthcoming with Ms Ryan, in the preparation of her book; and is also one of her main sources.

Certainly Ms Ryan had excellent sources, and has contributed important research. An itemized comparison of the inconsistencies between her view of the ambush and Feehan's was initially contemplated for inclusion here.

Regrettably, such an examination of all that may be said about her book has been found beyond the scope of the present work.

Apparently styled a darling of anti-Treaty sympathizers, it must be observed that her narrative seems to pursue an agenda to convict the anti-Treaty men in Collins' death; and to avoid questions about his own bodyguard's performance. This kind of approach may ring a bell, our discussion below.

Was there an anti-Treaty plan to kill Collins?

It has been alleged that somewhere in Cork that week, some anti-Treaty partisans made specific plans to assassinate Collins; and that those plans were based on reliable foreknowledge of his itinerary, his planned route, etc.

Amoung the arguments for this scenario is the contention that there was no other route open back to Cork City; and that for this reason his passing through Béal na mBláth a second time was a certainty.

The source for this argument seems chiefly to be Ryan. As her book attracted a great deal of attention, this argument has been accepted in some quarters. Yet this is another one of those points on which all verifiable sources seem to refute her. Deasy (anti-Treaty), Dalton (Free State) and others agree that a number of routes were available.

At the same time, it was standard practice for Collins, in a career always fraught with grave security issues, to retain the option to change his itinerary at will without prior notice.

Conclusions: What the Witnesses Tell Us

> *If a proper inquest had been held all members of the escort would have been cross-examined and this would have determined the exact details of the ambush and of the events leading up to it. What drink was consumed en route, the sobriety of the officers and men, the reason for taking the Béal na mBláth road, the composition of the escort, the tactics adopted when fired upon and all other relevant details would have come out in the open. As well, the medical evidence would have determined the location and number of wounds, ... the calibre of the bullet, the direction from which it came and the distance at which it was fired. If such an inquest had been held there would be no mystery whatever surrounding Collins' death. ... Where the Commander-in-Chief was killed, a full military inquiry would, under normal circumstances, take place at once. ... But there was no formal inquiry of any kind.* [62]

Above, we have explored the titular question of this section: what then do all these contradictions and corroborations add up to? We find that, taken altogether, the witnesses' statements raise questions:

What we don't know

It is interesting to note that *not a single witness ever says that he was shot by the ambushers*. While several witnesses, on both sides, explicitly

---

62 J Feehan

state their belief that he certainly was *not* (McKenna, as well as the ambushers themselves.) Medical testimony also indicates that his wounds bore signs of having been inflicted at point blank range.

This does not look well for the conventional wisdom. It means that not only we don't know who shot Collins: we don't even know *which side* shot him.

The convoy came under what kind of fire?

One of the most blatantly suspicious features of the ambush, at first glance, is that Collins was the only fatality. Certainly, had the convoy been under the kind of fire described by Dalton, Smith, Corry and J O'Connell, this could hardly have been so. It's hard to imagine how four occupants of a canvas-roof car with the top down could have escaped injury. If "*heavy machine gun fire*" had "*swept the road*" before and behind the touring car, shattering the windscreen, someone behind that windscreen would certainly have been hit.

This is the military equivalent of "the dog ate my homework." It's like the size of the fish that got away. It has a tendency to grow. So it is when a military party fails spectacularly in their mission: the truth about the numbers and firepower they were facing is often the first casualty. It's what men in such a situation, if they're going to lie, would be most tempted to lie about. It's the easiest thing to lie about. No one may be able to prove they were lying. And it is the first place any military investigator would look for "misrepresentations" (report-ese for "lies".)

Dalton, Smith and Corry are precisely those who had the most to lose, if the answer were any different; on this very key question of how much and what kind of fire. They were all directly responsible for the man who died. The only one they brought back dead, was precisely that man whom they were there to protect: at the cost of their own lives, if necessary. That's the bodyguard business. All in all, these Free State accounts do not speak well of themselves, on this important issue.

On the other hand, the various anti-Treaty accounts, as to the numbers and arms of all present, seem to tally remarkably well with each other and with both McKenna and McPeak. These sources seem to have been more definitely independent of each other. All were speaking after the dangers and passions of the Civil War had long subsided, and at the end of their lives.

McKenna is the only Free State account whose provenance cannot be called into question: who was personally interviewed, by a reputable researcher, whose identity can be confirmed. Whatever critique could be made about McPeak's interviewers at the Irish Independent, at least we know who they were. Whereas we may never know exactly who wrote down either Smith's or Corry's statements; and Dalton's shows definite symptoms of having been dramatized by a professional ghost writer.

This is a point in which both could not be true. What the witnesses seem to tell us, is that accounts which claim the convoy came under heavy fire were exaggerated, for obvious reasons. And that the numbers, weaponry, intensity and duration of the ambushers' attack, was probably more like the version shared by McKenna, McPeak and the anti-Treaty witnesses.

Unanswered questions

Literature should offer questions, not answers. - C N Adichie

To attempt to answer the questions surrounding Michael Collins' death is an ambitious project indeed; which no researcher today, however qualified, can approach with complete confidence of success. What we can be sure to accomplish here is to identify questions. While many of these have been asked before, we may also hope to pose some anew.

<u>My questions</u>:
Why there?
Why with that crew?
Why at that time?
Why in the teeth of all known dangers?
Why didn't all those soldiers protect him?
Why with Dalton but without any other of his usual bodyguard?
Who ordered the ambush?
Why did he "stop to ask directions"?
Why in a bright yellow convertible with the top down?
What did Michael Collins know and when did he know it?
What was the meaning of his extraordinary comments, noted by friends, relatives and associates, immediately preceding, and some on the very day of his death? Such as:

"Would you like a new boss?" *"Would you like to kill me?"*

"I'll make no girl a wife only to make her a widow"

"I'll end this business if it doesn't end me first"

"Whatever happens, my own people won't shoot me "

"No one in my own county's going to shoot me."

Why was there never any public, official investigation?

I would also like to consider important questions raised by Feehan.

John Feehan's unanswered questions:
Why so many trips to Macroom in two days?

Why did he use the same route on his return trip, in violation of standard military procedure?

When were Collins' clothes searched?

Where is the safe-conduct document for his journey through the south, signed by a prominent anti-Treaty leader?

Where are other documents he is believed to have been carrying, concerning ending the Civil War and merging the two armies?

Part 2

A new analysis

The difficulty is that which exists in all cases in which there is a mass of feeling to be contended against. So long as an opinion is strongly rooted in the feelings, it gains rather than loses in stability by having a preponderating weight of argument against it. For if it were accepted as a result of argument, the refutation of the argument might shake the solidity of the conviction; but when it rests solely on feeling, the worse it fares in argumentative contest, the more persuaded its adherents are that their feeling must have some deeper ground, which the arguments do not reach ...

- *John Stuart Mill*

Provisional Government Cabinet meeting, 1922. Michael Collins, leaning forward, on the left. WT Cosgrave at the head of the table, Ernest Blyth and Kevin O'Higgins facing Collins.

Chapter 4

Cabinet Counter - Revolution?

Many readers of this book, will have at least some previous familiarity with Collins' life and times.

Like other crimes of this kind, his assassination did not take place in a vacuum. It can hardly be described, without discussing the political crisis which led up to it. Details of that situation had everything to do with exactly what happened, on that isolated stretch of road where he died.

The following is intended to set forth that political turmoil and its relation to his death; to explore and, hopefully, explain something about the key events and characters, as they relate to the issue of his end; especially focussing on analysis and arguments which may not have appeared elsewhere.

However, this is *not* an in-depth study of the Civil War, or of all the events leading up to it. Readers with an interest are encouraged to investigate more complete accounts in the full biographies, in histories of the period; as well as in several books published by his comrades, contemporaries and opponents of that time.

*　　*　　*　　*

We find, then, two independent bodies with a very direct interest in getting rid of Collins, viz, the junta within the cabinet and the British secret service. [63]

Ireland's independence was not achieved by a letter-writing campaign. Constitutional means had been tried, and constitutional victories won. On paper, Ireland had Home Rule before World War I. And by 1916 it seemed clear that not even that modicum of autonomy would ever be enforced: except by force.

Without the Squad [64] *and the Active Service Unit, the revolution in the city of Dublin would have fallen flat.* [65]

63　J Feehan
64　"The Squad" also known as "The Twelve Apostles" were an elite unit of

As often happens, once the insurgents had won the victory, it was a politicians' job. And, as often happens, some politicians who were keen on keeping their jobs and dominant position, were not comfortable with a constituency of fighting men and women who had recently proved their capacity to topple a government; who had a powerful voice, strong opinions about the new national direction; a determination to get what they'd fought for, and what they'd watched comrades die for.

> *[Some members of the Cabinet] ... wanted civil war long before it started so that they could crush the republicans with all the means in their power. They had now little time for any form of nationalism and if Ireland were to become a loyal part of the Empire then the sooner these republicans were defeated and neutralized the better. Collins was the big obstacle in their way.* [66]

Ireland, like much of the world, was in the midst of great social upheaval in the opening decades of the 20th century. Home rule was not the only question. A formidable labor movement was rocking the nation, and joining forces with the independence Volunteers. Wildcat socialist insurrections broke out in isolated pockets here and there, throughout the country: ousting owners and setting up workers-controlled cooperatives. Women were demanding the vote and political enfranchisement. This was at the same time that wars for self-determination and socialist revolutions were turning things upside down in other places as far-flung as Russia, China, Germany and Mexico.

This was a global metamorphosis of unprecedented proportions, absolutely unseen anytime in history. Things were getting very hot indeed for the traditional ruling classes; and they were sweating bullets. The shots then heard round the world were shaking the windows and rattling the walls of powers-that-be everywhere. At least.

---

sharpshooters. As part of the War of Independence, they carried out strategic, surprise executions, against key adversaries, on a guerilla, hit-and-run basis.

65   D Neligan

66   J Feehan

> *[The agitators] were too strong to be ignored, and ... some new measure ... must be conceded ... The coach must be allowed to run down the hill ... . But let us have the drag on both the hind wheels. And we must remember that coaches running down hill without drags are apt to come to misfortune.*
>
> *- A Trollope*

Counter-revolution is a feature of every successful revolution. What rebellion sets in motion, has to come to a stop somewhere. Or at least pause for a deep breath. But where? When? And who will decide? Counter-revolution in this sense may not be always an entirely bad thing. It can apply the breaks to a spiralling juggernaut. However, it usually is even less planned and foreseen by the revolutionists, than the revolution itself.

WAS THERE A "JUNTA"?

> *We have won the right of the Irish people to rule in their own country, and I am not going to surrender that right to any junta.*
>
> *- Arthur Griffith 1922*

Coogan argues against the existence of a cabal in the Cabinet; but not very persuasively. [67] As seen from the above quotation from Griffith, the question was contemporary, and taken most seriously by the President of the Dáil. Coogan however agrees that Collins' policy on the North was *"unwelcome to his Cabinet colleagues and of course to the British."* In this he supports that Collins was serving on the Cabinet with men whose agenda for the future of Ireland was closer to the British, than to his own. This in itself speaks volumes.

> *Collins never concealed his contempt for [WT] Cosgrave, whom he regularly referred to as "that bloody little altar-boy." He detested [Ernest] Blythe and distrusted Eoin MacNeill and the feeling on their side was mutual, although for political reasons he had to have them in the cabinet.*[68]

---

67 He fails to answer issues about this raised by Feehan.

68 J Feehan

From Chairman to Commander - in - Chief

There has been much debate about the change in Collins' title which was effected very shortly before his death. Michael Collins, as Chairman of the Provisional Government, (equivalent to Prime Minister) headed the Cabinet, and Arthur Griffith was President of the Dáil. On 21 July 1922 (exactly one month before his assassination) he relinquished this title in favor of that of Commander-in-Chief of the armed forces.

It has been argued and also demonstrated from Collins' own memos to Griffith at the time, that this was his own decision, that there was no question of any "coup" having taken place.

However, as Feehan puts it, those in the Cabinet who wanted to get rid of him (who have been referred to as a "junta") " ... *persuaded him that the great priority at the moment was to win the Civil War, that he was the only one who could do it and that he should relinquish other posts, temporarily of course, and devote himself entirely to this task.*"

This is believable and seems very much in character for Collins. Until the Treaty negotiations, he had always been very much a team player on the Cabinet. Although he could be autocratic in his own sphere, the role of chief executive was one he never sought, but was forced on him by the Dáil split.

After that devastating heartbreak, he struggled under a herculean weight of government portfolios, which no man was meant to handle alone. Although ever fiercely tenacious, he was nonetheless a very young man, who was in way over his head, with the whole weight of the world on his shoulders.

One can imagine, at this point, what a relief it might have been, for someone to tell him what to do. Such advice as this was ingeniously calculated to appeal to everything in his character.

It is also possible that, in doffing his Government title, and assuming a more purely military one, Collins was registering a protest of sorts. Was this a way of saying that it was not his choice, to pursue war against former comrades? Finding himself a minority in the Cabinet, he was again "*merely obeying orders.*" [69] This is a theme he returned to several times in this tumultuous period. In this, he repeatedly refused to be a "dictator" of any kind. And also perhaps, sought to set an example to his own erstwhile troops: that it was time for obedience to a government. That it was necessary to bow to the new Irish government in Dublin: even when it was not everything one wanted in a government;

---

69 See Appendix 5: Collins' reply to mediators.

even when one disagreed with its policy.   As he cogently observed in this period:

> *Rebellion, like other powerful remedies if indulged in too often, can become a habit: a body and soul-destroying habit. ...*

However, this change in Collins' title was not announced to the press or public at the time. Those familiar with intricate details of some palace coups in British history may note an ominous resonance here: subtle, secretive legal enactments, hurried through committee; which soon after prove to profoundly affect a highly-placed personage with powerful enemies. Enactments which prove fantastically convenient for those enemies, when heads begin to roll, shortly afterward. It is a *modus operandi* with a distinguishing odiferous quality: it smells of handlers from the very, very old school of British imperialism.

As it was, exactly one month before the C-in-C's untimely demise, W T Cosgrave (former Minister for Local Government, and, until then, not a luminary in national affairs) became Chairman of the Provisional Government in Collins' place.

Think how convenient it was, one month later, that Collins' successor was already sitting at the head of the Provisional Government when both Griffith and the C-in-C suddenly died within two weeks of each other. And with them, all hope of an amicable settlement with honor to the Civil War. All hope of merging anti-Treaty heroes from the War of Independence into the leadership of the Free State Army. All hope of continuing armed resistance against unionist pogroms in the north.

The Collins-Griffith government became the Cosgrave government, indefinitely. With a very different direction for Ireland indeed: from there, the Free State seemed to become everything the anti-Treaty side said it was.

What can be said with certainty is that Collins' change in title entirely altered the color of his demise. In a very real sense, it turned down the "heat" on the perpetrators. As an assassinated head of a national government, his death would have been many times bigger news. Far more official scrutiny and even more public outrage would have been unavoidable. It would have been elevated to even more international interest. As Commander-in-Chief, his death was confined to Irish affairs.

Which causes us to wonder: without this change in his title, from civil to military leader, would it have been possible *not* to hold a public inquiry into his death?

The Cabinet and the death of Collins

> *Much as has been said against [the Cabinet,] I have never heard it seriously suggested that they planned and ordered his death.*

We cannot dispute this sensible observation by Feehan. Yet, once Collins had made for himself, on Ireland's behalf, such powerful enemies as the British secret service and their handlers, all the Cabinet needed to do to get rid of him was *do nothing*.

Members of the Cabinet profited enormously from their positions as heads of the new Irish State. With Michael Collins at the helm, those positions would have been considerably less secure, less autonomous and more demanding. "*He worked sixteen hours a day and expected everyone else to do the same.*"

Was the Treaty and the Civil War which it ignited, in a sense, the "counter-revolution"? A strategy to put the breaks on the independence struggle; to extirpate its most effective leadership; and replace that leadership's agenda? In this case, with a Dublin government less staunchly opposed to cooperation with imperialist interests: even willing to perpetuate old policies of colonialistic exploitation?

> *There are a lot of unanswered questions and mysterious incidents which [the Cabinet] could have cleared up and did not, and if the finger of guilt is sometimes pointed at them they have only themselves to blame.* [70]

---

70   J Feehan

Chapter 5

The Authors of the Civil War and their purposes

Was the Civil War on some level, a kind of assassination campaign in itself? Was that hell paved by the best intentions of many of the brightest and most dedicated in Ireland, in truth a trap set by the British establishment (who emerged from the wreckage its sole beneficiaries)? If so, it did exactly what it was intended to do, by its true planners.

> *A prime factor, of paramount importance ... was the wholehearted cooperation and support of the people, without which the War of Independence could never have been waged.* [71]

Unity was Ireland's most powerful weapon in the War of Independence. More than any single individual, party, region or strategy, this was the key factor which spelt Britain's defeat. By the dawn of the 20th century, after four hundred years of famine and cultural devastation, the notoriously factious Irish were ready to agree on one thing: British rule must go.

Their opponents in London were keenly cognizant of this. By 1921 the British had to face that there was no conventional military solution. It was time to change tactics: only their formidable arsenal of diplomatic chicanery could now salvage anything from the wreck of British dominance in Ireland. This they brought into play with consummate subtlety and skill. *"Come into my parlour, said the spider..."*

During the Truce, when Collins encountered Lord French at a diplomatic event in London, he had the characteristic gall to mention that "*my boys*" had had the former Lord Lieutenant in their sights on his last visit to Dublin. "*But I called them off.*" To which French quipped that he could do Collins as good a turn by meeting him at dinner in London. (Now we know what he meant.)

> *What are parties given for in London, but that enemies may meet?*

---

[71] L Deasy

— Henry James

In the Treaty negotiations themselves, Churchill is quoted as having countered certain objections from the Irish delegates with the explicit statement, "*In that case, there would be civil war.*" It is the first mention on record of the possibility of civil war in connection with Irish independence. Perhaps the author may be excused for admitting that this scene raises in the mind's eye a vivid image of that famous English statesman salivating and "washing" his hands like a stage villain as he spoke these words.

It was a self-fulfilling prophecy indeed. Particularly in view of the fact that it was this very same Churchill himself who was to take such pains to personally see that the Civil War got started, in the teeth of Collins' resistance.

After Collins had handled the explosive situation at Four Courts with kid gloves for two months, it would be Churchill's ultimatum, and his threats of all-out British invasion of Ireland, which precipitated the Free State army's bombardment of the anti-Treaty garrison, which marked the real beginning of the Civil War.

THE NORTH

The spreading [Civil War], marked by the cessation of IRA operations in the north, was correctly interpreted by the unionist government and armed loyalism as effectively removing the threat of concerted assault on the northern state.[72]

That threat was more real and present than most people, (including many historians,) realize or acknowledge. A shooting war between Irish troops and their British / loyalist counterparts in the northeast flared up continually throughout 1922. It included both IRA guerrilla actions and Free State regulars, British troops and loyalist paramilitaries combined. It moved Churchill to call for defense preparations against a Dublin-sponsored invasion of Ulster.

Before the ink on the Treaty was dry, even as he smiled and shook hands and signed agreements, Churchill was funding, directing and protecting military aggression in Ulster (both on and off the record.)

---

72 E Phoenix

Michael Collins, not to be outdone, cooperated without hesitation in republican units' response there (while smiling and shaking hands and signing agreements in London also.)

On 1st and 2nd August 1922, the C-in-C met with northern officers at Portobello Barracks in Dublin. He told them, "*The civil war will be over in a few weeks and then we can resume in the north. You men will get intensive training.*" Collins explained that, until the Civil War was resolved, IRA in the north would have to remain defensive and avoid engagements. A small, specially paid "Belfast Guard" would be created to protect Catholic areas from sectarian attacks. The Dublin government in the meantime would apply political pressure. Said Collins, "*If that fails, the Treaty can go to hell, and we will start again.*" [73]

Following the British soldiers' killing of two adolescent girls near the northern border, an outraged Collins wrote to WT Cosgrave:

> *I am forced to the conclusion that we have yet to fight the British in the northeast. We must by forceful action make them understand that we will not tolerate this carelessness with the lives of our people.*

In other correspondence:

> *[Northeast Ulster] must be redeemed for Ireland, and we must keep striving in every way until that objective is achieved. The northeast must not be allowed to settle down in the feeling that it is a thing apart from the Irish nation.*[74]

> *Six counties implies coercion. South and east Down, south Armagh, Fermanagh and Tyrone will not come into Northern Ireland.*

> *The Boundary Commission ... would be certain to deprive "Ulster" of Fermanagh and Tyrone ... Shorn of these counties,*

---

73 Affidavit of Thomas Kelly, quoting Collins from meeting of Northern Division commanders, in Officers Mess at Portobello Barracks, August 2 1922. It is lamentable indeed to see, in such otherwise laudable efforts as B Feeney's fine history of Sinn Fein, language which accuses Collins of a dismissive or opportunistic attitude toward the north; when this is so entirely disproved by the record.

74 M Collins, letter to DeValera 1921

she would shrink into insignificance. The burdens and financial restrictions of the Partition Act will remain on northeast Ulster if she decides to stay out. No lightening of these burdens can be effected by the English Parliament without the consent of Ireland. Thus union is certain. The only question for northeast Ulster is "How soon?". [75]

During his final journey, he allegedly carried with him terms on offer to the anti-Treaty side. It is believed that these included a plan for honourable compromise with "die-hard" elements: those determined to go on fighting, would be welcome to do so: in the north, with Dublin's blessing.

Collins' death put an end to all that. Not less a blow was the utter loss of the backbone which had made it all possible: widespread support by the Irish public for the underground military. The excesses of the Civil War, falling exclusively on the heads of Irish men and women themselves, disenchanted popular cooperation. This was one of the biggest casualties of that conflict. Such mass support for armed struggle was never again forthcoming, until Sinn Fein's landmark electoral victories of the 1980s.

With Collins removed, subsequent Dublin governments were content, or reduced, to leave the northern nationalists twisting in the wind.

*   *   *

Thus it may be seen that removing Collins would have been critical to the fulfilment of British imperialist agendas for the north: agendas which such elements proved demonstrably willing to kill for, and to go on killing for, indefinitely.

It is offered that the disastrous split in nationalist ranks, which plunged Ireland into disaster, had its ultimate source in the British Empire's war room. If that is the "why", the "how" concerns our next chapters.

---

75   M Collins, London Treaty negotiations, October 1921

CHAPTER 6

DEVALERA

ARCHITECT OF THE CIVIL WAR

Collins' death was directly attributable to the Treaty dispute among the Dáil leadership, and the resulting split in the army. This split was led and actuated by DeValera, ostensibly on the argument that the Treaty negotiators had betrayed Ireland, by failing to secure London's agreement to the immediate establishment of an independent republic.

In some quarters, this debate still rages. Yet the documentation now entirely proves beyond any doubt that it was DeValera himself who agreed with British authorities in advance, that there would be no republic at that time.

It is generally allowed that had it been DeValera who returned from London with an agreement which Collins didn't like, there'd have been no Civil War. It was DeValera who turned the guns away from British targets and toward Irish comrades, with his infamous *"rivers of blood"* speeches. Michael Collins questioned him to his face in a meeting, *"Are we the members of the Irish government whose blood is to be waded through?"* To which DeValera replied, *"You are two,"* (addressing Arthur Griffith [76] as well.)

DeValera had a hand in Collins' death ... only in the sense that he was the principal architect of the overall civil war situation. [77]

All the casualties and disaster of the Civil War rest squarely on DeValera's shoulders. In that sense at least, Collins' death included. There were no winners in the Civil War; with the exception of the British and DeValera himself: everyone who could really compete with him for the political leadership of Ireland died in 1922.

---

[76] In a previous attempt to split the Irish independence movement, DeValera had contested the presidency of Sinn Fein against Arthur Griffith in 1917. In typical Griffith style, the organization's founder manoeuvred to prevent disunity, during this critical period in the wake of the 1916 Rising. Thus it was through an agreed settlement with Griffith, that DeValera first acquired the presidency.

[77] T P Coogan

Author of the "Free State" Dominion compromise

> "Any news, Dave?" [asked Collins.]
> "Yes, Cope met DeValera in town last night," [Neligan] answered.
> "How the hell did you hear that? ... Yes," said Collins, "there's a peace move on, but it is supposed to be a dead secret."

DeValera was the main Irish negotiator, for the preliminary meetings which established the terms upon which talks would be based. With the Government of Ireland Act 1920, partition was a *done deal before* negotiations opened. The British King had, with supreme political irony, made his great conciliatory speech calling for compromise in the War of Independence, at the opening of the new mini-parliament for the north.

> Michael Collins: The northern parliament is a joke.
> Lloyd George: It will function tomorrow.
> Arthur Griffith: It will never function. Our people will never consent to remain subject to it. [78]

This means that DeValera's blood and thunder tirades about how Collins had "*betrayed the Republic*" were pure grandstanding. It means that he issued his call for civil war, not in any idealistic confusion, but with the most cold-blooded foresight. If so, it can only have been for one purpose, and that is the purpose it achieved: to secure to himself the dominant political position in the new Ireland.

DeValera was entirely sincere about "*wading through Irish blood.*" Was the Civil War his plan to climb to domination over the dead bodies of his countrymen? Did that not prove to be his path of promotion to the lofty plane of semi-permanent presidency? Was the slaughter of so many great heroes of the War of Independence, the bereavement of countless families, the gutting of the national economy: all these plagues which the Civil War unleashed, was this the cost he calculated as fit to win him that prize?

---

[78] F Parkenham *Peace By Ordeal*

DeValera and Lloyd George

In 1921, Lloyd George and Eamonn DeValera were two men with serious political problems.

> *No doubt [Michael Collins] is the head and front of the movement. If I could see him, a settlement might be possible. The question is whether the British people would be willing for us to negotiate with the head of a band of murderers.*
> - Lloyd George, 1921

> *I must get out of the straight-jacket of the republic*
> . - E DeValera 1921

For years, the London authorities had bombarded their public with the most vituperative propaganda, swearing that there was no problem in Ireland, except only a band of bloodthirsty cutthroats beneath the notice of decent government, led by a vicious thug named Collins. They now found themselves backs to the wall, with no choice but to negotiate with the very man himself: while their own secret service was baying for Collins' blood (not an agency it was wise to alienate.)

Lloyd George had learned that Collins would be a tough customer to deal with for the next fifty years. It was clear that a post-war government headed by Collins was going to pose many more grave future problems for British imperialist interests, than a post-war government led by ... just about anyone else.

Meanwhile, Mr. DeValera had arrived back in Ireland just in time to miss all the shooting. He had barely touched soil when he began voicing his resentment at finding that Collins, a man he considered his lieutenant, now towered head and shoulders above him in public stature. He was now distinctly in the shadow of Collins, who was universally regarded as the effective leader of the movement. The fact that Collins welcomed him as president, that Collins had always chosen and adhered to a role just peripheral to that of chief executive, did not seem to comfort him. As he stepped off the boat where he landed, DeValera ominously growled, *"I'll show them who's a big fella."* [79]

---

[79] Reported by Batt O'Connor, who was one of the party which met DeValera at the boat.

At the same time, DeValera and his associates were eager to come to agreement with Britain. Yet from the first exploratory communications, it was clear that a republic was not going to be on the table.

How could DeValera re-establish his position as titular head of the new Ireland? How would he ever step out of Collins' now overpowering shadow? One thing was certain: he wasn't going to win any popularity contests by being the bearer of the bad news that we're going to settle with the British, for something less than a republic right now. That would surely be the death knell of his now precarious career.

We know that he did indeed escape from the *"straight-jacket of the republic."* And we know how he escaped: a veritable political Houdini.

Two statesmen with problems

By August 1921, DeValera's private meetings and correspondence with Lloyd George had agreed partition, in exchange for a Dublin-based Irish government in the south. But they knew well that let whomsoever be the bearer of this bad news, the Irish public, especially its most militant elements, would be ready to "kill the messenger."

> *Michael Collins ... will have a republic and he carries a gun and makes it impossible to negotiate. DeValera cannot come here and say he is willing to give up Irish independence, for if he did he might be shot.*
> — Lloyd George, memo to cabinet April 1921

In a long, private *tête-à-tête* with Lloyd George, the substance of which was never revealed, these two consummate politicians could not have taken long to realize that there was one answer to both their problems. It is offered that this is when DeValera did the political "dance of the seven veils": that he promised then to deliver Collins' head on a silver platter. And in return, Lloyd George promised that DeValera would dominate Ireland for the rest of his life. Both their problems would be solved.

> *DeValera: "How can I come over and negotiate a Treaty if I know in advance there can be no republic?"*

Lloyd George: "You don't have to come. Send somebody else!" [80]

No doubt DeValera fully appreciated that the British establishment would now need some "very special help" to achieve their goals in Ireland. That very special help would have to be someone who understood the Irish people thoroughly, as well as the movement, and the army. It would have to be someone so highly placed in the provisional government, that it would have virtually no secrets from him. And, above all, someone who knew Michael Collins intimately.

Someone who knew how to find Collins; but was cagey enough never to give the game away. Someone who knew all about the way Collins used intelligence and how he planned an action. Someone who knew not only his tactics, but also his personality through and through: what he cared about; how to get his goat, what he would fight for, how much he could take, what he would sacrifice and what he would not. *The way his mind worked and what would break his heart.*

> *When I was caught for this delegation, my first thought was how easily I had walked into it. But having walked in, I had to stay.*

In this letter excerpt, was Collins writing of his first inkling about betrayal by someone close to him, in the highest echelons of the provisional government? Someone with the motive, means, opportunity and the cold-bloodedness to sacrifice the C-in-C and countless others, on the altar of his personal ambition? In another letter around that time, he was more explicit:

> *The Treaty will not be accepted in Dublin, not by those who have in mind personal ambitions under pretence of patriotism.*

DeValera had extremely valuable assets to offer: he knew Collins' character thoroughly. Unlike anyone in London, DeValera could, in a word, predict how the elusive mastermind of the War of Independence would react in a given situation. He knew his loyalties, and his *modus operandi*.

---

80 J Feehan: Collins had excellent intelligence sources within the British administration. This is a version of what had passed in DeValera's secret tête-à-tête with Lloyd George, which reached him shortly afterward. Subsequent events would seem to support it.

Remember that a proclamation ... may fling the enthusiast into the bosom of the opposite party to the one which he has served all his life.

- Stendahl

He knew that, so very far from any "dictatorial" aspirations, Collins would always bow to the majority's decision. He knew Collins was a "*realistic idealist*". And that, once convinced of the necessity of settling the war now, on the best terms available, he would pursue that agenda with all the herculean energy at his command. He knew that Collins' best advisers would surely counsel him to do just that. He knew that Collins would go to great lengths to prevent the kind of all-out British military bombardment which Ireland had suffered in 1916: would do anything to avert that kind of massive destruction and loss of civilian lives.

The political Houdini act

If DeValera's ambition was to position himself as the greatest man, somewhere, then the country's state of upheaval was a golden opportunity, for one ready to seize it. If only he observed that key principle, long recognized by politicians on the island: that the British authorities must be appeased.

Collins refused to bow to that principle. He, and the hard-line republican military behind him, would be the chiefest obstacles in DeValera's path to hegemony. To appease the British and win the dominant role for himself, what DeValera had to do was to engineer the neutralization of the nationalist military who had won the war. And "keep the con": that is, assure that it would never be generally known, that this is what he had done. (At least, as long as his career was to survive.)

DeValera had quite simply stolen republicans' clothing and would wear them for the rest of his career. [81]

This meant that the operation would entail not only some physical assassinations, but character assassinations as well. DeValera, after compromising with the British in early negotiations, would have to

---

81   B Feeney

publicly disassociate himself from that compromise. Somehow, he would have to steal away the mantle of hard-line republicanism, slip Collins into the role of moderate ... and then scream, *"Traitor!"*

In the tinder box of a nation torn by revolution, this was the political equivalent of shouting *"Fire!"* in a dark and crowded theatre.

With some advice from Lloyd George, the plan was set. It was time for the political Houdini act. DeValera would effectively switch roles with Collins. With a bombastic flourish of publicity, he would denounce Collins as the base betrayer of Irish republicanism: as a drunkard who had been seduced by the wine, women and luxuries of London, into signing away the republic, by the stroke of a pen. And portray himself, DeValera, as Ireland's only savior from this catastrophe.

Sell this analysis to a lot of "die-hard" republicans, who had formed the core of the clandestine Irish army (especially focusing on local commanders who, due to past friction with Collins' sometimes abrasive personality, might relish a reason to challenge him.) This would decimate the bodyguard which had kept him alive. Seduce away from him, under this banner, men like Harry Boland, Cathal Brugha and Rory O'Connor: just the ones who were bound to be most problematic to DeValera's leadership, in the future dominion state which was now on the cards.

Make stirring calls to "*wade through rivers of blood*" (meaning the blood of DeValera's political competitors): in colorful terms which would be appealing to the pugnacious spirit of these elements. And generally thus paint DeValera as a firebrand of republicanism.

The ensuing civil war would create sufficient confusion to camouflage Collins' assassination, and that of many others, in the general welter of violence. It would decimate the underground military which had dealt Britain its defeat. It would totally undermine the Irish unity which had made it all possible. It would assure that the revolution would stop here: saying "*thus far and no further, to the progress of a nation.*"

All of this would place DeValera in the enviable position of being London's major creditor, indebted to him *for life*. Not incidentally, it would exterminate everyone who could compete with DeValera for the national leadership. And that is what happened.

This man, who was present at Béal na mBláth on the day of Collins' assassination, was uniquely qualified to provide that very special help the British so needed. [82]

DeValera and Liam Lynch

> *[At] a meeting of the IRB in Parnell Place, Cork in November [1921] ... It was a large gathering including practically every centre of south Munster ... Before going into the meeting Michael Collins had a private talk with Liam Lynch, Florrie O'Donoghue and myself ... Collins said privately but quite definitely that there would have to be some compromise in the current negotiations in London. There was no question of our getting all the demands we were making. Lynch asked Collins not to repeat this at the meeting or else it would "blow up." ... Thinking back on that meeting I wondered if Lynch was wrong in stopping Collins from issuing a warning that a republic was not on the cards?* [83]

More than any other single factor, the Civil War may be largely attributed to failure to adequately inform and prepare the ranks to understand what was happening in the Treaty negotiations. Here we see Lynch himself actively endeavoring to prevent transparent, direct communication between Collins and the army on this pivotal issue.

This eloquent episode would also seem to establish beyond reasonable doubt that Lynch himself was very well-informed. Clearly he knew first-hand that Collins was dealing in good faith as a negotiator. He knew that Collins himself wanted to discuss the progress of the talks in London, openly with the assembled ranks that day in November 1921, before the Treaty was ever signed. *And it was Lynch himself who persuaded him not to.*

This casts an interesting light indeed on Lynch's subsequent role in the war; and in Béal na mBláth. If DeValera was the political leader of

---

[82] Anomalies in the 1916 trials and sentencing of DeValera and of C Marckievitch raise questions as to whether these two may have won preferential treatment at that stage, (or earlier,) through promises of cooperation. It would go far to explain DeValera's tactical retreat to America until the fighting was over, and his extremely divisive role thereafter. Dublin Castle's list, offering a reward for the capture of certain Irish leaders, omitted DeValera: orders were not to arrest him. Upon his return to Ireland in 1920, he pressed for a retreat from war against England; and pressured Collins to go to America. All of which would have fulfilled British goals. For a full examination of this question, see J Turi.

[83] L Deasy

the anti-Treaty cause in the Civil War, Liam Lynch was its supreme military chief of staff. The two cooperated very closely; but perhaps never more so, than in the days leading up to Collins' assassination.

DeValera's movements in Cork shadowed those of Collins' last days. Reportedly, witnesses who were present at rendezvous between DeValera and Lynch (hosting farmers, drivers, etc.) have read into the record enough sound bytes from those meetings to leave little room for doubt that the political and military leaders of the anti-Treaty side were planning to do away with the C-in-C, and directing more than one attempt to do so. [84]

---

84 One such account has them lamenting together that a mine laid in the path of Collins' car, near Cobh, had failed to explode.

Chapter 7

Why and How did the Civil War start?

We, the undersigned officers of the IRA,[85] realising the gravity of the present situation in Ireland, and appreciating the fact that if the present drift is maintained a conflict of comrades is inevitable, declare that this would be the greatest calamity in Irish history, and would leave Ireland broken for generations.

To avert this catastrophe we believe that a closing of the ranks all round is necessary.

We suggest to all leaders, Army and political, and all citizens and soldiers of Ireland the advisability of a unification of forces on the basis of the acceptance and utilisation of our present national position in the best interests of Ireland, and we require that nothing shall be done that would prejudice our position or dissipate our strength.

We feel that on this basis alone can the situation best be faced, viz.:
1) *The acceptance of the fact - admitted by all sides - that the majority of the people of Ireland are willing to accept the Treaty.*
2) *An agreed election with a view to*
3) *Forming a Government which will have the confidence of the whole country.*
4) *Army unification on above basis*

    Dan Breen   Tom Hales   Owen O'Duffy
    H Murphy   S O'Hegerty   Gearoid O'Sullivan
    F O'Donoghue   Seán Boylan   Miceál O'Coileáin[86]
    RJ Mulcahy

---

[85] This statement, known as "The Army Document" was published on 1 May 1922, and signed by equal numbers of both pro- and anti-Treaty officers of the Irish volunteers.

[86] "Michael Collins" (Irish spelling)

Why did it start?

During the Truce and the Treaty negotiations, the Irish partisans who had just won the War of Independence looked to the Dáil for political leadership. Their split into armed factions did not precede any move by the elected members, but followed. If the Dáil leadership had remained united regarding the Treaty, the army would have fallen in behind them. There may have been, at worst, some peripheral splintering. There would have been no civil war.

> *For me it had all begun with the Truce on 11 July 1921, continuing with the signing of the Treaty, and culminating in the fatal Dáil debate followed by banning the Volunteer Convention in March 1922. From there on events had marched rapidly ...* [87]

As the Dáil split, many in the army which had won the victory, and in the political leadership who negotiated the peace, began to eye each other with apprehension. Flaws in keeping the ranks up to date on the peace process had caused alienation. Suspicion began to circulate, that the cause was being "sold out".

The Volunteers' national convention had been scheduled in March, to discuss the issues. That same month, anti-Treaty forces seized several buildings in Limerick. This led to GHQ's decision to ban the convention. This instantly compounded the very tensions which it was intended to quell. Anti-Treaty leaders refer to this as one of the key mistakes which led toward civil war. It assured that the convention, which took place anyway, was attended preponderantly by those ready to defy the authority of GHQ. The new Army Executive elected at this convention was therefore populated by the most militant anti-Treaty faction. Thus the ban seems to have been self-defeating: it exacerbated problems with the army.

Florrie O'Donoghue, who remained neutral during the Civil War, has provided an excellent nutshell of the two factions, as expressed at an IRB meeting in January 1922:

---

[87] L Deasy

Those in favour of accepting the position created by the Dáil vote argued that to do so would be in line with well-established IRB policy, that there was nothing dishonorable in advocating such a course, that it was a matter of expediency and not of principle ... The country had made substantial advance towards its goal of complete independence. The people were war weary. Wisdom and practical common sense suggested that the advantages which had been gained should be seized and utilised, and that it would be foolish and irresponsible to commit the Irish people to war again for the difference between the Treaty and the most that could be attained with our present strength.

The other side was presented with equal sincerity. The Republic had been established and ratified by the votes of the people at two elections, therefore no analogy existed between . .. any previous crisis and the position now. Acceptance of the Treaty would disestablish the Republic, and for the first time in our history the people would have, by their own deliberate act, accepted foreign domination. The country was being partitioned, ... nationalists ... in the partitioned area were being abandoned to the blind fury of the Orange mob ... to eradicate and destroy them. We were not beaten in the field, we were in a better position ... than at any time since 1916; and above all, ... [they] had solemnly bound themselves on oath to maintain and defend the Republic, and should be the last to desert it.

At the same time, others sought to exploit the uproar. Instead of striving for the good of "*all the children of the nation*," [88] cynical opportunists seized upon the transition, as a chance to eliminate competitors. The passions and fighting spirit which the War of Independence had unleashed were a powerful force, still in motion. At this critical moment, the fate of the nation depended on bringing that juggernaut in for a safe landing. Some saw in this their chance to secure high positions, by letting it spin out of control, slaughtering the best and brightest.

A few remarkable characters stand out boldly from the pages of history, as either black or white: completely devoted, either to the common good, or to their personal ambition alone. Many ordinary

---

88 From the 1916 Proclamation of Irish independence.

people in extraordinary circumstances partook some of each. It was not difficult, in this crisis, for sincere patriots to be led astray, when the controversies of the cause became intermixed with personal grudges and jealousies.

This syndrome is not unique to Ireland, but an occupational hazard for all popular revolutions.

Michael Collins: first of the "die-hards"

It was Collins who had always consistently opposed entering into negotiations until a republic was offered. But when overruled by his colleagues in the Dáil, he dutifully bowed to the majority's decision. However, early in the first parlays, Collins did momentarily break ranks. He simply refused to end the war; and proved he had the power to do so.

This was occasioned by initial prisoner exchanges. Sean McEion was one of the war's most effective leaders outside Dublin. The British agreed to release all imprisoned Irish combatants: except McEion. Collins responded swiftly with an announcement that there would be no settlement without McEion's release. He did this on his own initiative, without Dáil approval. Because he could. It was effective. McEion was freed.

This episode spoke volumes. It was, in a sense, a mini-civil war in a teacup. Like many of those who ultimately formed the anti-Treaty side, Collins was initially suspicious of the peace process, and at least half-expected the war to resume before long. (He was not far wrong.) He intimated to friends his intention to "*go back to West Cork, to fight in the open, among my own people, if the war breaks out again.*"

A man who could, by his word alone, grant or withhold a ceasefire? Who could have Dublin's entire British secret service presence shot in their beds in one day? Who could elude the world's most sophisticated intelligence service while living right under their noses? To disappear into the hills of West Cork and carry on the war where they'd never see him again? This was the British authorities' worst nightmare.

Just imagine, what might have been the outcome, with Michael Collins at the head of the "die-hards"! Once the Civil War began, many anti-Treaty hold-outs were convinced that he would soon realize "*he was fighting on the wrong side.*" While Collins lived, Deasy continued to hope that he would ultimately join them.

Were they far wrong? As seen above, many of his off-the-record remarks suggest that such a development may not have been entirely out of the question. Right up until the bombardment of Four Courts, Collins continued to cooperate with anti-Treaty comrades, in clandestine operations against Orange terror in the north. In public and private, he was explicit: he was entirely prepared to break the Treaty over the treatment of Catholics in Ulster, if necessary.

> *If the so-called government in Belfast has not the power nor the will to protect its citizens, then the Irish Government must find means to protect them.* [89]

The British were still bleeding from their last wrestling match with Mr. Collins. They did not want another. Had he carried out this alternate contingency plan, say, in case of intolerable developments in the north, the possibilities would have been utterly unpredictable.

This is precisely the scenario which, with some "very special help," the Civil War was created to render <u>impossible</u>.

How did it start?

> *The Civil War had only begun when initiatives started to bring it to an end. ... We were well and truly beaten long before this. In fact almost from 20 June when we had declared our support for the men in the Four Courts, it was a losing battle.* [90]

Just the same, the Civil War by no means broke out instantaneously or thoughtlessly. Tremendous efforts were carried on, for months on end, to avert the outbreak of hostilities. The Army Document (shown in its entirely at the head of this chapter) was only one statement, produced in one round of meetings. Countless such parlays convened, from January (when the Dáil split) thru June 1922. The most painstaking debates were carried on interminably, by those who had risked every danger together for years.

Many strove desperately to find some means of going forward without civil conflict. Indeed, there is an awesome sense of tragedy, in reviewing the transcripts of these debates: to hear echo again the penetrating observations, poignant pleas, passionate oaths, of the

---

89   Michael Collins' speech at Wexford 9 April 1922

90   L Deasy

greatest hearts and minds of that heroic era; many of whom would soon be silenced forever. Silenced by the outcome of their own relentless march: into the disaster which they all knew that this war would bring.

Yet still some could listen, unabated in their determination to turn the guns on comrades, far less eager to avoid that at all cost. (It must be noted that Liam Lynch was not a signatory of The Army Document.)

No war ever begins for just one reason. All the factors set forth so far, in the sections above, may be seen as a powder keg: the explosive elements which placed the country in danger of war breaking out. In that sense, the siege of the Four Courts was the fuse, and the assassination of Sir Henry Wilson the spark, which together set off the conflagration; which cost so many lives, and broke out afresh in the northern Troubles of the 1970s -1990s.

Of all 20th century Ireland's critical turning points, these twin triggers to the Civil War's outbreak, have been among the most understudied. Both events remain at this writing still shrouded in mystery and controversy.

The Four Courts occupation

> *At best the Four Courts could only be considered as a protest in arms with failure as the inevitable end.* [91]

On 14 April 1922, anti-Treaty military units occupied the Four Courts and several other prominent public buildings in Dublin. Their argument was essentially that they rejected anything less than an entirely independent Irish republic immediately; and vowed not to lay down their arms for intermediary arrangements which accepted any British role in Ireland's government whatever.

Rory O'Connor, one of the leaders of the Four Courts garrison, did not mince words: "*Some of us are no more prepared to stand for DeValera than for the Treaty.*" Clashes between the Free State army and anti-Treaty units broke out in several regions around the country. Anti-Treaty guerrilla campaigns sought to disrupt the country with sabotage and destruction of public property. Their strategy seems to have been to block the Free State dominion government from coming into effect, by a reign of general anarchy (wherever they could not replace it with their own anti-Treaty councils.) [92]

---

91   Ibid.

The most important building seized was the Four Courts: a palatial Greek revival pile on the River Liffey. Since the 18th century, it had housed Ireland's superior courts, and other key administrative offices, such as the national archives. This latter included masses of priceless, irreplaceable records, such as every census ever taken, and ancient vellum scrolls stretching back to the island's misty, semi-mythical past. [93]

It cannot be disputed but that in handling this situation, Collins practiced extreme restraint and reluctance to fire on former comrades. His unwillingness to rush in, with the kind of aggressive military response which some Cabinet colleagues were calling for, was the subject of continual friction with them, which has been well recorded. Until June 23, Collins, as head of the military, continued to treat the anti-Treaty presence at Four Courts as a "protest in arms."

Not all his fellow ministers may have realized that Collins, still on the Supreme Council of the IRB, had been engaged throughout this period in continual conferences within that still-secret brotherhood. Pro- and anti-Treaty therein endeavored to find a basis for unity, and avoid civil war. *"Here, if anywhere in the distracted ranks of republicanism, many members thought, some hope of internal peace must lie."* [94]

One such IRB meeting took place on 19 April, just days after the seizure of Four Courts and other buildings. *"Incidents which had taken place throughout the country led to heated exchanges between some of those present. ... The atmosphere of the meeting was tense and explosive."* O'Donoghue goes on to describe:

> *Collins, who could be explosive himself on occasion, was grimly cool and calm. He said that ... the [new national] constitution*

---

92   At the zenith of their campaign, anti-Treaty forces gained practically complete control of Cork City and large parts of Munster, where virtually all active Volunteers went against the Free State. For a short time, they ran local government, collected taxes, supervised news media, managed the harbour ports, etc.

93   The destruction of the Four Courts' vast ancient records was a catastrophic loss which can never be calculated: not only for the nation, but for world history as well. Yet contrary to popular belief, it was not the bombardment which destroyed the archive. A lorry filled with gelignite, parked next to the records office, was somehow set off. It was the biggest explosion in Dublin's history. Evidence suggests that this took place after the bombardment and surrender were over. A point which might reward further investigation.

94   F O'Donoghue

would be available in three or four weeks, and that in it may possibly be found a basis for unity.

So while his Cabinet reproached him with "*procrastinating*" on military action against the rebels, Collins remained under secret obligations to his IRB brothers, including those garrisoned at Four Courts. He had made an undertaking to try to produce a constitution: one which would provide republicans with a way clear to lay down their arms, and participate in the new Irish state.

The Free State Army

"You'll get none of my men for that," said Collins.
"That's alright Mister Collins, ... I'll get men of my own." [95]

During the Truce, the composition of Ireland's armed forces was radically overhauled: true to this ominous promise which had been uttered by Cathal Brugha, not long after DeValera's return from an extended tour of America.

Collins retained the loyalty of the majority of the GHQ of the IRA, of his intelligence corps, and the Squad, as well as men like Sean McEoin, but a majority perhaps of the IRA throughout the country went on the other side, among them units that had done little or nothing in the war with the British.[96]

While Collins was overwhelmed with political battles in which the Treaty dispute ensnared him, the armed forces of Ireland were made over. Since the Truce, his military role had been progressively somewhat overshadowed by his statesmanship (the war being officially over, for the time.)

As the Treaty debates raged, British troops in Ireland, when demobilized, were invited to join the new Free State army. Dalton and Mulcahy oversaw this recruitment process. In addition, "*Soldiers ...*

---

95   This famous exchange was occasioned by a plan put forward by DeValera and Cathal Brugha, ostensibly to machine gun civilians queuing at cinemas in England.

96   L Ó'Broin

discharged at Colchester Barracks [in England] ... found, affixed to their discharge papers, slips inviting them to join the Irish Free State army 'where you will be heartily welcome.' " [97]

> [The army] had probably comprised around 3000 fighting men at the time of the Truce. But an unhealthy mushroom growth took place after that so that by the "beginning of November 1921, nominal IRA strength was listed as 72,363." Most of these "Trucileers", as they were called, were poorly disciplined and (a great source of suspicion and tension to men who had fought all through the Black and Tan War) were former British Army men. [98]

The upshot of all this was that a substantial percentage of the volunteer force who had won the War of Independence under Collins, joined the anti-Treaty side *against* him; leaving the C-in-C with an army heavily loaded with new recruits who were, in frightening numbers, British Army soldiers yesterday. It was during this period that he reportedly said to a friend,

"*If this is to be the Free State army, I want no part of it.*

The Pact elections

While the armed sit-in at Four Courts continued, Collins and others moved feverishly to patch the country back together. Ten leading officers, from both sides of the Treaty dispute, signed the statement shown above (known as the Army Document.) Their declaration therein, that the civil conflict now threatening "*would be the greatest calamity in Irish history, and would leave Ireland broken for generations*" was prophetic enough.

Although the Four Courts men rejected the Army Document, "*it ... could not be entirely ignored.*" [99] Liam Mellows, a member of the garrison, made a presentation to the Dáil, as did Kathleen Clarke,[100] who,

---

97 J Feehan
98 T P Coogan

99 Ibid.

100 Widow of Thomas Clarke, one of the organizers and martyrs of the 1916 Easter Rising. Mrs. Clarke remained active in the movement for independence and, later, in the Irish government, throughout her life.

like many prominent women in the independence movement, opposed the Treaty.[101] Sean O'Hegerty *"reminded a hushed assembly that the national position, which for some time had been drifting, was now driving toward disaster. He called upon the Dáil ... to find a solution which would save the country from civil war."* [102] The anti-Treaty army faction thus expressly pleaded with the civil branch to provide leadership: which would enable them to lay down their arms, with honour.

Ultimately all these efforts culminated in the Collins-DeValera Pact. This stipulated that new elections be immediately held: candidates for the Dáil would stand as either pro- or anti-Treaty, and a national referendum would decide on whether or not to accept the Treaty. No matter which side proved more numerous, pro- and anti-Treaty representatives would cooperate together in a coalition government. (This would be the Third Dáil.)

Meanwhile, London was calling, to express their discontent with the continued occupation of government buildings by insurgents. It also seems that Churchill was considerably displeased at the news of this peaceful resolution between Ireland's factions. He ridiculed and ran down the entire idea.

Such a coalition government as envisaged would require a constitution which excused anti-Treaty members of the Dáil from any objectionable oath of fealty to the British Crown. Collins, Griffith and their constitutional committee painstakingly thrashed out a draft, with a revised version of the oath. Then, in accordance with the Treaty, they had to literally take it to London. After several days of more exhaustive niggling with the wily British ministers, they returned with little left which would allow anti-Treaty deputies to take their seats.

The Pact elections took place on 16 June 1922. Pro-Treaty Sinn Fein won 58 seats; anti-Treaty had 35; Labour won 17, Independents had 7, Farmers 7; and 4 Unionists were elected by Trinity College Dublin.

---

101 During this epoch-making period for women, their full participation in politics was still quite controversial. In Europe and the US, women's right to vote was then still at issue, or only recently won. In the Treaty crisis, Cumann na mBan succumbed to a failing common for women upon their first entrance into a male bastion long forbidden them. There was an onus upon them never to be seen to lag behind, never to appear "soft" on hot topics. Thus the women took the "hard" line: Cumann na mBan *"practically unanimously"* opposed the Treaty.

102 F O'Donoghue

Just a week after the election, which seemed to promise peaceful resolution, Sir Henry Wilson was assassinated. Following Wilson's death, Churchill issued his ultimatum: that unless the Provisional Government in Dublin immediately dislodged the rebel occupation at Four Courts, the Treaty would be deemed broken, and a full-scale British invasion would be launched.

How did the bombardment of Four Courts begin?

> *Notices should be served on the armed men in the illegal occupation of the Four Courts and Fowler Hall that night, ordering them to evacuate the buildings and to surrender up all arms and property, and that in the event of their refusing to do so, the necessary military action would be taken at once.*
> — Provisional Government decision 27 June 1922

The bombardment began on 28 June; but precisely how it began, or who gave the order, has never been adequately established. In light of his remarkable role elsewhere, it seems significant that Emmett Dalton was directly involved: ostensibly as officer in charge. This raises serious questions.

It seems difficult indeed to believe that Collins could possibly have delegated this action to any underling whatever. He was painfully aware that Ireland's fate was hanging on the outcome of the siege at Four Courts. This crisis dominated his life for months, during which he consistently strove to handle it with kid gloves: in hopes to avert the explosion, which would so likely be fatal to himself.

The hindsight of history demonstrates that he was among the leaders who clearly foresaw just how terrible a disaster these hostilities would bring. Amidst all the trigger-happy factions, baying for blood at that juncture, in the Free State government, in London and in anti-Treaty camps, Collins by far most strenuously and continually resisted giving battle.

Everything for which he had faced death daily, had lived years as a hunted man, had watched friends and family die for, was at stake in that building on Inns Quay.[103] No matter how exhausting his schedule, it is impossible to conceive that he sent twenty-something Dalton down to

---

103 Contrary to B Feeney, there were for Collins no "*bigger fish to fry elsewhere.*"

Four Courts, saying, "Take care of that little matter, will you?" It's a great square peg sticking out, which does not fit the puzzle.

> *It is still not clear how it started. According to the republicans, they were loading their arms onto lorries and would have evacuated the Four Courts by 8AM in the morning. Had the shelling not started at 4AM, they say, there would have been no Civil War.* [104]

This in itself casts doubts on whoever was in command of the Free State units when the bombardment began. Reputedly, Collins had given strict orders that the anti-Treaty men were to be forced out by cutting off food and water. All records of his communications and meetings on the subject illustrate that his priority was to avoid an actual battle at all cost.

As subsequent events proved, his judgement on this was excellent. It was that explosion of the Four Courts, which he was so keen to avoid, that set off the chain of events which, ultimately, took his own life.

In this context, even if Collins had accepted that he might be obliged to shell the building, it was firstly as a bargaining chip that artillery would have been most useful to him: "Alright lads, it's time to come out, because we'll be knocking the building to atoms with the cannon now." Any negotiator, in any such stand-off, would naturally first seek to take maximum advantage of the *threat* of imminent bombardment, to try to secure a surrender instead.

Unless ... they didn't *want* to give them a *chance* to surrender. Unless ... they *wanted* to start a war.

Certainly, shelling at 4AM did not facilitate such last-minute parlay. On the contrary, it was rather calculated to *prevent* it. Further, it suggests that the Free State officer(s) on duty sought to shroud the artillery under cover of darkness. It means that whoever started the shelling at that hour meant to *surprise* the anti-Treaty men. This announces an agenda to preclude either surrender or escape; thereby inflicting maximum harm.

In view of the anti-Treaty account (that this ill-timed bombshell fell at the very hour when they were preparing to evacuate): Does this suggest that their surrender plans might have been leaked? From inside

---

104   J Feehan. Deasy as well supports this timetable.

the Four Courts? To powerful players with a capacity to arrange for a slight military error? Such as...?

> *Indeed there is as yet no adequate study available dealing with the role of the British secret service in the Civil War. No one really knows how far their promptings were responsible for starting the Civil War or indeed for the subsequent shooting without trial of so many Republican prisoners.* [105]

This was manifestly *not* Collins' strategy. Feehan, with his unique access to contemporary army sources now lost forever, expressly states that Dalton personally "*borrowed artillery from the British and shelled the building,*" and that he did so in direct contradiction to Collins' specific orders. [106]

If this is so, it raises one glaring enigma: why, in that case, would the C-in-C have gone on to entrust Dalton afterward with other such massive responsibilities as the amphibious invasion of Cork City, peace negotiations there, and with his own bodily safety on that fateful journey?

These are questions which we are better able to ask, than to answer here, at this writing. However, it must be observed that, in the Free State Provisional Government, Collins' approach to the anti-Treaty problem was in a distinct minority. Even the usually moderate and reasonable Arthur Griffith found fault with the C-in-C's continual avoidance of a shooting war with the insurgents.

At the same time as all this, Collins was still managing an overwhelming array of cabinet portfolios. He was Chairman of the Cabinet. He was writing the national Constitution. He was commanding an army which had just been decommissioned, then split in half, then re-populated, inflated to enormous numbers, and reorganized.

He was also not the only one giving orders, either in the government or in the army. Several of his colleagues, in both spheres, vocally opposed any delay in aggressive action against the Four Courts

---

105   J Feehan

106   For a discussion of Dalton's connections with British intelligence, see chapter devoted to him below.

garrison. And at 4AM, even in those days, even Collins, was most likely to be at home in bed.[107]

This raises the possibility that the bombardment may have commenced under the guise of an order given on someone else's watch, a bureaucratic misunderstanding, an error in communication, etc. Whether accidentally or otherwise. In any case, Dalton apparently managed to escape blame; even if he was indeed personally responsible for the commencement of shelling, at that hour.

Collins' state of mind

As shown throughout his career, Collins did not favor any public airing of the nationalist government's dirty laundry, which it was possible to avoid. Although he could be notoriously abrasive with colleagues in person, he would not disparage them to the public. He might call his minister an "eejit" in private; but he would shoulder the blame for their errors, rather than publish censures, which could undermine confidence in Ireland's new non-British government.

Evidence of his state of mind, as shown in his personal correspondence contributes to the mystery. His letter to Kitty Kiernan dated June 28 (just hours before the bombardment began) is of particular interest:

> *Even in the midst of today's business I stop for a short while to write you a word, as of course you may be inclined to worry. ... At the time of writing this, there is nothing very exciting going on, but I'm looking forward to an interesting evening, although for the sake of the people I hope the thing won't last very much longer. ... I do wish you'd come up for the weekend or some time very very soon. Of course there is no chance of getting away and as for coming up, I suppose that had better be left until we have an end to the present business.*

"*The present business*" and the "*interesting evening*" he's "*looking forward to*" are apparently references to the siege of Four Courts; and his expectation of some special developments there, to take place that night. His words suggest that it's rather a girl thing in her, to be "*inclined to worry*" at this juncture; while he seems sanguine in his *"hope the thing won't last much longer."*. (If the date of his letter is correct, this

---

107 As his personal correspondence attests.

would seem to indicate that the 4AM shelling would have been on the night of the 28th, actually the morning of the 29th.)

In this context, the relaxed, sociable, even romantic tone of this letter is of great significance. The fact that he's asking her to come to town for the weekend speaks volumes; including his half-hearted retraction in the next sentence that of course they'd better wait. Clearly he was not expecting the destruction of O'Connell Street and burning of the Gresham Hotel to commence in a few hours. It seems abundantly clear, from this letter, that a war beginning that night was not part of his plans or expectations at that writing.

This can be directly compared to his messages which immediately followed. He did not write another normal letter to her until July 12. Nothing but short, terse one-liners. The post ceased to function, and he sent mostly telegrams. You can feel the state of emergency in these wires. His emotional tone is extremely tense, when not at wit's end. On July 5:

> *Am still all right. Have not heard from you for several days. ...*
> *God be with you.*

*   *   *

Whatever happened, Collins' agenda to avoid outright war, was demolished in the rubble of Four Courts. There is no conclusive record as to who actually gave the order for shelling to begin: to begin without warning, in a manner offering no opportunity for last-chance surrender.

Did Collins so suddenly and inexplicably diverge from his entire strategy, and give the order to begin the bombardment? If it was not the C-in-C, then who was it? This single act so blatantly served a war-mongering agenda, that it can hardly be attributed to mere "error".

The evidence casts considerable doubt as to whether this ever came from himself. If investigation was called for, it would have been inevitably delayed by the war on his hands. Which he did not survive: he outlived the first shells to hit Inns Quay, by only fifty-five days.

In this sense, the mysteries surrounding the bombardment of Four Courts are directly related to the death of Collins: who may with justice be called one of its first casualties.

> *There clearly seems to be a need for a definitive study on the actual commencement of hostilities.*[108]

CHAPTER 8

THE ASSASSINATION OF SIR HENRY WILSON

> *I was given good reason to suspect a close relation between the shooting of Sir Henry Wilson and the shooting of Michael Collins, but when I tried to investigate this line I found every door closed on me - indeed some banged in my face.* [109]

Controversy likewise continues to surround the assassination of Sir Henry Wilson. At the very same time that the anti-Treaty men were sweating it out in the Four Courts, two members of the London IRA shot Wilson dead, on the doorstep of his home in London, in broad daylight. This was months after hostilities with the British were officially ended: after the Truce, after the Treaty had been signed; "out of the blue" as it seemed.

The shooters were obeying orders. But from whom? Who gave the order? The mystery has never been solved.

It has been rather carelessly conjectured, in several previous works, that this "job" was an old outstanding order to the London IRA, which had been issued before the Truce. The logic is that, due to an oversight, an order to shoot Wilson somehow missed being rescinded, when the ceasefire was declared.

This is patently absurd on its face. All active service units had stood down at the Truce: at which all such outstanding orders were automatically set aside. This is a self-evident aspect of any such cessation, affecting any military body. As surely as a white flag means "Hold your fire."

Allegations that either Collins or the anti-Treaty leaders ordered the operation do not hold water: these amount to no more than rumour, and are abundantly refuted by more substantial accounts. Yet Wilson was unquestionably shot by members of the London Brigade of the IRA.

The British newspapers (particularly those which served as mouthpiece for the conservative parties) unleashed a tidal wave of shrill invective in the vein of *"that's what you get for negotiating with the*

---

108   J Feehan
109   J Feehan

Irish" "*Of course any truce or treaty with those savages in Dublin is not worth discussing,*" etc. The journalistic wolves joined their voices in a one-note chorus of "*Revenge!*" This may be said to have (conveniently or otherwise) obliged Churchill to issue his ultimatum that the Dublin government end the rebel occupation at Four Courts or face military invasion. This is the bottom line of *how* the Civil War began.

Wilson's death was seized upon and exploited as a pretext for the British to threaten to declare the imperfect-but- hard-won Treaty null and void.[110] In short, it set in motion those events which led directly to the death of Michael Collins. For these reasons, any re-examination of Béal na mBláth should not omit another look at Wilson's mysterious, unsolved case.

WHO WAS SIR HENRY WILSON?

In this narrative, it is necessarily Irish leaders who have come under close scrutiny. However, that is not to say that British generals and politicians were above comment. Or that internal cabals and conflicts were unknown in London. On the contrary, Westminster's dirty laundry had frequently been a most untidy public spectacle, throughout the same period.

Wilson was, by birth, an Irishman: albeit fiercely devoted to the English Crown, as an Ulster Protestant of the Anglo Ascendancy. His family had a long history there as landlords and soldiers for the King. In a brilliant military career, he had made the highest echelons of command his "home town". At last reaching the lofty Parnassus of British Army ambition, in 1918 he was appointed Chief of the Imperial General Staff (CIGS).

He was also, to his own colleagues and superiors, a notoriously "difficult" character: pugnacious, outspoken, a political intriguer who courted the press and had become their darling. Rather a lone wolf, he could be both doggedly devoted, and frighteningly unpredictable. His famous demise was only the last of several celebrated scandals, of great concern to the British government, in which he played a key role.

He had been a conspirator in the Curragh mutiny, as it was called: when, in 1914, the London cabinet floated a proposal to send British troops to Ulster, to quell any violent resistance there to the

---

110 Not unlike the way a shrill one-note press exploited the destruction of the World Trade Center in 2001, to support Bush Administration military agendas; a martial campaign which proved similarly disastrous for all concerned.

implementation of Home Rule for Ireland (which, on paper, had by then been legislated at Westminster.) Over fifty British Army officers (of Ulster origin) replied to their superiors that they would refuse to obey orders to enforce Home Rule in Ulster, preferring to be dismissed from the army instead. In the political fracas which ensued, Wilson stage-managed the public embarrassment of Sir John French, (CIGS at the time,) as well as that of Lord Asquith. French was obliged to resign.

This was the least of London's problems with their generals. Lloyd George alleged that in 1918, "a military clique" formed a plot to overthrow the War Cabinet. Certain top British generals conducted a personal "war within a war" against their own government, while World War I was still raging. In the course of this political tussle, one of the heads of the British Army leaked Britain's war plans to the press. In that scandal, Wilson was an ally of Lloyd George, who supported his appointment as CIGS. But it is an example of the kind of shenanigans that British government had to fear. Rex Taylor described the personality which ultimately did little to endear Wilson to statesmen:

> ... *a mind of his own, a flair for independence and ... a sharp tongue ... He never hesitated to express his contempt for politicians ... Many of Wilson's enemies - Asquith for example - were not prone to forgetting and forgiving. ... To Lloyd George and Winston Churchill, to name only two, he was scathingly critical and bluntness itself ...*

Wilson had avowed enemies in London, in very high places indeed. By 1922 he was at daggers drawn with Lord Asquith, Prime Minister Lloyd George and Winston Churchill, over Ireland. George himself wrote that Wilson " ... *gave warrant for the suspicion and lack of confidence so widely felt in him ... One can understand the imputation of treachery which was associated with his name*" and that "*Asquith hated him for his implication in the Curragh mutiny.*"

To Irish nationalists, Wilson was widely considered a devil incarnate. He was known to be the official who, in 1917, had aggressively advocated conscription for Ireland in World War I. He had used his powerful influence to insist on it; although, thanks to John Redmond's Irish Parliamentary Party (IPP), Ireland had already provided 350,000 volunteers to those trenches, from which so few ever returned. It proved Britain's greatest single political blunder in Ireland. It drove literally millions of moderate voters overnight into the arms of Sinn Fein.

This was brought about almost single-handedly by Wilson, and his maverick political manoeuvring. It was not overlooked by his critics, on both sides of the Irish Sea.

For Wilson, the Irish problem was a military problem. Yet, as a self-willed, lone wolf of high politics, he did not always tow Westminster's line. Military discipline was his deity. As such, he was appalled at Sir Hamar Greenwood's introduction of the Black and Tans' random reign of terror. Wilson and Greenwood were both Anglo Ulstermen, and both unrepentantly anti-Home Rule. Yet that seems to have been where their agreements ended. Wilson wrote a vigorous letter of protest:

> *I told them, Lloyd George and Bonar Law, what I thought of reprisals by the 'Black and Tans', and how this must lead to chaos and ruin ... I pointed out that these reprisals were carried out without anyone being responsible; men were murdered, homes burnt, villages wrecked ... I said this was due to want of discipline, and this must be stopped.*

Interestingly, on this issue, there is evidence that he may have found allies in unexpected places; even co-religionists in his revered cult of military discipline:

> *Sir Henry's brother, [Deputy Lieutenant] James Mackay Wilson, living at Currygrane House, County Longford, received a visit from Commandant Sean MacEoin, commander of the Longford Brigade of the IRA. Pointing to two houses burning in the distance, MacEoin informed James Mackay Wilson that he should write to his brother and tell him that if such destruction continued, Currygrane House would be burned as a reprisal.*
>
> *In return James Mackay Wilson told MacEoin that his brother would pay no heed to such a request. "Well," said MacEoin, "in that case it will be too bad for Currygrane and you." He went on to say that if James Mackay Wilson tried to leave Currygrane he would be executed before he reached Edgeworthstown or Longford. On the other hand, if the battle were left simply to the military forces of both sides to fight it out, MacEoin would, in the name of the Republic, guarantee protection of life and property.* [111]

MacEoin's manoeuvre got Wilson where it hurt: they shamed him with his own side's guilt in that which he himself so loudly deplored: undisciplined thuggery and terrorism. This demonstrated detailed intelligence about Wilson's opposition to the Black and Tan elements. This direct appeal to Wilson's character was calculated to woo his respect. It was a hands-on rejection of the "murder gang" tag, which Wilson was particularly fond of hanging on the nationalist forces.

Another mark against Wilson had been his personal implication in the death of Kevin Barry: an eighteen-year-old schoolboy, who was captured during an IRA raid, because his gun jammed. During Barry's trial, it was established that his gun had been inoperable and had not fired a shot that day. Yet he was convicted in the raid's only fatality: a British soldier. Barry's barbarous torture by interrogators at Dublin Castle was also well-known. The case sparked widespread outrage. Nationalist leaders lobbied heavily for his reprieve. Collins [112] was observed to weep openly when discussing the case, and feverishly hatched several failed plans to spring Barry from jail.

E A Aston, a Dublin businessman, who was the employer of Barry's sister, wrote an eloquent letter of protest to the *Irish Independent* newspaper. Aston had travelled to London to intercede for the boy. He tried to see Lloyd George, and managed to get as far as a Colonel McCabe (a friend of Hamar Greenwood.) He was given information alleging that Greenwood and Prime Minister George were both against the execution of Barry; that no member of the Dublin Castle government in Ireland opposed a reprieve. But that Sir Henry Wilson insisted on Barry's execution, on pain of Wilson's resignation.

Apparently, this version was according to Greenwood's friend(s); and/or Prime Minister George's office in London. Yet Wilson's own correspondence belies it entirely: as shown in his letters to Macready [113] of 23 and 29 October 1920:

---

111   R Taylor

112   Collins was particularly affected by the report on Barry's torture, from his spies in the Castle. British interrogators had hissed in the boy's ear, "*What can Michael Collins do for you now?*" To which Barry famously replied, "*Nothing. But I can do something for him. I can die for him.*"

113   Sir Nevil Macready, one of the chief British military commanders in Ireland.

> *If this fellow hangs we are in for a spate of real trouble over there. ... . As much as I detest thuggery and sneaking terrorists, the balanced view, in my opinion, is to hold our hand in Dublin. It means that we shall have weakened our right there because of one man. But to execute is to invite the pot to boil over and we couldn't control it.*

A good call, as events ultimately played out. But does this mean that Wilson was set up, by British and unionist enemies of his own, to take all the blame for Barry's execution?

THE ASSASSINATION

On 22 June 1922, after delivering a speech at the unveiling of a World War I memorial, Wilson took a taxi to his home on Eaton Place. Two IRA men of the London Brigade, Reginald Dunne and Joseph O'Sullivan, had been lounging in front of the house for some time. As they saw Wilson, they split up and spread out, flanking him on both sides as he got out of the car. Wilson stood outside and paid his fare. As the driver let out the clutch to drive off, he heard a shot. Thinking it might be a blown out tyre, he looked over his shoulder. He saw Wilson shot four more times, as he stood facing the door to his house.

> *In London for his own safety [Wilson] was given police protection.* [114]

The most obvious question is, where was the police bodyguard which supposedly had been assigned to Wilson? Because of his prominent role in Ireland's troubles, he was considered at risk of assassination. Yet the two gunmen simply walked up to his house, stood about for a half hour or so in plain sight, and then took positions and cut him down unopposed. It's not as if he was hit by a hidden sniper.

The gunmen seem to have had no escape plan. Indeed, bewilderingly, one of those who carried out the assassination had a wooden leg. This would seem to be almost suicidal. They simply ran down the street and were soon overtaken by a crown of bystanders and police. (Apparently the latter were not so far away after all.)

The shooters were taken to Gerald Road Police Station, and apparently severely beaten as well as interrogated. Dunne took this

---

[114] R Taylor

philosophically, *"They hadn't expected to be given a cup of tea."* Throughout, they both maintained the most stoic silence.

Collins, the IRA and Wilson: who gave the order?

I shot the sheriff. But I didn't shoot the deputy. - Bob Marley

It cannot be denied that Collins was entirely capable of deciding and carrying out such an assassination. During the War of Independence, Wilson had certainly been a potential target in his "book". He would not have hesitated, had he seen it as a tactically effective means to further the Irish cause.[115] It seems that a tentative order for Wilson's assassination had probably been issued at some time, to be carried out under certain conditions, in the event of such-and-such.

However, Wilson's death, at that particular moment, was a tactical disaster. It did nothing whatever to further the Irish cause. It was the worst thing that could happen for Collins and his already beleaguered fledgling Irish government in Dublin. In the course of the War, tactical errors had been occasionally made in Collins' command. But it was entirely uncharacteristic of him to have anything to do with a strategic blunder on this scale, of such massive ramifications.

Sean McGarry, representing the Supreme Council of the IRB, unequivocally denied responsibility, on behalf of the IRB as an organization and Collins personally: *"Since the IRB has been instrumental in bringing favour to the Anglo-Irish Treaty, is it likely that the Supreme Council would blindly throw away what it had fought and schemed for since 1858? I reject any suggestion that the IRB or Michael Collins, as Head Centre of our organization, had anything to do with Wilson's death."*

The official response from the Provisional Government was penned by Arthur Griffith. In it, he recognized Wilson as a native of Ireland, whose *"political views were opposed to those of the vast majority of his countrymen."* He expressed his confidence that the vast

---

115 At the height of the War of Independence, a list of invited guests was copied to Collins, for the wedding of an officer from Dublin Castle. It included practically Britain's entire reigning military and civil leadership. Collins exclaimed enthusiastically, *"We'll plug the bloody lot of them!"* Accordingly his Squad was sent to lay in wait. Fortunately for the bride and groom, none of the high dignitaries on the list turned up. The snipers retreated unseen. (D Neligan)

majority would condemn "*this anarchic deed.*" This definitely disassociated that deed from any official sources in Dublin. In doing so, he encompassed his colleague, Minister Michael Collins. This excused Collins from making any statement individually; and he never did make any. DeValera in his response "*did not approve*" and disavowed any knowledge of who the perpetrators were, but hinted that Wilson fell due to outrage over pogroms in Ulster.

Likewise, Earnan O'Mally publicly denied responsibility on behalf of the anti-Treaty garrison occupying the Four Courts. He was seconded by Rory O'Connor, "*We had nothing to do with the shooting of Wilson. If we had, we would admit it.*" Interestingly, Sir Nevil Macready, Commander-in-Chief of the British army in Ireland, soon afterward declared that, "*so far as he was aware there was no evidence*" of O'Connor being connected.

This conclusively discredited a statement issued under the name of a Frank Martin that the order to shoot Wilson had come from the Four Courts men, to the London Brigade of the IRA, who were, Martin said, wholly anti-Treaty, except for himself. But the London Brigade didn't know any Frank Martin.

It appears that there were indeed both pro- and anti-Treaty members in the London Brigade of the IRA. It is important to emphasize that, at the time that Wilson was shot, that did not keep them from talking together; or from continuing to carry on operations side-by-side. There was as yet no civil war. Internal differences over the Treaty went on much like any other controversy, in any large organization run by democratic process and debate. Pro- and anti- were at this point still largely a "band of brothers", whose chief loyalties were to each other.

Yet some of the mysteries around Wilson's death suggest that it may have involved intrigue within the London Brigade; and that this was divided along anti-Treaty lines. [116] Despite these categorical disavowals, there were IRA men who reputedly issued statements to the contrary: even specifying that Collins had expressly given the order; and that he had given it while the Treaty negotiations were in progress, when he was in London. This version, attributed to Sean McGrath, Chief Intelligence Officer of the IRA in Britain, specified that Collins himself had personally

---

116   It should be noted that this unit was by no means immune to infiltration. Jameson, the first British mole to penetrate Collins' cell in Dublin, received his entrée on recommendation from the London Brigade.

conveyed the order to the London Brigade. (This would deflate Coogan's courier theory.[117])

This is the point in our inquiry where Capt. Joe Dolan first distinguishes himself: by stating that Collins issued the order. However, this testimony seems to have been given years later, to Rex Taylor, for that author's book about Wilson. Which is to say he never pointed a finger while Collins lived: as it would hardly have become him to do, while serving in the C-in-C's bodyguard, in London and at Béal na mBláth.

Following Wilson's death, Denis Kelleher, of the London Brigade, was summoned to appear before Collins in Dublin. Due to Collins' death exactly two months later, we have only Kelleher's account of what took place in that meeting. As a direct result of the assassination (that is, in result of the arrests and executions which followed it,) Kelleher was now acting commander of the London IRA. Rex Taylor relies heavily on Kelleher: apparently having interviewed him at length. Kelleher speaks to a great many crucial points of the story. However, it should be noted that everyone, who could either corroborate or contradict his account, died immediately after the events described (i.e. Collins, Reginald Dunne, Joseph O'Sullivan.) As a key figure in the London Brigade, which was certainly involved in the disaster, this could be seen as remarkably convenient for him.

Dunne, (one of the two shooters who were convicted in Wilson's killing) reputedly wrote a letter to Kelleher, after the trial and before his execution: in which he stated that Wilson's killing was never planned or ordered, but just "sort of happened." Taylor talks about the contents of this letter at length, but gives no indication of having actually seen it himself. He appears to be reporting Kelleher's account of the letter's contents. It seems we have only Kelleher's word that such a letter ever existed.

---

117 Coogan's consideration of Wilson's assassination is marred by his indulgence in a peculiarly flimsy "conspiracy theory" of his own. He recounts a family anecdote concerning a friend of his mother's, who was a London courier for the Irish Volunteers under Collins. This lady never saw the contents of the communications she carried, nor was ever told who they came from or where they went. She sometimes had a "feeling" it came from Collins. She reported having experienced this sentiment, about a letter she carried to London, shortly before Wilson's assassination. On that basis, Coogan confidently announces that her "feeling," about papers she never read, and of which she never knew either the author or addressee, proves that Collins ordered Wilson's death!

Joe Dolan told Taylor that he was sent to London by Collins to reconnoitre escape possibilities for Dunne and O'Sullivan; and that he met there with Sam MacGuire and with Sean Golden, Quartermaster of the IRA in London. Kelleher, meanwhile, disputed whether Dolan ever met with Golden.

Which ones lied?

And so it seems that, in comparing such details around Wilson's assassination, we find ourselves on a carousel of conflicting statements, very much like that encountered around Béal na mBláth. As in Collins' own case, these concern a high-profile shooting which no one wants to take credit for, on orders which cannot be traced, amidst enigmatic confusion in the chain of command. Like Collins' case, the details have remained mysterious, because the Civil War reduced the relevant authority (the IRA / IRB) to such disarray, and slew many of the personnel concerned.

They cannot all be telling the truth. Which is to say, some of them were lying. Which ones lied? What was covered up? Why? Did some have more reason to lie than others? Whose interests were served?

It would hardly make sense for Collins, while he was in London for Treaty negotiations, to order Wilson's shooting. Collins had long been on the British "most wanted" list. He was about as comfortable in London as a canary in a cattery. He was in the den of the powers who had been seeking to capture and kill him, any way they could, for years. A small airplane with two pilots were kept on twenty-four hour alert, for his quick escape, in case of a break-down in talks. He would hardly have wished to bait the lion, while still in the beast's den, and under its paw.

What does seem to be the case, is that Collins, as usual, did not walk into a dangerous situation unprepared. The plane and pilots were apparently only part of a formidable contingency plan, made ready to put in motion, whatever happened in London. These included orders to be carried out in the event that Collins were either imprisoned or assassinated there himself. The shooting of Wilson appears to have been one of these contingency plans.

Said Denis Kelleher, "*I state emphatically that instructions for the liquidation of Sir Henry Wilson was contingent upon the breakdown of the peace negotiations. This order was not subsequently cancelled.*"

As it happened, the peace talks did not break down. Collins was never flown out, and neither were the other plans ever carried out. The Treaty was signed. But it's easy to see how a high-ranking player in all this, with a detailed knowledge of these top-secret arrangements, who was well-connected with the command of the London Brigade, could do a great deal of mischief.

A fundamental sinew of military discipline is indisputable records as to exactly what orders were issued, by who, to whom, when, etc. These are precisely the questions so strangely unanswered in the cases both of Collins and Wilson. If the relevant authorities had mounted the kind of full-scale investigation which these catastrophes merited, each of these conflicting testimonies would have been carefully scrutinized and cross-examined.

As it stands, the IRB, the Provisional Government, and the anti-Treaty leaders all disavowed responsibility. None of these entities had anything to gain by this act. None of them did gain anything by it. On the contrary, it was an unqualified disaster for all of them. Nor did it fit their tactical profile. These Irish leaders had not risen out of obscurity to talk terms with an empire, by being in the habit of making foolish moves. Their disavowals seem more substantial and believable than conflicting statements from the peanut gallery, which have been set against them.

So the question remains: who gave the order?

Wilson and the Treaty

By getting rid of Wilson, it was hoped to smash the Treaty, damn Collins in British eyes, and turn the Irish people against the IRB. With a few shots you killed three first-class birds.
- Sean McGarry, IRB

In any cursory survey of the events of 1922, the most striking feature is the sudden death of the most brilliant nationalist leaders of the period, who could compete with DeValera for the domination of Ireland. But there were other remarkable developments as well.

It was shortly before his death in 1922 that Wilson, the high priest of Britain's military, suddenly abdicated his cherished coronet as CIGS, resigned his commission in the army, and stood as MP for north County Down.

Wilson ironically had something in common with the IRA "die-hards" at Four Courts: he also was violently opposed to the Treaty. The opening line of Wilson's letter to Sir James Craig demonstrates his stature and influence among the top unionist leaders; as well as his very vocal contempt for Prime Minister Lloyd George:

You have asked for my opinion and my advice on the present and the future. Here they are.

Owing to the action of Mr. Lloyd George and his Government, the 26 counties of south and west Ireland are reduced to a welter of chaos and murder, difficult to believe, impossible to describe. A further consequence of the course pursued by Mr Lloyd George is seen by the state of unrest, suspicion and lawlessness which has spread over the frontier into the six counties of Ulster.

The dangerous situation which obtains in the 26 counties will increase and spread unless: (1) a man in those counties rises who can crush out murder and anarchy, and re-establish law and order. ... (2) Great Britain re-establishes law and order in Ireland. Under Mr. Lloyd George and his Government, this is frankly and laughably impossible, because men who are obviously incapable of holding the Empire, are still more incapable of regaining it.

Wilson's letter is copied here, minus a snide comment (between his items (1) and (2), which seems to allude to his belief in the traditional creed of his national minority: that the Gaelic Irish were a sub-species, fundamentally incapable of self-government. It is particularly interesting to consider the letter, with that edit. Wilson's prominent mention of item (1) as a potential solution is highly significant. Apparently, in even mentioning such an eventuality to his loyalist crony, he felt obliged to reaffirm his embrace of old school racism, in the same breath. Yet it still clearly offers that even a competent (heaven forefend!) Gaelic leader in Dublin, if he had the "right stuff", would be more acceptable to Wilson than a *"welter of chaos and murder."*

COLLINS & WILSON..?

Shake hands with the devil

Nationalist efforts to reason with Wilson were illustrated in MaEoin's "friendly visit". This attention to Wilson's personal details, loyalties and pet peeves demonstrates keen interest in him by the Irish leadership. MacEoin was Collins' right-hand man in the area; a region close indeed to the C-in-C's heart: he frequently visited

Edgeworthstown, County Longford, as the rail stop for the home of his fiancé, Kitty Kiernan.

In view of the extreme secrecy required, in any parlay among the passionate factions of a country teetering on civil war, all of these factors together raise a fascinating question: was Collins courting Wilson? Facing the necessity for negotiation with violent unionists, certainly he would have been shopping for a devil he could deal with. Clearly Wilson, by his stubborn opposition to the Black and Tan terror, had won Collins' attention. The C-in-C had already attempted, with varying success, to come to agreements on the north with Sir James Craig (the recipient of the preceding letter from Wilson.) Taken together, all of the above strongly suggests that Collins, as a man who would restore order and, above all, maintain military discipline, might be, in Wilson's mind, a devil in Dublin he could live with.

Collins in Dublin and Wilson in Belfast? An unrepentant physical force republican, and an unrepentant former Chief of the Imperial General Staff? Imagine what that might mean!

One thing is clear: these were two who would not hesitate to see the military problems, and face them as military problems. Both hated misrule, and loved discipline. Both would oppose the deterioration of the island into anarchy.

Is it possible they might have come to an understanding? If so, there is no question that between them, they'd have been more than a match for any external foe. Is this what Westminster *feared?* Could this be placed on the list of their "worst nightmares"?

LLOYD GEORGE AND WILSON

Following is the full text of Wilson's last public letter, to the Editor of the London Evening News. The editor had written seeking his opinion on the situation in Ireland. In it, Wilson heaped his scathing contempt on Lloyd George's government: implicitly calling for the Prime Minister's removal. His incisive comments on that statesman's relations with Collins, Griffith and DeValera are particularly interesting.

> *June 11, 1922*
> *Dear Sir - Yours of June 1 just received on my return from a fortnight's cruise.*

The situation in Ireland is indeed grave, but it is nothing to what it will be later if the present Government is allowed to remain in power.

No self-respecting citizen of the 26 counties will have further communication with the Imperial Government except to dictate and impose terms.

It was only 10 months ago that DeValera was proclaimed as 'that Chieftain who represented the vast majority of the people of the south and west of Ireland!' Then he became discredited because he was honest, and Collins became the Darling of Downing Street.

Now, he too seems to have fallen from grace, and a desperate effort is being made to cling to the Griffith wreckage; a little later and our Government will be alone; and then we shall have gone back to 1798. What a tragedy! And all from ignorance, incompetence, and various forms of cowardice.

You ask for some 'plain words on the Irish nation.'
Alas! there is no Irish nation nor has there ever been one, and so there is no address to which one can post 'a few plain words.'

Eleven days after the date of this letter, Wilson was dead. Oddly enough, the date of his death reflected that of Collins: both died on the 22nd.

Prime Minister Lloyd George hotly declared that, "*Documents have been found upon the murderers of Field Marshal Sir Henry Wilson which clearly connect the assassins with the Irish Republican Army and which further reveal the existence of a definite conspiracy against the peace and order of this country.*" Collins and Griffith immediately demanded a chance to review the documents George cited. None were ever produced. Records suggest that the only papers on the shooters was a copy of the IRA newspaper, which was at the time freely sold at London newsstands.

It does not speak well of George, that he should act in a manner calculated to shatter the fragile peace which he himself had just negotiated. If no such documents had been found on Dunne and O'Sullivan, why would George claim that there were? This behavior also begs the question: once a crime has been committed, who is naturally most anxious to knowingly, loudly and falsely point the finger at the wrong suspect?

> *If his methods of gaining a particular objective were not in the best diplomatic tradition, it was indisputable that when the smoke of battle had cleared David Lloyd George commanded the field.* [118]

WILSON AND THE NORTH

Wilson may have worshipped discipline in the military sphere, but politically, he was a loose cannon. Throughout his life, the British Army had been all in all to him. But now he publicly denounced the government, resigned from the army, and took up his position decidedly in Ulster. It was issues in Ireland that seem to have brought about this final breach. His story illustrates the grave internal tensions which existed on the British side of the Irish question.

It appears that a struggle for control of the new northeastern statelet was under way. Already Anglo Ulster was finding that, however they cherished union with the Crown, their interests and London's agenda might be two very different things. Wilson was distinctly squaring up on the Ulster side of that struggle, in open opposition to Lloyd George and his government. He snapped his fingers at London.

Now Wilson shed the uniform which had previously kept him safely separate from the sphere of ministers and secretaries. As MP for north County Down, he was no longer on their leash. He was deeply initiated in the mysteries of Westminster's wizards. They could hardly hatch an intrigue, but Wilson's penetrating gaze would see to the bottom of it.

Wilson had been making powerful enemies at Westminster for some time. Now, some of these very players (Lloyd George and Churchill) were planning a coup in Ireland. It was a tangled web they wove. It would require the utmost delicacy on the part of all those in the plot; and the most tomb-like silence in any who, though not in the plot, were capable of both understanding it, and making their opinion heard by the public. This last category had perhaps a population of only one: Sir Henry Wilson. No one was more deeply involved in Ireland than

---

118 R Taylor

Wilson: a man who could be trusted to be silent as the tomb ... only when he was in it.

In short, Wilson had unquestionably come to be seen by some as a political liability. Is it possible that Lloyd George, Churchill and their cabal came to the conclusion that, in realizing their scheme for Ireland, Wilson would be worth a great deal more to them dead than alive?

WHO GAINS?

Who had motive, means and opportunity? The yardstick of gain, and of *modus operandi*, jointly tend to exonerate both Collins and anti-Treaty leadership; and to cast suspicion in the direction of London.

But Wilson was unquestionably shot by members of the IRA. How could Westminster be responsible for that? The IRA didn't take orders from them. At the same time, there is a certain resonance between these twin key disasters which set off the Civil War. Both seem to turn upon a muddling of military communication. Both were effected in such a way as to implicate Collins. Both unfolded in a manner which assured that he would not come forward to accuse anyone else.

Of course, that "very special help" mentioned above could have arranged it: if it were someone who understood the IRA chain of command intimately, and had complete access to all standing orders ever issued. Someone whose allies in the London Brigade might be persuaded to cooperate discreetly: either with or without being fully informed about the real origin, purpose or consequences of this action.

Who could have fulfilled all these requirements? It could only have been someone practically as high up in the Irish leadership as Collins himself. Who answered that description, and also had anything to gain by the outbreak of civil war? Who was also in close cooperation with Lloyd George?

Yes, if London was culpable, and DeValera cooperated, all of this was entirely feasible.

If not ... Then how else could it have been done?

WHAT IF WILSON HAD NOT BEEN SHOT?

In this context, we should pause to consider another alternate reality. Wilson's murder, at the precise moment of crisis when Ireland teetered on the brink of Civil War, set off the conflagration. What if that spark had not been lit? What if they gave a war and nobody came? If Wilson had not been shot, could the Civil War have been forestalled?

Up to that time, Collins had successfully managed to avoid giving battle to anti-Treaty forces. As long as he continued so, there was no war. Meanwhile, Collins and Griffith negotiated desperately with the British to allow for a few minor adjustments in the fine print, which would make the Free State palatable enough for the insurgents to lay down their arms in good conscience. The new Free State constitution which was taken to London, was designed expressly for this purpose.

Without the public furor aroused by Wilson's assassination on British soil, could Churchill have gone on saying "no"? Without that "weapon of mass distraction" it would surely have become known, that the Colonial Secretary's perverse niggling over a mere form of words was about to plunge Ireland into fratricidal strife, which might cost thousands of lives and millions in damages (much of it to property owned by British citizens.)

It is offered that, without Wilson's assassination, Churchill could not have held out against Collins' and Griffith's moderate and reasonable pleas for semantic adjustments, to save the country from civil war. A constitution more acceptable to anti-Treaty sentiment might have been implemented, and disaster averted.

Chapter 9

Collins, Griffith and Boland

In this climate, the chances are about a million to one against there having been anything either "accidental", "random" or "natural" about the sudden death, within days of each other, of Collins, Arthur Griffith and Harry Boland. The odds are simply astronomical. Even in the dangerous environment of the Civil War, it would be about equivalent to being struck by lightening while holding a winning lottery ticket.

Arthur Griffith

> *[The Cabinet "junta's"] first step was to isolate Arthur Griffith ... shortly before his death [P Moylett] found Griffith sitting alone with not even a secretary or typist available to him.* [119]

If Collins' assassination was part of a secret palace coup and/or counter-revolution, Griffith's demise would have been absolutely necessary to the same game-plan. No post-war government led by Griffith would ever be supine either to British interests, nor to DeValera: who would never have the most potent political voice in Ireland, as long as Griffith still lived.

At the time, Collins was working intimately with Griffith on a daily basis, in the Provisional Government. He by no means took Griffith's death so much for granted as historians have been willing to do. As shown in his personal correspondence:

> *The death of poor Mr Griffith was indeed a shock to us all, more so naturally to those of us who had been intimate with him, and who thought that his illness was a very slight thing indeed. We shall miss for many a day his cheerful presence and his wise counsel ... He had sounder political judgement than any of us, and in this way we shall feel his absence very keenly.* [120]

---

[119] J Feehan
[120] P Beaslai and M Collins' personal correspondence August 1922

Although no bounding youth like the C-in-C, at 51, he was hardly decrepit. The negotiations with Britain, the deterioration of the country into Civil War, certainly would place a tremendous strain on anyone in his highly responsible position. Yet, lest we forget, the War of Independence was not exactly a walk in the park. Since the founding of Sinn Fein in 1905, Griffith had lived in the eye of a political storm. His life had been unending controversy, continual persecution; in the course of which he had endured years of imprisonment, and the constant threat of arrest or assassination.

Yet P S O'Hegerty was even more shocked at Griffith's demise:

Until the last few months, he never lay in a sickbed. Whoever else died, we felt sure that it would not be Griffith - Griffith with the iron will, the iron constitution, the imperturbable nerve. Griffith, whom we all thought certain to live to be one hundred and write the epitaph of all of us. Griffith, upon whom we all leaned and depended.

Clear and present threats to Griffith's life

At the time of his death, the Civil War was in full swing. The prisons were overflowing *"with defiant political prisoners."* A list appears to have issued from some quarter, indicating that members of the Dublin government were to be shot on sight at the first opportunity. Government Buildings had become for Griffith and other ministers *"a place of internment,"* for their own safety. Kevin O'Higgins' wife had been forced to flee their suburban home, shortly before shots were fired at it. O'Higgins reported that, when he went out on the roof of his office for a smoke, the glowing end of his cigarette was hit by a sniper's bullet. [121]

Thus, danger to the safety of members of the Provisional Government was certainly clear and present. Mr. Griffith was without question the most important member of that government, who was in Dublin at the time. When entering St. Vincent's Nursing Home, Griffith checked in under the fictitious name of "Mr. White"; apparently as a personal security measure. [122]

---

[121] As Free State Minister for Justice, later responsible for the executions of many former comrades from the War of Independence, O'Higgins continued to be a particular target of the anti-Treaty hold-outs. He was ultimately assassinated in 1927.

P S O'Hegerty quotes Griffith himself as saying, in their interview on June 30, *"Of course, those fellows will assassinate Collins and myself. DeValera is responsible for this, for all of it. There would have been no trouble but for him."*

Poison: possible

Griffith's health certainly seems to have sharply declined around the time of his sojourn in London. This is exactly the same period which set in motion the events that led directly to Collins' death.

An appearance of natural decline, which camouflages murder via certain chemical substances, is by no means confined to the realm of fiction, but has been well-documented, from the Roman Empire to the 21st century. It was not unheard of at the period in question. As with other technical fields in the Victorian era, clandestine chemical warfare was then undergoing a new renaissance and refinement.

There are well-known substances that can bring on either heart failure or fatal cerebral hemorrhage (such as reputedly claimed Griffith's life.) Substances which, even with modern forensics, may be undetected in any subsequent medical examination. Simple, old-fashioned arsenic is one of these.

> *He complained of headaches, sore throat, depression, and sleep deprivation, all symptoms which could be attributable to arsenic or a similar type poison.*[123]

In this profoundly dangerous situation, in the presence of multiple death threats, Griffith was living in an environment where any number of people could gain access to his food, drink or medications.

> *Free State ministers, including President Griffith, [were living] in the adjoining College of Sciences, where acquisition of arsenic, cyanide, or other poisons was a relatively easy matter ... Food was delivered from Mills Restaurant on Merrion Row and/or from the*

---

122 P Colum

123 J Turi (Just as this book was being finalized, this author was happily surprised by the appearance of another new work, by a writer entirely unknown. Synchronistically enough, John Turi's 2009 biography, *"England's Greatest Spy: Eamonn DeValera"* concurs with several of the most controversial points raised herein; and supports them with a mine of meticulous research.)

Bailey ... These public restaurants were freely accessible to anyone.[124]

The death of Arthur Griffith
Dr. Gogarty reported that Griffith had suffered an attack of *"acute tonsillitis on Monday 31st July,"* [125] which *"passed off in a few days. No operation was necessary."* The doctor then *"prevailed on him"* to recuperate in a nursing home *"for the benefit of his general health."*

Turi points out that, once away from Government Buildings, and the restaurant food provided to him there, his health returned *"rapidly."*

Griffith was set to return to his duties when, *"two female visitors, reportedly his nieces, ... bearing chocolates"* paid him a call. Immediately upon their departure, *"he stooped down as if to fasten his shoe and slumped on the ground."* [126]

Because he died in hospital, under a doctor's care, there was no autopsy or inquiry into Mr. Griffith's death. For ninety years afterward, his demise has hardly been questioned as suspicious. Certainly not by historians or biographers.

Poison: alleged at the time

"The curious rumor that Arthur Griffith died from the effects of poisoning and that his body was to be exhumed has been persistent in the city for some days past." [127]

Yet there is some indication that the C-in-C himself did question his President's sudden end. This can be seen in his correspondence, his verbal comments, as well as in some film footage of him at Griffith's funeral.[128] He hardly had a chance to do more, as he himself was taken exactly ten days later.

---

124 Ibid.

125 This was the day after Harry Boland was shot.

126 Report of Mother Ignatius, St. Vincent's Nursing Home, Dublin

127 *New York Times* September 7 - 8, 1922

128 The film shows the C-in-C staring into Griffith's grave, lost in thought. As he looks up, he glowers into the camera, not with grief, but with an expression of *anger* and *suspicion*.

WT Cosgrave seems to have assumed that Griffith's fate could not be unconnected with the general state of siege the Cabinet was living under. On the day Griffith died, Cosgrave immediately dashed off a page-long message, which was apparently intended to be read in the event of his own imminent death: complete with prayers for the forgiveness of his sins, and assurances that he forgave anyone who shot him! (The message was filed away and preserved for posterity.)

Shortly afterward, the Chicago Tribune reported:

> *Reports that Arthur Griffith was poisoned circulated in Dublin at the time of his death three weeks ago and have again become prevalent. ... A leading physician [says] that there is some talk of exhuming the body and clearing away any doubt ... [by performing] an autopsy ...*

On September 7, the same paper announced not only that the proposed autopsy had taken place, but that poisoning was the verdict, and that arrests had been made as a result!

> *... two reliable men who have just returned from Dublin [inform us] that the Free State authorities have exhumed the body of Arthur Griffith and found traces of poison. A doctor and two nurses are said to have been arrested. The news is said to have been suppressed by the Dublin censors.*

The timing of Griffith's death, so close on the steps of Collins' and Boland's, his pivotal leadership role, the political developments around him, the dangerousness of the times and of the powerful players involved; combined with all these other suspicious factors, together give reason to question whether there might have been foul play. While the lack of any inquiry means that there is no conclusive proof that there *could not* have been.

Who gains?

Arthur Griffith and Michael Collins were the lynch-pins of Ireland's new independent government. As individuals, their public stature was head and shoulders above and beyond all other Irish leaders in recognition value, savvy, integrity and genius. Joined together as twin heads / partners they were a formidable team indeed. The Treaty debates and subsequent elections had both proved them an unbeatable combination.

They were the personification of the best and brightest of the nationalist old guard and new: Griffith representing non-violent Sinn Fein, the cooler heads and traditional values of the movement's 19th century luminaries. Collins the young, aggressive military and economic agenda for total independence.

While these two lived and joined forces, DeValera would always be relegated to "second fiddle" in the politics of Ireland.

Harry Boland

Harry Boland TD, a Volunteer since 1913, was a close friend and associate of Collins and, like him, a member of the IRB's Supreme Council. He played a leading role in the War of Independence, and would have been expected to hold a Cabinet seat or other high office in the post-war government.

Boland's death took place in the very opening days of the civil conflict, before it had really developed into all-out war. According to Deasy, it was attended by *"mysterious circumstances"* and *"was another serious blow to the moderate wing"* of the anti-Treaty side. That is, it drove another nail into the coffin of hopes for a swift reunification of the victorious War of Independence army.

War man, peace man

"During the dreadful first week of civil war [Boland] was constantly moving between DeValera and Collins trying to patch up a truce." [129] *The Free State was still pursuing a "policy of moderation" in "hopes of a negotiated settlement."*

Away from the debating chambers and podiums, where accusations flew, Collins and Harry Boland continued on relatively friendly terms.[130] Throughout this time, Collins continuously cooperated with anti-Treaty leaders Rory O'Connor and Liam Lynch, in co-ordinating

---

[129] D Fitzpatrick (Most quotations in this section are from Fitzpatrick's excellent work *Harry Boland's Irish Revolution*, unless otherwise noted.)

[130] Kitty Kiernan expressed her anxiety to Collins that he should not be going out for drinks with Harry.

IRA efforts to protect Catholics from pogroms in Ulster. Right up until June, all of them had attended regular IRB meetings together, in which they strove to find some means to avoid violent conflict. Boland moved freely about Dublin, eating with friends in a well-known restaurant on Nassau Street, staying at the home of his mother and of Kathleen Clarke.

At the same time, Boland was instrumental in organizing major shipments of arms and ammunition for the anti-Treaty troops, in preparation for war. His correspondence included explicit details. Some of these letters were seized in a raid. *By asking [Sean T O'Kelly] to attend [Clan na nGael's]* [131] *convention in quest of guns and ammunition, he had laid both of them open to being treated as gunmen rather than politicians.*

This was while the stinging arrows of a well-oiled anti-Treaty propaganda machine, were daily demonizing Collins, tarring him with every outrage most heinous to the Irish public's imagination. Boland's confiscated letters provided the besieged government with a necessary opportunity for rebuttal. *Collins himself advised that "they ought to be given to the press exactly as they are."*

Still those letters were not made public until 31 July: the day after Harry was wounded. In the meantime, Collins sent off his oft-quoted letter to Boland of 28 July. It should not be omitted here:

> *Harry - It has come to this! Of all things it has come to this. It is in my power to arrest you and destroy you. This I cannot do.*[132]
> *... If you will think over the influence which has dominated you it should change your idea. You are walking under false colours. If no words of mine will change your attitude then you are beyond all hope - my hope.* [133]

---

[131] Clan na nGael was an Irish-American organization which had provided support and funds to the independence movement in Ireland, since the 19th century.

[132] Emphasis is this author's.

[133] In characterizing this message as "histrionic" Fitzpatrick seems to forget that this is personal correspondence between intimates, in an emotionally-charged situation. As such, its language is entirely appropriate: a classic distillation of the tragic dilemma shared by all caught in civil conflicts, which turn "brother against brother." Collins can cause fastidious discomfort in academics, accustomed to dry history, when he thus jumps off the page as "too human." Yet even his worst detractors have been unable to deny the sincerity of grief, and determined plea for reconciliation, which these few words set forth so eloquently. Biographers tend to

TDs are not to be shot

Shortly before Boland's death, the Provisional Government had made a clear decision to differentiate between armed combatants and politicians. "*On advice from Collins*" they agreed unanimously on 17 July 1922, not to arrest elected representatives, propagandists, nor "*mere political suspects ... except of course, those actually captured in arms.*" The date of this resolution, particularly urged by Collins, was just fourteen days before the incident which took Boland's life.

So officially, the Provisional Government policy in place was, no arrests of TDs, nor of unarmed political opponents. Boland was unarmed when taken. This was never disputed by either side. *Why then was a military manoeuvre mounted to seize him?*

What happened?

On July 30, he made a trip to Skerries, a seaside village nineteen miles north of Dublin. He was accompanied by an associate named Joe Griffin. The area had little anti-Treaty presence, but was surrounded by formidable Free State army garrisons, in the neighboring villages of Swords, Balbriggan and Julianstown. It is not known precisely what errand he was on. Accounts are fragmentary and conflicting. Yet it seems noteworthy that he shares this enigma with Collins: that his reasons for being in the obscure location where he died, have remained shrouded in mystery ever since.

Some say that he had visited this out-of-the-way spot repeatedly in preceding weeks. Of course, for those concerned in arms shipments, contacts with America and Liverpool, etc., an isolated seaside village might have attractions. These factors also raise the possibility that a secret rendezvous may have drawn him there. For men on the run, such meetings are always fraught with the danger of entrapment.

On arrival, Boland and his companion booked a room together at the Grand Hotel, Great Strand Street. They had a few drinks in the hotel bar, then went to bed about 1 or 2AM.

What followed next is only discernible through a haze of conflicting reports. (A confusion which resonates disturbingly with the tangle of tales around Béal na mBláth.)

---

champion their subject; and so, sadly, we cannot always expect complete fairness to Collins, in Boland's chroniclers.

The Free State version

The Free State army journal published an account[134] ostensibly given by "*the anonymous officer in charge.*" It stated that this officer "*got information*" at 1AM, as to Boland's whereabouts. He reported that he took a detachment of 12 soldiers and surrounded the building, front and back. Then he and just one other officer went in to confront Boland and his companion. He says he "*found them occupying two beds in a room.*" There was no mention of knocking, announcing their presence or talking through the door. He says Boland was in bed when he entered. Boland reportedly asked to be left to his sleep, giving an undertaking to report at any place and time requested. The officers would not agree. He got up to dress. As the second officer went through some papers in the room, Boland reportedly "*sprang upon him*" and tried to wrestle his gun away. The first officer says he fired warning shots over Boland's head, and that Boland rushed down the corridor. The officer says he then shot the TD in the back as he was running away. Some newspaper reports quoted army sources as alleging that he had been shot accidentally while struggling for the soldier's gun.

The anti-Treaty version

Reports from the anti-Treaty side differ from the above in some important points, and confirm others.

Joe Griffin, his companion, said that he was wakened by "*footsteps and a knock*"; that Harry was "*already up,*" Griffin said he gave warning to Boland and then tried to slip away unnoticed "*as he had slipped away from Four Courts.*" Harry "*made for the door*" before Griffin "*heard a scuffle and a shot.*"

One anti-Treaty publication was not far from the army estimate of 12, in giving the number of soldiers as 16. Others reported "*28 or 30 Free Staters in armoured cars.*"

The Cork Examiner, which was under anti-Treaty control at the time, published another account. This agrees that both men were in bed and that two soldiers entered. The army journal said that they had first "*searched*" another building nearby. The Examiner quoted someone who was wakened by a soldier in error, when a second one by the door said, "*That is not the man.*" This seems to chime in with various reports that the party had brought a man with them expressly to identify him.

---

134 A fortnight after the raid

Boland himself, in the two or three days he lingered on, said that he was shot by a man he knew, who had been in jail with him.

The Examiner went on to say that "*Joe Griffin was taken out into another room,*" and that shots then rang out immediately. It agrees with the army journal account that he was shot in the back. It speaks of "*marks in the corridor,*" which are not described (bullet marks? bloodstains? scuff marks?) and "*assumes*" that he tried to escape that way.

In the same newspaper report, a priest, who visited the hotel shortly afterward, said that he believed Boland must have been shot in his bed: because only the bed was blood-stained, and there was no sign of blood anywhere else. It was also alleged that he was left in the bed without medical attendance and not taken to hospital until 7 hours later, at 8AM. Father Ellis, a local priest who attended him, said he found Boland lying on the bed, surrounded by 6 soldiers. The Irish Independent said he was attended by a doctor and removed at 6:30AM (for a very bumpy nineteen mile ride to Dublin.)

All accounts agree: the hotel was surrounded; Boland was unarmed; he was shot by soldiers who had come to arrest him.

Who gave the order?

The government had made it official policy, two weeks before, (17 July) that political representatives were not to be arrested. That policy had not yet been published; but neither had there been any public allegations that Boland was anything but a TD and a non-combatant. As Boland's biographer observed, *The government was spared the indignity of having to admit that its instructions had been ignored.*

The Free State army version gives his death as an unfortunate accident, caused entirely by the victim's actions. Other reports cast some doubt on this. There is no explanation as to why so much military might was mobilized to seize an unarmed TD, whom they weren't even supposed to arrest!

Among the fragments of evidence, are anecdotal reports that Boland was betrayed by a publican; that a former comrade from jail and from the Dublin Brigade was waiting in a pub where he stopped en route; that these cooperated to summon the soldiers.

Yet there are indications that some considerable clandestine operations had gone into preparing to take him; (i.e., that the raid did not take place on the spur of the moment, in spontaneous answer to a report received at 1AM, as the officer claimed.) The services of a man who could identify Boland had been secured, and at this ungodly hour, were at the ready.

All this being undertaken in the dead of night, does not support the army's assertion that everything was on the up and up.[135] Why the pre-dawn raid? Why such efforts to assure that he would be in bed when they arrived? So that he could be shot while he lay in it (as at least one witness suggests)?

Secret paths mark secret foe. - Scott

Who ordered this? Who organized the arresting party (of two, four or six soldiers)? Who was "*the anonymous officer in charge,*" whom army sources declined to identify? Boland was a top minister, a key member of the Dáil government since 1919. If a decision had been made that it was necessary to bring him in, well and good. If it were made responsibly, in good faith, certainly particular care would have been taken to prevent any mishap.

As mentioned above, considerable planning and special personnel seem to have been chosen. But not, it would seem, with a view to preventing tragedy. Boland's character and *modus operandi* were thoroughly well-known in the army. Indeed, his opponents were his former intimates and guerrilla comrades. The Irish Volunteers had handled many a delicate mission since 1920. From commandeering supplies to kidnapping dignitaries. *Why were not sufficient measures taken, to assure that Boland be overpowered without bloodshed?*

In short, the operation which set out to take Boland that night was characterized by many suspicious features, which do not fit the picture. Boland's death was a terrible blow to the efforts of Collins and others to cool down the hotheads and avoid civil war. In this delicate situation, and with the tremendous stature of Boland in the movement, there was no excuse, in letting some fly-by-night loose cannon bring the TD back with a large hole in him.

Where was Collins?

The suggestion that Collins ordered Boland's killing was fostered by some anti-Treaty propagandists during the Civil War. Historians have not found much merit in it. It is favored only by the most shrill Boland

---

[135] One of the first reforms of the French Revolution was that no one was to be arrested after dark.

biographer, in the context of flagrant Collins-bashing; and without the offer of any noteworthy evidence to support it. Even DeValera scorned to associate himself with allegations that Boland's death was intentionally sought by Collins: "*I do not think Mick Collins willed the death of Harry Boland or that his killing was in any way premeditated or deliberate.*" Senator Gerald Boland, Harry's brother, although a political opponent of Collins, likewise cleared him of any involvement.[136]

Collins had been in Cork on 24 July. On 30 July, apparently about the same time Harry was heading for Skerries, the C-in-C wrote his fiancé that he was leaving that moment on an inspection tour to the south; ("*but not all the way south*," he added, apparently meaning not as far as Cork this time.) He sent notes to army staff on 1 August, describing conditions in various barracks about the country which he had recently inspected. Evidently, he was making frequent, short inspection trips to outlying areas: around this time in general, and on July 30 in particular.

His personal correspondence gives a strong impression that he was probably *not* in on any plans to hunt down, seize or otherwise endanger Boland. He and Miss Kiernan discussed Harry in their letters not infrequently: touching on everything from personal to political concerns about him. Collins' regular missives to her at this time show no special emotional tension or concern with regard to Boland, such as he tended to express, on the eve of major operations. He wrote to her on 28 July specifically asking her to come to town to spend time with him. It seems hardly likely he would have done so, had he been planning the shooting of their close mutual friend Harry to take place two days later. While his well-known letter to Harry of 28 July (quoted above) explicitly states that he "*cannot*" bring himself to have his friend arrested.

Yet three days later, on the 30th, Boland was taken: apparently as part of an elaborately well-planned siege, which could not have been mounted without considerable advance preparation. Was such preparation undertaken without Collins' absolute knowledge?

Later (that is, in the 20 days between Harry's death and his own,) Collins protested to his Director of Intelligence Joe McGrath "*you have not sent me any copies of the letter which was found in the late Harry Boland's notebook. Please send me one or two.*" Whether he ever received it remains a mystery: the letter Collins was so concerned about in the last days of his life, now appears to be lost forever.

---

[136] M Forester

Collins, Boland and Wilson
All told, a remarkable number of peculiarities characterize both Boland's and Collins' death. Both cases concerned:
a) an isolated location;
b) in hostile territory (i.e. held by the opposing military);
c) unsolved mystery as to what he was doing there;
d) indications suggesting he was called there for a secret meeting of some kind;
e) prominent moderates, who had been continually involved in negotiations to prevent and/or end the Civil War with speed (i.e. Collins and Boland);

At the same time, Boland's death may with justice be said to have been to the anti-Treaty side, what Sir Henry Wilson's assassination was to the British: it created a furor, in which the voices of moderates could no longer be heard, over extremist shrieks of "*Revenge!*"

Within weeks, the shooting of Collins set off a similar reaction on the Free State side. Were these three men marked for death, in order to shatter the fragile and controversial truce between these three major players: the Free State, the anti-Treaty IRA & the British?

*   *   *

MORE INVESTIGATION IS CALLED FOR
It may be interesting to note that Michael Collins, Arthur Griffith and Harry Boland all died within exactly 20 days of each other. Boland succumbed to his wounds on 2 August; Griffith 10 days later on the 12th, and Collins 10 days after him, on the 22nd. What are the odds?

All things considered, this writer cannot accept that Griffith's sudden, unexpected death at that particular moment could possibly have been an "act of God", marvellously fortuitous to certain political interests. Nor will a verdict of "regrettably unavoidable" stand up, under a close examination of the circumstances in Boland's suspicious killing, only days before.

Certainly the "weaker men" who succeeded these three found them at least sometimes more convenient in death than in life. The names "Collins and Griffith" became a useful mantra for the Cosgrave government, trotted out at critical moments, to fan flagging support; most often for policies which those "dear departed" would themselves have most fiercely opposed (such as the execution of Erskine Childers, Rory O'Connor, and others.)

It is offered that the ends of these great national heroes, Arthur Griffith and Harry Boland, so closely associated with Michael Collins, deserve much more anxious scrutiny, than they have yet been accorded.

CHAPTER 10

THE PEACE NEGOTIATIONS

Efforts to bring the Civil War to an end began immediately after its outbreak and were continued, by different groups and individuals, up to its conclusion. [137]

Peace was the bait used to lure Collins into the trap. Attempts on his life during this trip were carried on under cover of a safe-conduct, to attend peace negotiations with anti-Treaty leaders in West Cork. Notably, with DeValera.

"I'm going to put an end to this bloody war as quickly as possible." [138]

"Tonight I must get back to Cork. I will not leave Cork until the fighting is finished." [139]

"Twill soon be over," so the C-in-C assured *all those he trusted*, wherever he went, on his last journey through his home county of Cork.

All during the day it was freely rumoured among [the ambushers] that the war would soon be over, and as one of them said, "We had no great mind to shoot anybody."

His journey's relationship to peace negotiations is a key aspect in the discussion of what happened. This is particularly illustrated in the controversy which questions it.

The Mallow IRA have stated openly that they removed all the mines from the Cork-Mallow road, so that Collins and his convoy could get to Cork safely. [140]

---

137   F O'Donoghue

138   Capt Sean McCarthy recounted Collins' words to him at Rosscarbery on 22 August 1922.

139   The C-in-C's brother, Sean Collins, reported this from their conversation at Sam's Cross on 22 August 1922.

If the Mallow IRA did take such measures to assure the C-in-C's safe conduct, ... Why would they have done so, if not on the instruction of their leaders?

> After his death it was discovered that Collins had been guaranteed safe-conduct throughout his journey to the south and during his tour there. The document bearing this startling information was signed by a prominent anti-Treaty leader. [141]

This author is willing to wager that, could this document yet be discovered, the signature by "*a prominent anti-Treaty leader*" would belong to ... Liam Lynch.

Significantly, Dalton appears to have been the go-between in Cork, who actually received a list of blown bridges, etc., from anti-Treaty representatives. Yet orders were given to ambush Collins' convoy. While at least one account reports Lynch and DeValera chatting about the mines they had planted in his path.

This explains something about why the question of whether he was or was not there to seek peace is so important. There have been conflicting reports, even among eye-witnesses and prominent representatives of both sides, as to the purpose of his journey. The rather shrill insistence, in some quarters, that he was not there for talks, must be considered in this interesting light.

Peace negotiations at that time were highly sensitive, and not without danger. Not all Collins' colleagues on the Free State side favored an early settlement. The anti-Treaty men he needed to meet with were officially outlaws on the run. The possibility of a trap was clear and present in the minds of delegates on both sides. It was difficult for anyone in this maelstrom to know whom to trust, who's side anyone was on, what was really going on.

> It is also known that some of his cabinet colleagues, who had now finally settled for membership of the British Commonwealth

---

140   J Feehan (Followed by Feehan's observation that, once Collins reached Cork City, it would have been in the hands of other units.)

141   R Taylor

> *and who had abandoned the republic, were strongly opposed to [Collins'] moves and regarded him with suspicion ...*
> *Their feeling was that they were winning the Civil War and that they should continue without negotiation until the IRA were brought to their knees and surrendered unconditionally.* [142]

This helps explain why we have little or no record as to exactly who on the anti-Treaty side was engaged in these negotiations with Collins and with Dalton at Cork. Feelings running high as they were, there could be risk to the life of advocates for peace. As will be seen below, there certainly was such risk.

> *Dan Breen told Liam Lynch: "In order to win this Civil War you'll have to kill three out of every five people in the country and it isn't worth it."* [143]

Collins was painfully aware by this time that he could not necessarily trust everyone with whom he had to work closely; nor everyone who might have access to official information about his movements. The danger was not only from opponents in the Civil War, but also from the British secret service: whom Collins knew was hot on his trail, and at the bottom of numerous attempts on his life in the days / weeks leading up to August 22.

Significantly, immediately after leaving Collins (earlier in August, on another leg of the same "inspection tour") Frank Thornton was ambushed en route to peace negotiations. He was the Free State's contact to reach Dan Breen [144] in County Kerry. His entire party was massacred, Thornton alone surviving, but severely wounded. The peace talks in question never took place.

---

[142] J Feehan. Once Collins was removed, this was certainly the strategy pursued by the Dublin government.

[143] Ibid.

[144] See Chapter 1 re: Breen's pivotal role in the War of Independence.

THE MEETINGS

> *It is known that he had arranged to meet secretly with some high-ranking neutral officers in Cork the following evening to try and get negotiations started.* [145]

Certainly a remarkable number of meetings between key people seem to hover around the time and place of Béal na mBláth.

Some of Michael Collins' meetings
(possibly related to peace negotiations)
- early August 1922 with Tom Malone (E Limerick anti-Treaty IRA) re: negotiations;
- early August 1922 with Frank Thornton re: contact Dan Breen for negotiations;
- 21 August with cyclist messenger from Liam Lynch at Ballincollig barracks;
- 21 August with neutrals at the Imperial Hotel, Cork City;
- 22 August Macroom;
- 22 August Bandon long meeting with General Sean Hales re: peace negotiations;
- 22 August with Collins family at Sam's Cross (during which Collins was reportedly absent about a half hour for a private meeting, possibly with contacts for anti-Treaty forces);
- (22 August scheduled to meet with DeValera on this date(?) At Béal na mBláth(?)
- 22 August scheduled to meet on this evening with prominent neutral IRA officers at the Hotel Imperial in Cork City, including Florrie O'Donoghue and Joseph Derham
  (Collins dead on arrival there.)

Some anti-Treaty officers' meetings (related to ending the war)
- 20 August meeting between DeValera and Liam Lynch;
- (20 August(?) meeting including DeValera, Tom Hales, Erskine Childers, Liam Lynch near Ballyvourney
- 21 August DeValera meeting with Deasy, re: ending the war

---

145   J Feehan

- (22 August (?) between DeValera and some anti-Treaty officers at Béal na mBláth?)
- (22 August DeValera scheduled to meet with Collins on this date(?) At Béal na mBláth(?)
- 22 August major conclave of senior anti-Treaty officers scheduled at Béal na mBláth; ending the war on the agenda;
- 13 October Crookstown (near Béal na mBláth): major meeting of Free State and anti-Treaty officers, on the subject of ending the war.

Deasy confirms that the Cork Number Three Brigade Council had scheduled, on its agenda for the meeting at Béal na mBláth on 22 August 1922, a motion calling for withdrawal from the war. Collins' death caused the meeting to be cancelled: the motion was never voted on.

Feehan records that there were two versions about the half-hour Collins slipped away from his family's gathering at Sam's Cross. One says this was a secret meeting with anti-Treaty representatives; another that the meeting was with relatives. However, he left a family reunion to attend this meeting. All the relatives were already there. What would be secretive about a meeting with relatives, and why would it be separate from the reunion already in progress? There are indications that Collins used the term "*relatives*" freely to cover his secret contacts with anti-Treaty envoys on this trip. His family circle was a natural resource for mediation with republican elements in West Cork. If he went from this family gathering to a hush-hush parlay, it seems more likely that it might have been connected to negotiations with men on the run, than with "relatives".

Florence O'Donoghue was one of the prominent officers of the Neutral IRA, who were scheduled to meet Collins at the Imperial Hotel in Cork City on the evening of 22 August. He was one of the founders of the Neutral IRA, who had abstained from taking sides in the Civil War, and tried to act as intermediaries, to promote reunification of the two sides. Another prominent neutral, who took part in the meeting with the C-in-C at the Imperial Hotel on the previous day, 21 August, was Joseph Derham. Derham had been a veteran of 1916, a comrade of Michael's from the siege of the GPO, and captain of the Volunteers at Skerries.

Coogan quotes Jimmy Flynn, an officer accompanying the "*principal architect of the whole civil war situation*," who confirms that

DeValera "*was in the area to meet Collins, that arrangements had been made to bring them together.*"

THE TERMS

> His last words to General Sean Hales in Bandon that fatal day were that he did not want to injure one Irishman or even to humiliate in the least the proud spirits of those of his countrymen who may have been opposed to him. [146]

For all the noble rhetoric, it was already becoming clear to many anti-Treaty leaders that military victory was not attainable. Deasy reports that he and DeValera explicitly agreed on this, in their meeting of 21 August. Yet anti-Treaty forces were unwilling to simply give up the fight, without having won anything at all. They still held out for certain terms: they wanted to get something honorable out of their military "last stand." Liam Lynch, to the bitter end, clung to the belief that their campaign would "*force them to negotiate.*"

There were questions as to amnesty versus penalties; future position in the new establishment, or ostracism; recognition and reward for the victory against Britain which they had won, etc. These concerns are reflected in communications between Collins and Dalton, on foot of this journey to Cork. According to neutral representatives acting as go-betweens, these were issues the anti-Treaty side wished to address, as conditions for cease-fire. (See Appendix 4)

Feehan summarized all he could learn about the peace terms then under discussion (gleaned from the above-mentioned correspondence and interviews with survivors.) He believed that Collins intended to secure for the anti-Treaty officers the option of joining the new Irish army, confirmed in their previous rank; or alternatively, they would be offered jobs in the civil service (which required no oath of allegiance to Britain.) Any "die-hards", who refused both these options, would be supported in carrying on underground military resistance to Orange terror in the north.

In this context, the C-in-C and General Hales privately declared their plan to gradually dismantle the Treaty's most objectionable

---

146 Ibid.

aspects: until former anti-Treaty hold-outs could play a formative role in developing the new state, which they had brought into being.

WERE PEACE NEGOTIATIONS COVERED UP?

In view of all this, it is surprising that, in describing his discussion with DeValera about ending the war, Deasy says that he felt many men in his Division would not accept "*unconditional*" surrender. This indicates that "*unconditional*" ceasefire was all that DeValera suggested, in that meeting. Deasy demonstrates no knowledge about the kind of terms which had already been outlined in communication between Collins and neutrals in Cork City. Nowhere in his writing does Deasy show any awareness that such terms were ever under discussion with Collins.

Had they been aware that the Free State was offering something better than unconditional surrender, that Collins was considering such terms, Deasy's men might have found peace more attractive. This would in turn have enabled Deasy and other moderate anti-Treaty officers to lead them in that direction.

Yet apparently they never heard about such an offer. The existence of those terms, and of the negotiations which might have secured the army's reunification, were shrouded in oblivion.

If supporting documentation was on Collins' body when he died, it was intentionally removed. If so, it was removed for one purpose: in order to keep this alternate outcome, and the C-in-C's role in it, a profound secret, never revealed to the public. Above all, it concealed Collins' support for favorable terms with the anti-Treaty side. It erased from history the fact that his death was directly connected with his efforts to reunify the army; and that *he died trying to secure such terms for the anti-Treaty troops*.

This concealment of the true purpose for his journey was an important component of posthumous disinformation and character assassination. This is what rendered his presence at Béal na mBláth a mystery. The unresolved question of "why there?" and the blank thus created, have enabled lame speculation. Thence proceeded baseless allegations, used to excuse and justify his death: such as suggestions that his convoy was on an aggressive military mission.

DIPLOMACY AND PROVISIONAL GOVERNMENTS

In her poignantly personal and poetic biography *The Lost Leader*, M Forester very intelligently observed that "*A Commander-in-Chief does not fling himself on his stomach behind a ditch with a rifle to take pot shots at the enemy. Nor, for that matter, do heads of government.*"

However, she erred in comparing Collins to statesmen like the British: secure in the enjoyment of a firm and wealthy dynasty, backed by centuries of relative stability, with the happiness to be free from armed conflict, on the steps of their own government buildings.[147]

A young provisional government, guerrillas only yesterday, faced very different obligations and challenges. Struggling to emerge from a violent military occupation, their society was turned upside down, their civil institutions in flux or non-existent, fraught by enemies within and without.

In such contexts, a Salvador Allende might find that the Presidential Palace (where certain death awaited) was perhaps precisely the place he had to be. It can likewise be seen that Collins, both in his role as C-in-C, and as head of the Provisional Government, was fulfilling his appropriate role: pursuing diplomacy and negotiating peace.

But he didn't have a nice, quiet 10 Downing Street at which to hold his conference. Nor could his conferees have come there.

Maybe the only way to make that happen, the only way to prevent imminent national disaster, was to take his life in his hands, into the wild back roads of West Cork; *now*. As it happened, perhaps that very place, at that moment, was where he was obliged to appear: because no one else had the authority, as well as the credibility, in addition to the will, and the power, to negotiate this peace, with these forces.

And, lest we forget, assassination en route to peace parlays, has historically been an occupational hazard for Gaelic leaders, who venture to negotiate with London.

---

[147] Just the same, Mr. Churchill may indeed have gotten his chance to hit the dirt in London later on: when war came home there in the 1940s. A development not unrelated to British foreign policy discussed herein; as will be touched upon in Part 3.

Collins' death and further peace negotiations

As seen in a number of issues discussed herein, Collins' fate had an enormous impact on the Civil War's subsequent turn for the worst possible scenario.

With regard to peace talks in particular, Béal na mBláth was the death knell for all chance of a negotiated settlement "with honor" for the anti-Treaty side. The political posture of those who thereafter led the Dublin government, is one reason for this. With Michael Collins died Free State political will for any negotiation with the insurgents.

Another is the fact that, as seen above, a number of people at the time were indeed aware that Collins was travelling on a supposed safe conduct from anti-Treaty leaders, when he met his death, in an anti-Treaty ambush.

This meant that there would be no question of a parlay on the basis of such "safe conduct" *ever again*. Free State "hard-liners", who insisted on unconditional surrender or nothing, would get their way. Moderate anti-Treaty leaders, who were ready for a negotiated end to the war in August (less than a month after it began,) now had no hope and *no means to be heard*.

It meant that there was now nothing to slow the disastrous snowball toward total slaughter.

*(ARR-2) Rolls Royce armoured car, "Sleivenamon"
(in Irish "Sliabh na mBan") from Collins' convoy*

Chapter 11

The escort

Michael Collins was the most important man in Ireland at the time, and because of the number of British agents whose deaths he was responsible for, as well as the hazards of a Civil War, he was particularly vulnerable to an attempt on his life. ... Consequently, the greatest care should have been taken in choosing any escort for him and each member of that escort should have been thoroughly screened. ... That was not done. They seem to have been selected haphazardly, and there were many ex-British soldiers in their ranks.[148]

Controversy still surrounds the question of how the convoy's personnel was chosen, why and by whom. Some Army sources say that it was Dalton who picked the crew.[149] While Dalton was in charge at Cork and could have decided any changes made there, much of the escort started with Collins from Portobello Barracks in Dublin. It's hard to see how Dalton, from Cork City, could have taken part in what happened there. (Due to the war, telephone lines were reputedly inoperable between Dublin and Cork that week.)

However, as noted before, he was head of the bodyguard party which set out from Cork City on 22 August. As such, as Feehan observes:

Before leaving the city Dalton should have provided a bodyguard of Irishmen who knew the West Cork countryside and who had experience of rural guerrilla warfare. He had enough such men under his command in Cork.

Shockingly, Coogan, although he does give six individual names as members of the anti-Treaty ambush party, he does not account in any detailed way for the escort party: who was in it, how and by whom they

---

148 J Feehan

149 More than one of the author's personal contacts with special access to archival material have corroborated this, independently and unknown to each other (speaking on condition of anonymity).

were chosen, etc. (It is one of the strange blind spots, in the vast exhaustive detail of his research.)[150]

It has been lamented above that none of Collins' party were ever questioned afterward in any formal way. What surpasses this omission, is the fact that we don't even know who exactly made up his party! We all know that the first thing an investigator does is to find out the name and personal details of everyone concerned. In seventy years, no one ever bothered; and/or the army never released the information. This certainly would have been the Free State's job.

This of course severely limits what subsequent researchers can say on the issue. Nevertheless, some comment is both possible and necessary.

THE DRIVERS

"*The night before their departure for Cork*" the C-in-C's usual driver "*was told that he would not be driving Collins*". From the statement of Collins' regular driver Jack Swan, it was not Collins who told him this. Neither was the decision made by himself, the usual driver. The decision therefore was made by some unnamed third party. Armoured car driver Jim Woulfe was reputedly asked by Capt. David Coates to drive "*because usual driver Jimmy McGowan was sick*"

The driver of the Leyland touring car who replaced Swan was Private M B Corry, an Englishman with a pronounced Cheshire accent. The armoured car driver, the armoured car machine gun operator(s) and the motorcycle scout were all strangers to Collins' usual compliment, and chosen specially for this journey. Those particular choices are quite significant.

The only ones near the C-in-C, with any chance of seeing events around him clearly at the moment when he fell, would have been Dalton, the drivers; and perhaps some of the armoured car crew as well.

Continual motor trouble plagued the C-in-C throughout this inspection tour (including the earlier leg, in Kerry.) It should not pass without comment that providing for adequate, functional equipment would have been at least partly the driver's job. (Dalton also must share some responsibility in this, from Cork City on.)

---

150   The list of escort members given in Appendix 1 is a compilation of all published accounts. M Ryan's list seems the most complete; but in view of other issues in her version, its uncorroborated points are not entirely relied on herein.

As will be seen below, the drivers' role in the disaster which followed merits scrutiny.

JOCK MCPEAK

As the gunner who operated the Vickers machine gun in the turret of the armoured car, McPeak, his conduct, and the performance of that gun, were most central to events at Béal na mBláth. In Part 1, we've seen his actions and words cast conspicuous doubt upon his veracity and character; and also discovered how critical is the question of whether or not McPeak's gun worked fine, or malfunctioned.

McPeak is quoted as saying that jamming was known to be a problem with that specific gun. This does not say much for him as an operator. Assuring that they had the right equipment, in good working order, would have been part of his job. To undertake a mission as bodyguard to the Commander-in-Chief of the nation, a mission in which the armoured car would represent the "big guns", the flagship centerpiece ... To embark on this mission knowing that your most important weapon was a specially faulty one, ... This is worse than negligence, on the part of the technician with, according to himself, particular knowledge as to which guns worked, and which ones had chronic problems.

Yet, in the 1971 interview, he attributed jamming not to any chronic problems with the gun, but to the lack of a trained second gunner to refill the gunbelts. But other witnesses, notably Dalton and the ambushers, do not say that the gun jammed; on the contrary indicate that it was fiercely active throughout the engagement.

It is necessary to consider in this context McPeak's subsequent desertion and theft of the armoured car, [151] and the controversy that surrounds those suspicious actions. Could an examination of the gun turret have cast doubt on someone's version?

McPeak's story is highly questionable indeed; so as not to say bizarre. It concerns a notorious fatality, at the scene of which he was present and played a key role. He was one of those most directly responsible for the protection of the C-in-C's invaluable life, and physically nearest to him at the moment of his suspicious death. He was reportedly the object of acute suspicion among his fellow soldiers; suspicion which seemed justified soon after by his desertion and theft of the armoured car.

---

151 See Part 3

In view of all the mysterious factors connected with him, hardly any other conclusion would be reasonable but that, if Collins met his fate through the agency of traitors in his own bodyguard, then McPeak was either involved, or had some knowledge of what happened. If so, his account published in 1971 might be expected to contain inaccuracies, calculated to conceal something he knew. (That is, he would be one who may have lied, had more reason to lie than others, etc.)

JOE DOLAN

Dolan was a member of the Squad; according to Coogan "*one of the toughest members.*" His memoire has contributed significantly to our record of the War of Independence; particularly his first-hand accounts of "jobs" they executed. Neligan remembers that he always wore a pin in his lapel, with the motto "*For King and Country*", entwined with red, white and blue ribbons. "*When the Tans and Tommies saw it, they passed Dolan through the cordons murmuring, 'one of our fellows.'*"

This officer apparently cooperated with both Margery Forester and Rex Taylor in preparing their biographies of Collins. He is quoted by them and by others. It seems remarkable that Feehan never mentions him. Pearas Beaslaí lists Capt. Joe Dolan as included in the convoy that left Portobello Barracks, Dublin with the C-in-C on 20 August 1922. Forester says that he joined the party at Limerick. Apparently having interviewed him, she says that he was on the back of the armoured car at Béal na mBláth. While M Ryan places him in the Crossley tender.

Like Dalton, he formed part of Collins' bodyguard in London during the Treaty negotiations. He appears again, in connection with the assassination of Sir Henry Wilson (as discussed above.) Finally, he was present at the killing of his chief, at Béal na mBláth.

Thus he must be of considerable interest to this inquiry. Is there anything remarkable about his association with these three episodes? The Treaty negotiations, the death of Wilson, and that of Collins were not unrelated. They were intrinsically intertwined. All theories aside, there were definite causal links between them. The Treaty and Wilson's death both can be said to have led directly to the C-in-C's assassination. Collins certainly has some responsibility for the Treaty, and was accused of being responsible for Wilson's end.

Dolan comes to history's attention chiefly in the context of these three closely related, yet-unresolved controversies. Before and after, he tends to fade into a background of foot soldiers in general.

Dolan's previous membership in the Squad indubitably identifies him as a key, highly trusted member of Collins' War of Independence team. Yet, as we know, many bonds of loyalty were shaken and sundered in the Civil War. It is also generally allowed, that Collins had enemies who did not openly declare their purpose, with such forthright honesty as did his anti-Treaty opponents at the Four Courts.

According to Dolan's own account, he was asleep on the back of the armoured car when the shooting started. This can add nothing to our esteem. In itself, it immediately casts suspicion on him: for dereliction of duty, at least. It also raises questions. If Dolan could not be trusted to stay awake, while acting as bodyguard to his chief, (arguably "the most important man in Ireland,") in what can he be trusted? Should we then trust his testimony?

If he was asleep in broad daylight, in hostile territory, in wartime, on duty, as one of the guards closest to the C-in-C's priceless person, in an area *"with probably more dangerous ambush sites per mile than any road in Ireland,"* that is bad enough. Yet this is so unbelievable, that we cannot omit to ask: is that the truth? Is he covering up something? Did he only *say* he was asleep?

One thing that can be gleaned from a reading of Dolan's service on the Squad: he was a sharpshooter, with a lot of practice in executing his "targets" consistently, swiftly and efficiently, with no more than one shot or two. He had a reputation as "*quick on the draw*." [152] He had been trained and acclimated to take orders to kill, and to shoot on command, men who were strangers to him, for reasons which he may have understood in only a general way. It was not pleasant work. He undertook this difficult and demanding job for his country, in wartime; and cannot be faulted in that context.

Yet there is danger in training young men to become cold-blooded killers. It is the danger which must be faced, whenever peacetime follows any great martial effort by a nation. As Collins himself (one of the chief organizers of arms shipments to Ireland) observed:

> *A gun is a dangerous thing for a young man to have. Some day he might use it in a quarrel, over a girl, or over a shilling, or over a word.*

---

152   D Neligan

The C-in-C's fundamental dilemma in the Civil War, is that large numbers of the troops who had been organized and trained for one purpose, were swayed away from his control, for another purpose. It is one of the occupational hazards of popular revolution. In the collapse of old, corrupt authorities, it is not always easy for troops to know whom to follow.

Fellows like Dolan were persuaded by some of their countrymen, that the patriotic thing was to shoot a man, because another man said, that this was the man to shoot. Does that mean that he could never be convinced, by say, some third man, that it was his duty now to shoot the man who had told him to shoot the other man before? Could he have been persuaded to yield to such pressure, because his loyalty had been weakened by a personal quarrel, *over a girl, or over a shilling, or over a word?* What seems black and white from the distant perspective of history, may have been a much more difficult call at the time, for a lot of very young men.

This is not intended to accuse Dolan. It is intended to illustrate that he was not above suspicion: that someone *like* him *could* have been involved. That neither are others in the convoy, from the Dublin Brigade or the Squad, exempt from scrutiny. We certainly cannot place members of the convoy beyond questions, which their own words or actions seem to raise. Nor would any thorough military inquest ever have done so. This must be considered in light of the C-in-C's own apparent suspicion that someone, as near to him and as trusted as these, could be cooperating to eliminate him.

In the following pages, we shall explore reasons why each and every Free State man, at that end of the convoy where Dolan was, must be scrutinized.

THE FREE STATE OFFICERS

It is astonishing that, with such a large number of high-ranking officers in the convoy, during the ambush, there seems to have been practically *no leadership*. That is, if the statements of witnesses are believed.

The fact that half the convoy allowed the dignitary, whom they were there to protect, to get out of their sight, in itself suggests a shocking laxity. It is certainly not what one would expect of any military bodyguard moving through hostile territory.

The question of drink

> MILITARY ORDER [27 July 1922]: It is prohibited to supply members of the National Army in uniform with intoxicating liquor. Where a member of the National Forces is found under the influence of drink in a licensed premises the licence of such will be immediately cancelled and fine imposed.

The C-in-C was well-known throughout his brief, brilliant career as the sworn enemy of alcohol while on duty. At the GPO garrison in 1916, he distinguished himself by pouring barrels of porter down the gutter, which had been brought in with provisions; grimly vowing that no one was going to accuse the Irish troops of drunkenness, on this watch. In his ragtag army of shopkeepers, clerks and farmers, this was one of his key principles. It was by this means, that he managed for three years to maintain sufficient discipline to disturb the rest of generals like Wilson and Macready.

> If not for Collins, drink or informers would have finished us in two weeks.
>
> *- Vinnie Byrne (of the Squad)*

He was rarely seen, during the war, to imbibe more than a glass of sherry. [153] On this journey, Collins was on one of the most deadly serious and dangerous missions of his career. Everything he'd worked for, and the nation's entire future, was at stake. He was keenly aware that his life was under clear and present danger, every step of the way. It is hardly likely that he would have chosen this time for a relaxation of discipline, in the bodyguard he was depending on, in the most basic first principle he had always insisted upon.

Reputedly there are conflicting accounts about this, apparently from spectators who were nearby, in the various towns they passed that day. That is, some reported and some refuted, that there was any drinking by the C-in-C's escort, of a nature to interfere with their duties. They cannot all be telling the truth. So some of them spoke in error.

---

[153] Collins had sown some wild oats as a teenager in London, but was never known as a heavy drinker. He was seen to be visibly intoxicated only on rare occasion, such as Christmas 1920 (after the Auxiliaries' raid on his Christmas dinner party nearly ended his career.)

Some may have lied. Allegations of riotous debauchery were one of the tactics of Collins' political enemies. Such allegations, never heard of before then, formed part of a character assassination campaign which immediately preceded his death.

In those days, it was a time-honoured practice throughout Ireland and England, for visiting officials to provide a round of drinks for everyone in the house, at each stop they made. As a representative of the new government, which was still striving to win the hearts and minds of a divided population, the C-in-C could hardly have refused to do as much. He seems to have fulfilled this duty of hospitality on that tour, where cheering crowds surrounded his car in every town. This alone, of course, could have given rise to rumours that he himself and/or his men were drinking at every stop.

In this context, Collins was acting as the Free State's goodwill ambassador. This required him to show not only a friendly face, but also to demonstrate that theirs was a competent and disciplined government, which could be trusted with the nation's future. Throughout his career, one of the keys to his success was his astounding ability to win over and inspire the confidence of extremely diverse people, wherever he went.

The Military Order at the top of this section was published in the newspapers, a few weeks before, and would have been common knowledge. He could hardly be seen to publicly flout that order, or fail to enforce it, in his own bodyguard. For him to have done so, in the course of public appearances, undertaken to secure cooperation and confidence, would have been entirely out of character.

Coogan suggests that some mischief may have broken out while Collins was away for short periods, during his various meetings. However, the convoy was bristling with officers: one Commander-in-Chief, one major general, one commandant, three captains, two lieutenants and one sergeant. Nine out of twenty-five. That's one officer for every two and a half enlisted men. If between them they couldn't keep the soldiers from getting drunk, they'd never have won the war.

Generally speaking, the balance of evidence does not support the idea that alcohol interfered with anyone's performance that day.

Officers' meeting at the Curagh, early August 1922, left to right: Col Dunphy, Commander-in-Chief Collins, Major General Emmet Dalton, Comdt General P. MacMahon, and Comdt General D. O'Hegerty

Chapter 12

Dalton

Emmett Dalton seems to come to public attention first as Collins' London bodyguard, during the Treaty negotiations of 1921. He ostensibly served the Irish delegation there as "military advisor". He is seen in many photographs of the delegates' arrival at 10 Downing Street. Just previous to this, during the Truce, he held a position of great responsibility as Volunteer Liaison Officer at the Gresham Hotel Liaison Office: a nerve centre and contact clearing house for Collins and his operatives. He was a very young man, not much above twenty years old at the time of these events. His prominence lasted a very short time, and he left the army not long after the Civil War ended.

He was a native of Dublin. His brother, Charlie Dalton, "*though only a boy*" had been a member of the Squad, where he had "*rendered excellent service.*" [154] Emmett Dalton had served in the British Army. This was not unusual for youth in Ireland, and did not in itself prove sympathy for the English cause. Economic conscription was often a matter of survival: the imperial army the only career open to the young and unemployed.

Reputedly, Dalton's British Army service in World War I was with the intelligence corps. Army sources now confirm that, in World War II, he was with British Army intelligence again. This is but a short step from the secret service.

"*Not everyone on the Free State side trusted him ... .There were many who believed that he, like Childers, was a British agent.*" [155] While this is hardly proof, this report on what was widely "*believed*" is not without value: Feehan had a long career in the army, which brought him into contact with War of Independence veterans still serving. Many contributed to his research.

Of course, if "*many believed*" this, the C-in-C himself could hardly have been unaware of the charge. However, it is necessary to understand the context in which he worked. The British administration was riddled with Collins' operatives; all of whom titularly "worked for" the enemy, while secretly aiding the fight for independence. A number

---

154 D Neligan

155 J Feehan

of his men had been in the British army; and, as explained above, this was no shame. His organization went all the way to the heart and dizzyingly high up in Crown administration. Associates were at times shocked or alarmed by some of his contacts; or doubted whether they could be trusted. Therefore, although he listened attentively to everything said,[156] others' suspicions might not necessarily convince him.

Needless to say, this was a dangerous game, involving many calculated risks. And lest we forget, Collins did play it with astonishing success: he beat the British secret service at it. The complex nature of it is interestingly illustrated by an episode which took place after the Truce. At the end of an exhausting journey to London, a tired and irritable Collins was working alone in his train compartment. A British officer *"named Shaw or perhaps Shore"* asked to see him. Collins' aide knew that the Big Fella was in no mood for socializing. The officer said, *"Oh, he'll see me, alright."* At first Collins was angry at the interruption, but when he learned who it was, said, *"Yes, I'll see him, of course."* The officer had been one of the heads of the British forces who had hunted Collins and his organization for years. As the astounded aide gaped in horror and fascination, the two sat down and engaged in a long conversation about the past conflict. In the course of it, they even discussed double agents whom they had both employed. *"He was really working for you, wasn't he?" "Oh no, he was your man, always."* [157] As close as the killer to his victim.

At a time when Collins was experiencing grave doubts about his closest associates, Dalton came to be entrusted with the C-in-C's personal safety: in preference to other confidantes, in a situation which he knew to be life-threatening. It is offered that these factors may not be unrelated: a person who was that close to him might be well-positioned to take advantage of the situation.

One of Feehan's colleagues put it, *"Yes, he was a shrewd man, but he was also a man of great likes and dislikes. If he liked someone he tended to trust that person. The British secret service knew that and they cleverly exploited this trait. It was also no problem to them to infiltrate the convoy. It would be going a little too far to say that Collins could not be deceived. Such a claim can be made for no man."*

---

156 One of Collins' qualities was his truly democratic esteem for the input of all he met, however humble. *"He took advice from his chauffeur."*

157 T P Coogan

It is significant that Dalton's short-lived prominence coincides with the Treaty negotiations and Civil War: which entire scenario had all the earmarks of a profound British strategy to isolate and eliminate first Collins, and then the best of his comrades in arms.

Despite all the indications that Collins trusted him, and that he was well-established in the movement, it is impossible to exonerate Dalton in the events at Béal na mBláth.

One of the very few points on which all testimony, including Dalton's own, agrees, is that Dalton was the one physically nearest to Collins' person throughout the ambush. Widely accused of complicity in Collins' death, and of being a British agent, he *never denied* either charge. On the contrary, he even publicly admitted that he might have shot Collins himself ("accidentally")!

All in all, Dalton, by word and deed, has spoken so cogently for himself, as to merit special examination of his testimony. His account deserves in-depth critique; especially because it is the most often and most thoughtlessly quoted today.

DALTON'S VERSION OF EVENTS

Everyone knows that Saint Patrick brought Christianity to Ireland. And everyone is wrong.

- Richard Warner

Dalton's account of the amount of fire they came under, is one of the most excessive of all the eye-witnesses. It is also the least plausible. Obviously, if an open car with four passengers had been swept before and behind by "*a fierce fusillade of machine gun fire*" which shattered the windscreen, people in the car, behind the windscreen, could not have escaped injury. But this is what Dalton asks us to believe.

The public has been made familiar with the oft-repeated tale of how Dalton said, "*Drive like hell,*" but was countermanded by the C-in-C's "*No stop & we'll fight them.*" But for this, we have none but Dalton's word alone. It is not corroborated by anyone else. It is contradicted by the only other witness on record who was within hearing: the driver Corry, to whom these words were supposedly addressed. [158] (See Appendix 6, Myth 3)

---

[158] This version of events has turned up elsewhere: but only in the mouths of those who were not there at the time, but are apparently repeating Dalton's version.

An interview with Dalton in 1968 added a few points to his account of 1923. [159] In it he expressly denied that he sent Collins' body to the British military hospital at Shanakiel, but claims it went to Bon Secours instead. The medical testimony here agrees in contradicting that, and McKenna supports them. Press reports also list Dalton as being present at the removal from Shanakiel. He is the only eyewitness who insists that Collins suffered one wound alone.[160]

Shanakiel was a British military hospital. Why would the chief of the Irish national army in Cork send the body of his Commander-in-Chief to the British military? Why would he insistently lie about it later on? [161]

DALTON AND THE PEACE NEGOTIATIONS

McKenna states that he saw decoded messages exchanged between Dalton in Cork and Collins in Dublin on the subject of possible peace terms to end the Civil War. (See Appendix 4)

He further testified that Dalton knew the C-in-C was making this trip through West Cork in order to negotiate with anti-Treaty leaders there, for an end to the Civil War. He averred that Dalton had received details from the anti-Treaty side about mined roads and blown bridges, *"as a kind of assurance of safe conduct and goodwill."*

He thus corroborates several critical points:
1) that Collins was there for peace talks;
2) that Dalton was in the C-in-C's confidence as to that purpose;
3) that Dalton had
    a) acted as a go-between for at least some communications from the anti-Treaty side, in opening these negotiations; and
    b) in planning the itinerary and meetings to take place on this subject in Cork; and

---

159 More of this interview is reproduced in J Feehan.
160 Among commentators after the fact, M Ryan is the most insistent partisan of this view.

161 This may ring a bell for British history buffs: At other key turning points of history, the news of a great leader's demise was a closely guarded secret. Certain elements were keen to have it first, and to keep it to themselves for as long as possible. One can likewise hardly escape a shiver, remembering the ancient barbaric war practice of literally sending the head of a vanquished foe to one's superior. In view of all of the above, certainly it might have been a matter of concern to the British, to absolutely confirm if the C-in-C were truly dead.

c) therefore that Dalton apparently lied about all this, later on.

Deasy also confirms:

> One of [the negotiations to end the Civil War] was initiated by Emmett Dalton who occupied Cork City in August [1922]. Through intermediaries he made contact with some republican officers and he was actively assisted by Tom Ennis.

They are corroborated by Florrie O'Donoghue, that peace negotiations of *August 1922* were initiated *by Dalton* from Cork City after it surrendered to the Free State forces under his command. While Sean MacEoin reported:

> General Collins agreed to a meeting on the night of 22nd of August. Republican forces supplied Dalton with details of laid mines, mined bridges etc. and generally speaking assured a safe conduct for the Commander-in-Chief. As time would not allow the contacting of every outlying post, and for that reason only, an armoured escort was included, to serve as it were both as deterrent to possible attack and as an identification. [162]

All these authoritative sources, independently of each other, confirm that Dalton, while Free State commander in Cork City, acted as a negotiator.

Yet Deasy, only two pages earlier, (in *Brother Against Brother*), expresses his bewilderment at what Collins could possibly have been doing at Béal na mBláth that day; and finds it difficult to believe that his presence there could have been the merest happenstance.

In his description of said peace moves of August 1922, Deasy specifies that nothing was on offer to the anti-Treaty side, except unconditional surrender; and that this is the reason the talks failed. He appears to have had no knowledge whatever of any of the terms outlined in said correspondence between Collins and Dalton on the subject. He makes no mention of Collins in connection with peace negotiations, and demonstrates the utmost ignorance that Collins was involved in discussion of such terms.

---

[162] Sean MacEoin papers

In this context, let us consider Dalton's 1968 interview with Cormac McCarthy: [163]

MacCarthy: *Did you and Collins meet any neutral members of the IRA to consider peace while in Cork?*

Dalton: *He met several people but I do not know who they were. ... He met several civilians whom I understood to be relatives. In fact, I do not know who they were. Collins did not say. He did not discuss any matter other than of a military nature with me.*

MacCarthy: *... You had been in Macroom that morning and also on the previous day. Had these visits to Macroom any political significance?*

Dalton: *None whatever.*

Dalton states first that he never discussed anything but military issues with the C-in-C. He says he knew nothing about people Collins met with on this trip; says Collins never told him anything about it. In the same breath, he is then most positive that he did know whether there was or was not a political purpose of their repeated circling of Macroom: that negotiations were *not* involved. (The following statement is true. The preceding statement is false.)

In this Dalton denies that he had any connection with peace negotiations. Yet the record indicates that he certainly did work closely with the C-in-C in this respect,

Deasy also mentions Dalton's part in peace moves of September 1922 which "*had the authority of the Free State Government*"; resulting in yet another major anti-Treaty meeting about ending the war, also near Crookstown, County Cork, in October 1922. "*But because they insisted on unconditional surrender they had no hope of success.*"

---

163 For *Agus* magazine.

Peace negotiations and the suppression of evidence
If Dalton was quite active indeed as a negotiator for the Free State in seeking an end to the Civil War, and lied about it later, then, in these subsequent denials, *he was "covering-up" of the fact that Collins was killed while travelling under safe-conduct, for peace negotiations.*

This points out Dalton's prominent role in concealing from posterity Collins' true position with regard to the Civil War. It directly implicates him in the defeat of the C-in-C's peace mission that day, which ended in his death. Because by covering up Collins' intention to make amicable terms with the anti-Treaty side, he took part in demolishing, both tactically and ideologically, all hope of reuniting the forces which had won Ireland's freedom.

Hiding Collins' endorsement of reconciliation was a powerful propaganda tool, in that policy of all-out war against the anti-Treaty side: which the C-in-C so ardently opposed, and died trying to prevent.

Collins' successors cynically used his death as a stick to beat the "die-hards," while concealing facts about that catastrophic fatality on their watch. Or to be more precise, on Dalton's watch.

WHO SEARCHED COLLINS' CLOTHES?
The unusual lack of formal, written records has deprived us of a reliable inventory of what was in the C-in-C's pockets when he fell. Discussions by previous authors are not drawn from any documents of that kind. They refer only to scattered remnants, gleaned from various sources. Apparently Dalton would seem to have been the ultimate source for any such items or information from the scene of the ambush. Following is a list of such alleged items:

Items alleged to have been found on Collins' person, at his death
1) A small scrap of paper, bearing Lady Lavery's signature. This includes nothing of a remotely romantic nature. It seems to be an excerpt from precisely the kind of letter, often written by Lavery as a go-between for 10 Downing Street. While certainly friendly, its polite compliments in no way exceed the standard style employed by political hostesses of the time. Collins had previously given some of these letters to Ms Kiernan, expressly in order to show her that his contact with the English lady was strictly business (contrary to gossip-mongering London tabloids.) [164]

---

164 The fragment from Lady Lavery reads: "...*how fine and impressive and marvellously*

2) A fragment of an undated letter written by Collins, does not include the name of any addressee.[165] Apparently we have again only Lady Lavery's word as to the all-important question of provenance: exactly where and when it was found. Biographers have freely quoted the note she wrote on this letter, that it was "*written the day he was killed - found in his pocket.*" However, as it includes no names or dates, we must ask how either its projected addressee, or its date were ever identified, and by whom. Once again, it seems, we are dependent on Dalton, as the first person to take charge of the C-in-C's remains.

3) A copy of a Shane Leslie poem, on the subject of Lady Lavery's portrait. (This seems doubtful, in light of Collins' known dislike for Mr. Leslie.)

4) Also according to Lavery (whether or not via Dalton remains uncertain) a small brooch of hers was "*kept in his scapular case.*" [166]

Some of these items were reportedly stained; apparently with blood (ostensibly the C-in-C's.) His field diary, which he was certainly carrying at the time, was never listed. Nor were any other papers related to army or government business ever alleged to have been on his person when he died.

The report that his pockets contained nothing when he died, except a personal letter and tokens connected with Lady Lavery, is in itself a flashing red light, with bells and whistles.

---

organized it all is - I am so proud Michael how can I say it all 'at all.' Your letter has just come to me from London. May God keep you. Hazel"

165 The letter in Collins' hand reads: "*must face realities ... so goodbye - I read your letter again this morning before going to sleep. When I woke the pages were by my side. God bless you, I am mo mhuirnin yours, M.*"

166 Whether Collins possessed such a thing as a scapular case is open to question. He was admittedly not a very actively practicing Catholic. At the GPO in 1916, he was distinguished as the only Irish combatant who went into battle without having received the sacraments beforehand. His correspondence with Ms Kiernan documents that it was she who particularly pressed him in this period, to be more religiously observant. He carefully reports to her on many occasions that he went to mass, lit a candle in church, etc.; and also explicitly acknowledges to her, both that he would not have done so without her influence, and that it has done him good.

For a man in the C-in-C's position, on a demanding official tour, filled from morning til night with one meeting after another, a man with a mania for constant note-taking and paperwork; a man in the eye of such a political storm, the focus of so many dangerous enemies, and the victim of a violent death, attended by so many unanswered questions ... any self-respecting researcher should find this highly suspicious. It should announce to any penetrating examination, that there was something very, very wrong with *whoever handled his body first,* following his death.

> *If this is true [that Collins had been guaranteed safe-conduct] then it poses the question: When were Collins' clothes searched and where is that document now? This question of who searched Collins' clothes and when, needs a great deal of further investigation.* [167]

Collins' pocket diary, in which he continually marked down his minute-to-minute observations on this trip, disappeared from his person after his death, and according to Feehan, only "*turned up*" [168] forty years later. Coogan states that Dalton himself offered the notebook for sale, years afterward. Documents outlining terms for ending the Civil War, and for merging the two armies back into one, also believed to have been on his person, likewise went missing.

Dalton was in an ideal position to rifle the C-in-C's pockets: but was not alone in having abundant opportunities to remove some documents and to replace them with others. If members of the convoy were culpable, this could easily have been done as soon as he hit the ground; or in the darkened vehicle on the inordinately long journey back to Cork City. Dalton claims to have knelt beside the body, held it in his arms all the way, etc. But no one else corroborates the pious purposes in his account, of shedding tears and saying prayers: not even his picked men who second him on other key points.

---

167 J Feehan

168 Ibid.

Chapter 13

Lady Lavery and the Churchills

One of the lowest tactics used by the political authors of the Civil War to smear Collins' good name, was invidious gossip of sexual liaisons with fashionable ladies in London. The Countess Marckievitch went so far as to bring into the Dáil her allegation that he was engaged to marry the Crown Princess! (A calumny which history has shown to have been entirely baseless and irresponsible.)

This "psy op" [169] was aimed to sting the public in a particular place. It tended to portray Collins, not only as swept away by the luxuries and flattery of London. But as fundamentally *unfaithful* in character: to his most sacred, most personal ties; to his Irish woman. And, *therefore*, in the deeply poetic, symbolic sensibilities of Irish public perception, to Ireland "Herself."

Dalton and the Lady Lavery letters

It is significant that more letters from Lady Lavery, in which the supposed affair with Collins is again supported *only by her* statements, were addressed to Dalton personally. And have recently been donated to the National Library by Dalton's son.

Dalton was widely believed to be a British agent. Lady Lavery was alleged to be a British agent. Both had remarkably close access to Collins' person around the time of his death. Both contributed to calumnies against his character which were particularly identified with British sources and associated with the Treaty controversy.

Because of the connection between character assassination and physical assassination, we should take a moment to consider the question of Lady Lavery.

Lady Lavery

Hazel Lavery was an American from Chicago who became well-known as one of London's foremost society hostesses, following her marriage to John Lavery, a genteel Belfast-born painter. She was also a

---

[169] "Psychological operations": actions calculated to have a propaganda / psychological effect, conducive to British goals. Although the term has been coined relatively recently, the technique has a long pedigree in Anglo-Irish relations, reaching back to the 16th century.

notorious *femme fatale*; whose shenanigans at one point inspired women in her sphere to create a Husbands' Protection Society, in her honour. When a teenage Collins was first being secretly sworn into the IRB, her salon was already a famous watering hole for British government and diplomatic circles. That is, for precisely those powers-that-be who would bend all their considerable might to capture and execute Michael Collins and his nationalist "brothers".

THE LAVERIES AND THE CHURCHILLS

The Churchills have a long history of intimate service to the British royal family. They originally acquired position through a lady who was a personal favourite and confidante of Queen Anne, in the 17th century. Lady Sarah Churchill's husband later distinguished himself as a general. Credited with the famous victory at the Battle of Blenheim, the family was generously rewarded indeed. The Churchills were created Dukes of Marlborough,[170] receiving a former royal residence (Woodstock) and ample means to transform it into the present Blenheim Palace: renowned for vast magnificence, hardly excelled by princes.

All of this is to say that the Churchills' special relationship with the Crown, although at first amorous, was of a definite military character. In Collins' time, this manifested notably in Lord Randolph Churchill's ominous slogan: "*Ulster will fight. And Ulster will be right.*"

Long before the 1916 Rising, the Laveries were already clients of the Churchills, and the Churchills their patrons in the upper echelons of high society. It was through the Churchills' patronage of John Lavery that he was commissioned to portray the royal family in 1913. As an official illustrator for the British army, during World War I, Lavery did much artwork of a military nature; some of which may have been connected with intelligence work. It is worth noting that during the First World War, when pleasure trips were largely discouraged, the couple continuously travelled abroad. One of his prestigious accomplishments was the official portrait of Admiral Beatty dictating terms to the defeated German command.

In short, the Laveries rose to fame as the darlings of the British military: he was knighted, and became "Sir" John Lavery. His wife organized the official Victory Ball at the Albert Hall. They were known as

---

[170] With an unusual provision that, if lacking any male heir, ladies of the family could succeed to the title as Duchess in their own right.

shining members of "the Asquith set": frequenting that Prime Minister's summer home as well as 10 Downing Street.

This brilliant social position must be seen to far overshadow the Laveries' dalliance with London's Irish community. It also sheds a particular light on their presence there. In the general balance of evidence, it is far more likely that their visits to London's Irish were made in their capacity as representatives of the Churchills and the British military; rather than vice versa. All things considered, the fact that they had met Collins and his sister before 1916, through London's Irish social circles, may well have been merely good routine British intelligence. It does nothing to suggest that the Laveries were not servants of the Empire throughout.[171]

It is indeed difficult to conceive how writers on Collins could pass off Lady Lavery as some kind of Irish patriot. Or even as merely a London Gaelic League enthusiast who was an American of Irish descent.

> *My dear Hazel,*
> *I had a very pleasant talk with MC this morning* [172] *and hope to see him again on Monday. I am very glad he and his colleagues are dining with you tonight. I am sure your influence will be exerted in the cause of peace ... I ought, I think to let you know "confidentially" that my colleagues take a most grave view of the Constitution.*
> *- Winston Churchill letter to Lady Lavery, June 1922*

During the Treaty negotiations, the Laveries emerged as go-betweens for Churchill. Sir Lavery's studio was used for Churchill's meetings with Collins. After the Treaty was signed, Lady Lavery continued to act as courier from Churchill to Collins. This would have made it impossible for Collins to refuse to see her or to resist her communications. It may have made it necessary to flatter her,

---

[171] C Osborne suggests that there may have been a dating relationship between Lady Lavery and Collins during his early work life in England. However, she offers no evidence, and this appears to be pure conjecture, possibly based on post-Treaty gossip. The most dazzling high society hostess in London would hardly be seen stepping out to the theatre with an obscure Irish clerk on her arm. Such a thing could have been fatal to her career! Once Collins became famous, many were ever after eager to claim more connexion with him than they had.

[172] This may be some kind of code: none of Churchill's talks with Collins in June 1922 were "*very pleasant.*"

important not to offend her, and difficult to absolutely refuse her attentions.

Still, Lady Lavery's political role, and her influence on the C-in-C, have at times been inflated by her fans and eulogists. Notably her husband, in his autobiography, claimed that the real reason Collins signed the Treaty was because Lady Lavery told him he should. (Not very likely; and utterly belied by Collins' detailed arguments during the Treaty debates.)

All this did, however, place her in an excellent position to be the one apprised of his daily schedule. In the week of his death, she continued to be so. On the eve of his departure for that last journey, she was reported as arriving "*in his train*" as "*his abject admirer,*" [173] at a dinner party which he attended. There was an attempt on him by a sniper during the festivities.

Hazel Lavery's behaviour throughout seems to have been rather out of character for an upper class Lady of that era. She went to extraordinary lengths, not to conceal, but to publicly claim that she had an affair with Collins. Although believable for readers in the 21st century, this was not at all normal conduct for a married woman in her social milieu at the time. In those days, and even more recently, such behaviour in a woman was considered to be a serious and permanent setback not only for herself, but for her whole family. It could be expected to finish a husband's career. It is hardly believable that she would have broadcast it, *if such an affair really existed*. It should also be noted that she never dared make such claims, as long as Collins was alive.

It is inappropriate, and shockingly naïve, that Collins biographers have been willing to rely heavily on the British author Shane Leslie, in the question of Lady Lavery's supposed affair. Leslie himself was Winston Churchill's first cousin: hardly a disinterested source. His mother was sister to Winston's mother, Jennie Jerome: a Brooklyn, New York-born society dame, from the same American nouveau-riche milieu as Hazel Lavery. Born John Randolph, he "espoused" the Irish cause in 1908 and changed his name to "Shane Leslie". Such British / American "recent converts" in general, and those so closely connected to the Churchills in particular, must be taken with a grain of salt. The year 1908 was one of great ferment in the Irish nationalist movement. And so also for British informers who hovered around it.

---

173 Lady Gregory, personal correspondence

Collins' own closest associates in the army, who were most in his personal confidence, absolutely refused to give any countenance to Lady Lavery's performances. This was particularly demonstrated in prohibiting any flowers to be laid on his coffin, excepting only a single lily from Kitty Kiernan.

KITTY KIERNAN

In view of all of the above, Lady Lavery should be beneath any comparison with Kitty Kiernan; and we should be above mentioning them in the same breath. However, Ms Kiernan cannot be relegated to a footnote here, but merits a few choice words on her own account; especially because some historians have been obliged to play down Michael's fiancé, in order to support their theories about Lady Lavery, and about his death.

There is no basis for the erroneous characterization of Ms Kiernan as politically naïve. It is, at best, a gloss of inexcusable carelessness. The contention that Lavery would have had more capacity than Ms Kiernan, as a political confidante, is entirely refuted by the record.

Writers seem to have presumed on the fact that Lavery was a famous society hostess, who moved in high British government circles; while Ms Kiernan was merely the proprietor of a small hotel and shops, in a modest country town, in rural Ireland; her name unknown to the public, outside of her relationship with Collins. Collins biographers seem to have written off Ms Kiernan as clueless and useless politically, on this basis alone. [174]

Clearly Collins did not think so; as an attentive reading of their letters illustrates. Such an assumption does not demonstrate adequate acquaintance with their correspondence, with her education, her family's prominent, albeit secret role in the War of Independence; nor with the level of political sophistication general among Irish people of her time, place, class and social standing.

---

[174] That is, those writers who must be presumed free from any archaic attitudes, that the intelligence, looks, or attractiveness of an upper class English "Lady" are automatically superior to those of all women from other classes, nations, races, and in the eyes of all men, of every kind. Some comments on Lavery have been marred by rather sophmoric romantic partisanship (particularly in female writers of English background;) and by eagerness to include anything which adds "spice", however doubtful.

On the contrary, as muse, hostess, networker, companion and confidante, the Kiernan sisters and their hotel may be called the Irish nationalist counterparts, of a London lady's political *salon*.

With Ms Kiernan, Collins could feel secure that he was not confiding in a British agent: the Kiernan hotel had been a key safe house for Volunteers throughout the War of Independence. In their correspondence, she and Collins frequently discussed the political situation; of which she demonstrated a keen grasp, often providing insight and encouragement. The C-in-C, for his part, explicitly declared that Kitty was more and more necessary to him in these stressful days, and that *"there's no one like you."*

Ms Kiernan came from precisely the same sort of background as he: a traditional Irish farming family, hard-working, upwardly mobile, successful in business and adaptable to town life. Both were products of a progressive, republican education. Both were ambitious, modern and stylish. In Collins' world, Ms Kiernan was an elegant lady, and the female of his own species.

Michael Collins' love letters

The C-in-C's correspondence "pact" with Ms Kiernan, rendered him particularly vulnerable to a certain kind of intrigue. In 1921, he and Kitty had made an agreement to write to each other daily (or as nearly so as possible.) It was an important part of their somewhat complicated courtship. Collins was at great pains to convince her of his sincerity; which could be quite a challenge, for a man obliged to live and work many miles away, who had little personal time to devote to romance.

The British Post Office had continual access to their intimate communications. They handled Collins' own love letters: a great number of them.

Michael and Kitty's correspondence has been catalogued. From this, it is known that they definitely exchanged considerably more than the over 300 letters now indexed. We may never know exactly how many, or what became of them.

Their letters explicitly document that they were agreed to burn certain types of long letters, immediately after reading. A number of times, they also discussed acute concern that their communications had been tampered with; and that this was done by the C-in-C's political opponents. They mention that some letters have gone astray, were never received, disappeared, etc.

Their own messages clearly record that these concerns suddenly became more serious in the last month or two of his life. The impression is that something particularly alarming had happened, which caused them to exercise more caution than ever. They began to avoid the post and favor wires, whenever he was in London. On August 2, 1922, he wrote, *"It was no imagining about that letter which you did not get ... I fear it must have been captured by the Irregulars."*

No love letters for Lady L

> *Letters from Collins were shown to Lord Birkenhead by Lady Lavery and he noticed that the occasional romantic passages were interpolated in a woman's handwriting, valiantly, if unsuccessfully disguised.* [175]

There exists only one complete document, in Collins' hand, to support any alleged affair with Lady Lavery: a single page, of a few words. The syntax is very much like some of Collins' most affectionate notes to Ms Kiernan, such as he dashed off on several occasions, just after seeing her. The name "Hazel" is written on it three times, but always in a peripheral way: in front of the word "Dear" and after it (no other words on that line.) The handwriting of the name does not precisely match the rest of the letter. Michael and Kitty's voluminous correspondence cannot be compared with this single, dubious bit.

C Osborne entirely misleads with an insinuation that a few poems in Lady Lavery's scrapbook outnumber the lines written by Collins to Ms Kiernan. Said poems are the only other evidence offered for any rival to Ms Kiernan in the C-in-C's affections. They are alleged to have been written by him, to Lavery. However, we have only Lady L's word for it. The poems in question exist only in Lavery's own handwriting, in her scrapbook. The claim that Collins wrote any of them originates solely with herself. While the poems themselves have a distinct Shane Leslie ring to them. (Leslie's poetry was addressed to Lavery frequently, avowedly and publicly, during the same period.)

> *If Hazel did make romantic interpolations in Collins' letter in a disguised hand, as Birkenhead averred, it is not impossible that*

---

[175] Terence DeVere White

others may have done the same, perhaps to an even greater extent.

Coogan follows the above paragraph with a detail of suspicious indications of forgery, in letters which have been attributed to Collins; apparently with the specific purpose to fabricate a personal attachment between him and British government circles. [176]

All of this strange carry-on, like so much else in this inquiry, dates from the time of the Treaty.

Clandestine love and war

Michael Collins was a clever, politic man; clever enough to outmanoeuvre an army on his trail, for years on end. No scandal concerning a woman was ever attached to his name for the first thirty years of his life. Although, from the maturity and restraint he demonstrated with Ms Kiernan, she was probably not his first passion.

On the contrary, he had spent his teenage years sowing a good deal of wild oats; exposed to the pleasures of London; with enough disposable income to attend the theatre regularly, take classes and join clubs. Yet he appears to have conducted himself with such discretion, that no record of any female trouble for him has ever been substantiated.

It is to be supposed that a man who could run a guerrilla campaign, under the very noses of Dublin Castle, could manage to exclude unwanted spectators from his sex life. Evidently he did manage his personal intimacy, as men of good character in those days were expected to: without noise, without publicity, without exploitation of the innocent, and without scandal.

The period for which we are asked to believe that he carried on affairs with more than one British noblewoman, is from the time of the Treaty negotiations on. This is when he became overwhelmed with the most mind-boggling workload of his remarkable career. In addition to this, he was spending every weekend possible, and many weekdays,

---

[176] A letter without signature or addressee, written in pencil, is one of those discredited by Coogan. It has been closely guarded by the descendants of Lord Londonderry, and rarely seen. It is certainly odd that these should be anxious to allege that Lady Londonderry (or any other Lady) was unfaithful to her husband, and with a gun-wielding republican at that. Any cursory examination of the house of Londonderry, their ancestral position and loyalties, indicates that these were the last people on earth for such bedfellows; either literally or figuratively.

with Ms Kiernan (as their correspondence abundantly documents.) In view of all this, that he either would or could have indulged in an on-going sexual liaison with a notorious London society siren (or two,) in the full glare of publicity which his frequent meetings at 10 Downing Street now suddenly trained on him ... This is in itself beggars belief.

But that anyone would ever catch him doing it? That for the first and only time in his life, he would have failed to keep private, anything which he did not wish to be known, anything which it would behove him to conceal ... This is demonstrably incongruous, and entirely contradicts his *modus operandi,* in every other comparable question.

The idea is further belied by the profound attention which Collins always paid to the Irish public, with its peculiar symbolic sensibilities. A major contributor to the movement's astounding success was the talent and skill with which he ever "played to the audience." He lived in the utmost consciousness that his public character was a powerful propaganda tool. He had used it skilfully to inspire nationalists to take on an empire; and later, to win the population's confidence in its untried young native government.

At the period in question, that public confidence was an enormous issue. No one would have been more sensitive than Collins, to the negative impact on that confidence, which such a scandalous affair would have; an impact which might change the fate of the country. Just now, when his life's work was at last within reach of success.

For the Treaty negotiations, he emerged from a life spent in hiding, constantly dogged by professional surveillance. Collins was painfully aware that he had never been under such painstaking scrutiny, as he was in the goldfish bowl of the dreaded British capital.

That he would have chosen such a moment as this, to risk all and let his hormones lead the way, is believable only by general readers, who are unacquainted with the extraordinary self-discipline and circumspection, which were the keys to his success at all times.

Commander-in-Chief Collins entering his car, surrounded by crowds, outside O'Donovan's Hotel, Clonakilty, 22 August 1922

CHAPTER 14

WHAT DID MICHAEL KNOW AND WHEN DID HE KNOW IT?

As seen in the preceding chapter, Collins' very private personal life has been seen to bear upon unanswered questions about his death. In this, the often secretive nature of his work has frustrated the job of historians again and again. It seems that practically no one was entirely in his confidence regarding his business in West Cork on that last journey (with the possible and lamentable exception of Dalton.) This has led to erroneous conclusions and exasperated despair by biographers, "What was he thinking? What could he possibly have been thinking?"

A good rule of thumb is to avoid the pitfall of deciding that we're smarter than he was; or that we know more than he did about what was going on. With this, much can be gleaned from a re-examination of the facts which his many chroniclers have uncovered.

He knew of clandestine operations circling him

> *The Government is aware of plots to murder the members of the Government who are carrying out the people's mandate to restore order to the country. They are further aware that certain Officers in the Army whose military services are well known are marked down similarly.* [177]

As director of the most successful intelligence war ever waged against Britain's espionage past-masters, Collins was an expert at detecting and unravelling surreptitious operations. He had come to know the players intimately. He knew their personalities, their style, their *modus operandi*. He could smell a British secret serviceman at fifty

---

[177] 4 August 1922 Michael Collins sent this draft to WT Cosgrave, which he wished to have published " *... as an official statement either now or at some more suitable opportunity.*" Do these underlined words (emphasis added) suggest that there had been dialogue, and resistance, within the Cabinet, about making an official statement regarding such threats? Certainly its publication at that time would have had a profound impact on the public dialogue, and on the historical discussion since. Prevalent presumptions that the C-in-C was blithely ignoring the danger of assassination would have been impossible. Considering the number of prominent deaths which immediately followed the date of this draft, one must wonder precisely who or what prevented its publication, apparently keenly desired by the C-in-C.

paces. He could differentiate between one of them, an Auxie, or a Black & Tan by the cut of their clothes and the swing of their step.

> *It is very difficult to shadow such a man. He has been in tight corners, has developed a sixth sense. He adopts many tricks of evasion, ... When one's life is at stake perceptions are sharpened until danger can be scented in the very air.*[178]

He knew his former comrades from the War of Independence. He knew by sight and/or by name members of virtually every unit around the country. He knew what kind of weapons they had. He knew what kind of actions they were likely to mount and equal to carrying out.

As attempts on his life multiplied in July - August 1922, he would naturally have been making careful note of these attacks: and of any features thereof which might identify their source.

He knew he had an infiltrator close to him

As noted above, several attempts on his life in the weeks before Béal na mBláth demonstrated very timely information about his daily schedule. This included one such attempt made at the dinner party he attended, just the night before setting out on his last journey.

It is offered that, while "psy ops" by his powerful opponents worked to undermine the army's trust and the public's confidence in Collins, a corresponding campaign was also under way to undermine Collins' trust in his own associates. He voiced such concerns on numerous occasions in this period.

> *"I'm looking at friends, and wondering if they are friends."*

"How would you like a new boss?"

Collins posed this question to both Sinead Mason, his personal secretary, and to Joe O'Reilly,[179] his all-around personal assistant, in the

---

178 D Neligan

179 Neligan refers to Reilly as *"confidential courier"* and Liam Tobin as *"chief personal assistant."* He goes on to describe Tobin as the number two man in Collins' intelligence network. Without differing, it seems more precise, in view of O'Reilly's multifarious role, to call his work all-around "*personal*" assistance; while Tobin's seems to have been more specifically as second-in-command to the Director of Intelligence.

days preceding his death. If Collins had reason to believe that his innermost circle had been infiltrated, such remarkable comments may have been calculated to sound them for any burning hidden desire to see him removed.

His relationship with those he most trusted could be quite complex. Ms Mason had been favoured by some in the Collins family as a possible future Mrs. Michael Collins. There are some indications that the news of his engagement to Kitty Kiernan did not pass entirely unnoticed by her. Joe O'Reilly was described by Collins as "*my closest friend*"; by other biographers as "*the only one who always knew where Collins was*"; and as a man who "*lived only for Collins.*" [180] However, Michael " ... *was a hard taskmaster, sparing none, least of all himself.*" He was known to subject Joe and other associates at times to some playful teasing, which could get quite rough; even reducing O'Reilly at times to tears. He was reproached on occasion for this. Collins protested that he valued no one more highly, and that Joe "*prays for me every day.*"

> *I'm sorry if I may be appearing to be unpleasant to you. And it's my real friends that have to suffer these things, and please don't you blame me. ... I hope you have written to Mrs. D. I'm making her life a misery at the present time, but again it's a case of my real friends.*
>
> *Yes, it was a lovely party, but I was unpleasant, as I have really too many things to carry out at the present moment. It is not right for me to inflict myself on people.* [181]

He was not insensitive to the fact that he sometimes went too far, with his intimates. He apologized for this sort of thing regularly; in his personal correspondence, and in funny, poignant gestures which were fondly recalled by recipients, decades afterward.

Yet does his enigmatic query not suggest that he may have been asking himself whether some one of these ... had decided not to forgive him?

---

[180] D Neligan, F O'Connor

[181] Michael Collins, personal correspondence

O'Reilly responded to his question about "*a new boss*" with absolute horror, abjuring that he never wanted to work for anyone else. Sinead Mason reported the C-in-C's comment with wonder and dismay. In a note to Susan Killeen, a former girlfriend, and a supporter of the independence movement, he apologized for breaking a date for the theatre: adding at the end in Irish "*Do you want to kill me?*"

For a man in Collins' position, such language was not without meaning. It certainly seems significant, not only that he asked such singular questions, but exactly the same question, to more than one of those he most depended on, and at that moment in particular. From their reactions, it would seem that he did not ask it in the merest joking manner, but with enough emphasis to raise sincere concern. Was he not asking, "Have I hurt this friend enough for them to seek my death?"

There is no question that many former friends and colleagues took sides against him in the Civil War. It is well-documented that this was not his only worry, but that, in this terrible period, he often found himself obliged to entertain serious doubts, even about those who claimed to be still on his side.

If Collins had to ask himself this ... Don't we have to ask also? Similarly, if evidence suggests that there may have been treachery among members of his bodyguard at Béal na mBláth, it does not suffice to say, "Well, this one was from the Dublin Brigade, so it couldn't have been him." It is necessary to review each player's actions realistically, such as it is; whatever their past service or association with the C-in-C may have been.

He knew and did not underestimate the dangers

Characteristically swift and decisive, as soon as peace was in sight, he commenced serious plans for his post-war life, without delay. Not long after the Treaty was signed, he announced his engagement to be married.

This was a man, fond of feminine companionship, distinguished by his charm with ladies, overflowing with peasant health and good spirits; who had postponed a normal conjugal life for the sake of his country. He was now thirty-one, and evidently had no inclination to put off normal happiness and fulfilment any longer. His wedding was first scheduled to take place on 21 June 1922. But when civil war loomed, he re-scheduled it.

> *""I'll make no girl a wife just to make her a widow. The wedding will keep for a few weeks; in that time I'll end this business, if it doesn't end me first."*

Here, he openly acknowledged that he might not survive the conflict. The new date was set, ironically, for 22 August 1922. This is striking indeed, in more than one respect. On one hand, it suggests that in June, when he cancelled the first wedding date, (explicitly due to danger that the Civil War might end his life,) he estimated 22 August as a date at which said danger could be expected to be past. That is to say, he believed he could put an end to hostilities by that date. What we now know about peace negotiations indicates that his prediction was astonishingly close: if not for his death, he would have been, on that very day, on the brink of ending the war. On the other hand, as events fell out, his estimation seems positively eerie.

Following his arrival in Cork City on the evening of August 20, Collins met with his sister, Mary Collins-Powell, and her son Sean, who was on active service with the Free State army. His enthusiastic young nephew expressed a keen desire to join his famous uncle's party, on the convoy through West Cork. The C-in-C absolutely would not allow it. His firm refusal clearly illustrates that, despite his cheerful assurances to colleagues who had tried to dissuade him from this trip, he was vividly aware that it involved real and present danger.

He knew of plans for an ambush

> *"What struck me ... was the rapid transit of news to Collins. Happenings in remote areas of West Cork were reported to him in a matter of a half-an-hour."* [182]

They didn't call Cork "the rebel county" for nothing. It had earned this reputation long before 1916; indeed, for centuries past. Collins' closest personal relationships there, family and friends from boyhood, formed a strong and far-flung network throughout the region. Many of these had been deeply involved in the movement from the beginning. He was by no means the first or only member of his immediate family who was an accomplished organizer for Irish freedom. His sisters, brothers, cousins, even the housemaid, were only less active than their famous "kid brother."

---

[182]   D. Neligan

Before and during the Civil War, right up to the last minute of his life, Collins never lost touch with the Cork brigades. Key leaders there remained sympathetic. Many of these had profoundly mixed feelings about the wisdom of this conflict. Throughout the War itself, there were continuous efforts by cooler heads to bring others to reason, and to the bargaining table. Collins, acknowledged past-master at clandestine communication, never ceased trying to negotiate with these comrades.

Among the anecdotal evidence of that day, is the report that a local postman, while making his rounds, assured his garden gate gossips that *"Collins is gone west, but he won't go east."* [183] This was a tactful way of announcing his certain knowledge that the C-in-C would meet his death in West Cork on this journey. While another resident of the area has claimed that the ambush was *"an open secret."*[184]

If the postman knew this, certainly the Collins clan knew as much. In view of all of the above, the C-in-C's last family reunion, at Sam's Cross, just hours before his death, could not have left him in the dark about any intelligence and/or local gossip which could be expected to interest him.

He was well prepared for ambush

Despite Collins' assurances that *"No one in my own county is going to shoot me,"* the presence of a full military escort of twelve soldiers, two machine gunners and an armoured car, clearly indicated that he took the threat to his own safety quite seriously. He was armed with substantial defensive measures and prepared for action.

The C-in-C had a minute acquaintance with anti-Treaty forces' weaponry and personnel, and his preparations were entirely adequate to "brush aside" anything the lads in West Cork could throw at him. Machine guns were at that time a relatively new war technology. Armoured cars had not often been seen outside the major cities. In view of the relatively primitive conditions which prevailed in rural Ireland (not only in the 1920s, but even into the 1980s,) Collins' convoy was a show of force calculated to awe and overpower.

---

183 T P Coogan

184 This is hard to reconcile with other testimony, stating that Collins' presence there, and the laying of the ambush, were unexpected and unplanned for, until that very morning. At the same time, other reports exist, that more than one ambush was lain on his route that day.

This was not altogether inappropriate in the context of peace negotiations. Believing the appropriate officers to be well-informed that he was coming with an olive branch, it was not impolitic to simultaneously send a powerful message to the under-supplied insurgents, as to the futility of further military resistance. In this sense, his entrance could "*speak softly and carry a big stick*," in typically dramatic Collins style.

He did not underestimate his opponents

> *Tis better to be vile, than vile-esteemed; when not to be, receives reproach of being.*
>
> *- Shakespeare*

Criticism of Collins' performance in the Treaty negotiations was public. A vicious print campaign of personal smears included allegations that he was a traitor to the British side, planning a London-sponsored military dictatorship; or that he had personally ordered the murder of his close friend Harry Boland. These were widely disseminated by anti-Treaty propagandists during the Civil War; and by DeValera apologists ever since.

But Collins never indulged in such tactics against his opponents. He would not stoop to personal insults or calumnies against Irish leaders; not even against his worst enemies, not even if he believed them to be true. Because to do so would cast aspersions on Irish independence itself.

In private conversation, he expressed his opinion of DeValera plainly enough; but such off-hand comments were never committed to paper by him. This speaks volumes when compared with the assessment of DeValera which he reportedly gave to journalists like Hayden Talbot. It is clear, from other writing and speeches, that he did not really believe DeValera to be a naïve schoolteacher, a mere pawn led astray by radical elements (as reported by Talbot.)

However bad his opinion of political opponents, he would not publish anything to undermine public confidence in the new Irish-led government. He might call DeValera's policies disastrous. He might say that a DeValera-led government would bring catastrophe. [185] But he never explicitly accused him of being a turncoat for British interests;

---

185 See Appendix 7 *"Free State or Chaos"* by Michael Collins

even though personal correspondence indicates he suspected this. Responding to DeValera's *"rivers of blood"* speeches, he said in a speech shortly afterward:

> *We would not be hearing those blood and thunder speeches, we would not be seeing the revolver, if argument could have prevailed. Our age-long enemy, when "constitutional ways" failed, also used the revolver to try and suppress us, and threats to frighten us into submission to his will - to exercise our "free choice" in the way he wished.* [186]

Here, he left it to his listeners to draw their own conclusions; and to the politically penetrating to understand precisely what he had just said. (Why say more to anyone else?)

Most of the worst suspicions which arose in his own mind regarding his closest associates, or for that matter his worst enemies, were never made public. His motive in this was less personal kindness, than the national welfare. This is abundantly illustrated in his contemporary political writings, such as are now collected in *The Path to Freedom*. The theme he returned to again and again was building public confidence in an independent Ireland. This was certainly a bottom line issue at the time: after centuries of brutal subjugation, and of British propaganda that the Irish were congenitally incapable of self-government.

As he wrote in 1922, the worst possibility was not only that the British might come back, but *"that they would be welcomed back."* [187] "Selling" Irish government to the public was the first order of business. Schisms and conflict among Irish leaders complicated the job, and were very bad publicity. Another factor in this, is that any negative statements from Collins, in this volatile situation, could actually endanger those concerned.

Shakespeare may be forgiven his exasperated observation (quoted above) that villains may prosper in popularity, while integrity silently endures denunciation. Honesty is the best policy. Yet Collins' cause suffered, *because* of his integrity; not only in the turbulence of the Civil War, but in the history books. His British enemies knew the value of controlling history. And had the benefit of DeValera's intimate

---

186　Ibid.
187　M Collins, *The Path to Freedom*

comprehension of Collins' inner motivations: when he would speak and when he would be silent.

Accomplished biographers, who ought to know better, have frequently overlooked these factors, especially when assessing his state of mind leading up to 22 August. Thence have proceeded contentions that he was blithely wandering about West Cork enjoying himself, relaxing discipline, oblivious to any danger, etc. On closer examination, it becomes clear that nothing could be further from the truth.

"My own countrymen won't shoot me."

Of all his highly competent chroniclers in the past, who has offered a satisfactory explanation, regarding this bewildering assurance, made on the eve of his death? So poignant, so telling, in view of the event which immediately followed ... But what exactly does it tell us? His biographers have been unable to restrain themselves, with all due respect, from noting the ridiculous in these words. With the most dignified language, they've literally scratched their heads, and confessed themselves puzzled. Their reason baffled, they have been pitifully reduced to explanations which don't make sense. They have conjectured that he was absolutely innocent of any knowledge of imminent danger to his life; while knowing that this could not be the case.

These "famous last words," on the very brink of disaster, are so positively tragi-comic ... That one begins to detect a twinkle in his eye.

Ah, but didn't the Big Fella love a joke? Wasn't he good for a laugh, even in the midst of mayhem, with his life on the line? Throughout the deadly struggle of the war, his keen appreciation for the absurd, his sense of comedy, were continually put to use; for the most serious purposes possible.

He mystifies us still. Yet a careful application of plain common sense might decipher the message. He was not speaking thoughtlessly. Collins repeated these words so many times on this last journey of his life, as to demand particular attention to these statements. Was he trying to tell us something?   Let us examine them in the full light of all we know about him and his situation at the time.

He is first reported saying this, in relation to this journey, at Portobello Barracks on August 20, the day he started out. Coming down to breakfast at 6AM, he talked about a dinner party the night before: where shots had been fired at his car. *"The end can sometimes be so near,"* he mused.

Shortly after, he had to encounter objections from Joe McGrath, then Director of Intelligence, who advised him not to go. *"Whatever happens to me, my own fellow countrymen won't shoot me,"* he answered. Within the same hour, Joe Sweeney came to plead with him not to go; so strenuously that they almost came to blows over it. Again, the C-in-C assured him, *"No one in my own county's going to shoot me."*

He repeated the same statement, almost word for word, at several meetings along the way to Béal na mBláth. Most significantly, to his own family, who fêted him near his boyhood home, just hours before he fell, again, *"My own countrymen won't shoot me."*

Note, he *never* said that *no one* would shoot him. On the contrary, over breakfast he had recounted an attempt to do so, just the night before; and mused on the potential nearness of death. Such attempts had become frequent occurrences. He qualified at least one such statement with the ominous *"whatever happens to me ... "*

Clearly the C-in-C was not unaware of attempts on his life, and the danger thereof which he dealt with every moment, wherever he went. Nor did he deny their existence. Nor was he speaking thoughtlessly. The only *reasonable* conclusion, which *fits the facts*, is that he was *trying to say something* of a serious nature, which he *very much wanted his people to know*. Something which he *could not discuss explicitly*. Not even with those closest to him.

There could be many reasons for cryptic language on his part in this context, which do not require improbable guesswork. On a whirlwind tour, with crowds surging round him at each stop, he had little private time or space for lengthy exchanges with his many friends, relations and colleagues in County Cork.

But most of all, if he suspected that the predator on his trail was the British secret service, and possibly involving an operative very near him, he was likely to exercise extreme caution in discussing what he knew. This would be basic normal procedure in the cat-&-mouse games of espionage he had mastered and survived thus far. Personal security, as well as diplomatic reasons, may have prohibited any explicit statement by him, on this, at the time.

Under such conditions, he could hardly know whom to trust, how nearly he might be overheard, or how widely his words repeated. In that case, a false impression of carefree unconsciousness of any danger might be exactly what he wished to project: except to those who knew him best. This was in keeping with his technique for dealing with danger, throughout his heretofore brilliant career of astounding survival.

In this light, his words are not so difficult to understand: *Whatever happens to me, IT'S NOT MY OWN COUNTRYMEN who did it. Whatever I have to fear, IT'S NOT THE LADS IN WEST CORK.*

So very far from clueless about the dangers, Collins not only knew of plans to assassinate him: he knew *it was being planned so as to blame the IRA.* He also knew, and wanted his confidants to know, that this planning *came from outside Ireland entirely.* Which was to say that *he knew British elements were planning to assassinate him, and blame it on his own countrymen, in County Cork.*

He very nearly evaded the ambush altogether

The ultimate outcome at Béal na mBláth has diverted our attention from the fact that Collins' times of arrival (both morning and evening) all but entirely circumvented anti-Treaty military preparations there.

This sort of manoeuvre was completely in keeping with his usual *modus operandi.* As illustrated by his practice while directing the clandestine war in Dublin: Ever an avid theatre-goer, one evening the Auxiliaries raided the Gaiety, while a performance was in progress, which he was attending. He simply slipped out a discreet doorway, waited until the raid was over and the Auxies gone away; then resumed his seat for the rest of the show.

At Béal na mBláth he "happened by" with full military convoy at an hour of the morning when there were virtually no defensive measures in place, except a solitary sentry. When he returned, the original ambush party had grown tired of waiting, decided he wasn't coming, and gone home. All of this was absolutely typical Collins.

In this his judgement was sound. The five men left clearing up the road equipment were hardly any match for twenty-five soldiers with two machine guns and an armoured car.

His death alone is what seems to belie this. Yet, the more closely we examine the evidence, the more doubtful it appears that the anti-Treaty men's part therein may have been anything more than unwitting cover for the real killer.

Chapter 15

The usual suspects

Those who believe in the murder theory are convinced that it was a British secret service job.

- J Feehan

I am of course aware that the continuing suspicion is, and always will be, that Collins in some way fell victim to the British secret service.

- TP Coogan

It seems self-evident, from a realistic and detailed examination of the facts, commensurate with what is known of the man himself, that his death could *not* have been any fluke nor random act. Even in the unsettled state of the country, he was not an easy target, but very difficult to kill.

If Collins' death was not accidental in any sense, then it was murder. If murder, there are basically two suspects: either the anti-Treaty men (aka IRA) or the British secret service.

These two suspects are differ from each other in one very telling point: the IRA always claims their actions. *And the British secret service always remains silent.* The ambushers, as seen from the published accounts, consistently denied any intent to assassinate him, and explicitly accused his own escort party.

There is evidence in the State Papers that during the Truce he was regularly followed by British secret service men.[188]

It is the British secret service which most abundantly fulfils all requirements for a believable suspect in Collins' death. The crime entirely fits their psychological profile and their *modus operandi*. They alone had all three cardinal requirements of *motive, means and opportunity*.

In fact, it's safe to say that no other entity concerned could possibly have mounted such an operation. If eye-witness testimony, many army men at the time, and the ambushers themselves were

---

[188] J Feehan

correct in believing that it was *not* the anti-Treaty men who shot him, Collins had no other opponents with the resources and sophistication necessary to get at him, except the British secret service.

> *The second group of people with a particular interest in seeing Collins out of the way was the British secret service. They are and were a world-wide body operating in every country with hundreds of years of experience behind them and millions of pounds of public money at their disposal. ... It is a basic tenet of their organization to take revenge when one of their agents is killed - this they must do as proof to their members that no one will be allowed to get away with such killings, so it is not hard to imagine their feelings for Collins, who killed not one, but at least a hundred. ...* [189]

Lest we forget, the British secret service had not always been so hopeless of ever catching The Big Fella, as the long shadow of heroic legend now implies. Shortly before the stunning Bloody Sunday coup which broke London's spirit, Collins himself exclaimed, of one of their targets therein, "*If we don't get him, he'll get us, and soon!*" [190]

> *They believed that if they could get Collins, dead or alive, Irish military resistance would be broken and yet another revolution suppressed.* [191] *They picked sixteen of their best secret service agents from all parts of the world, assembled them in Cairo, where they underwent a special briefing course on Michael Collins, his appearance, his habits, his haunts and everything known about him. They then travelled singly to Dublin under false names with the sole object of getting Collins. It is said that a sum equivalent in our money to £200,000 was offered to whoever would kill or capture him.*

The secret service had been getting to know him for quite a while. They knew what kind of undercover operations had been aimed at him and failed. They had an idea by now how he would catch on, and also how quickly. They may have realized how well he knew their methods.

---

[189] Ibid
[190] D Neligan
[191] History would seem to have proven them not far wrong.

With a little of that "very special help," they could learn a lot more: enough to use his own intelligence expertise against him.

There is hardly any entity which *could have* arranged his death, and shrouded it in so much mystery, for so long, who was any less formidable than the British secret service. There was no other player involved who had sufficient clout to bring together all those who *had to* cooperate for such an outcome to be achieved: Irish former officers of the British army who were close to Collins, members of the Free State Provisional Government Cabinet, DeValera and members of subsequent Dublin governments.

A MATTER OF EMPIRE

> *If Healy was a spy he changed Irish history, being the most active of Parnell's opponents in the disastrous split of 1890. Had Parnell succeeded, Home Rule would have been conceded and a child born that year, Michael Collins, would probably have become a prosperous business man in an un-partitioned Ireland.* [192]

It was not only a question of past scores to settle. The future was at stake. When he secured the conclusive defeat of Britain's police state in Ireland, Collins was only scratching the surface. If he remained in power, there was more bad news to come, for the long arm of British interests there.

At the time of his death, he was hot on the trail of a Crown operative who did not merely lurk in the background, but held high office in the new Free State government: a man who was one of the oldest pillars in the nationalist movement. Code-named "Thorpe", Collins had unearthed his track, through old records left behind when the Irish took over Dublin Castle. This mole had played a remarkable part, during the great movement for Irish independence led by Charles Stewart Parnell in the 1880s. Notably, that effort also had been undermined, at the moment of success, by a sudden split in the

---

[192] Collins' investigation of "Thorpe" is discussed in detail by both Feehan and Coogan. Tim Healy, a high dignitary of the Irish independence movement, is alleged to have served British interests under the operative name of "Thorpe". His nephew Kevin O'Higgins (five rows behind Collins, in Griffith's funeral procession) was propelled to the highest office, as a direct result of the C-in-C's demise. O'Higgins became a pet of Lady Lavery and Dublin's British horsey set. Healy became the first Governor General of the Irish Free State.

movement: a split in which said mole was instrumental. It is believed that the C-in-C had identified the culprit, and planned to deal with this on his return from Cork. As we know, he never returned. The intelligence assistant who was working on this for him, reported that the files concerned disappeared from Collins' office at Portobello, immediately following his death.

This case alone shows how much further than anyone imagined, throughout the Irish establishment, did the tentacles of British authority extend. It also demonstrates how that authority continued to function undisturbed and undetected, for decades on end: until Collins. His continuance in high office, his relentless pursuit of British operatives, his aggressive defence against such clandestine interference in Ireland's national interests, ... had only just begun.

And that was just in Ireland. As the 20th century dawned, republican revolutions were seething, roiling and breaking out all over the Empire. The British authorities were painfully aware that they were sitting on a powder keg, which any spark could set off. They knew it was only a matter of time, and that Ireland would be only the beginning.

Collins had put the fear of God into the British imperialist establishment; which was no mean feat. They were impressed. He was good. He had earned their sincerest form of flattery. *"Where was Michael Collins during the Great War?"* Lloyd George's secretary Tom Jones complained, *"He'd have been worth a dozen brass hats."* That is to say, they were convinced that he had more leadership in him then the traditional army "brass" they were accustomed to.

During the Treaty negotiations in London, he was approached. They spread a map of the Empire before him and said, *"You're an able fellow. Why don't you help us?"* But he had other plans.

In connection with international lobbying for the Irish cause, Collins had made an interesting acquaintance, several years before, with a certain T E Lawrence. [193] Lawrence was also a legendary leader of indigenous insurgents. He also had accomplished amazing things, at a very young age. He had been Britain's man in the Middle East. And he was not happy.

---

[193] The great international conferences which led up to the Treaty of Versailles, were attended by many petitioners from "small nations"; including an Irish republican contingent. They lobbied vigorously for Ireland's right to independence; particularly asking the American President Wilson to put pressure on London. T E Lawrence also attended. His book about his experiences in the Arab Revolt was later the basis for the award-winning feature film *"Lawrence of Arabia"*

Lawrence had been sent to organize disgruntled Arabs, with promises of civil rights and national independence. In a long and bloody campaign, he had led men to their deaths on the strength of those promises, and on his word. Then the Crown pulled the rug out from under them. They had no intention of abiding by engagements made to a lot of restless natives. The promised united Arab Middle East, never materialized. Instead it was divided into the problematic fragments we know today.

Lawrence had been used, and he took exception to it. In a public presentation at Buckingham Palace, he mounted the royal dais to, figuratively speaking, fling his decorations back at the king. The gesture was quite shocking at the time. He resigned his commission and went into early retirement, turning his back on the army.

Lawrence was also, on one side of his family, partly Irish. For some time, Collins had been trying to persuade him to help the Irish cause. Imagine the implications! Here were two of the most able military strategists in Europe. Each of them individually had proved his capacity to organize an army, from the ground up, fit to overthrow the world's top guns. Collins had already bested every British general they could throw at him. Lawrence in Arabia and Collins in Ireland!? By God, they'd have the Empire encircled! This were an alliance to mar imperialists' rest. [194]

They had learned a healthy respect for Collins; the hard way. They knew this was a man who could get things done and make things happen. Big things. He was a man who thought big. And he was only beginning. He was a fit, young man, at the very start of his career. He was going to go on thinking big, and making big things happen. He was, as Lloyd George observed, *"the head and front of the movement."* He was now head and front of the new Irish-led government next door. As a future player on the stage of world statesmanship, there was no telling where he might lead.

They could bet on just one thing: the big things he was going to do were *not* going to be in the interests of Empire. Collins was going to be a big problem. As long as he lived. And the longer he lived, the more difficult and dangerous it would become, to try to remove him.

---

[194] T P Coogan, although often dismissive of "conspiracy theorists" refers to Lawrence' own death as *"mysterious,"* to an extent which *"generated controversy."*

> *In the background, dominating everything, was the British cabinet who knew well what Collins was up to, but who could do nothing publicly to stop him so long as he remained within the framework of the Treaty. They also knew that if he were eliminated they would have no problems whatever in dealing with Cosgrave, who had now accepted fully and finally the idea of permanent membership of the British Commonwealth.*
>
> *If the British secret service decided or were given orders to murder Collins how would they go about it? With such a long experience behind them they would certainly not have him picked off in the street or in his bedroom which would be too obvious. Far better to have him killed in an open engagement where the IRA could be blamed.* [195]

If the British secret service meant to assassinate him, arranging for blame to fall on the Irish was part of their well-established *modus operandi*.

As argued above, this plan would have been highly time-sensitive. If he were not "taken out" immediately, he might succeed in reuniting his War of Independence forces, and sending them north.

> *A surprise peace settlement with the insurgents would eliminate the usual IRA suspects in the death of Collins and the British would be hard-pressed casting blame on anyone else. It was critical for the British to act prior to any settlement and Collins' assassination was shifted into fast forward.*[196]

If such British elements as these wanted him dead enough, fast enough, badly enough, ... They were not going to chance it on a half-hearted shot from the hillside by his friends and neighbours. They would have to infiltrate his bodyguard. It would have to be point blank.

---

[195] J Feehan
[196] J Turi

Summary: Let us count the ways

> *I feel a kindred spirit with the arrogant personality of Collins, and I also believe that I'm in much the same situation as he. Basically, I have no place in organized politics.*
> — Bernadette Devlin, 1969

It has been shown above how a number of powerful elements concerned had compelling motives to eliminate Collins from any post-war government, at all cost.

> The cabinet had settled for permanent membership of the Empire and wanted none of Collins' republican 'stepping-stone' policies. Indeed the thing they seemingly wanted most was to get rid of him. His former comrades, now fighting against him, believed they were fighting for a republic, but in reality they ... were pushing the republic further and further away. Sections of the army he commanded, having failed to shoot down Irishmen when they were with the British, were now having a field day doing so under an Irish flag, and under [Collins'] leadership.

There was the British imperialist establishment. Collins had been bad for them. Very bad indeed. He continued to be bad for them. They had first met him as, in their view, a virtual gutter-snipe. A minor clerk, a poor labourer, ducking about the shadows of Dublin; whom their men could exterminate in any dark alley with impunity, anytime they caught him.

But they never caught him. Now he was a head of state, whose arrogant manners they were obliged to endure at official functions in London. If permitted to consolidate his now extremely strong position, he showed great promise of being as dangerous on a grand scale, on the world stage, as he had proved fatal to their age-old sovereignty in Ireland.

There was the British secret service. Their abundant motives for wishing to eliminate Collins have been set forth above. They also had the future to consider. For generations, Ireland had been a clear field of endeavour for them. They had occupied every public institution, and none could say them nay. No one in authority had the will, skill or power to attempt it. Until Collins came along. A government headed by the strategist who had broken their power in Ireland was not a future they welcomed.

There was the Provisional Government Cabinet. Collins had, as Stendahl quipped, been landed by a fluke of politics in the lap of those elements least congenial to him. He had friends in this Cabinet, but only a few. Were any of his opponents there cynical enough to cooperate (either actively or passively) in his death? What motives had they?

What kind of career could some of these men look forward to, with the ever-demanding, ever-blunt Collins over them? What if he succeeded in reuniting his precious army of gun-wielding republicans? Just when this Cabinet had risen so high in their absence? How secure would their seats be then? On the other hand, how rosy their professional landscape might look, minus that glowering taskmaster, and his mass of armed insurgents. Why, without him around, they would look like big men indeed.

> *The old are seduced by gold, youth by pleasure, the weak by flattery, cowards by fear, and the courageous, by ambition.*
> *- Scott*

Nor can fear be discounted as a motive in such possible cooperation. Precious few have ever dared to envision or attempt an Irish government which was less than supine to the long arm of British interests; an arm wielding all the secret service' formidable arsenal and clandestine powers of "persuasion".

Then there was DeValera: a man, by his own avowal, determined to "*show them who's a big fella.*" A master of political intrigue, admitted by his worst critics to be the best negotiator of his time. A man whose finesse could exasperate a British prime minister. A man determined that no one's shadow should fall across his own ascending career. A man who could not brook political associates willing to differ from him in public. His particular means, motive and opportunity, have been discussed at length above.

> *The IRA did not want Collins dead. On the contrary, they realized he was their only hope.* [197]

---

[197] J Feehan

All in all, Michael Collins was going to be a real problem for many of the major players in Dublin and London.

In fact he was going to be good for only one thing: for Ireland. For her people and her future. For a land which had been prostrate under foreign vassalage for centuries. For a people at the moment between national governments and largely without functioning civil institutions. For a nation which had as yet hardly even come into existence; and a future which had barely been dreamed of, by anyone but him. In short, for a country which had great need of his protection; but was hardly in a condition to protect him.

We staked our lives for a city that had an existence only in desperate hope.
- *Thucydides*

Thus Collins, after doing so much to win freedom which had been "*beyond our wildest dreams*" [198] in 1916, came to be denounced, by many who had lionized him, so shortly before.

To defame a man is to shed his blood.
- *The Talmud*

In this case, as often happens, character assassination paved the way for physical assassination that soon followed; and camouflaged the tracks of the assassins ever since.

---

198 M Collins see Appendix 7

CHAPTER 16

UNANSWERED QUESTIONS REVISITED

In light of all of the above considerations, let us now return to some of the unanswered questions posed at the end of Part 1.

Why at that time?   *Why in the teeth of all known dangers?*
Collins went to Cork for something which was worth risking his life to get. He went for something which could not wait: which he had to do everything in his power to realize without delay, *at all cost*. He went to avert the Civil War's bloodbath; and its legacy of lasting, crippling national division, which he could see was coming, if it were not stopped in time.

This is corroborated by many reliable witnesses from both sides, abundantly documented in related correspondence, recorded in his private conversations; and is thoroughly consistent with his character, behavior and priorities throughout the period.

It is easy to understand the urgency expressed in his many comments, on that journey. Up until the C-in-C's assassination, the general damage incurred had been relatively minimal. "*The [anti-Treaty] moderate wing ... even at this stage was anxious to and hopeful of ending the clash with some honour.*" [199] Collins felt deeply the death of his intimate friend Harry Boland, and was determined to prevent the loss of more comrades. It must be remembered, that he knew most all of the key military leaders of the independence movement. Many were personal friends,[200] having served together in 1916, in Frongach prison camp, and in the IRB.

The Civil War was never strictly black and white. Throughout the fighting, there were profoundly mixed feelings, in some of its leading players. There were both hotter and cooler heads on both sides. Efforts broke out continually to achieve a settlement. There were frequent conferences among prominent anti-Treaty officers, debating the wisdom and/or practicality of continued resistance.

---

199   L Deasy

200   The same claim cannot be made for DeValera, who, after the 1916 Rising, was never deeply involved in the military arm, and had virtually side-stepped the entire struggle from 1919 - 1921. Nor was he ever similarly renowned for many affectionate personal friendships among comrades.

"*I want no rancor.*" Collins was particularly anxious to avoid any lasting animosity. He understood that, to avoid it, his former (and, as he hoped, future) comrades would need terms which they could accept as honorable.

Feehan observed that the IRA had no motive nor desire to assassinate Collins; that, on the contrary, they were well aware that he was their "*only hope*" in the Free State government. If so, in view of the holocaust which ensued after his death, they were right. It cannot be over-emphasized that the Civil War before Collins' death and the Civil War after Collins' death were two entirely different animals. And that it was his pivotal leadership presence which made the difference.

Why there?

> *There has been no satisfactory explanation of why so many visits to Macroom were necessary within the space of twenty-four hours ... Why did the convoy not go the direct Bandon - Macroom road? Instead they went via ... Béal na mBláth, a round-about way with probably more dangerous ambush sites per mile than any road in Ireland. Again why did they commit the cardinal military offence of returning by the same route they came?* [201]

"Béal na mBláth Cross" is a major four-way crossroads, with clear routes stretching directly to the north, south, east and west of Ireland. This is not the high road, certainly. But it is a major four-way artery of what may be called the low road. That is, the kind of back channels which would naturally be favoured by men on the run. Nearby Macroom would be a natural contact point for units roughing it in the nether reaches of West Cork: a key anti-Treaty stronghold.

This location was chosen to facilitate talks, not only with local commanders in Cork, but as a safe meeting place for anti-Treaty representatives from all regions. As Deasy confirms, "*several Divisional Officers ... who had been forced to retreat from Limerick, Kilmallock and Buttevant ...* " had gathered there on August 22. There was a Brigade Council meeting scheduled to take place at Béal na mBláth that evening, which was attended by a number of senior anti-Treaty Divisional,

---

[201] J Feehan

Battalion and Brigade officers. The future of the war was on the agenda, including the possibility of ending it.

22 August was not the only date on which a major anti-Treaty conference on ending the war was scheduled there. The same site was chosen for the same purpose, for 13 October 1922, just a couple of months after Collins' death.

It is this author's belief that the C-in-C also chose West Cork like a skilful guerrilla strategist: as *his* chosen ground for talks. There he had the strongest local network, the warmest personal ties to the most recalcitrant anti-Treaty leaders; the best chance of surviving the journey. To secure peace would require a major conference with such commanders, on rebel territory, including representatives from every region. Where in Ireland could Collins have had more reasonably planned it? Where would he have better local resources to support his chances of bringing it off successfully and in one piece?

In view of all of the foregoing, this entirely explains why he was so determined to make this trip, why so many passes around Macroom, why that particular obscure back road; and why none of this was discussed with colleagues in Dublin.

Why in a bright yellow convertible with the top down?

It doesn't take much rumination to realize that a man who had recently been a target for would-be assassins, and who was travelling in a country which was widely believed to be teaming with hostile belligerents, would not usually drive around there, in an open car with the top down.

It is not exactly military equipment. The convoy's canvas-roof Leyland touring car struck a strange contrast indeed to the armoured car next to it: the two diametrical extremes of the maximum protective armour and the complete absence of armour. And the man who was at greatest personal risk, the man whom all that armour was there to secure, was travelling in the most vulnerable, exposed position possible.

Auto trouble plagued Collins on this tour. He mentioned this to Mulcahy in a communication on the Kerry leg of his tour, earlier in August; and again to Fionan Lynch as they set out from Dublin on the 20th. He recorded his surprise & dismay in his notebook: commenting on these unusual mechanical problems, and wrote a reminder to get *"manifest on vehicles,"* noting that *"Normal preparation and planning should have averted."*

In view of all this, one can't look on the Leyland touring car as one which was carefully chosen by the C-in-C. But if the top was folded back, that would seem to have been a deliberate choice. Because it made so little sense in terms of the hazardous situation, it becomes another red flag in the puzzle of Béal na mBláth: it boggles the reason. It certainly seems to have been deliberate. Yet it doesn't make sense.

If one applies to the conundrum everything we do know about Collins, and about the journey, there is nothing wrong with this picture. And its meaning seems to spell itself out in red letters across the frame.

This was a man who had eluded an all-out manhunt by the world's most sophisticated intelligence network; sometimes, even while riding in the same car with them! He was a master of perception and appearance. He understood what people would see, what they would notice, and what they would not notice. When he didn't want to be seen, he would not be found.

The ambush was set because the C-in-C's car stopped in Béal na mBláth in the morning, ostensibly to ask directions; and the lad whom they asked just happened to be an anti-Treaty sentry. And the sentry recognized Michael Collins sitting in the back seat. If the C-in-C had hidden behind his hat in the back of a closed-top car, the sentry at Long's Pub need not have recognized him, and there may have been no ambush.

Obviously, he *intended* to be seen. One need only look at the photos from the trip: he was positively advertising his presence. This was connected to secret negotiations, with men who were living on the run. In the context of such negotiations, it would have been necessary to broadcast to the other parties that he was on for the meetings. This may have been a necessary sign of good faith: that he was really coming, and that the rendezvous was not a trap.

Above, MacEoin's papers explicitly confirmed that Collins' armoured convoy was planned partly as a signal, expressly to increase his visibility, clearly identifying the C-in-C's party to anti-Treaty men in the region, who were supposed to be expecting him. MacEoin also specifies that Collins travelled in Cork under a safe conduct from anti-Treaty authorities; that the safe conduct came through Dalton; and that the armed escort was meant as a "deterrent" against attack by "*outlying posts*" whom "*time would not allow contacting*" in advance about the peace talks.

He *intended* to be seen, because *that was the signal which had been arranged:* to confirm that he would be there for a parlay that evening. Only ... no one told the lads at Béal na mBláth.

Why with Dalton but without any of his other usual bodyguard?

Collins being clearly aware that this journey was likely to be life-threatening, why was he not accompanied by Liam Tobin, Tom Cullen, or Joe O'Reilly, at Béal na mBláth? How did Dalton come to have such full, nearly sole charge of the C-in-C's safety? Why did Collins suddenly seem to trust Dalton so implicitly, and at the same time seem to distance himself, on this mission, from his usual stalwarts?

Sowing dissension and distrust among the Irish was an old tactic for the British secret service. In this volatile period, when so many past allies had proved false, it might have been entirely possible to excite Collins' distrust of his most intimate associates: and so distance him from the shield which had always protected him. Consider the following scenario, as a possible explanation how and why this *might have* happened:

If the secret service sought to place their man not only close to Collins, but past more experienced comrades who formed the C-in-C's inner bodyguard, how could their operative eclipse others, and attain a pre-eminent position as Collins' especial confidant, and with speed? (*As Dalton did.*)

Perhaps by the oldest trick in the book: by feeding the C-in-C intelligence. An oldest trick, but one which could not be shabbily brought off with Collins. He had won London's respect. After years of continual, failed attempts to capture or kill him, they knew that his shrewdness merited the most carefully planned, full-scale, top-class operation.

They knew that no counterfeit currency would entrap the C-in-C. It would have to be valuable intelligence, which he really needed. It would have to be proved. It would have to convince him that it couldn't be bait set by the secret service.

If Collins suspected that one of those closest to him was connected to the numerous recent attempts on his life, he was correct. One might even ask whether some of these attempts were not calculated to advertise to him that the planners thereof had excellent, timely access to his daily movements: such as could only come from one of his inner circle. With an operative very close to him, acquainted with his daily schedule, he could be subjected to "attentions" which would clearly demonstrate this to him.

Then, the operative himself wins Collins' confidence by "revealing" the presence of such a mole. He might have skilfully forged evidence, which seems to implicate just those confidants whom he aims to supplant in the C-in-C's estimation. With the number and frequency of attempts on Collins at the time, he may even have an opportunity to "save his life." Such an incident could be staged so as to convince his superior of his devoted courage and readiness to risk his own life in the process. If you're the British secret service, all this could be arranged.

During the Truce, Dalton, a former British soldier, acted as Liaison Officer at the Gresham Hotel nerve centre of the provisional government. There he was responsible for putting people in touch with Collins. For that reason, he had both excellent access to the C-in-C, and was easily available to Dublin Castle's British authorities as well.

In this capacity Dalton had personal contact with Andrew Cope, who is known to have met with him privately (at least at said Liaison Office.) A protégé of Lloyd George, Cope was highly placed in the Castle, and oversaw recruitment for the British secret service.

"Join the IRA, old boy," said the Major, "and if you catch Collins it will be £10,000 for you." [202]

Could every young man resist such persuasion? If the secret service wished to eliminate Collins, they'd have been shopping hard for an ally as close to him as possible. In that case, it is hard to imagine that Dalton would *not* have been approached by Mr. Cope, in the course of several, private encounters, to act as a British operative. He was ideal for their purposes in every way.[203]

> *Hearing an English voice I thought, "That is Cope." He seemed to be saying 'good-bye.' I dived into an empty bedroom just as Dalton's door opened and Cope went down the stairs. Slipping into Dalton's office, I startled him: 'Where the hell did you come out of? Did you see Cope?"* [204]

---

202   With these words Neligan was welcomed into the ranks of the British secret service, which he joined as a mole for Collins.

203   That is, if Dalton ever really withdrew from British military intelligence, whom he served in World War I.

204   D Neligan

The British secret service were master manipulators, who excelled at psychological warfare. Whether by promises, bribery, threats against loved ones, control of people in prison or in the military ... The means they had at their disposal to secure cooperation, willing or unwilling, were all but unlimited. If they needed to convince a 24-year-old that betraying Collins was the right thing to do ... Who could doubt they had the means to do it?

Despite Collins' assurances that "*No one in my own county is going to shoot me,*" the presence of a full military escort of twelve soldiers, two machine gunners and an armoured car, clearly indicated that he took the threat to his own safety quite seriously. He was armed with substantial defensive measures and prepared for action.

One possibility which would answer the titular question of this section is: *that it was Dalton who alerted Collins to the fact that he had a mole in his inner circle.* He produced proof. With careful coaching from his handlers, he could "uncover" the secret service' actual infiltration: just enough to *win Collins' trust*; and to distinguish the bearer of such revelations as wonderfully sharp, loyal, keen and devoted to his commander's safety. By his means, it might be possible both to unsettle the C-in-C's confidence in his closest aides; and simultaneously, raise the actual mole himself (Dalton) into their role, and *place him above suspicion*.

Overwhelmed by the weight of the entire government dropped in his lap, by the disaffection of half the Dáil, by the deaths of Arthur Griffith and Harry Boland as well, the C-in-C *had to delegate*. In the scenario suggested above, it would be entirely reasonable that Dalton might have been placed in a position to hand-pick some of the crew for this convoy. *As, reputedly, Dalton did.*

WHO ORDERED THE AMBUSH?

It's hardly surprising that no one wants to take responsibility for Collins' death. The question of precisely who ordered the ambush is fraught with contradictory accounts.

The ambushers' 1964 statement specifies that it was set in keeping with general policy to attack Free State convoys; and not with intent to eliminate anyone in particular.

Tom Hales was the officer directly in charge of the ambush party. Yet it is unlikely that he could have planned it, at a gathering of more senior officers, without their input. The "last day of the war" was rumoured to be at hand. Hales was a close personal friend of Collins. His own Divisional Commander, Deasy, was a moderate; but ostensibly away most of the day.

Deasy particularly commented on the more bellicose mood of some of the Divisional Officers there, who had recently retreated from other areas.

In view of all of the above, there could easily have been, among these, a senior officer (or officers,) in the plot, who could exert the necessary "suggestions" on Hales. We all know what a "suggestion" from the boss is like. If Hales did act, to any extent, in response to such suggestions, it would not be unlikely for him to keep silent about this later on. Taking the blame for a boss's error, is considered by some an obligation, which needs no explaining.

If Hales ever accepted responsibility for "deciding" to set the ambush, that may have been more magnanimous than precise. Others allege that, at a meeting at Murray's farmhouse that morning, Hales alone opposed setting an ambush.

Deasy, who has been accused of ordering Collins' death, claims his role on the day was peripheral; although the 1964 statement places him among those who prepared the ambush. He does not name others, and certainly not Hales, as having ordered it.

Is there an indication here that some present were chiefs of equal rank to himself, not controlled by him, although he was the titular commander of that area?

DeValera at Béal na mBláth

Deasy gives a fairly detailed account of DeValera's presence there. [205] In summary:

On the morning of 21 August, Deasy arrived at Gurranereagh, his temporary Division headquarters, about three miles from Béal na mBláth. Waiting for him there was Liam Lynch's dispatch from his own headquarters at Fermoy-Glanworth; in which Lynch announced that DeValera had just left him, and was coming to see Deasy, for a parlay on the subject of ending the war. Lynch expressed his refusal to accept DeValera's *"arguments and suggestions"* on that subject; and requested that Deasy should also reject them.

That evening, DeValera arrived at Gurranereagh. He and Deasy discussed the war situation *"far into the night."* DeValera argued that there was no chance of military success, and that a withdrawal would now be

---

205   With regard to Collins' end, some of the most important details in *"Brother Against Brother"* concern not the blow-by-blow twenty minutes of the ambush itself (at which Deasy was not present,) but significant related events, which took place before and after, in the anti-Treaty enclaves around Béal na mBláth

honorable. Deasy, "*although agreeing in my heart with him*," felt that the thousand men of his Division would not accept an *unconditional* cease-fire.

The next morning, 22 August, Deasy and his host "*conveyed*" DeValera to Béal na mBláth, arriving at about 9:30AM. From there DeValera was to return to Lynch at Glanworth via Ahadillane.

At Béal na mBláth Cross, an anti-Treaty sentry, Denny Long, was on duty, as protection for several Divisional officers who were billeted there. Long reported that an armed Free State convoy had stopped there earlier that morning, to inquire the road to Bandon. He gave details of the convoy's vehicles and armaments, as well as the presence of a famous passenger. He had recognized Michael Collins in the touring car. Jehr Long, the proprietor of the village pub, had watched from the window and confirmed all this. Deasy says that then:

> *DeValera asked me what was likely to happen now and I replied that the men billeted in this area included many of those who had been forced to retreat from Limerick, Kilmallock and Buttevant and in their present frame of mind would consider this incursion into the area which was so predominantly Republican ... as a challenge which they could not refuse to meet. I felt that an ambush would be prepared in case the convoy returned. DeValera then remarked that it would be a great pity if Collins were killed because he might be succeeded by a weaker man. DeValera then left us to rejoin Lynch ...*

As Feehan points out:

> *In view of [DeValera's] important and perceptive statement [that "it would be a pity, etc.,"] it is extraordinary that he did not use his influence to scotch the while idea of an ambush. If he had done so it seems reasonable to assume he would be listened to.*

Deasy recounts that he himself then returned to Gurranereagh, to spend the day in administrative work with Tom Crofts, his Divisional Adjutant.

Who met with whom when?

The anti-Treaty officers' meeting at Béal na mBláth, was scheduled in the usual way for men on the run: to begin whenever all the officers turned up. This was the reason why a large body of anti-Treaty foot soldiers were gathered and waiting around there, on that day: as bodyguard for the officers' meeting.

M Ryan states that this planned meeting did commence in the morning, on 22 August. She says that DeValera took part in this morning meeting, at which a decision was made, in response to the appearance of Collins' convoy a little earlier: a decision to postpone the conference, expressly in order to set an ambush for him instead.

Yet Deasy describes DeValera's stop at Béal na mBláth as only a changing from one conveyance to another. He describes his own meeting with DeValera of the previous night (21 August,) but does not suggest DeValera attended any meeting at Béal na mBláth on that morning of the 22nd. He recounts DeValera's infamous words about Collins' possible death being "*a pity*," then says that DeValera "*left us to rejoin Lynch*" in north Cork. Deasy says he himself also left the village soon after.

"*I believe Dev's knocking round this area.*" [206]

Does this raise a question? Did DeValera really leave the area when Deasy thought he did? Did a meeting take place without Deasy, but with DeValera and some officers, after Deasy had left? The 1964 ambushers' statement seems to indicate that Deasy took part part in a morning meeting, in deciding to set the ambush, and at least in preparing it.

Jimmy Flynn [207] confirms that DeValera "*was in the area to meet Collins*." According to him, DeValera "*spent the day pleading*" with the men there, not to ambush Collins. He goes on to explain that DeValera was overruled in this, as having no local authority, by officers there who were following orders from Liam Lynch. [208]

If all this were so, DeValera was in an excellent position to send warning to Collins, and/or to change the time or place for their proposed meeting. Such last minute schedule changes were a routine security measure, for the Irish leadership-on-the-run, throughout the War of Independence.

DeValera does not seem to have informed Deasy that Collins' presence there was as a negotiator, under safe conduct, coming to attend a

---

206 Collins' comment at breakfast on 22 August, reported by Capt Joe Dolan to M Forester.

207 Flynn was ADC assigned to accompany DeValera on that day.

208 L Lynch was soon after rendered permanently unavailable for comment.

scheduled peace conference with himself. Neither does Deasy report any "*pleading*" from DeValera, to prevent an ambush. Deasy certainly demonstrates complete ignorance of any safe conduct having been promised the C-in-C, any peace negotiations involving Collins that day, or any of the terms which the C-in-C had in hand. It would seem that DeValera did not mention any of this to him; not on that morning of 22 August, nor during their long conference the night before, expressly on the subject of ending the war; nor at any time after.

Coogan quotes TP O'Neill as stating that DeValera later denied that a meeting between himself and Collins had been planned for that day. However, that DeValera and Collins both turned up at one particular obscure, back-country crossroads, within hours of each other, merely by chance, beggars belief.

One is tempted to ask, what else could DeValera possibly have said afterward? That Collins came by arrangement, to meet with him, and was there fatally ambushed by DeValera's men?

There is, of course, the farmer near Béal na mBláth at whose home DeValera seems to have mislaid his field glasses. DeValera wrote a polite letter to the farmer, asking for their return, explaining that he left them there on 22 August 1922. The farmer kept the letter, and the binoculars.[209]

Perhaps the man who had started the war, with his exhortations to "*wade through rivers of blood of some members of the Irish government*" really did spend the morning pleading with those who had risen to that call, and begging them not to obey it. But, in any thorough overview of his whereabouts and actions that day, it is impossible to clear DeValera of implication in the decision to ambush Collins in West Cork.

*　　*　　*

For the rest of our unanswered questions, it will be necessary to proceed to Béal na mBláth, and a new analysis of what happened there.

---

[209] T P Coogan

Commander-in-Chief Collins seated in the rear of the touring car, next to General Dalton, leaving Clonakilty, 22 August 1922

Béal na mBláth, aerial photo, Ordinance Survey. On the right side of the road, just below the lane intersecting from the right, stands the monument. The ambushers fired from the parallel lane on the left. A stream runs between the road and the lane.

CHAPTER 17

WHAT HAPPENED AT BÉAL NA MBLÁTH?

The following is a new analysis of events on that fateful day. It is the first detailed re-examination to be offered with the benefit of all the research and discussion which has been published since John Feehan's key work of the 1980s.

This is an opinion: what this writer *thinks* that all of the above adds up to. To omit it would be unfair to readers who have come thus far. But the author would not seek the public's attention for this opinion: unless deeply convinced that no other explanation fits the evidence.

*   *   *

> *We were aware of IRA Flying Column being about at various places during our journey down to Cork; but not a shot was fired at us.* [210]

If, on his final journey through West Cork, Commander-in-Chief Michael Collins, under cover of a routine tour of inspection, was travelling on a safe-conduct for the purpose of peace negotiations, ... That is to say, ostensibly, no one was supposed to shoot at him!

However, neither was he careless of his personal safety, nor unmindful of the hazards of travelling in anti-Treaty territory. He came with a full military convoy which was well-equipped to make short work of any "loose cannons" who might take a shot at him: either through ignorance of his peaceful mission, or betrayal thereof.

> *"[anti-Treaty] Brigade Officers ... were [at Béal na mBláth] to attend a Brigade Council meeting at which the possibility of ending the war was likely to be discussed."*

> *All during the day it was freely rumoured among [the ambush party] that the war would soon be over, and as one of them said, "We had no great mind to shoot anybody."*

> *"Dev's mission ... was to try to bring the war to an end ... "*

---

210   Private Corry, driver

> "I will not leave Cork until the fighting is finished."

> I found it hard to accept that the convoy was travelling merely on a social visit to West Cork. ... that the convoy did return by the same route ... for Collins ... was inexplicable and in military terms baffling. [211]

The Brigade Officers were there to discuss peace. The soldiers on the hillside were freely talking about peace. DeValera was discussing peace with Deasy, and reportedly was scheduled to meet Collins there for talks. Soldiers in the convoy believed they were escorting a peace mission. All day long, and all though this journey, Michael Collins was talking about peace.

These several quotations make it difficult to conceive that the C-in-C could have been, contrary to his own statements, the only prominent player heading to Béal na mBláth that day who was *not* there to talk about ending the war.

Deasy could not believe Collins was there by chance. Yet, writing fifty years later, was at a loss to explain what the C-in-C was doing there. He claims to have known Collins "*intimately*." Yet the wild guesses he muses on (in his memoire) are diametrically wide of the mark. Deasy said, "*I considered him then to be the greatest leader of our generation and I have not since changed that opinion*." Yet his next sentence reads: "*This last expedition of his may have been the gesture of a man who felt that reconciliation was no longer possible.*" The following statement is true. The preceding statement is false. At a loss, he flounders and gropes for some explanation; finally offering one entirely at variance with everything he knew of the man.

Because, though Collins was clearly convinced that he was going to bring the fighting to an end on this trip, *no one informed the anti-Treaty officers gathered at Béal na mBlath that Collins was there for talks*.

How could Deasy have failed to make the obvious connection between the dots, after fifty years of trying? Is it not equally evident, then, that being painfully close to the tragedy, the obvious conclusion was simply too excruciating for him to consider: that the C-in-C had been lured there for negotiations. And that Deasy and the other anti-Treaty officers had been, if not directly responsible for his death, duped into both taking the blame, and inadvertently camouflaging the assassins' retreat.

In this light, we should reconsider Deasy's statement that both himself and most of the officers gathered at Béal na mBláth had all recently

---

211 Ibid.

arrived from far away. This was out-of-the-way back country, off the beaten track; and these all were men technically "on the run", dependent on a clandestine network for communication with the outside world: a network controlled by Liam Lynch (who may have been controlled, or manipulated, in this matter of Collins' death, by DeValera.) Under these circumstances, it is believable that they could have been kept in the dark about secret peace negotiations with Collins; as were many others.

As Sean MacEoin mentioned, "*outlying units*" might have been unaware of the negotiations, and of the safe-conduct. But DeValera could not have been.

How could this have been done?

>"Good Iago ... Honest Iago." [212]
>
>*- Othello, Act II Scene III*

For the trap to be successful, in both eliminating the C-in-C and in placing the blame on his former comrades, only one man in Ireland could hold all the threads in his hands. To set the trap, DeValera (possibly assisted by Lynch,) would have had to be the source of communication with Dalton from the anti-Treaty side. Hardly anyone else was in a position to contact all the players involved: all the leaders of the anti-Treaty forces, Collins, and the British secret service.

DeValera was in a position to convince the C-in-C that he was assembling the anti-Treaty leaders for a major peace conference, while at the same time, keeping those leaders ignorant of DeValera's secretive invitation to Collins, and in the dark as to Collins' intentions to make terms. Hardly anyone was so well-positioned to cooperate with the British secret service plans to exploit the Civil War, as a cover for assassination of the C-in-C.

Thus could be struck down at one fell swoop, the two remaining major threats to DeValera's future political domination of Ireland. For it was Collins' death that set the stage for the execution of the War of Independence' major military leaders, which could only take place over his dead body.

---

[212] Shakespeare's classic villain Iago was distinguished by a genius for inciting conflict and death in those around him; while each one perceived him to be the merest, well-meaning bystander.

DeValera had to be at Béal na mBláth that day: because if he had not turned up in the immediate area, Collins would have known it, and detected the trap. It was likewise necessary to assure that anti-Treaty commanders be called to a major conclave there, and that they should not fail to arrive. Lacking this, the C-in-C's intelligence sources would have noted a surprising absence of any major meeting such as had been promised, and smell a rat.

However, due to factors mentioned above, Collins would *not* be put off if anti-Treaty commanders either did not admit or did not know of peace negotiations underway with the Free State. It does not weaken the case for the existence of such talks that not all the perspective participants were informed of them. *"Yes, there's a peace move on, but it is supposed to be a dead secret."*

Why did he "stop to ask directions"?

> *Nobody knew better than Collins the area through which he would pass.* [213]

> *It is a basic principle of military movement that maps are always used. A military convoy travelling through hostile territory does not stop casually and ask the way as if they were tourists. If it is absolutely necessary to seek directions, then the person from whom such directions are sought must be arrested and brought with the convoy so that he cannot inform anyone as to its destination.* [214]

It was *not* because he didn't know the way, that Collins stopped at Béal na mBláth on the morning of August 22. It is offered that he had been instructed to do so, as a signal to anti-Treaty commanders that he was in the area and would attend the conference there that evening. It was not a coincidence that *"several Divisional Officers were billeted in Jerh Long's public house"* [215] when the C-in-C's convoy just happened by to ask the road to Bandon. Only, ... those commanders were never informed of these arrangements.

---

213   L Deasy

214   J Feehan

215   Ibid.

The bend in the road

The ambush site basically consists of an extended "S" curve. Although its two interlocking bends do not appear terribly sharp on paper, they are sufficiently pronounced, so that passengers on the ground quickly lose sight of each other, at a very short distance.

If the barricade in the road were visible as soon as they came out of the lower (southern) curve of the "S", they would not have proceeded any further. Therefore the barricade which impeded the first vehicles was probably tucked away in the upper (northern) curve of the "S", so as to be invisible to drivers in the long straightway which separates the two curves. The logic of the ambush planners was probably to stall the convoy thereby, in the long straightway, between the two curves. Commander-in-Chief Collins, in the touring car toward the rear of the convoy, seems to have halted while still in the lower curve of the "S", well before coming into the straightway.

When the convoy stopped, the four vehicles were spread out over the road. The motorcycle scout and lorry of soldiers, near the barricade at the forward end, were approximately a quarter mile from the armoured car which brought up the rear, and separated from the C-in-C's touring car by a sharp bend in the road. As reported by McKenna and confirmed by several others:

> When the shooting ceased they could hear firing at the Bandon end of the ambush site but could not see anything as the armoured car and touring car were around the bend.

Who fired when and who took cover where?

One must ask why anyone with an armoured car handy would have lain down next to a ditch only two feet high, which must have left them still all but entirely exposed to fire from the ambushers, who were elevated more than 20 yards above them. The armoured car would have afforded the best protection, both visually, and in terms of a substantial shield against gunfire. Wouldn't it have been more natural to take cover behind it? [216] Dalton's account does say that the C-in-C did do so, at least at one point.

---

[216] Feehan points out that the logical thing for any bodyguard to do, would have been to get the C-in-C into the armoured car, and drive him out of harm's way, until the shooting ceased.

Collins did **not** recklessly expose himself

All relevant accounts agree that, after the firing began, Collins *got out* of the touring car and *moved back* toward the armoured car behind them. This was natural and reasonable, if the first shots from the ambushers were a quarter mile *ahead* of his position. In that case, there would have been little or no fire at his end of the convoy, when he got out.

Collins, far from clueless, had a very clear perception of what kind of fire was coming at him from the local lads. He did *not* carelessly expose himself to the ambushers. He moved *back* from the touring car, because their fire came mainly from directly *in front* of his car, on the road ahead.

Did the armoured car fire first?

The combination of various accounts strongly suggests that, at his end of the ambush site, it was the armoured car's Vickers machine gun which *fired the first shots*. And that it continued to mercilessly rip up the dirt around the ambushers' positions until after Collins was dead: assuring that the anti-Treaty men could hardly have poked their heads out to see what was happening on the road below.

Consider the amount of fire such a weapon spews out in minutes. Yet the ambushing party consisted of only five men, only three of whom had rifles, who were widely spread out over a quarter of a mile; and by their own account, "*whatever firing they did was very half-hearted.*"

McKenna maintains that the ambushers' fire, at the forward end of the ambush site, lasted no more than about two minutes. Apparently, return fire from the Crossley tender also ceased with it. Only then, in the ensuing quiet, they heard firing on the road behind them, but couldn't see what was happening there.

" ... *The [armoured car] gunner ... literally tore the ditches in shreds with the fierce fusillade of bullets from his machine gun.*" [217] The sound of continuous machine gun fire is one of the dominant impressions which is consistently corroborated. It did not come from the ambushers, because they had no machine guns. It was heard by the Crossley tender crew after everything was over at their end. So it was not their Lewis machine gun. It had to be the Vickers gun on the armoured car.

---

217   L Deasy

Why with that crew?
If the C-in-C was shot at close range by a member of his own party, it would of course have had to be by someone who was near him when he fell. Separated visually from the rest of the escort by the bend in the road, only someone immediately around the Leyland touring car could see him, so as to aim such a shot.

It is offered that isolating Collins from the rest of the party in this way, was key to his assassination. The C-in-C could hardly be attacked in the presence of such a numerous escort. The greater the numbers present, the more complicated the efforts required to contain potential testimony as to what happened. One or two men might succeed in deceiving perhaps two or three subordinates who were young, inexperienced and peripheral to the action. It would be much more difficult to be sure of a whole lorry full of soldiers (such as rode in the Crossley tender.) For the same reason, the presence of this full complement of soldiers lent credence to whatever explanation was later published.

To effect such a plan, it might therefore only be necessary to be sure of certain members of the convoy in particular: such as one or more of the drivers, one or more of the gunners, perhaps a scout. (A number of these personnel were reportedly either hand-picked by Dalton, changed from Collins usual crew, and/or replaced in Cork.) These would be the only members of the convoy who could have any idea what happened at his end of the road.

This is not to say that all these were necessarily privy to any plot on the C-in-C's life. However, someone planning such an action might wish to ensure, for instance, that the driver would *not* be Collins' usual personal chauffeur. It might be enough for such purposes to assure that the driver would not be one who was especially sharp, devoted and reflexively attentive to Collins. It might be enough to select a driver who was young, inexperienced and unfamiliar with West Cork. Or not known to the C-in-C, but overawed by their famous passenger and naturally looking to Dalton for orders. Who was, in a word, easily led.

The Vickers gunner in the armoured car would also have a key role to play. If fire from ambushers at his end of the ambush site was negligible, then it was only the sound of the Vickers gun which created the *illusion* that his end of the convoy was under any significant attack. This illusion would cover the assassin's work. When the C-in-C was found struck down by a bullet, no one would ask for an explanation.

Why didn't all those soldiers protect him?

Commandant Sean O'Connell was the officer in command of the twelve soldiers in the Crossley tender: these made up the bulk of Collins' bodyguard. As such, he had a great responsibility and a great deal to answer for at Béal na mBláth. Yet no one seems ever to have questioned him or his actions.

Why did the mass of his bodyguard never make any move toward the C-in-C during the ambush? Why did they let his car remain out of their sight while under fire? Why did they not fall back to surround and secure Collins' person? Why did they *all* remain a quarter mile away, exchanging shots and moving the barricade? Why did they only inquire a fatal ten minutes later as to the C-in-C's condition; to find that their precious charge had in that time been killed under their noses?

It is offered that, if the C-in-C were not killed by the ambushers, but by someone in his own party, ... It would have been necessary to be sure of one other in the convoy, in addition to the drivers and the armoured car gunner: the commander of the Crossley tender.

The soldiers in the tender, under military discipline, were not in a position to make any move without the authorization of their commander. Whatever actions the soldiers in the tender took, must have been what they were *ordered to do*.

McKenna describes in most detail what actions this party took and when, and is largely corroborated by Smith, the ambushers and Priv J O'Connell. Smith clearly states that the men in the tender proceeded as they did under the express orders of Commdt Sean O'Connell. McKenna does not explicitly say that they were so ordered: because it is entirely unnecessary to say it. If, as he says, the party instantly detailed themselves into two sections: one to move the barricade, the other taking cover and returning fire, it is the same as to say, "*Our commanding officer gave orders for us to ...* " In view of the outcome, it would be a point of natural tact and delicacy to leave this unsaid; knowing that anyone with a clue of military procedure would not need it explained.

McKenna reported that Commdt. O'Connell "*wept openly*" on their return journey to Cork City. While not wishing to take an excessively cynical view, it must be observed that such emotional display was in direct contradiction to his actions during the ambush. In a darkened vehicle at night, it would not have been difficult to give a convincing appearance of weeping (especially when this was in keeping with the mood of everyone around him.) *If* O'Connell *were* in the plot, this would have been intelligent policy: at the cost of a few grunts and sobs, perhaps one hand pressed to his eyes ... suspicion arising from his actions might be instantly dispelled.

What happened?

As the convoy came into sight, the ambushers fired a warning shot or two; which were probably not aimed at the convoy and did not hit anyone.

The cyclist "scout", when he encountered the barricade, did not act as a scout. Instead of flying back to his commanding officers in the rear, to inform them of the barricade (as one would expect a "scout" to do,) he got off his motorcycle and stood about; with his hands on his hips (so to speak.)

The Crossley tender, having received no information from the "scout", who had "scouted" the barricade first, then came up to the same spot and stopped. The cyclist had a key role in allowing all this to happen: his failure to immediately alert those behind him, while there was still a chance to take evasive action, cannot be excused. It directly resulted in more distance between the C-in-C and most of his bodyguard.

In the barricade they encountered an obvious and ominous indication that they had run into a trap. At the very same moment, the C-in-C's Leyland touring car was obscured from their view. At these double dangerous developments, the commander of the tender did not act like a bodyguard. The tender was *not* ordered to back up and close with the C-in-C's car in case of attack. Instead, the tender, incomprehensibly, stayed where it was. The soldiers in it were ordered to get out.

Only after they got out were they fired upon. They came under rifle and pistol fire, from the anti-Treaty men at that end of the site. They were then ordered to form two parties: one to move the barricade, one to return fire. No one to protect the C-in-C or see if he was still alive.

A few minutes later, when the ambushers ceased fire at this forward end of the site, the soldiers from the tender could hear firing from the direction of the C-in-C's car. Once again, their commanding officer's actions, or lack thereof, is inexcusable. Although they were no longer under fire at their end, his "bodyguard" party apparently stopped there passively listening to the gunfire around Collins' car, a quarter mile away. They stayed there and let the C-in-C take the bullets, while they waited for the shooting to stop.

Precisely what was happening at Collins' end of the convoy, we may never know. In view of tall tale-telling in the semi-official stories, it is impossible to rely on the accounts we have from the C-in-C's end of the ambush site. Anything could have happened there. This writer's deductions from the evidence are as follows:

The touring car stopped (possibly by Collins' order) when shots were heard ahead, near the Crossley tender. The four occupants of the touring car got out. Collins, and perhaps others, probably moved back toward the armoured car. At least some of them commenced firing from behind the two-foot ditch or bank (possibly in response to only a couple of warning shots from the hill, and before they ever came under any fire, at that end, themselves.)

It seems unanimous that the armoured car gunner opened up and began sweeping the hillside with machine gun fire. (If there were no anti-Treaty casualties, it wasn't his fault.) In view of the ambushers' probable fire and fire power, this would seem to have been overkill. It also makes it extremely unlikely that the two (or, at most, three) anti-Treaty men at that end could have got off such a carefully aimed shot as would have been necessary to account for Collins' fatal wound. They fired in the convoy's general direction, but they could hardly have lifted their heads.

Perhaps this intensity of machine gun fire from the armoured car was a zealous defensive measure. But, under the circumstances, what was Collins likely to think of it? Travelling into a rebel stronghold on a highly sensitive peace mission, in a volatile and unsettled situation, he might have been prepared to expect a few random shots from a hillside. But it's difficult to imagine that he would consider such aggressive bombardment from his party as the kind of message he wanted to send, at that particular time and place.

In this context, what would have been the convoy's standing orders? They wouldn't have been simply piled into vehicles and driven away without a word of instruction as to their duties, objectives and desired comportment on this mission. Certainly not while accompanying the Commander-in-Chief on top secret negotiations entailing the fate of the nation!

It's safe to assume that the entire convoy must have been briefed in some way. Such orders may have played a role in the soldiers' impression that they were there to negotiate peace (as reported by McKenna.) That they should have some clue to that effect, would naturally have been desirable. "*Whatever happens, don't get trigger-happy!*" would certainly have been the Prime Directive of the day, on any such mission.

Indeed, all things considered, it's not hard to imagine Collins getting out of the car furious, and pounding on the armoured car turret, commanding the gunner to cease fire. This is conjecture. But unlike many surmises around Béal na mBláth, it's a reasonable conjecture which fits the facts and what we know of the man, what he was doing there, and his leadership style. Let's follow this as a hypothesis: and explore just how very far from some Free State accounts, events at that end *could* have been.

If he did so, he would certainly have had to approach from the side of the armoured car away from the ambushers: that is, away from the direction in which the Vickers gun was firing. This would have been logical, keeping him clear of "friendly fire" as well as covered from the ambushers.

If he did so, no one would have seen it except Dalton and his picked drivers in the touring car. No one else could have heard him, over the machine gun in the armoured car.

The next thing that happened, the reaction he then got from those men, with whom he now found himself isolated, on a deserted road, with a lot of guns and a lot of bullets flying, ... May have caused it to instantly dawn on him, that he had fallen into a trap.

"*My first thought was how easily I had walked into it.*"

Like any other man, he could be trapped: with enough information about who he was and how he worked, the right bait could be set. But he was not slow. In an instant, he may have realized his situation. His excellent instincts would then take over.

> *It is very difficult to shadow such a man ... When one's life is at stake, perceptions are sharpened ...*

Did Collins, in that moment, realize he was betrayed by his bodyguard? Did he take the alarm from what was happening at that end, and try to clear off from his own party, in a last ditch effort to save himself?

It is significant that in Dalton and Corry's versions, there seems to have been some pains taken to account for Collins being separated from them and some distance back in the Bandon direction on the road, when he was found hit. Dalton's account explicitly specifies that Collins went behind the armoured car and then "*ran 15 yards back up the road.*" The ambushers' account says that the Free State officers "*ran up and down the road.*" Corry says that everyone from the touring car walked back up the road "*about 50 yards*" while under heavy fire.

Why would he and how could he (or anyone) have run or walked up the road while they were under heavy fire? Bear in mind that Dalton, Corry and Smith's accounts of the amount of fire they were under seem to be exaggerated and unreliable.

It is offered that Collins ran up the road, away from the touring car and armoured car, at a time *when there was little or no fire coming from the ambushers at that end*. If so, it's clear that he did not get far. Dalton would have been anxious to account for this, in case any of the anti-Treaty men on the hill above may have seen it.

All witnesses, even those who seem most likely to be concealing something, agree on one point: it all happened near the armoured car. Dalton and Corry mention unidentified "other officers" with them, near to Collins, who were part of the armoured car crew.

If he were killed by an entry wound high on his forehead which exited behind his ear, his assassin would have had to shoot from above him. If he were also shot at very close range, as Dr Gogarty and other medical examiners suggest, how could anyone have delivered such a shot, at such an angle and point blank? Collins was not a short man. He would have had to be kneeling or prone. Or the assassin would have to be standing on something. If the C-in-C were not crouching, but were fleeing when hit, someone standing on the armoured car would have been in the best position to inflict such a wound.

The armoured car was also mobile, and had no obstruction behind it. If Collins attempted to flee his own associates, the armoured car could have pursued, come up to him quickly, and a sharpshooter standing on it could have dealt the fatal blow.

It was necessary to assure that there were no witnesses: not only in the complement of soldiers in the Crossley tender, but also among the ambushers on the hill. The armoured car fills this gap as well. It was the only equipment large enough to conceal a man (and what was happening to him) from observers on the hill above.

A point on which all Free State accounts surprisingly agree, is that about the time Collins died, the firing stopped.

It is offered that the ambushers had already retreated when Collins was hit. *That is why none of the anti-Treaty men saw any casualties on either side.* At that point, there was no fire at that end, except for the Vickers gun in the armoured car; which stopped firing when the C-in-C was dead. It stopped firing then, because the purpose of its inordinately intense bombardment had been accomplished: it had camouflaged the sound of the assassin's bullet(s), and created an auditory illusion of intensive fighting at that end, to account for their only casualty.

Could this be the way it was?

Bearing in mind that, for this to work, all of it had to be planned, and had to go according to plan: is it feasible, that such a plot could have been made and carried out? That the bend in the road, the spot where the ambushers would wait, the places where the various vehicles would stop, etc. could have been worked out in advance?

Yes. If DeValera and Lynch were in the plot, they were in a position to assure all of those factors. If they had the cooperation of Dalton, who could control the drivers of the touring car and armoured car, as well as the commander of the Crossley tender, all of it could have been carried out in this way. Under the guise of projected peace talks, they could designate points of Collins' itinerary, and his appearances at Béal na mBláth. They would have also been in a position to influence young Tom Hales as to the advisability of setting up an ambush and precisely where.

> *DeValera then remarked that it would be a great pity if Collins were killed ... then left us to rejoin Lynch ... "* [218]

Qui tacit consenti. Once the trap was set, playing his favorite role of the innocent bystander, DeValera, while saying he wanted peace, walked away without lifting a finger to avert such an attack; nor to warn Collins, whom, the evidence strongly suggests, he himself had invited there for negotiations.

> *DeValera knew of course that news of his presence in Béal na mBláth might well seal his death warrant.*[219]

All of this further explains why the issue of peace negotiations in connection with the C-in-C's journey to Béal na mBláth remains controversial. If it had been more generally known that Collins was lured there by the promise of talks, questions would have been asked, much sooner after the fact than this, as to just who had made that promise.

Anti-Treaty representatives would have compared notes, and might quickly have realized that DeValera had to be at the bottom of it. To anyone with a solid background in the history of Ireland and Scotland's conflicts with their nearest neighbour, the entire *modus operandi* would stink to high

---

218   L Deasy

219   T P Coogan

heaven of British involvement. Within weeks, the whole business could have been the death-knell for DeValera politically; if not otherwise as well.

Thus we see the fantastic foresight necessary to bring this off, with all the benefits to DeValera and to British imperialist interests which ensued: It was not only necessary to keep Collins' shrewd associates permanently confused about what happened, but to keep the anti-Treaty leaders equally in the dark. It was necessary to completely deceive DeValera's insurgent comrades as to his actual role; while at the same time set them up to take the blame. And, not incidentally, the bullets.

* * *

It fits the facts. Collins, at the centre of a united Ireland, the spearhead of its best and brightest, could beat the British secret service. Collins at the epicenter of a shattered Ireland, his inner circle broken, half his best comrades turned against him, isolated from his usual bodyguard, from the tactical and emotional support which had made it all possible, overwhelmed by herculean government roles meant for ten men, ... was a much more vulnerable target. He himself had decried the Truce's dangers for his clandestine combatants: observing that they'd now be as vulnerable to their adversaries as *"rabbits come out of their holes."*

The Treaty and Civil War thus rendered the Big Fella far less well equipped to hold his own against that hydra-headed agency who had lost so many of their star operatives at his hands.

BÉAL NA MBLÁTH: CONCLUSIONS

Tell them in Sparta that, faithful to their commands, we perished here.

- inscription at Thermopylae

The IRA never claimed any intent to shoot Collins. The ambushers themselves did not believe that he fell at their hands, even accidentally. Not a single eye-witness statement before 1960 *ever said* that he was shot by the ambushers. Members of his own escort believed that he was not killed by the ambushers. Which is to say that they believed he was a victim of foul play by Free State men in the convoy. Dalton was later a target of accusations that he colluded in Collins' death. For decades he issued no denial, but even admitted he may have shot Collins himself "accidentally."

These were no "conspiracy theorists." They were *there*.

Twenty-five professional soldiers travelled out as escort to the Commander-in-Chief. Following an encounter with a force of five men, with vastly inferior arms, they brought the C-in-C back dead. There were no other fatalities or serious injuries on either side. [220]

There was no inquest; although, even in that unsettled period, such inquests were routinely held in deaths of much less renown, and attended by far less questionable circumstances. Those present at Collins' death were never formally questioned by any official authority.

If this analysis is not the answer then what is? If it cannot be proved, neither can it be refuted. Other explanations have been suggested by biographers and historians: but hardly with more than half-hearted conviction in the writers themselves. Unlike such previous hypotheses, all the evidence supports this analysis: as opposed to other theories, which do not match all the known facts, and tend to contradict themselves.

Of course, this must be expected to spark more dispute and inquiry. That is precisely what it should do. If this entire work were to serve no other purpose, it would be worthwhile for that reason alone. Anyone who can prove this wrong, and/or offer a better explanation, is welcome to do so. In the process, they might hopefully shed yet more light on a murky conundrum of history.

To those who remain unconvinced by the arguments herein, the author appeals to the strength of their convictions: Demand a full, independent, scientific investigation now. An examination of Collins' remains, with the benefit of modern forensics, could answer today many key questions: such as the number and location of his wounds, from which direction, at what range, and from what kind of weapon. This alone would go very far in culling true from false in the many conflicting statements of witnesses.

It is also past time for all Michael Collins documents and correspondence to be assembled, archived, catalogued and published for the benefit of the public, historians and academic research. When this is done, it will greatly facilitate any efforts to improve on the analysis offered above.

---

[220] The alleged injuries of the motorcycle scout, Lieut. Smith, as explained elsewhere herein, merit no more than a footnote.

Part 3

Aftermath,
legacies and ramifications

Chapter 18

Aftermath

The death of Collins evoked the same strong feelings in ordinary people of Dublin as Daniel O'Connell and Parnell. [221]

Collins' death was passionately mourned by the Irish public *en masse*. It was acknowledged, even by many opponents and anti-Treaty partisans, as a national catastrophe. Fifty-thousand people watched, as his body was carried to City Hall, from the ship which brought it from Cork. "*Vast throngs*" made an "*endless queue*" [222] for three days, to pay their respects as he lay in state there. Millions silently lined the streets of Dublin for miles, as he was slowly carried to Glasnevin cemetery.

The Irish public's consciousness of him has never faded, as undisputed "head center" of the active independence movement on the ground. Intervening decades of "silent treatment" from official sources seem to have had remarkably little impact on his fame. Despite rigorous efforts to "air-brush" him out of history, public consciousness of him has never ceased to burn hot and bright.

What was the response to his demise in official quarters? What was the sequel there?

The Free State government

Certainly there were high stakes indeed for the Free State government, in any investigation of Béal na mBláth. Had many of the basic facts become generally known, it would have seriously undermined their credibility. It's not going too far to consider whether the nation might not have gone over to the anti-Treaty side, in a body, had some details of the C-in-C's death been known. In any case, it would have been sure to further destabilize an already shaky national situation. Feehan cites this as one of the reasons offered to excuse the Free State's failure to investigate his death.

While this is plausible, in the big picture, it does not wash. It does not explain the Cabinet's astounding lack of curiosity regarding Collins' fate. If

---

221   Doherty & Keogh

222 *Freeman's Journal*   25 August 1922

the facts were too hot for publication, surely his trusted, devoted colleagues in government, must have wished to inform *themselves* as to precisely what happened?

Claims have been made that an official inquiry into Collins' death was made, but that it was kept secret, due to the volatility of the issues and the unstable state of the country. However, it must be remembered that, if such an inquiry took place, it was without the benefit of testimony from eyewitnesses. Feehan found:

> *It has been suggested ... that a private inquiry was held by the army. I cannot find a shred of solid evidence to support this ... None of the escort with whom I spoke were questioned in any formal way or asked to attend an inquiry.*

Some may consider this too controversial for comment even at this writing. But the fact remains that there are only two explanations possible for this amazing failure to inquire: *they knew what had happened*; or *they did not wish to know.*

It does not speak well, that the few statements we have from members of the convoy came almost exclusively from those particular personnel who demonstrably would have had to be in the plot, if Collins were killed by one of his own bodyguard.

Those accounts appeared in most of the newspapers, credited to representatives of the army (Lieut. Smith, and a year later, Dalton.) Therefore, they naturally tended to be accepted by the general public as constituting the "official story".

Government neither explicitly approved nor disapproved those accounts. In this they effectively avoided personal identification with them; and at the same time, excused themselves from making any further inquiry. Much in the Pontias Pilate style of washing hands, or the DeValera tactic of "*standing silently by*": associations deeply resonant with the British tradition of political chicanery.

Coogan asserts that there was "*nothing sinister*" in this cover-up. However, that is a fundamentally flawed concept, which does not hold water. There is always something sinister, in any cover-up concerning a fatality. Wherever human life is lost, there is a fundamental need and right to know. In a murder investigation, there is no privacy. No one can judge for the public, as to which details they do or do not need to know. Because every bell that tolls, tolls for thee. In the words of President Kennedy, "*We are all mortal."* What happened to one, can happen to others, or to ourselves, next. Or to the next generation.

> *The Free State government derived immense propaganda value from blaming his death on [the anti-Treaty side.]* [223]

Mass outrage and grief at Collins' death was immediately exploited as a public relations coup, to undermine support and sympathy for the anti-Treaty forces. A reprisal fever took hold in the ranks:

> *Vinnie Byrne, to give but one example, told me that for "four or five days [after Collins' death] I'd have shot any bloody [anti-Treaty man] I came across."*

From the evidence it seems that there was an agenda in the Free State government to blame the IRA for Collins' death: for the express purposes of reaping political dividends, and justifying extreme measures in the war. This paved the way, both for legalized slaughter, and for unconditional surrender. It cannot be separated from the practice of widespread summary executions, which formed part of the same policy. Executions of men to whom that same Free State government directly owed its very existence.

This in itself does no honor to that government. It does less when combined with what was, at best, an inexcusable lack of routine inquiry into the suspicious death of their most important member; at worst, deliberate cover-up of the evidence.

McPeak and the Theft of the Armoured Car

Following the ambush, the armoured car gunner continued to be closely attached to Dalton, serving as personal driver to him and Tom Ennis in Cork.

There are a number of wild rumours about McPeak, ostensibly coming from former Free State soldiers. These include reports that he was accused, interrogated, beaten and charged with Michael Collins' murder (but that charges were dropped for lack of evidence.) Others said that, in his cups, McPeak boasted that he had killed Collins. Another witness claims that McPeak admitted the C-in-C fell "accidentally" to "friendly fire".

---

[223] J Feehan

The truth is the strangest tale of all: three months after the ambush, McPeak deserted to the anti-Treaty side. In doing so, he just happened to drive away, not with just any armoured car, but that one in particular, which took such an important part in Collins' death.

Many excuses for his conduct were on offer. It was said that he experienced a change of heart about the Free State army, after witnessing the beating and shooting of anti-Treaty prisoners. That he had a girlfriend who talked him into it. That the IRA wanted the armoured car.

Another reason given is that fellow Free State soldiers put him in fear for his safety, with continual accusations about Collins' death. As Feehan points out, this is another instance of suspicion against the escort crew, which was general in the army at the time. It also suggests that comrades had no very high opinion of McPeak himself.

All of these explanations are plausible. But none of them are nearly so likely, as that his absconding with that great hulking piece of evidence had more to do with that single most important event connected with it, and with him: the C-in-C's untimely demise.

After turning over the armoured car to the anti-Treaty side, McPeak went back to Scotland. It's said that he was arrested there in 1923, and extradited to face charges in Ireland.

He was prosecuted for the theft of the armoured car; but, strangely, not for desertion. Nor was the death of Collins ever mentioned at his trial. He is said to have then spent six years in prison for that theft; always adding that he was usually in solitary confinement. [224]

It seems fair to point out McPeak's own testimony that, in the British Army (where he'd formerly served,) if an armoured car ever fell into enemy hands, it was the gunner's duty to disable it, so that it could not be used by them. Thanks to McPeak, the armoured car and its all-important Vickers gun turret were lost forever to history, soon after Collins' assassination. This constituted destruction of evidence. which could have told tales about eyewitnesses and their testimony: his own in particular.

GENERAL SEAN HALES AND CALLS FOR AN INQUEST

General Sean Hales was the ranking Free State officer in the district encompassing Béal na mBláth. He immediately set about trying to organize an official investigation: seeking to have all members of the convoy

---

[224] Why has this been made a special point? Is it necessary to account for no one having seen him in the prison?

returned to Bandon, so that a court of inquiry could be held. To obtain the necessary authorizations, he made several trips to Dublin, where he met with representatives of the Cabinet and army headquarters. They refused to cooperate.

He would not be dissuaded, but travelled to Dublin again to press his suit for a full investigation. His driver and constant companion Jim Woulfe told Feehan that Hales never accepted Dalton's story. A letter from Woulfe to Feehan states, " ... *His chief topic of conversation was Michael Collins. He told me that he would leave no stone unturned until he got an inquiry or inquest held on Michael's death. ... At this time he was about three times in Dublin but all to no avail. The 'big brass' in Dublin would not listen to him. He told me so himself.*"

Hales took his appeal to the highest Free State civil and military authorities. This means that the lack of inquiry was no oversight, but was defended in the teeth of continued demand. It also directly implicates WT Cosgrave, Richard Mulcahy, Kevin O'Higgins and other key figures. Certainly these are the people Hales would have been speaking to.

Genl Hales and Dalton

Just at the same time that Hales was pursuing this campaign, the following remarkable announcement appeared in the Cork Examiner:

> *Now I, the undersigned, being the competent military authority for the County of Cork hereby order that no inquest shall be held in the said County unless written authority for the holding of same shall have been first given by me.*
>
> *- Major General Emmett Dalton*

This announces that, while Genl Hales had to go begging mother-may-I, Dalton himself had the power to initiate inquests; and that he expressly failed, neglected and refused to hold one in Collins' case. In view of his having this authority, it is probable that he was one of the officers whom Sean Hales (a considerably older and more experienced man) would have contacted.

The implications for Dalton's own character, as a responsible member of the escort, are devastating. Any young officer of integrity, in such a position, would naturally be eager for a full public enquiry; rather than allow doubt and suspicion to dog him all the rest of his days. *As Dalton did*. Dalton seemed to be curiously unconcerned in this sense. How could anyone have continued under such circumstances, *unless secure in powerful protection*?

Responsibility falls on the same Free State leaders for this unbelievable travesty: the man who was the chief bodyguard present, at the suspicious death of his Commander-in-Chief, invested with the authority to silence all inquests, in the very region where that fiasco took place! That Dalton should have been invested with such authority, or allowed to retain such authority, after he himself had been present at the killing of his superior officer, is inconceivable in itself. His personal blocking of all inquests into same cannot be viewed in any benign light. It can hardly be called by any other word than incriminating. Incriminating not only himself, but also to the Dublin political and military leadership which allowed it.

This would be like giving a bodyguard from President John F Kennedy's motorcade in Dallas, authority to prohibit the convening of the Warren Commission.[225] Such a thing would not have been dreamed of. It would have set off immediate public outcry and suspicion of government involvement in his assassination.

Although excuses were put forward, connected to unsettled conditions, etc., Feehan could find no evidence that any other military authority, anywhere in the country, ever placed similar restrictions on inquests, in the same period.

The assassination of General Hales

Travelling again on this matter, Hales went to Portobello Barracks, where, as a general of the army, he normally stayed while in the capital. On his arrival, he was informed that the Barracks had no accommodation for him. This forced him to move to a hotel: on the doorstop of which he was assassinated the next day.

Witnesses saw two British soldiers at the scene, with their guns drawn. These same soldiers testified that Hales was shot by two unidentified assailants, whom no one else had seen. The British soldiers' version became the official story, accepted at the inquest.

The IRA have consistently denied responsibility. Notably Moss Twomey, one of the top anti-Treaty commanders for Dublin at the time,

---

[225] The commission appointed by the US government in 1964 to investigate President Kennedy's assassination. It was notoriously flawed, peopled by many of Kennedy's direct political opponents; and has been the subject of controversy ever since. It was at least not prohibited to convene, by a member of Kennedy's Dallas bodyguard!

"always maintained that no orders whatever were given to shoot Hales and it was not the IRA's doing." [226]

Coogan quotes a *"secret IRA communiqué ... initialled by Liam Lynch,"* which seems to contradict Twomey. However, nothing is offered to account for this remarkable discrepancy, between the *"communiqué"* and the regional officer in Dublin. It should be noted that Twomey seems to have survived the war, long enough to have *"always maintained"* his position on this point repeatedly. On the other hand, Lynch was not around for questioning, as to the authenticity of this *"secret"* document. His name is connected with it, ostensibly by his initials (but not by a signature.) No one claims that Lynch wrote it. In fact, no information as to its exact origin or real author is ever provided.

THE RIDDLE THAT WAS ERSKINE CHILDERS

Another prominent member of the anti-Treaty party who was near Béal na mBláth that day was Erskine Childers.

Although Childers did not live to give his side of the story, Frank O'Connor did. O'Connor wrote that he himself was in the company of Childers and Sean Hendreicks *"on a hillside ten miles from the place of ambush. ... We did not know of the death of Collins until we read of it in the newspapers."* M Ryan also places Childers at the same distance from Béal na mBláth on the day (Moneygave near Enniskeane); producing *An Phoblacht* [227] on a hand press at the home of Richard Woods. She also alleges that Childers took part in a meeting with DeValera, a few hours before the latter met with Deasy (evening of August 21,) and on the same topics.

Childers was a product of the Anglo-Protestant land-owning "Ascendancy". In his youth, the Empire fired his imagination. He had burned to "do his bit" for King and country. He subsequently fulfilled that ambition, and gave distinguished service to the British army, in conflicts overseas.

Yet he was also born in Ireland; and reputedly was not unmoved by Ireland's wrongs under the London government. He came to prominence for his involvement in the Howth gun-running, prior to the 1916 Rising. In the 1919-1921 period, he was elected to the Dáil as a Sinn Fein TD. He

---

226   J Feehan

227   "The Republic" anti-Treaty newspaper.

served briefly as editor of *The Irish Bulletin*, the Volunteers' newsletter; and later became a leading anti-Treaty propagandist for *An Phoblacht*.

Childers' contemporaries varied widely in their assessment of the man. From the usually mild-mannered Arthur Griffith, he drew more than one explosion of public denunciation. At one point he told Childers to his face, before the entire Dáil, that they had his record as a British secret service agent on hand. [228] Yet we have no record of Collins taking part in that denunciation. Others openly lauded Childers as a man of outstanding noble qualities.

There seems something remarkable in Collins' own attitude to this enigmatic figure. During the Civil War, when his intelligence team sighted Childers in Liverpool, the C-in-C was asked what should be done with him. British sources advocated charges of treason / sedition. As can be seen from Childers' ultimately tragic fate, he was considered a ringleader who might be held accountable on serious charges. Yet Collins' orders came with a palpable tongue in cheek: "*Charge him as a stowaway.*" (This would seem to be a satiric dig, making reference to the plot of Childers' best-selling novel, *The Riddle of the Sands*.)

When the question arose of sending the "stowaway" back to Dublin to face prosecution, Collins said to keep Childers in England on a misdemeanor. If carried out, this plan would not only have neutralized him as a threat, but would also have preserved Childers' life until the Civil War was over. Comrades and commentators agree that Collins would have opposed Childers' ultimate execution.

If the worse ever alleged against Childers were true, Collins may have been anxious to monitor men like this, precisely in order to keep his hand on the pulse of such elements. It is known that the C-in-C employed double agents, who worked for the British, and for the Irish as well. Some of the greatest heroes of the struggle, like David Neligan, could be so described: he was Collins' man in Dublin Castle. Childers had played a famous role in gun-running to the Irish Volunteers. A keen yachtsman, with excellent knowledge of the Irish Sea, the English coasts, and British institutions, his assistance may well have been invaluable during the War of Independence.

---

228 Churchill's famous public denunciation of Childers is often referred to by historians as evidence that he could not have been a mole for the British. However, if Childers had been secretly working for them, they would hardly be expected to announce it. Such public disparagement is a standard technique for screening such operations. It proves nothing in itself.

Whatever he had done, clearly Collins, unlike Griffith (at times,) did not consider him an outright enemy; British secret service record notwithstanding.

The Childers' were reputedly on quite friendly terms with Collins, from early in the struggle. Biographers are by nature prone to lionize their subjects, and Childers' chroniclers tend to play this up; even suggesting that the wealthy, educated Childers family mentored the unsophisticated farm boy from West Cork. But there is little evidence of this. Childers himself, even while serving the anti-Treaty side, was fond of displaying a small, toy-like pistol, and bragging that it had been a gift to him from Michael Collins. Ironically, it is supposed that this was the very gun for which, after Collins' death, Childers was arrested on weapon possession: thanks to Cosgrave's Execution Bill, a capital crime, which he would die for.

It is this author's surmise that Childers was in fact a double agent: that in the Irish question he played both sides against the middle. The reason that his character has remained an unresolved enigma to this day may even be because he himself was not quite sure which side to be on. It is entirely possible that he laboured under a severe identity crisis throughout the Irish struggle.

Or perhaps he was one who fancied himself too clever for either side. He may have succumbed to the heady intoxication of revolution, and inwardly declared himself a sovereign independent entity. He may have sincerely supported independence, but still cooperated with a cabal which was manoeuvring for a British-friendly version. He may have done so without any moral qualms whatever; even without strictly violating his Dáil commitments.

If there is some truth in all of the above ... If the absolute fact lies somewhere between these extremes and unsolved riddles ... If Childers was willing enough to serve the republican cause to a point; if he was also ready to help split the country in two, if doing so would achieve some Ascendancy political goal, to be gleaned from the wreckage of Civil War; and if he was near Béal na mBláth around 22 August 1922, in DeValera's company ... He certainly may have known something about workings behind the scenes on that tragic day.

Childers was a key anti-Treaty tactician. He worked closely with DeValera, on a range of Civil War strategies: political, propaganda and military. His presence in anti-Treaty circles near Béal na mBláth on that day, may have given him direct knowledge of DeValera's role there. He was a decorated former British Army officer, accused as a secret service agent, and certainly had excellent connections in London. Therefore, even if entirely innocent of any foreknowledge about the attempt on Collins, he was likely to have a penetrating awareness of many details and secret manoeuvers, which have since been lost forever.

We have examined above DeValera's evident contradictions and cunning throughout this saga. How allies and opponents alike may have suffered and fallen, for their willingness to rely on his constantly shifting lead. If DeValera was less than entirely candid with both sides in the Civil War; if he participated in luring Collins into a death trap; if Childers knew something about all this, and if, as evidence suggests, Childers was not without some friendly feeling for Collins, ... Perhaps the independent double agent side of Childers may have felt tempted to play his own hand. He may have taken exception to Collins' murder. Or simply held his knowledge of DeValera's part therein, as a card to play in future.

Childers was an elected member of the Dáil. His shocking summary execution took place against a backdrop of bloody purge, cover-up and file-burning. In light of all of the above, we should ask whether his killing could have had anything to do with his inside knowledge about what happened at and around Béal naBláth.

The end of the Civil War

> Efforts to bring the Civil War to an end ... were all unsuccessful: the end did not come through negotiation. [229]

By January 1923, there had been fifty-five executions of anti-Treaty combatants. The Free State had embarked on a policy of slaughter which has with justice been called atrocity. Fundamental principles of humanity and justice, as well as international conventions regarding the treatment of prisoners of war, were discarded   Prisoners were shot without trial. There were beatings, torture, and summary executions by the side of the road. If anti-Treaty soldiers gave battle, prisoners in the region were killed as a reprisal. Others were reportedly deliberately bound together and blown up with grenades, in reprisal for Free State deaths from anti-Treaty mines.

> It was evident that military victory was no longer a possibility for them, and it was becoming equally certain that their opponents were determined to deny them the means of ending the struggle honorably by negotiation.[230]

---

229   F O'Donoghue

The Cosgrave government's Execution Bill declared weapons possession a capital offense. This was a renewal of the British establishment's policy during the War of Independence. It brought new waves of arrests, and death sentences mounted.

> Tom Crofts especially expressed the fear that this [Execution Bill] would create a new wave of bitterness where, up to now, there was at least some hope of a mutual understanding. To both of us it seemed provocative and unnecessary ... We were at all times on the defensive and constantly retreating.[231]

Captured while recuperating from illness, Deasy called for an end to hostilities in early 1923.[232] Yet although DeValera had told Deasy in August 1922, that a military victory was not possible, he was reportedly the author of the anti-Treaty Executive's answer, rejecting this call for a cease-fire.

The death of Liam Lynch

As war-weariness descended on the anti-Treaty ranks, it seems to have become clear that Liam Lynch was another who kept the war going. Many, even among his friends and admirers, referred to him readily as a fanatic. While his apologist comment that "*men like Michael Collins must be shot,*" in itself identifies him as an accessory to that catastrophe, whether before or after the fact.

Did Lynch not realize that he was paving the way, logistically and ideologically, for the bloodbath in which many of his fighting men were executed *en masse*?

In early 1923, when other anti-Treaty commanders were calling for a meeting of the Executive, to discuss ending the war, Lynch repeatedly resisted and blocked it from convening. When it was clear to all that military success was impossible, Lynch continued to issue communiqués, assuring the ranks that victory was within their reach, that their position

---

230 Ibid.

231 L Deasy

232 The circumstances, and a detailed account of his reasons, are given in *Brother Against Brother*.

had never been so strong, etc. As long as he continued that stand, many others would not abandon the fight.

Although Lynch had continually declared that an anti-Treaty victory was at hand, events proved his judgement fallible. Even F O'Donoghue, while praising his character, admitted he was "*a man of more than ordinary capacity. But he had no abnormal intellectual gifts and he was not a military genius.*"

A detailed account of Lynch's death is given in his biography "*No Other Law*". [233] Following a meeting of the anti-Treaty Executive, there was a particularly thorough combing of certain regions by Free State troops. A few days later, they closed in around a mountainous area where Lynch's party was preparing for breakfast. The anti-Treaty men took to the hills, but were encircled by several units. Reportedly, Lynch took a bullet through the abdomen, while retreating through the mountains, outflanked by a formidable Free State presence. Reportedly, against their strenuous objections, he issued a direct order, that his companions leave him, so as to carry important documents to safety. Identifying himself to the Free State men who soon came up, he was carried down the mountain on an improvised stretcher made from an overcoat and two rifles.

He died of his wounds after a few days, on 10 April 1923. And so went to his grave perhaps the only man who could ever reveal DeValera's exact role in the assassination of Michael Collins. Twenty days later, on 30 April, the Civil War came to an end: in unconditional surrender.

What did the Civil War achieve?

The Army Document, rejected by Lynch and others, proved signally prophetic. The Civil War did prove to be one of the worst disasters in Irish history; certainly in the history of the movement for independence. It did indeed leave the country "*broken for generations.*"

The nightmare that Collins chanced his life to head off, was allowed to unfold, in all its disastrous legacy of bitterness, bloodshed, and disabled national development.

Though declared in the name of republicanism, the Civil War achieved *only* British goals: a neutralized republic incapable of resisting partition; its formidable underground military de-fanged and decimated. It

---

[233] However, we should not omit to note that, like Collins and Boland, the only witnesses to Lynch's death were those directly involved themselves; and so there is no objective testimony.

put an end to Collins, its greatest strategist, and many of the most effective officers under him. With them ended plans to lend support from Dublin to guerrilla defenders against unionist pogroms and partition in the north.

Only over Collins' dead body, came the waves of shocking executions without trial of Ireland's most heroic Volunteers; as well as beatings and brutality by Free State authorities against anti-Treaty partisans, which poisoned nascent national pride and hope; with lasting shame which continues to this day. The Civil War ended in Ireland's triumphant unity shattered, her greatest leaders dead, her economy sunk by millions in damage, her heart broken.

In this light, Collins' death certainly would have been a key British goal of the Civil War. In this sense, the war served largely as a cover for the elimination of himself, his closest associates and most able commanders, like Harry Boland, Rory O'Connor, Liam Lynch. At the same time, it conveniently provided a scapegoat, to draw culpability away from the British; while simultaneously sowing division among the Irish, and discrediting their self-government.[234]

The Free State got their unconditional surrender; but it proved something short of peace. The Cosgrave government's mentality of denial meant that the split of the Civil War, and many War of Independence issues, were never resolved. The conflict merely took another shape, in a civil cold war which smouldered for decades. Flaring up occasionally, it ultimately re-erupted in the conflagration of the Troubles (1970s-1990s).

The closing lines of Deasy's memoire, recalling the anti-Treaty surrender, are particularly significant:

> *On this same date seven years previously the forces of the Republic had surrendered to overwhelming British forces in Dublin and just as the leaders of that time saw not the end of a dream but merely a prelude to the resurgence of the Spirit of Ireland, we too felt that even in this bitter defeat we had advanced another step towards Ireland free and undivided.*

---

[234] A look at the Dead Sea Scrolls may give an idea of the great longevity of such tactics: Scholars believe that these venerable documents now suggest that the Hebrew philosopher we know as Jesus may have been in fact a leader of guerrilla insurgents against the Roman occupation. Consider the manner in which that famous martyr was likewise executed by colonial authorities; who then blamed his death on his own persecuted-but-tenacious ethnic minority. The London government may with justice claim an indirect descent from the Roman colonial administration; and certainly have been fond of styling themselves after that ancient empire.

We hope so. Yet, as a military strategy, the Civil War was above all a crashing military failure. As its military leader, Lynch is answerable for that catastrophe. The anti-Treaty officers, in taking up arms against former comrades, published their opinion that this course was preferable to the one Collins pointed out. In taking up arms against him, they expressly rejected Collins' leadership.

In the lifetime of those who survived, DeValera would at length adopt precisely the same kind of "stepping stone" strategy which Collins advocated: establishing beyond reasonable doubt that, even from the grave, The Big Fella remained the real leader of Ireland.

W T COSGRAVE

After Collins' assassination, when Cosgrave publicly assumed the Chair of the Dublin government, Churchill was lavish in his praise. "*In Cosgrave the Irish people found a chief of higher quality than any who had yet appeared.*" It seems, according to Churchill, Cosgrave was as brave as Collins and as wise as Griffith; with the added attraction of having no embarrassing British secret service blood on his hands.

The new Chairman was understandably eager to laugh this off, as due to nothing more than his having once made a polite inquiry after Churchill's recovery from a fall at polo. Yet history has spoken. There is no question that Cosgrave's accession solved a lot of problems for the British, and ended hopes for any immediate solution to certain Irish problems: partition, a pogrom regime in the North, continuous sniping from an alienated IRA, to name only a few.

Nor did Mr Cosgrave's hands in the end come away altogether clean. His leadership meant an end to chances for an early and amicable end to the Civil War, and dashed forever all hope for the reunification of the army. He presided personally over the Civil War's most horrendous escalation, as the Free State cast aside all possible terms except unconditional surrender, and embarked on an aggressive program of extermination.

The execution of many War of Independence heroes was a decision taken on his watch, which he stridently embraced and defended. This was the other side of the coin, to the "altar boy" minister, writing pious prayers, as he cowered in fear of gunmen in the streets.

Not unlike DeValera, his tenure in office threatened to be a fulfilment of the Protestants' bogey: "Rome rule". He proposed tearing down the GPO to build a cathedral in its place; and also suggested that all Dáil legislation should be submitted to the Church for approval. DeValera was swept into power in 1932 largely in reaction again Cosgrave's repressive regime (combined with global financial crisis which followed the 1929 stock market crash.)

THE BURNED FILES

> *The outgoing government had issued a directive that documents relating to three classes of incident were to be destroyed: those dealing with courts martial, executions and - the death of Collins.*[235]

As the years passed, questions about Collins' death multiplied; and also about the Free State government's role. *"With the ending of the Civil War ... [there was] mounting suspicion of government negligence"*[236] concerning Béal na mBláth.

Just before the accession of Fianna Fail in 1932, the Cosgrave government engaged in the systematic destruction of large numbers of official records. A soldier who took part in that burning reported seeing a large, well-bound file concerning Michael Collins; as well as files on the composition of courts martial, and firing squads in Civil War executions.

Of course, the obvious question is, as Feehan posed it, *"If there was nothing to hide, why were the documents burned?"* He details a list of papers *"believed"* to have gone up in smoke: Dr Oliver St John Gogarty's autopsy of the C-in-C, all Collins' confidential Civil War files, including his investigation of the high-ranking British mole *"Thorpe"*:

> *This particular charge concerning the burning of documents has been published on and off in books and newspapers over the past twenty years, yet neither the government, the army, nor the Fine Gael* [237] *party have contradicted it.*

It has been argued that the Dublin government's complicity in covering up the facts of Collins' death may be explained away in a benign

---

235   T P Coogan

236   J Feehan

237   The Fine Gael party, founded by WT Cosgrave, constituted the out-going government responsible for the order to burn the files.

fashion. That his killing was the accidental result of the fledgling Irish state's weakened condition, poor planning, embarrassing oversights, etc. And that these were kept secret for the public good: to prevent instability, anarchy, etc., during the Irish state's delicate formative years. In wartime or other national emergencies, the danger of panic or instability, might be said to justify keeping some information from publication. It does not explain what the government was still so anxious to hide, *ten years later.*

Coogan even suggests that facts about drinking by Collins' party, and sensitivity to embarrassment that this might cause his own family, was a reason. (That is to say, they burned all those papers because Collins had something to hide: not them!)

Whatever could be said to excuse a lack of transparent public inquiry in 1922, there was no excuse in 1932. The burning of records, ten years after the fact, could have no benign purpose. It strongly tends to indicate that facts were buried: to protect some parties, who still had a great deal to lose, should those facts become known.

THE NORTH AFTER COLLINS

Predictably, Collins and his circle were replaced by a government more conciliatory to Crown interests: in their supine acceptance of Britain's land-grab of six northeastern counties (without reference to wishes of the majority in Fermanagh and Tyrone); and in their hostility to republican resistance there. Under Cosgrave, no matter how many men, women or children were slaughtered in the northeast, the B-Specials would henceforth be safe from either protest or interference from Dublin.

> *Collins' death removed the one leader in the pro-Treaty side who had consistently made partition and the position of the northern nationalists a primary consideration in determining policy. ... [Said Belfast OC Seamus Woods] "The attitude of the present government is not that of the late General Collins."*
>
> *Cahir Healy, the Fermanagh Sinn Fein leader, then an internee on board the prison ship Argenta in Belfast Lough, was more caustic: "We have been abandoned to Craig's mercy."* [238]

The Civil War cemented partition, by destroying Irish unity, at the moment when it was sweeping all before it. As *"architect of the Civil War"*

---

238 E Phoenix

DeValera was the chief enabler of partition. If indeed he was the real secret turncoat for British imperial interests in this saga, he couldn't have served them better. As Coogan observed, "*The Border was not altered by one millimeter throughout DeValera's long reign.*"

DEVALERA: A LONG BUT NOT PROSPEROUS REIGN

It's my considered opinion that in the fullness of time, history will record the greatness of Michael Collins. And it will be recorded at my expense.

- Eamonn DeValera

By his own statement, DeValera explicitly and implicitly acknowledged his own belief that *he himself would be discredited, when the truth about Michael Collins was fully known*. There was no third way. DeValera could bask in his prominent position, only by virtue of maintaining a tight lid on the truth of what happened to Collins. He admitted this.

In 1922 DeValera had demanded "*rivers of blood*" to be shed, largely over the issue of an objectionable oath, required for taking government office. After presiding over the slaughter of those who had won the war in his absence, he took that same oath himself in 1932. When challenged on this, he said it was OK because he didn't really touch the Bible!

Just imagine how many lives might have been saved, if only he'd thought of this expedient sooner! If all the anti-Treaty TDs had taken this view, there might have been no Civil War!

DeValera came to power at the head of Fianna Fail, founded as an IRA electoral party. He styled himself as the ultra radical uncompromising champion of republicanism. Only for his supporters to learn the hard way that he was not. Brought into power as the IRA candidate, DeValera lost little time in unleashing vicious crack-downs and draconian anti-republican policies, on those to whom he owed his exalted office.

Collins died trying to reunite those forces which had proved so formidable against British hegemony in Ireland. But not everyone shared that goal. *Au contraire*, unquestionably there were some who *wanted* lasting division. Most obviously, division was the number one British post-Truce agenda. What can be said of elements in Irish government who favoured the permanent marginalization of those who sought to oppose partition? Who favoured Irish society's permanent division along the lines of the Civil War?

The fact that partition remains to this day was due to DeValera stampeding the Dail deputies in 1921 into accepting partition as one of Lloyd George's conditions for entering into peace talks; his civil war in 1922, his refusal to return to the Dail at the urging of diehards like Austin Stack and the Labour Party to cast a deciding negative on the 1925 Boundary Commission decision, and ... his 1937 Constitution and Neutrality scam during WWII. He followed true to form by ignoring or squelching any action contrary to British interests during each of these crises. [239]

The successful preservation of Irish neutrality throughout World War II, saved DeValera's skin, and assured more of the same to dominate the post-war period. Ultimately, one of DeValera's supreme gifts was his knack for convincing whomever he wished, that he would be great for *them*. He could always persuade people that he was what *they* needed. So Feehan himself was indebted to DeValera for keeping men his age out of the battlefields of World War II. (A grateful generation which could act as a buffer between DeValera and survivors of the War of Independence / World War I era, as the latter began to see the light.)

As for the British ... Having delivered them Michael Collins' head on a silver platter, the Empire was stuck with him. They could not afford to discard him; and besides, he knew too much.

And so proceeded the domination of the south by successive conservative governments: persistently passive on partition, tough on the IRA, friendly to domination by foreign investors, and limp on the economy.

These presided over a deafening dearth of official discussion about the events of 1919-1923: that is, of the developments to which they owed their position. This glaring omission was impossible without government suppression of evidence, for decades afterward. This phenomenon rests squarely on the shoulders of those who held highest office, most often, 1923-1973; who may with reason be called the Civil War's ultimate Irish beneficiaries: DeValera and his party.

---

[239] J Turi

Chapter 19

What if Collins had lived?

The responsibility of the historian is to give to each past the open future it once had.

- Professor Ronan Fanning

An early end to the Civil War

Collins was acting swiftly and decisively to end the war with speed. Just imagine if he had succeeded! In light of all of the above, consider how it might have been, if his purpose at Béal na mBláth had been achieved.

> ... no serious discussion can be conducted on issues of this type unless we specify at all times our assumptions about alternatives - about what exactly we think would have happened, if only what did happen hadn't happened. [240]

No wonder he asked the Dáil to delay its session a few days for his return.[241] Wasn't he planning, not a *coup d'état*, but a typical Collins *coup de théâtre*: to march into the most dangerous rebel territory in Ireland, and march out victoriously, with the golden ring of a win-win negotiated peace.

In one brilliant stroke, he would have politically demolished his detractors, masterfully shrugged off the "bad guy" image which had recently smeared his public character, and got back his white "good guy" hat. Re-united the army, brought all his beloved comrades back into the fold. Sent the die-hards to protect Catholics from pogroms in Ulster; thumbed his nose at the British secret service (again); and blown off Machiavellian manoeuvres by DeValera.

It was high stakes indeed: not only for himself. He understood, as clearly as anyone, that Ireland's entire future was in the balance. It is small wonder he was ready to risk everything to make it happen.

---

240   J J Lee

241   The Third Dáil (that installed by the Pact elections) never met in Collins' lifetime. It convened for the first time on 9 September, two weeks after Béal na mBláth. Despite undertakings to accept the results of the June 1922 election, anti-Treaty elements took the position that only the second Dáil, and no subsequent legislature, constituted the legitimate representatives of the Irish Republic; a position curiously adhered to in some quarters even to the present day.

If peace had been negotiated in August 1922, the Civil War would have ended less than eight weeks after its start. Its worst violence would never have taken place. All the outstanding War of Independence leaders and heroes who died after August 1922, would instead have lived on, and taken prominent leadership roles in the new Ireland. (Either in the Free State government, in constitutional opposition thereto, and/or in a later Dublin republic, achieved by Collins' "stepping stone" strategy of gradually wearing away the most offensive points of the Treaty.)

Men like Liam Lynch, Rory O'Connor and countless others would not have died then, but might have been re-integrated into a regular Irish army. Or carried on in clandestine campaigns against extra-legal British aggression in the north.

THE REALISTIC IDEALIST

"A hero stands between the people and their destiny."
- Professor Daithi O hOgain

Consider what Ireland might have been, if Collins had survived as long as did many of his contemporaries. If he, a younger man, more vigorous and fit, had remained as active and prominent in public life, as long as DeValera did? Consider, if it had been Collins who presided over numerous governments, reigned as Taoiseach and/or President, continually from 1922 until the 1970s.

As head of the new Irish government, he would have differed from others who later assumed that role, just as he had differed from them before, when they worked together in the War of Independence. Not in that he was talented and gifted. He was surrounded by talented people. Although perhaps none so gifted as himself. Not alone in his devotion to the cause. Many were devoted to it. Although perhaps few as dedicated as he. Not only in his astounding capacity for work. Many gave their all, and would do anything for their country. Although few could do as much as he could.

Vision and principle

It was above all his vision, and his principles, which, combined with other outstanding strengths, set him apart from his contemporaries.

It has been said of some other leaders of the period, that they seemed to love the *idea* of "The Republic" more than the people in it. Collins was exactly the opposite. He was about the people, and the reality of their situation. With him, rhetoric was always subservient to them; not the other way around. Nor was he inclined to sacrifice them on the altar of elusive totems such as "honor".

He was guided by principles which were humane, reasonable and practical. Anyone could understand his principles: which may be called a distillation of the best traditional Irish values, combined with a modern progressiveness, driven by the national knack for creative innovation.

From farmer to statesman

As the product of a traditional Irish farming family, Collins was in a minority at the top. Most of those who went on to form governments, tended to come from the educated middle class, the intelligentsia, and/or the gentry.

This was at a time when the majority of the population lived a simple, rural, agrarian lifestyle; often in poverty and facing considerable hardships. A lion's share of the fighting men who won the war came from that background. Few of Collins' colleagues in government did. Hardly any of them understood the reality of people's lives as he did; or so valued those people themselves, as estimable individuals, whom he knew, respected, even revered.

Yet while deeply rooted in traditional, rustic culture, his vision was far-sighted. When no one dreamed of breaking the British secret service in Ireland, he *visualized* it. Planned it. Concocted the ways and means to do it. He studied and found out his opponent's strengths and weaknesses. He looked around him and drew together the personnel and tools to make maximum impact.

Unique intellectual and organizational gifts

> *Eloquence ... may become almost a curse. Patriotism is suspected, and sometimes sinks almost to pedantry. A Jovian intellect is hardly wanted, and clashes with the inferiorities. Industry is exacting. Honesty is impractical. Truth is easily*

offended. Dignity will not bend. But the man who ... has ever a kind word to speak, a pleasant joke to crack, who can forgive all sins, who is ever prepared for friend or foe, yet never very bitter with the latter, who forgets not men's names ... He is the man who will be supported in a crisis ... It is for him that men will struggle, and talk, and, if need be, fight, as though the very existence of the country depended on his political security.

- A Trollope

Imagine Collins, then: a man with all of these gifts: honesty, industry, 'Jovian' intellect, and also the kind word, the joke, the absence of bitterness.

This vision and these principles were served by capacities which characterized himself in particular, and in which he seems to have surpassed all those around him. The way he seized the most staggering, immense situations head on. He seemed to take them apart, and throw everything he had at them, with a voracious creativity. He penetrated and analysed labyrinthine new dilemmas with breathtaking speed and accuracy. It was as if he had ten brains going full throttle, in that one head.

Then his dynamic organizational ability translated all this into coordinated group action. His genius in this area alone would have guaranteed him a place in history. A brilliant multi-tasker, he reputedly *"never lost a piece of paper."* While, with uncanny penetration, he could assess in a flash the special capacities of each person, win their trust and their commitment with a few words, and inspire them to daring new achievements.

It's amazing indeed to review his blueprint for Ireland's future. When the new state had hardly been born, even while overwhelmed by devastating national and international crises, Collins was already grappling with Ireland's economic needs and challenges. He developed detailed, innovative strategies for attacking these issues from all sides at once.

God knows when he found the time, but he read voraciously, magazines and journals of all kinds. He studied all the latest technology, and what was being done in other countries: from Switzerland's special techniques for cultivating vertiginous mountainsides, to Dutch reclamation of marshlands, to public education programs in Germany. He became a walking treasure trove of all the most progressive ideas, in that golden era of socio-political, technological and cultural ferment. The best and most useful he translated into his own Irish form of realistic idealism.

Then, he acted. He took comprehensive, decisive action, without hesitation or delay.

These were the reasons why, as Coogan observed, his personality formed a better rallying point than any others who came after him; and *"was better equipped than most to make his dreams come true."*

HIS VISION FOR IRELAND

Collins had already begun unfolding plans for the nation's future, in correspondence and published articles. In the following, he is thus able to speak largely for himself. (All quotations in the following section are from Michael Collins, except where otherwise noted.)

He understood the country's resources, potential, and chronic dilemmas. He knew how much wealth this land had generated for foreign profiteers, for centuries. He believed that such abundance could be turned to benefit its own people instead.

It's sobering to see how many of the dilemmas and possible solutions, identified by him, remain at issue in Ireland today.

National financial plan

It's apparent that his nine years as a young banking professional had not been spent concentrating only on how to win promotion or a fat personal portfolio. His mind had been occupied with questions *"touching the welfare of his country."*

During the Treaty negotiations, Collins presented the British ministers with his calculations of over a billion pounds in reparations owed to Ireland. Decades before the term was embraced by international institutions, he sought restorative justice, regarding London's role in arresting Ireland's economic development, over hundreds of years. Clearly a Collins government would not (like Cosgrave) have agreed to saddle the Irish public with millions in "annuities" payments to British barons, for the right to occupy their own country!

> *Millions of Irish money are lying idle in banks. The deposits of Irish joint stock banks increased in the aggregate by £7,318,000 during the half-year ended 31 December 1921. At that rate the total of deposits and cash balances in Irish banks was £194,391,000 to which in addition there was a sum of almost £14,000,000 in the Post Office Savings Account. If Irish money were invested in Irish industries, to assist existing ones, and to finance new enterprises, there would be an enormous development of Irish commerce.*

> The Irish people have a large amount of capital invested abroad. With scope for our energies, with restoration of confidence, the inevitable tendency will be towards the return of this capital to Ireland. It will then flow in its proper channel. It will be used for opening new and promising fields in this country. Ireland will provide splendid opportunities for the investment of Irish capital, and it is for the Irish people to take advantage of these opportunities.
>
> If they do not, investors and exploiters from outside will come in to reap the rich profits which are to be made. And, what is worse still, they will bring with them all the evils that we want to avoid in the new Ireland.

Prophetic words indeed. This paraphrases John Connolly's observation, that removing the British flag and running up the tri-color, would, in itself alone, change few of Ireland's chronic problems.

Socio-economic justice

The following demonstrates Collins' recognition that, as Connolly said, "*The cause of Ireland is the cause of labour; and the cause of labour is the cause of Ireland.*"

> What we must aim at is the building of a sound economic life in which great discrepancies cannot occur. We must not have destitution or poverty at one end and at the other an excess of riches in the possession of a few individuals, beyond what they can spend with satisfaction and justification. The growing wealth of Ireland will, we hope, be diffused through all our people, all sharing in the growing prosperity, each receiving what each contributes in the making of that prosperity, so that the wealth of all is ensured. [242]
>
> The keynote to the economic revival must be ... that the people have steady work, at just remuneration, and their own share of control.

---

242 This resonates with the principle "*From each according to ability, to each according to need.*" Statements in this section clearly illustrate that while foreseeing and critical of state communism's flaws, Collins was not deaf to socialist arguments, which took a prominent part in international debate in his lifetime.

The uses of wealth are to provide good health, comfort, moderate luxury, and to give the freedom which comes from the possession of these things.

Our object in building up the country economically must not be lost sight of. That object is not to be able to boast of enormous wealth or of a great volume of trade for their own sakes, nor to see our country covered with smoking chimneys and factories. It is not to show a great national balance sheet, not to point to people producing wealth with the self-obliteration of a hive of bees.

The real riches of the Irish nation will be the men and women of the Irish nation; the extent to which they are rich in body and mind and character. What we want is the opportunity for everyone to be able to produce sufficient wealth to ensure these advantages for themselves. That such wealth can be produced in Ireland there can be no doubt.

The Irish nation is the whole people, of every class, creed and outlook. We recognise no distinction. It will be our aim to weld all our people nationally together who have hitherto been divided in political and social and economic outlook. Labour will be free to take its rightful place as an element in the life of the nation. [243] *In Ireland, more than in any other country, lies the hope of the rational adjustment of the rights and interests of all sections, and the new government starts with the resolve that Irish labour shall be free to play the part which belongs to it in helping to shape our industrial and commercial future.*

Above, he speaks of curbing unbridled exploitation of the many by the few: (a syndrome which had been one of the unwelcome imports of British rule.) At the same time, he foresaw the foibles of "state monopoly" type socialism (which was to prove so oppressive in the then-nascent Soviet Union.) [244] In this he favored worker-controlled for-profit cooperatives:

---

243 This statement was made at a period when the right of laborers to organize into unions, and seek their rights through collective bargaining, was still highly controversial. In the 1920s deadly attacks on organized labor, involving numerous fatalities, were a common occurrence, in Europe and the US. Indeed, in many countries, we can hardly call this entirely a thing of the past, even now.

244 Economic justice, capitalism and socialism were hot topics in the 1920s, as revolution

The development of industry in the new Ireland should be on lines that exclude monopoly profits. The product of industry would thus be left sufficiently free to supply good wages to those employed in it. The system should be on cooperative lines rather than on the old commercial capitalistic lines of huge joint stock companies. At the same time, I think we shall avoid state socialism which has nothing to commend it in a country like Ireland, and in any case, is a monopoly of another kind.

Agriculture and Industry

Of manufactured articles £48,000,000 worth are imported into Ireland yearly. A large part of these could be produced more economically at home.

Agriculture is, and is likely to continue to be, our chief source of wealth. ... We must establish industries arising directly out of agriculture, industries for the utilisation of the by-products of the land: bones, bristles, hides for the production of soda, glue, and other valuable substances.

While the Irish seas are teeming with fish we have the Dublin market depending upon the English fish market for its supplies. The export of Irish fish is decreasing, and the fishing industry is neither the source of remuneration it should be to those engaged in it, nor the source of profit it could be to the country.

---

rocked some of the largest countries, around the world. An entirely successful alternative to capitalism remains, at this writing, a work in progress, one hundred and fifty years after the words "socialism" and "communism" entered our vocabulary. Wherever such new systems have been successful, they seem to vary according to the unique character of each nation. (It is worth noting that socialism seems to have had little to do with the Russian and Chinese models' notorious flaws: more attributable to survivals from their old regimes, which revolution *failed* to change.)

Michael Collins promoting the latest tractor design; Fordson's Factory, Cork, June 1922. Mr Grace, Managing Director of Fordson's at left

Land reform

On land reform, Collins' agrarian background was most useful. Unlike others at his level of government, he had travelled the land and evaluated these issues first-hand, with the keen eye of a professional farmer.

> *If room is to be found for our growing populations, land must be freely available. Land is not freely available in Ireland. Thousands of acres of the best land lie idle or are occupied as ranches or form part of extensive private estates.*

> *There are some 20 million acres of land in Ireland, and of this about 7 million acres or one-third of the whole consist of waste land and bogs. Walk along the banks of almost any of our rivers and you will find a few fields' depth on each side of that river, and all along its course, are quite useless lands for cultivation. Now, if you can only sink those river-beds and drain those bogs you would bring enough new land into being to stop the national haemorrhage of emigration for the whole of the year. There you have the practical politics of our new day.*

Energy

Collins was likewise remarkably far-sighted on the subject of renewable energy and energy independence.

> *Water power is concentrated in her 237 rivers and 180 lakes ... The development of this white power will also enable the means of communication and transport by rail and road to be cheapened and extended. And there is urgent need for cheap transit.*

> *In the opinion of experts reporting to the Committee on the Water Power Resources of Ireland, from the Irish lakes and rivers a total of 500,000 horse power is capable of being developed. The magnitude of this is more readily seen if it is appreciated that to raise the power in steam would require 7,500,000 tons of coal. With the present price of coal it should be a commercial proposition to develop our water power as against steam. ... [through a] national power generator ... What Northcliffe described as the "White coal of Ireland" - hundreds of great waterfalls all over the country ...*

Ireland free of incursions by foreign intelligence agencies

> *Although [the British secret service] suffered a severe set-back at his hands, it was only a temporary set-back. The moment the Treaty had been signed and Collins otherwise occupied, they moved back in force and penetrated almost every department of public life in Ireland, particularly the army, the new police force, and the civil service.* [245]

Consider an Ireland with a world-class, state intelligence system of its own, designed and nurtured by Collins and his associates, training future generations, developing national strategy over decades, with one objective: to keep British / imperialist operatives out of Irish institutions.

Public education films

Collins' renowned sense of the dramatic and theatrical led him to form detailed plans for the use of the then-new technology of film. While weighed down by all the crushing concerns of 1922, he was composing screenplays, which would fuel and direct the public's energy and imagination.

> *[Film has been used this way] elsewhere with remarkable success. I hear that Germany has used very largely the cinema. Great and*

---

245   J Feehan

> quick results are bound to flow from there ... to focus the people's minds on the great problems of construction and retrenchment.
>
> [Screenplay concept:] ... picturesque photos showing the broad seas, calm, wild, etc., with such captions as "The Atlantic gold-mine - full of wealth for the taking of it." ... [Other segments should show] the poor, ill-equipped little fleets of the poor people ... This section will show the reason they are so poor and go as harvesters to England and Scotland. Show then the well-equipped up-to-date trawlers of Great Britain which poach on them. [Then say] Fellow countrymen, this is one of the problems. It rests with us now to equip these fishing folk and make them as prosperous as the English and the Scotch. To do this we must have peace and stable conditions in our country.
>
> [Screenplay concept:] ... photos showing the appalling distress ... the awful little huts of ... the Gaelic-speaking people ... their poor dress, food, their barren fields, sowing corn growing among great boulders I have seen in Donegal. Other pictures could show [by contrast] 1) Our barren mountainsides as they should be, [like] Swiss mountainsides covered with areas of noble pines and other trees ... [show] what Holland has done to save and reclaim her little land.
>
> I have thousands of other possible films in my mind ...

He had *thousands* of film scripts in his head! In the middle of the Civil War!

Public arts

> Irish art and Irish customs must be revived, and must be carried out by the people themselves, ... helped by departments of music, art, national painting etc. Everybody being able to contribute, we would have a skilled audience criticising and appreciating, and not only, as in England, paying for seats to hear famous performers.

Collins was a great patron of the arts. During his youth in London, he haunted the theatres, at a time when the century's leading luminaries, like Bernard Shaw and Isadora Duncan, were at their zenith. His thoughts above show the influence of Duncan (an Irish-American,) whose writing and speeches on these subjects were widely disseminated at the time. She famously crusaded for the arts, not as mere merchandise, but as a basic human need, which governments should deploy, to enrich the life of every child in society. [246] Her pioneering work in revolutionary Russia soon after set a new standard for mass education, in physical arts and fitness: later carried throughout the socialist world by her students. (Multitudes practising Tai Chi together, at public squares in China, are a legacy from the soviet Duncan School.) Since that time, numerous studies have proved the benefits of such arts programs: not only for fitness, but also higher math scores and decreased juvenile delinquence.

Revival of Irish culture and language

> *We are now free in name. The extent to which we become free in fact and secure our freedom will be the extent to which we become Gaels again. ... The machine of the British armed forces, which tried to crush us, we could see with our physical eyes. ... We could put our physical strength against it. ... We could see their tanks and armoured cars.*

> *But the spiritual machine which has been mutilating us, our customs, our independent life, is not easy to discern. But ... we can replace it. We can fill our minds with Gaelic ideas, and our lives with Gaelic customs ...*

> *The biggest task will be the restoration of the language. How can we express our most subtle thoughts and finest feelings in a foreign tongue? ... Until we have it again on our tongues and in our minds we are not free ...*

---

246 Duncan, a darling of high society in her early career, continually lobbied the great and good, to sponsor her holistic system, as part of a state educational institution. During the same period that Ireland won independence, one new government finally accepted her offer: Bolshevik Moscow. Despite alarmist assurances that they would all be slaughtered at the border, she relocated her dance school to the new communist Russia. Returning to Europe to raise funds, Isadora found herself swindled by impresarios, blacklisted and outcast, for her association with the soviets. She died in destitution a few years later. Imagine if Collins had lived, and offered a haven in Irish education, to such famous contemporaries.

Programs to erase national identity, ethnic culture and languages have historically been a routine practice of racists, imperialists, and colonialists. People's right to their language and culture has come to be recognized as intrinsic as our right to personal identity, ideas and relationships. The extinction of a culture, however obscure, subtracts from humanity's resources of experience and understanding. Preservation and celebration of culture has become central to social justice everywhere; (in a context of diversity, not sectarianism.) It's played a key role in Ireland's emergence as a modern democracy.

Ireland a light unto nations

> *We are a small nation. Our military strength in proportion to the mighty armaments of modern nations can never be considerable. Our strength as a nation will depend on our economic freedom, and upon our moral and intellectual force. In these we can become a shining light to the world.*

When all else fails, read the instructions

> *The past is not only about what happened, it's also about what might have happened, but didn't.*
> *- Brian Friel*

Much of the above writings were published in his lifetime. It was a matter of public record. It is offered that this may be just one more reason why certain elements in the British establishment were determined to remove him with speed: before his leadership could create national momentum in these directions. Because a secure, prosperous, united (and more Gaelic) Ireland, as economic competitor next door, was someone's worst nightmare. [247]

How topical his observations remain today. How tragic, that chance was missed to take such new directions. How much good could have been done by bringing his ideas on board, at a time when the re-structuring of the nation was on the table. How much damage was suffered, by more

---

247 Although, as British endorsement of Adolf Hitler demonstrated, worse things could happen.

entrenchment of the same old wrongs, long after the Union Jack was lowered, and the tricolor waved above Dublin Castle. Without Collins, the new republic stagnated for decades in a profound economic morass.

It was not until almost forty years later, that Sean LeMass (a veteran of the 1916 Rising and the Squad) successfully ushered in a new era of national prosperity. He explicitly credited Collins as the source for his ambitious and innovative programs. Yet few since then seem to have followed the suit.

Today, it is interesting to speculate whether Ireland would have fallen so utterly victim to the economic catastrophe of 2008-10: either on Collins' watch, or in an establishment built upon his high standards of national economic independence.

A DIFFERENT NORTH

[General Collins told us that] partition would never be recognized, even though it might mean the smashing of the Treaty. [248]

If Collins had lived on, and secured peace terms like those outlined in his correspondence, then republican soldiers determined to fight on would have flooded north to support beleaguered Irish suffering pogroms and mass displacement in Ulster. Combined with tenacious political pressure from Dublin, such actions could have greatly curbed British / unionist extra-legal aggression there.

A Dublin government which included Michael Collins would not have supinely rolled over for Britain's annexation of Tyrone and Fermanagh, which violated the Treaty's provisions that the statelet would include only areas where a majority approved it. He and the kind of national leadership his associates fostered, would have gone further in holding Britain to its agreements on the north.

Imagine men like Collins, Lynch, Rory O'Connor, Tom Barry and Dan Breen still working together, leading their War of Independence force, still intact, and with nothing to fight for but Ulster. It is safe to say they'd have had an impact on the military situation there.

It has been frequently pointed out, that the sort of campaign which was successful in the 26 counties, would not work in the North; that such attempts only intensified Orange terror there. Although he is frequently

---

[248] IRA Second Northern Division report, 1922, (National Library of Ireland)

faulted for reprisals suffered by Catholics, his successes are less talked about.

Having learned the hard way that the campaign in the north would require a different approach, Collins was pursuing a double policy: speaking softly and carrying a big stick. Far from thoughtlessly ploughing ahead with whatever had worked elsewhere, he was carefully revising and recreating tactics, to suit the special conditions. These ranged from détente negotiations with Craig; to a massive guerrilla operation, in which forty prominent dignitaries were kidnapped in daring, coordinated, overnight raids: to be held as security for the lives and homes of northern Catholics.

> *Collins put forward the idea of using the existence of nationalist-controlled councils in Tyrone, Fermanagh and adjoining areas to make partition unworkable, "and to reduce the partitioned counties to four." This suggests that as early as January 1921 Collins was beginning to formulate a northern policy which would attempt to achieve Irish unity by reducing the size of a northern state to non-viable proportions.* [249]

Characteristically, he had thoroughly exploited his time spent wrangling with London's masterminds of Empire. A studious reading of his action on the north, in the last months of his life, demonstrates that he was learning their game very, very fast.

Simultaneously, he was developing both physical and moral force manoeuvres. He made Churchill's life a misery of constant protests, meetings and demands for inquiries on extra-legal Orange killings. At the same time, while pursuing all-Ireland institutions, provided for in the Treaty, he was preparing for the worst: to turn his triumphant, re-united War of Independence army north, if necessary.

On this track, chances of success were considerably greater than most historians acknowledge. With his astute political sense, he would soon have realized that London was powerless to follow up its threats of all-out military invasion. This was the reason they'd sought peace in 1921: because England could not afford to alienate the (largely Irish-)American public. They needed American cooperation with Imperial goals in Asia and the Pacific. This is the reason, as soon as Macready reported (in 1921) that they could not hold Ireland except by all-out invasion and martial law, the Crown had to throw in the towel.

---

249   E Phoenix

Twenty-six united counties, led by Michael Collins and his War of Independence chiefs of staff, determined to protect Catholics in the north from a minority mob; and Britain unable to resort to all-out military invasion ... things in the north were likely to have developed very differently indeed.

One source says [250] that Collins secretly met with Sir Henry Wilson during this period. If so, could this have been reason enough to assassinate Wilson? Were there elements that keen to prevent détente between these two formidable generals?

> *There was quite a sensation here when yourself and Craig met. People were stunned, and charmed, and the place is full of Belfast travellers, ...*

So Kitty Kiernan relayed to him public reaction on the ground in County Longford: near the island's center, and strategically close to the six counties. Around the same time, the Liverpool Express, "*a deeply Orange and anti-Catholic paper*" printed a letter from an ex-serviceman, praising Collins, admiring Ms Kiernan, and Ireland generally:

> *One of the prettiest pictures in the Express has been that of Ms Kitty Kiernan, the intended bride of the Financial Minister of the Irish Free State. Not for a long time has the public been so highly favoured as by the good fortune of inspecting the picture of this lady, whose presence would grace the life of any man however highly placed, and whose inborn native beauty is portrayed in every outline of her life.*

> *In a country of beautiful women the reputation is well retained by the choice of one whose sagacity has been so wisely proven in his efforts for the advancement of his native land.*

These last lines, referring to Collins, speak volumes. One would hardly have seen eulogiums of this kind directed at, say, Gerry Adams, in any "*deeply Orange and anti-Catholic paper*" of the 1980s! Such sentiments, so placed, had a distinctly political overtone. Was not the *Express* thus preparing its readers to accept that a Collins government in Dublin might not be such a bad thing?

---

250   On condition of anonymity.

As Coogan observed, "*His development plans were all set in a united Ireland context.*" In 1922 Collins wrote:

> *[These methods will] utilize the water power of the Shannon, the Erne, the Bann and the Liffey. It is probable that the Liffey and the Bann, being closely connected with urban centres, can be dealt with at once.*
>
> *A prosperous Ireland will be a united Ireland. With equitable taxation and flourishing trade our Northeast countrymen will need no persuasion to come in and share the healthy economic life of the country.*

The ultimate border of Northern Ireland was by no means etched in stone while he lived. It is entirely possible that, with Collins and associates at the helm, his plan to make the northeast statelet non-viable, and unity more attractive, (whilst brandishing a very big stick against anti-Catholic terror) might have succeeded; thus evading decades of bloody conflict later on.

* * *

WHAT MIGHT HAVE BEEN

> *If only DeValera had gone to London, if only Collins hadn't signed the Treaty, if only DeValera hadn't opposed it, if only he hadn't withdrawn from the Dail, if only Collins had attacked the Four Courts immediately Rory O'Connor occupied it, if only he had delayed the attack further, if only he hadn't attacked it at all, if only he had attacked Northern Ireland, if only he had withheld all support from the IRA in the north, if only he hadn't deluded himself that he could cod Churchill with a 'Republican' Constitution, if only he had defied Churchill's insistence that the Constitution must stick to the letter of the Treaty, if only he hadn't sought compromise in the Pact election with DeValera, if only he hadn't denounced the Pact, if only, indeed, he had taken a different route ... on 22 August, and if only ... he had lived for - how long - and with what assumed consequences. Even this cursory list, which could be easily extended, makes it clear how littered with 'if onlys' our judgements are bound to be.*[251]

It seems safe to say that, whatever doubts may exist as to what Michael Collins *would* have done, as to whether things would have been different had he lived ... whoever killed him did *not* doubt it.

Imagine a mature Collins, pursuing these agendas for decades on end, with all the resources and support of a nation whose victory over the British was unclouded by crippling divisions; which had known no armed strife since the British left Dublin Castle; a nation which, despite all factions, recognized and accepted Collins as a key architect of Irish self-determination; in a political landscape rich with the independence movement's brightest lights, working together throughout the 20th century, to re-build a new Ireland.

Who can set a limit to what the country might have accomplished? Where it might be today? Where could Ireland go now, with a fuller appreciation of these ideas?

With full publication of all Collins papers, the future might still benefit greatly from a complete collection of his writings on these subjects.

---

251   J J Lee

Chapter 20

Revolution: Don't try this at home

It does not require a majority to prevail, but rather an irate, tireless minority.

- Samuel Adams

As observed above, Americans, in dealing with the Kennedy assassinations, have been hindered by emotional factors. In a sense not unlike Americans, Ireland is a relatively young republic: comparatively new to the modern consciousness of itself as a united, independent nation. That is, we've been at it for mere centuries; not for millennia.

The Béal na mBláth end of his story is not the part most attractive for Irish men and women, nor most calculated to make them proud. So one can understand why it has never been told quite this way before; although there is hardly any new evidence revealed here for the first time.

Is this what nationhood is all about? An understanding that reality is not a patriotic recruiting poster? It's not a picture post card Oirish fantasy, nor a Norman Rockwell icon. It's not even Ireland's Proclamation of 1916 or America's Declaration of Independence. These are national treasures. They represent our highest values; our highest collective "self", if you will. They may be the moral keystones of our national identity. And ... but ... they are not the whole story of who we are.

Such a proclamation or declaration may be the crest of a great tsunami of social change, which has been swelling beneath the waves for generations. It's not the "happily ever after." It's not the end of the story by any means. It's just the beginning. It's a gauntlet thrown down on the bloody pages of history. Corrupt this. In a sense, it's a declaration of war.

If nationhood is what happens after the proclamation, then the story of Michael Collins may be called a microcosm, even a skeleton key, if you will, of what follows.

Adulthood, for an individual, entails clearly seeing and accepting one's own faults and weaknesses, as well as one's strengths. Similarly for the adulthood of a nation: Doesn't it mean facing the ugly facts of history, along with the heroic inspiration? And any nation with a memory longer than the last century may be painfully conscious that its own government can be its worst enemy.

You're a beast.

You're an angel.
You can crawl.
You can fly too.

- J Mitchell

So modern republics celebrate their founding revolutions, and canonize revolutionary leaders. But kids, don't try this at home. Revolution is always a gamble, of the highest stakes possible. Its outcome can be *"more unpredictable than the results of a first-rate European war."* [252] The "good guys" don't always win. Overturning an entrenched, abusive regime often means the shattering of social orders. Thus ripping the fabric of society opens the door to change: for better or worse. It can invigorate society with new ideas and opportunities; and/or expose it to opportunists and backlash, very far from the aims of idealistic insurgents. Because the jungle is always out there, ready to encroach on the civilizations carved out of it.

The assassination of great popular leaders, at a key cresting pinnacle of the monumental social upheaval which had brought them to prominence, in which they are the man of the hour ... is one of the terrible tragedies common in revolution. Assassinations often occur in the context of such great convulsions, when the institutions of society are in flux. Under such conditions, suspects are many, circumstances are complicated, and mutating in unprecedented ways as the situation unfolds.

Does it always take more than one generation? To extricate the tangled web in which the authors of such crimes know so well how to cover their escape? Because defeating popular rebellion, turning its weapons on itself, and slaying its best and brightest in the confusion: these are skills that go right back to the Roman empire. They're all covered in third level imperialism "101".

These are risks not to be undertaken lightly. Neither can any lunatic fringe jump-start such changes. The leaders themselves are often very much taken by surprise. Or, like President Kennedy, unexpectedly called to take a stand, by a long-suffering population who, one day, wake up to find they're *"fired up and can't take no more."*

Two kinds of courage enabled the nation to struggle out of bondage - the patient, enduring courage that willed survival in the long years

---

[252] George Bernard Shaw

of defeat; and the flashing, buoyant courage that struck manfully, challenging fortune. [253]

Revolutions are born, not made. A movement for political change which has lain dormant underground for years, decades or centuries may, like in Ireland, suddenly rear up, and sweep all before it. Their greatest leaders don't so much choose the time, as recognize, and seize it.

It is the necessary nature of a political party ... to avoid, as long as it can be avoided, the consideration of any question which involves a great change. There is a consciousness ... that the pressure from behind, forcing upon them great measures, drives them almost quicker than they can go, so that it becomes a necessity with them to resist rather than to aid the pressure which will certainly be at last effective by its own strength. The best carriage horses are those which can most steadily hold back against the coach as it trundles down hill

- A Trollope

Evolutionary appetite

The landless younger son ... who without power, privilege or patronage, rose meteorically to become the political leader of his country, and its most skilful general. This man ... has remained in popular belief the undoubted, undisputed hero of the Wars of Independence ... At the same time however, his character was vilified by English propagandists ... On one side, he was a patriot, a hero and a martyr; on the other a brigand, a traitor and a bloodthirsty outlaw ... In an era when the natural leaders - the earls, barons and great magnates and prelates betrayed their country for their own selfish ends, ... he shines forth as the one man who never swerved for an instant in his devotion to liberty. Almost miraculously he was to lead the common people in a struggle against the finest army in Europe, and defeat it. Such a hero must be endowed with personal prowess, physical and moral courage, a lofty devotion to duty and spiritual qualities ... Nevertheless historical research ... has gone far to confirm many things ... which

---

253 F O'Donoghue

for a long time were treated as imaginary and the real features of the man are found ... to be of an even nobler type.

Sound like Michael Collins? The foregoing paragraph is from J Mackay's biography of William Wallace, Scotland's great hero of the 14th century Wars of Independence. What do these popular leaders, so far separated by time and place, have in common? What was similar about their lives and deaths and struggles?

Consider also Emiliano Zapata (assassinated en route to peace negotiations); Augusto Sandino (assassinated under cover of peace negotiations); Che Guevara (eased out by former comrades as the revolution consolidated victory); Mahatma Ghandi, Salvador Allende, Martin Luther King, the Kennedies, Patrice Lamumba ... The list goes on.

Why would and why do such gifted people sacrifice themselves for the common good? Shaw observed:

There are forces at work which use individuals for purposes far transcending the purpose of keeping these individuals alive and prosperous and respectable and safe... Men will in the pursuit of knowledge and of social readjustments for which they will not be a penny the better and are indeed often many pence the worse, face poverty, infamy, exile, imprisonment, dreadful hardship, and death. Even the selfish pursuit of personal power does not nerve men to the efforts and sacrifices which are eagerly made in pursuit of extensions of our power over nature, though these extensions may not touch the personal life of the seeker at any point. There is no more mystery about this appetite for knowledge and power than about the appetite for food: both are known as facts and as facts only, the difference between them being that the appetite for food is necessary to the life of the hungry man and is therefore a personal appetite, whereas the other is an appetite for evolution, and therefore a superpersonal need.

Mainstream historians and commentators are frequently heard to reduce the aims of revolutionary leaders to the lowest common denominator; attempting to explain away extraordinary lives in ordinary terms

But the round peg of revolutionary heroism does not fit the square hole of day-to-day politics-as-usual. History demonstrates over and over that not only individuals, but entire peoples may, in a national emergency, rise in a body above the normal ruling drives of personal gain and personal preservation, for a great common good. While lives like Wallace, St Joan, and Collins inspire folkloric beliefs in the collective capacity of a given people to miraculously generate out of their own body politic, precisely the necessary new, dynamic leadership called for, just at the time and place it is most needed. Not unlike the cells of a human body generating a new chemical, to cure itself of a life-threatening disorder.

The culture of assassination

Just the same, this writer is no partisan of the "great man" school of history. Just someone who was seven years old in 1963; and twelve in 1968. Who witnessed and deeply felt the culture of assassination impinge on our life and world, in their most formative moments.

> *For what chance ever have the brave left captainless - what fate but to be trampled down by the fools and cowards?*
> *- Standish O'Grady "The Gael" 1903*

Assassination of key people, at key moments, is a key tool of imperialism. It is a favored tool, because it works. Its damage can be deep and lasting. It can set the world back twenty years.

This was no less true of Chile in 1973 than of Ireland in 1922. Both were examples of government-by-assassination. But such murders never stand alone. They form part of a context of slaughter, which enable other deaths. In both cases, the elimination of one man, who represented millions of voters, enabled the mass murder of virtually an entire movement, along with him.

Although a minute study and comparison of such assassinations may not form a department at any major university [254] ... It ought to. Until there is such a department ... your local conspiracy theorist may be as good as it gets.

Parallels between Collins' end and that of other outstanding political prophets are many. Like President Kennedy's, it inspired a dumbfounded prostration of grief in his public. Despite outrage and incisive questions in some quarters, those who most profited by his death were able to control

---

[254] *"Some criminology texts cover assassinations as political crimes; yet the discussion invariably is reduced to the assassin's psychology"* K D Tunnel, *Journal of Criminal Justice Education* Vol 4, Issue 1

and stifle public inquiry, for a generation after. Because people are dependent on political leaders to explain the politics to them.

There may be some comfort today in a circumspect appreciation of civil war and partition as the basic tools of imperialism: a standard antidote to successful revolution. Ireland may have been the first, but this genocidal game of bait-switch-and-partition has since had a long run in "theatres" of struggle all over the former colonized world, from Israel to Vietnam.

A systematic destruction of records, inscriptions, statues, monuments, etc., often accompanied regime change in the ancient world. The doctoring of official history through the control of academic institutions is likewise found in the standard tool kit of every imperialist regime since the Egyptians. Because forewarned is forearmed.

We will never tell anyone who we are until we know who we are.
We will never go anywhere until we know where we are.
- Malcolm X

The control of this history is still important: there remain prominent political elements today who continue heavily invested in preventing exposure of the facts regarding Michael Collins' death. It is uncovering those facts which will tell us most about why this should be so.

Epilogue

Europe 1933 - 1945

But in history, as in travelling, men usually see only what they already had in their own minds; and few learn much from history, who do not bring much with them to its study.
- John Stuart Mill

In terms of aftermath, it is important to consider another nearby development, which speaks to the victories and tragedies played out in Ireland. It has been observed that this drama was not isolated, but part of a larger context of explosive political ferment throughout Europe at that time.

Germany in particular was the cradle of the largest and most powerful socialist movement on the Continent. Like other countries, World War I wrote finis there to the old monarchist regime who'd spawned it. Yet Europe's rickety new republics often proved unequal to the economic crisis which the war had bequeathed.

About the time Collins was forcing an Empire to talk terms, an obscure corporal was convalescing in a forgotten bed of a German military hospital. Along with some others in his predicament, he could not accept the idea of Germany's defeat; and so became obsessed with the idea that it was anti-war agitation by socialists, Jews and liberals at home, which had cheated them of victory.

A few years later, now a fully qualified fanatic, this humble foot soldier joined the growing ranks of street corner soap box orators. He found followers. They formed a party. In keeping with the spirit of the times, they called themselves a socialist party. The Nationalist Socialist Party (known to us as the Nazi Party.)

Now, although government in London had been virulently hostile to Collins, it was less resistant to Adolf Hitler. All in all, influential British elements found him a more congenial character altogether. It could in fact be said with justice that Hitler owed much of his success to this friendliness from London. That is, he could hardly have risen as he did, when he did, without their cooperation.

Without the welcoming smiles of British Prime Minister Neville Chamberlain, the Third Reich's great war machine would have been stillborn.[255] Its panzer divisions might never have been built. Because according to the Treaty of Versailles, Germany was forbidden to re-arm. They were not permitted to have an army.

But Britain and their allies stood silently by when, after publishing his blueprint for *leibensraum* military expansion, Hitler began building his tanks and munitions factories. The Allies were empowered by the Treaty of Versailles to intervene, with physical force if necessary, anytime Germany should engage in such re-arming. They praised Hitler in their speeches, defended his rhetoric, and passively watched the tank divisions, bankrolled by American industrialists, grow. (Hitler's moving pre-war peace speeches should be required reading for every first year student of political science.)

Yes, Michael Collins and Adolf Hitler: just about exact contemporaries. Let's consider these two, side by side. Let's examine their ideas, their plans and vision, as set forth in their writings. Let's look at the welcome they received from Europe's great and good, and how far it carried them in their respective careers. Let's look at all they contributed to their countries, and to world history. Let's ask why was one promising statesman cut down so young, while the other flourished: first as London's friend, later as their foe

One born a subject of the British Empire; a days' journey from its capital. Yet, in his own view, obliged by patriotism to take arms against England. A brilliant organizer, tactician and statesman, he ultimately won the respect and admiration of even the very warlords whom he had humiliated. He was moderate in his political views, humane toward adversaries and generous to the vanquished. He opposed racism, sexism and sectarianism, welcoming "*all the children of the nation equally*" into the new Irish state. He abhorred religious strife. He never gave countenance to the politics of pogrom, but upheld the values of the 1916 Proclamation, eschewing "*cruelty, inhumanity or rapine*."

Hitler was the offspring of England's hereditary foe, the Austro-Hungarian Empire. He too had fought against the British in the World War I era (although with less success than Collins.) No one could plead ignorance as to what Hitler intended to do. He never made any secret of it. The war and the concentration camps and the mass genocide were all there in black

---

255 That young king Edward, so romanticized for abandoning his throne "*for the woman he loved*," was particularly cozy with Hitler. Absolute monarchy as a form of government was not nearly so dead an issue in Europe in the 1930s, as it seems now. Edward embraced much of the Nazi Party's outlook, and sought to import it: after all, he was king, wasn't he? His abdication was necessitated not only by his fiancé's divorce status: Wallis Simpson's chatty relations with the German embassy also set the British cabinet aghast. Edward was given a choice; and the rest is history.

and white, for the world to read at their leisure, in his bestseller "*Mein Kampf*". And he did exactly what he said he would do.

The one assassinated in his prime; arguably with the collusion of the British regime, at least; if not by their express order. The other patronized, coddled and enabled by London, to the devastation of their neighbours and allies on the Continent ... Until the viper they'd nursed in their breast turned on themselves.

The loss of life and property in the Nazi bombardment of London was one of the worst military catastrophes in English history; dwarfing by comparison all the casualties and damage attributable to Irish insurgency in a hundred years.

So much for conventional wisdom of the powers that be. What was really dangerous, and what was good, for British interests?

A secure, united, egalitarian Ireland next door? Or friendly fascists on the Continent?

Afterword

Republicanism and Michael Collins Today
Demonization or Canonisation?

Saint Joan of Arc was not canonized until six hundred years after her death. To this day, the religious authorities do not recognize her as a "martyr" *per se*. This is understandable: she was condemned to death by a jury of Catholic bishops. If she was a martyr, then the Church's own bishops executed its own holy saint, for her faith!

Joan is now considered one of the founders of modern nationalism: the idea that people of a given land, united by shared language, culture and history, have a collective identity, as a "nation"; and that such a national identity endows them with common interests, rights and responsibilities, in connection with that land.[256]

Interestingly enough, she finally got sainthood in the very year that Ireland's revolution was at its climax: 1920. Soon after, George Bernard Shaw (one of Collins' favorite dramatists) wrote his classic play. It is no coincidence that, in his preface discussing Joan's political predicament, Shaw made several references to the Irish struggle and its leaders: [257]

> *The fear inspired ... [by a mental giant is immeasurable and unbearable] when there is no presumption of guarantee of its benevolence and moral responsibility: in other words, when it has no official status. The legal and conventional superiority of Herod and Pilate ... inspires fear; but the fear, being a reasonable fear of measurable and avoidable consequences which seem salutary and protective, is bearable; whilst the strange superiority of Christ and the fear it inspires elicit a shriek of Crucify Him from all who cannot divine its benevolence. Socrates had to drink the hemlock, Christ to hang on the cross, and Joan to burn at the stake ... Many terrifying but quite comprehensible official scoundrels die natural deaths in all*

---

256 Under feudalism, the general population was not officially recognized as having any identity or relationships, outside of vassalage to the ruling baron, whatever he might be.

257 Shaw held that Joan's trial for heresy and witchcraft was more fair than the trial of Sir Roger Casement, for his part in the 1916 Easter Rising.

the glory of the kingdoms of this world, proving that it is far more dangerous to be a saint than to be a conqueror.

Although now officially canonized by Hollywood, Michael Collins is not a subject without controversy in Ireland at this writing. The Irish republican movement of today has its roots in the anti-Treaty side of the Civil War. It is still grappling with the yet unfinished business of that era. Ireland remains partitioned, and pogroms against Catholics still ring in living memory. A united 32-county republic remains a dream.

Collins is a painful quandary for this movement. Historically, there is a traditional identification with DeValera, as leader of the anti-Treaty side in the Dáil. Therefore a certain anti-Collins outlook has been inherited from anti-Treaty rhetoric of that period.

Is it time for a re-assessment? Family tradition, folk belief, and parochial pamphlets have struggled to fill the vacuum created by Dublin's failure to facilitate transparent, independent, public inquest and academic discussion. Such failures have fostered lack of faith in academic institutions and "official" histories: allowing outlandish rumours, long disproved, to be kept alive: such as that Collins ordered Harry Boland's death, or that his convoy in West Cork was hunting DeValera. [258] Careless analysis and irresponsible sensationalism has enabled and encouraged such posthumous character assassination. (Suggesting that, for some people, Michael Collins is still not quite dead enough yet.)

The promoter of the false charge simply expresses his gratification at finding that he had been misled [by erroneous information.] It is not customary for him to express gratification ... that, out of all the mud which he has thrown, some will probably stick!

- A Trollope

Is the demonization of Collins connected to guilt complex regarding his death? Is it linked to an assumption that the ambushers killed him?

If the anti-Treaty men did *not* shoot Collins, if they never had any intention of shooting him, never claimed responsibility for shooting him ... Does that require a new outlook on him in republican quarters? If the IRA is

---

[258] Certainly if Collins had had any intentions in that way, it would not have been DeValera who survived the war. It would also have been wholly uncharacteristic of Collins either to drive around in an armoured car for such a purpose, or to miss hitting his target.

off the hook, does that contribute something to the encroaching realization: that demonizing Collins is an obsolete analysis?

During the War of Independence, the Irish were far from perfectly united. But nationalism constituted one umbrella movement. With, by and large, widespread support from the common people.

Under the guise of the Truce and peace negotiations, the British ran the bait-switch-and-partition routine, which took that away. The movement was split up, set up and shot down. Yes, there were elements in leadership who, as the Irish have historically come to expect, sold out the popular victory for a piece of the pie. Some heroes of the struggle were shot by former comrades, some by former British soldiers in green uniforms, some by firing squads and some by secret service assassins. Some were beaten and died in Free State custody. Some fell to anti-Treaty mines.

> *Now two Russias will be facing each other. Those who were sent to prison. And those who sent them there.*
> — *Anna Akhmatova*

The Republic and the republican movement today have suffered from these flaws in their foundations. A lot of politics and policy have been based on what happened in the War of Independence and Civil War. Yet as Collins' story itself demonstrates, that period remains so controversial, that there is still a great deal of confusion about what in fact actually did happen. That child-bed of the nation was so recent, so chaotic and volatile, that public discussion and public record about it has been distorted: both in institutions of the south, and in republican rhetoric of the north. [259]

> *The perverting impact of the Troubles upon Irish history and historiography since 1969 is but an example of the axiom that truth is the first casualty of war. Thus arch-revisionism at its most extreme insists that nothing must be said or written about the effective use of violence in the Irish past, in case it gives comfort to those who use violence in the Irish present ... Some seem to have*

---

[259] B. Feeney's otherwise excellent *"Sinn Fein: a Hundred Turbulent Years"* is likewise marred by its assumptions identifying Collins with "sell-out" and DeValera with "hold-outs". However, Mr. Feeney fails to present any supportive evidence on that view, which would facilitate discussion.

tacitly embraced as their slogan John Cleese' catch-cry in the German tourist episode of Fawlty Towers: 'Don't mention the war!' [260]

With institutionalized suppression of historical research (see Forward) the public often had little but oral traditions to judge by. Without access to reliable, scholarly analysis, it has been all but impossible to make an accurate assessment of that era, or of its meaning for subsequent generations. We are only beginning to unravel that story now.

This has sometimes allowed mistaken analysis, misfired arguments, rumour or open wounds to stand in the place of history. Such errors have in some quarters been carried on and enshrined like some sacred scroll; as Ireland wandered through the wilderness of the 20th century.

Since the 1970s, new generations, wrestling with the legacies of the War of Independence and Civil War, have brought new hope, new conflicts, tragedies and victories. From abstentionism to hunger strikes to air strikes, the realities on the ground in partitioned Ireland have struggled toward the light of progress.

This process has frequently entailed the careful overhaul of traditional outlooks, which were handed down from past generations, who were closer to the Civil War. While revering the noble motives of anti-Treaty founders, this movement's greatest achievements have turned on the most terrible lesson of the 1920s: that a split in the army *must* be avoided *at all cost*.

It has long been recognized, by and large, that any canonization of DeValera was premature. It is hoped that, with better scholarship about the independence struggle, any lingering demonization of Michael Collins will soon be abandoned. Hopefully, it will be fully recognized, that his alienation from anti-Treaty republicans was the type of tragic error, which is an occupational hazard of revolution.

The records are no longer shrouded in mystery: Collins consistently resisted hostilities with former comrades, and continually sought terms acceptable for them. Only with his death came the terrible damage which he foresaw, and which he died trying to prevent: deep divisions of searing acrimony, which carried on for generations after. More than the demise of any one leader, it was these divisions, still not yet resolved, between nationalists themselves (north and south, insurgent and establishment,) which stopped the independence struggle in its tracks, and crippled its progress since.

---

[260] R Fanning

Throughout his short but brilliant career, Collins was determined to oppose partition, not passively, but actively. As long he lived, he continued military support from the south for embattled Catholics in the north. As leader of the Provisional Government, he assured that support from Dublin, with the backing of the State army. *Something which, after his death, never happened again.*

It can now be established, beyond reasonable doubt, that he lost his life in an attempt to end the Civil War without rancor. He died trying to bring friends and comrades back to their leadership positions in Ireland's military; to re-unite the army, and focus it on ending partition.

> *For no greater love than this hath any man: that he should lay down his life for his friends.*
> - John 15:13

Many of the tactics he fostered are still favored by republicans today. In the 26 counties, his plan was the one ultimately fulfilled: because his opponents had no other to offer. His argument was proved by the very detractors who had rejected it.

That unsuccessful rejection of his leadership created the split which launched the Civil War. The Civil War cemented partition: with his lifeblood, and that of so many other heroes of the War of Independence. Once these were divided or dead, there was no one able to stop it.

Likewise, the entrenchment of partition, the concurrent stagnation of republican militarism, followed by the IRA's revival, and the conflict of the 1970s - 1990s, have all seemed to prove Collins right again: that only an underground, guerrilla opposition could make headway against partition; while minimizing pogroms and civilian devastation. This again, turned out to be the very strategy embraced and carried to ultimate victory by the remnant of anti-Treaty republicanism.

Does exonerating Collins mean condemning DeValera? From his own statement ("*the greatness of Michael Collins ... will be recorded at my expense.*") DeValera seemed to think so.

Does all this mean we must choose between demonizing one of them? Yet perhaps one of the lessons here is that to kill for political domination is fundamentally *human*. Some will kill reluctantly, for national justice and self-determination. And this is *because* others will not shrink from slaughtering multitudes, simply to become or remain the most powerful individual in their place and time.

The record is clear: although Collins signed the Treaty, it was DeValera who secretly agreed to partition, as a pre-condition, before the Treaty could even be negotiated. DeValera long since ultimately proved soft on partition, tough on republicans and false to the movement. Albeit Collins was the bearer of the bad news, he was consistently anti-partition, and never abandoned the north.

The general public today is more sophisticated than in 1922. They are better acquainted with the pitfalls of negotiation; and with the Machiavellian divide-and-conquer tactics, which popular progressives must often face.

The tragic lessons of the Civil War have been learned; the hard way. Let us honor all those who bought us that precious experience, at the cost of their lives.

Appendices

APPENDIX 1: THE ESCORT

Convoy vehicles
One Rolls Royce armoured car,
> (Fleet number ARR 2, dubbed the "*Sliabh na mBan*" (English spelling "*Slievenamon*")

One Crossley tender
One Leyland Thomas straight-8 touring car
One motorcycle

Convoy's weaponry
Vickers machine gun (on a turret, in the armoured car)
Lewis machine gun (with the troops in the Crossley tender)
Rifles (.303(?) and pistols (troops in the Crossley tender, the C-in-C & other officers
and drivers)
Mauser pistols (the C-in-C, Dalton, possibly other officers)

Riding in the Leyland Thomas touring car
General Michael Collins, Commander in Chief
Major General Emmett Dalton
Private M B Corry, driver (replacing Collins usual driver, Jack Swan)
M Quinn, co-driver
(Fionán Lynch sat next to the C-in-C as far as Limerick)

Riding in the Crossley tender (lorry)
Commandant Sean (Paddy) O'Connell (commanding the tender)
> Capt. Conroy, driver; Sgt. Cooney, co-driver

Eight soldiers, reputedly including:
> Private Carmody   Private Barry
> Captain Peter Conlon   Private Coote
> Private William McKenna   Private Edmunds
> Private John O'Connell
> Plus two Lewis machine gunners (Lieut(?) Gough and Murray

(Total in the Crossley tender: twelve)

Riding in the armoured car
Private Jock McPeak (gunner for water-cooled Vickers machine gun)
Jim Wolfe, driver
Private Jimmy "Wiggy" Fortune, co-driver
Private Wally Cook

[Captain Joe Dolan(?)]
(Normal armoured car crew was four men; a second gunner was alternately reportedly changed at Cork City, left behind in Cork City or altogether missing from the usual complement.

Captain Joe Dolan is sometimes referred to as commanding the armoured car. He and/or another man, possibly an officer, may have ridden either inside and/or outside at given times.)

Riding the motorcycle
Lieut. John Joseph Smith, "scout"

Appendix 2:

The Accounts by Eye-Witnesses

1) Lieut. John Joseph Smith motorcyclist

When the party arrived at the scene of the ambush, fire was opened on them. I immediately put on full speed and rode right through for about 300 yards. One bullet struck the handlebar of my motorcycle and injured by left hand. I saw a large cart with a wheel off drawn across the road in the form of a barricade, and I dismounted and ran into the ditch for cover. The cart completely filled the road which is narrow at that point. After a minute or two I crawled along taking advantage of the little cover which the ditch afforded to see how the others fared. A few seconds elapsed and then the Crossley tender came up and stopped first where I was. I shouted to them to get under cover and under the direction of Commandant O'Connell the men dismounted and divided into two parties. Heavy firing was, of course, going on all this time, and our party had not yet commenced to reply. My motorcycle and the tender were left on the road. One party then immediately opened fire on the attackers at both sides of the road with a Lewis gun and rifles. Notwithstanding the heavy fire being directed on us the other party ran to the cart across the road, and attacking the barricade vigorously moved it aside, thus leaving the road open. This work occupied a very considerable time, during which we kept up a continued fire on the attacking party. Mean time the Leyland touring car and the armoured car had stopped some distance further up the hill and we could hear the fight going on at this end also. The attackers were spread out along the slopes at both sides of the road for fully a quarter of a mile. [One newspaper credits Smith with saying there were 200 ambushers.] The touring car was stopped by direction of the Commander-in-Chief, who with Major General Dalton and the two drivers took cover behind the fence about a foot high. This, however, left them exposed to the fire of the party on the other side of the road. The armoured car was in action a little further up. At the lower end of the road we kept firing and after some time drove back the ambushers on the right hand side of the road. They seemed to retreat over the top of the hill and the firing from this direction practically ceased. I went up around the brow of the hill after a little while in order to reconnoiter and as far as I could see this section of the irregulars had gone back over the hill. This gave us the opportunity to open a more intensified fire on the attackers on the other side, who were concealed around the farmhouse and amongst the shrubbery and bushes across the stream. We picked off a couple of them and could see them fall. Another was crossing a gap and was hit. Our party continued to fight fiercely and after another short space of time I decided to try and get in touch with the others to see if they were alright. I rushed over to my bicycle after telling the officer in charge and jumping on rode about 100 yards up the road. I was, of course, seen and had only got this distance when heavy fire was directed at me, so I again dived for cover turning the bicycle into the ditch and jumping clear. After waiting a little, I crawled along till I reached the touring car in which, of course, there was nobody. It was in the middle of the road and about 200 yards higher up I could see the armoured car in action. I crawled along until I came to a point opposite the armoured car. Then I saw the Commander-in-Chief lying wounded at the right hand side of the armoured car. Major General Dalton and Commandant O'Connell were attending him and were trying to bandage his head. General Dalton called me over with another of the party to get the Commander-in-Chief into the armoured car. We went over and as we were lifting the body I was hit in the neck. During all the time heavy firing had been kept up. The others eventually got General Collins' body onto the armoured car which then moved down the road to the Leyland car. This was the concluding stages of the engagement which had been going on for about an hour. It was then nearly dusk. The armoured car pushed the Leyland and after a while the efforts of the driver to start the engine were successful. We moved on to where the tender was halted, those in the armoured car keeping up the firing all the time. The body of the dead Commander-in-Chief was then moved onto the seat of the touring car and General Dalton stood there holding the body. I went to the front seat next to the driver as I had to abandon my motorcycle. In this way we went on past the cross to Crookstown.

2) Major General Emmett Dalton

Our motorcyclist scout was about 50 yards in front of the Crossley tender, which we followed at the same interval in the touring car. Close behind us came the armoured car. We had just reached a part of the road which was commanded by hills on all sides. The road itself was flat and open. On the right we were flanked by steep hills on the left there was a small two foot bank of earth skirting the road. Beyond this there was a marshy field bounded by a small stream, with another steep hill beyond it. About half way up this hill there was a road running parallel to the one we were on, but screened from view by a wall and a mass of trees and bushes. We had just turned a wide corner on the road when a sudden and heavy fusillade of machine gun fire swept the road in front of us and behind us shattering the windscreen of the car. I shouted to the driver: "Drive like hell!" But the Commander-in-Chief placing his hand on the man's shoulder said: "Stop! Jump out and we'll fight them." We leaped from the car and took what cover we could behind the little mud bank on the left hand side of the road. It seemed that the greatest volume of fire was coming from the concealed roadway on our left hand side. The armoured car now backed up the road and opened a heavy machine gun fire at the hidden ambushers. General Collins and I were lying within arms length of each other. Another officer, who had been on the back of the armoured car, together with our two drivers, were several yards further down the road to my right. General Collins and I, with the officer who was near us opened a rapid fire on our seldom visible enemies. About fifty or sixty yards further down the road and round the bend, we could hear that our machine gunners and riflemen were also heavily engaged. We continued this firing for about twenty minutes without suffering any casualties, when a lull in the enemy's attack became noticeable. General Collins now jumped to his feet and walked over behind the armoured car obviously to obtain better view of the enemy's position. He remained there firing occasional shots and using the car as cover. Suddenly I heard him shout: "There they are running up the road," I immediately opened fire upon two figures that came into view on the opposite road. When I next turned round the Commander-in-Chief had left the car position and had run about fifteen yards back up the road. Here he dropped into the prone firing position and opened up upon our retreating enemies. A few minute elapsed when Commandant O'Connell came running up the road under fire. He dropped into the position beside me and said: "They have retreated from in front of us, and the obstacle is removed. Where is the Big Fellow?" I said: "He's alright. He's gone a few yards up the road ... Hard, I hear him firing away." Next moment I caught a faint cry: "Emmett, I'm hit." We rushed to the spot with a dreadful fear clutching our heart. We found our beloved Chief and friend lying motionless in a firing position, firmly gripping his rifle, across which his head was resting. There was a fearful gaping wound at the base of the skull behind the right ear. We immediately saw that General Collins was almost beyond human aid. He could not speak to us. The enemy must have seen that something had occurred to cause a sudden cessation of fire, because they intensified their own. O'Connell now knelt beside the dying, but still conscious, Chief whose eyes were wide open and normal, and whispered into the ear of the fast sinking man the words of an Act of Contrition. For this he was rewarded with a slight pressure of the hand. Meanwhile I knelt beside them both and kept up bursts of rapid fire, which I continued whilst

O'Connell dragged the Chief across the road behind the armoured car. Then with heart torn with sorrow and despair I ran to the Chief's side. Very gently I raised his head on my knee and tried to bandage his wound, but owning to the awful size of it this proved very difficult. I had not completed my grievous task when the big eyes quickly closed and the cold pallor of death overspread the General's face. How can I describe the feelings that were mine in that bleak hour, kneeling in the mud of a country road not twelve miles from Clonakilty, with the still bleeding head of the Idol of Ireland resting on my arm. My heart was broken, my mind was numbed. I was all unconscious of the bullets that still whistled and ripped the ground beside me. I think that the might of the blow must have caused the loss of my reason had I not abruptly discovered the tear-stained face of O'Connell, now distorted with anguish and calling also for my sympathy and support. We paused for a moment in silent prayer and then, noting that the fire of our enemies had greatly abated, and that they had practically all retreated, we two with the assistance of Lieutenant Smith, the motorcyclist scout officer who had come on the scene, endeavored to lift the stalwart body of Michael Collins on to the back of the armoured car. It was then we suffered our second casualty, the recently arrived officer was shot in the neck. He remained on his feet, however, and helped us to carry our precious burden around a turn in the road and under cover of the armoured car. Having transferred the body of our Chief to the touring car where I sat with his head resting on my shoulder, our awe-stricken little party set out for Cork.

3) Private M B Corry, driver

There were two drivers in charge of the car, M Quinn and myself. Make of car was a Leyland Thomas Racing type, straight eight cylinder, no armour of any sort being attached at any time to bodywork or engine; canvas top folded back to rear. General Collins and Major General Emmet Dalton were seated in the back, the two drivers in the front seat. We were aware of IRA Flying Column being about at various places during our journey down to Cork; but not a shot was fired at us. We arrived in Cork City at 10:30 PM - due to obstructions, blown bridges etc.

The day of the ambush. ahead of us two Crossley tenders with ten armed men in each. Also one Crossley tender containing ropes, saws, picks, food, etc., for emergency use. Leading our column was a motorcyclist-guide. At the rear of our car, a Rolls Royce Whippet armoured car, named

"Slievenamon". Two men of the convoy observed that time of departure from Bandon town as being 8PM (GMT). After doing some five miles we came around a sharp curve and were then on a straight stretch of road. A single shot rang out from across the hill on our extreme left, some 440 yards away, approximately. General Collins' command "Stop" was obeyed at once. There was no obstruction on the road ahead of us at the time. On leaving our car we were met by heavy fire, but no one was hit. General Collins walked back some fifty yards, followed by Major General Dalton, Quinn and myself. We took cover at a hedge or ditch about two feet high. The firing was heavy at this time from enemy position right in front. On our extreme right our men were replying. On our extreme left a clear road. At our backs a steep hillside. Firing came from directly in front only. Major General Dalton observed that the armoured car machine-gun was not firing. He called to the gunner who replied, "Gun is jammed, sir." General Collins who had been lying firing from a position six feet from me now stood erect and after firing several rounds fell on the roadside with a gaping wound near the left ear lobe extending to the upper section of the skull. There was also a tear in the front of the forehead, and a hole ripped in the front of his cap close to the badge. Major General Dalton said to me: "The General's finished." We placed the body across the rear of the General 's car; my hands holding the head, Major General Dalton the feet of General Collins. Firing had ceased as General Collins died on the roadside. Nightfall was coming on and there was some drizzle as we started on our eighteen miles journey back to Cork.

4) Private John O'Connell

We arrived at Cork at half-past eight. Collins stayed in the Imperial and some of the escort stayed at the Victoria Hotel. There were no anti-Collins demonstrations, but there were chalked notices on the wall "Collins marches through Cork - why not Belfast?" The City was controlled by members of the Cork Civil Police.

The following night we were told to be ready to move out at four a.m. the next morning. In the morning the cars were brought round to the Imperial. The route was by Skibbereen and from there by by-roads to Bandon. From there we went through the Bandon demesne towards Clonakilty. Outside Clonakilty, near the workhouse, occurred the first hint of trouble, the way being blocked by newly felled trees. Collins, mentioning that the following day was fair day in Clonakilty, ordered the removal of the trees and he lent a hand. Eventually he decided that the work would take too long. They then retraced their route, going by another road to

Clonakilty where they breakfasted. To the commander of the garrison Collins gave orders for the removal of the trees. Proceeding from Clonakilty we travelled over four miles of mountainous road to Sam's cross. There Collins pointed out the heap of grass and stones, all that remained of his former home after its destruction by the "Black and Tans".

At the public house run by his cousin Jeremiah Collins treated each of us to two pints of the Clonakilty Wrestler, the local stout. Here Collins drank his last drink. We stayed about half an hour at Sam's Cross, while Collins talked with members of his family. At six o'clock that evening we went back through Skibbereen where Collins reviewed the local garrison. Then he had a conference with his officers and decided to return to Cork. We went through Bandon towards Clonakilty and found the way still blocked by trees. Meeting some soldiers Collins wanted to know why they hadn't been removed. The soldiers told him that a force of irregulars from which they had retreated had attacked them. But the convoy saw no force of Irregulars either before or after the meeting with the detachment. We travelled fairly fast and reached the valley of Béal na mBláth a place northwest of Bandon, but nearer to Crookstown than Bandon. The road narrowed, zigzagging into a series of blind corners. On one side of the road there was a swampy stream in which watercress grew. On the other side scrub following the slope of the hill. The touring car was now travelling ahead of the Crossley tender. From the tender Barry and myself could see that Collins had lifted his rifle from its customary position at his feet to lay it across his knee. The gloomy valley seemed a likely place for an ambush.

And so it proved. Coming out of a blind corner and with a straight road in front, we saw an old four-wheeled dray lying across the road with two of the wheels removed. The dray was loaded with cases and bottles - it was a brewer's dray - and immediately in front of it the road was strewn with broken glass. Almost at once machine-gun fire commenced, coming from the brush. There was a haze on the road and the light was fading quickly. Seeking cover we returned the fire. At the time of the beginning of the action the armoured car was almost half a mile behind the rest of the convoy. After a while it arrived but it wasn't very useful. Shortly after the guns began to fire the belts fell off. For a while the firing continued and then there was a lull during which we saw the attackers retreat in the direction of Cork. Lt. Smith and myself began a survey of the area and we found a black oil and a bag with black powder in it. There was more firing at this point coming from the direction of a farmhouse on the hill. Again the firing died down. Collins stood up to see how things were going. He was in the middle of the road, looking round, reloading his rifle. There was a single shot and Collins went down. A number of men went to help him but with that the firing around us intensified. It was nearly ten minutes later when we reached Collins. He was dead. There was a bad wound near his left ear. There was no more firing from the enemy. We put Collins in the back seat of the car. In the darkness we took the wrong road back to Cork and got lost. Eventually we had to go across country and the Crossley got bogged down. We made a carpet of coats and blankets and got the tender onto the road. But the armoured car got bogged down and the touring car wouldn't start, so we carried Collins across the tender and went to Cork in that. We arrived at Shanakiel hospital outside Cork at three o'clock in the morning.

5) Ambushers 1964
(Florence O'Donoghue Papers, MS. 31, 305 National Library)

On the evening of Tuesday 15th February 1964 seven of us sat down at the Metropole Hotel, Cork to try to record the circumstances in which Michael Collins was killed so far as they are known to the surviving members of the Republican forces who participated in the engagement.

There was present Liam Deasy, O.C. First Southern Division; Tom Kelleher, O.C. Fifth Battalion Cork No. 3; Jim Hurly, Brigade Commandant Cork No. 3; Dan Holland, O.C. 1st Battalion Cork No. 3; Pete Kearney, O.C. 3rd Battalion; Tom Crofts, Adjutant 1st Southern Division and myself (Florence O'Donoghue). All except myself were at Bealnablath at the time and I was asked to be present to record what could be established as the truth and because I had been given an undertaking by Capt. Sean Feehan of the Mercier press that he would not publish Eoin Neeson's book on the Civil War until we were satisfied that the part of it dealing with the death of Collins was in accordance with the facts.

The first information the Republican officers received of the presence of Collins in the area came to them on the morning of 22nd August. Denis Long was on sentry duty at Jehr. Long's public house on the night of 21st-22nd. Tom Crofts stayed at Murray's and Con Lucy stayed at Long's that night. In the morning, Denis Longs saw the Free State convoy pass in the direction of Bandon and reported it. Liam Deasy and de Valera, who had stayed at Gurranereagh on the night of the 21st, arrived at Béal na mBláth next morning. De Valera, in company with Sean Hyde, went on apparently to Ballyvourney but Liam Deasy remained. Four officers of Cork No. 3 Brigade assembled at Bealnablath in the forenoon to attend a Brigade council meeting called for the afternoon. This meeting was called without any reference to the possibility of an ambush and in fact it was not held until 11 p.m. that night.

Before these officers arrived at Bealnablath the decision had been take on Divisional initiative to lay an ambush 400 yards south of the cross for the Free State convoy on the assumption that it would probably return later in the day by the same route. When the four Cork No. 3 Officers arrived, the position was in the process of being prepared and occupied.

Statements which have been made to the effect that the Division and Cork No. 1 Brigade were aware of Collins' intention to visit posts in Cork and that a general order was issued to kill him and are without foundation and completely untrue. His presence in the South was known to the officers in the Division and of the 1st and 3rd Brigades only on the morning of 22nd and no order had been issued by either of the commands. The ambush was decided on as part of the general policy of attacking Free State convoy.

The ambush party numbered between 20 and 25. It included, Liam Deasy, Tom Kelleher, Jim Hurley, Pete Kearney, Dan Holland, Tom Hales, Tom Crofts, Con Lucey, Sean Culhane, John Lordan, Bill Desmond, Dan Corcoran, C. O'Donoghue, John O'Callaghan, Sonny O'Neill, Paddy Walsh, Sonny Donovan, Jim Crowley, Tady O'Sullivan and Jerh Mahony.

A mine was laid and a mineral water lorry with one wheel removed was used as a road block. A farm butt was also placed as a road block on the bohereen running almost parallel to the road on the eastern side..

The ambush party remained in position during the day but no action took place. In the afternoon a message was received from Bandon that Collins was there. It was considered unlikely that the convoy would return through Bealnablath and the decision was made, probably by Liam Deasy, to call off the ambush and evacuate the position.

When the main party moved, a Cork No. 3 section remained to cover the withdrawal and clear the road. This group consisted of Tom Hales, Jim Hurley, Dan Holland, Tom Kelleher, Sonny O'Neill, Paddy Walsh, John O'Callaghan, Sonny Donovan, Bill Desmond and Dan Corcoran. They had left their prepared positions and were helping to clear the road when the noise of a motorbike and lorries was heard approaching from the south. They realised that the main party moving back towards Bealnablath cross-roads were in a ravine and in a very dangerous position. They could not have reached the cross-roads before the convoy overtook them.

Immediately on hearing the noise of the approaching vehicles, seven or eight of the Cork No. 3 section took up poor positions on the bohereen west of the road and opened fire on the oncoming convoy. Jim Hurley fired at the motor cyclist and missed him. Tom Kelleher fired at the following vehicle. The convoy stopped and opened fire. The Republican party were armed with rifles and revolvers only, they had no machine guns, but there were two machine guns in the convoy and fire from them raked the section of the fence from which the Cork No. 3 section were firing. The action lasted between 20 and 30 minutes and, before it ended, darkness had fallen to the extent that it was possible to see the flashes from the gunfire. Conditions were such that it was not possible to get off an aimed shot.

Firing stopped at almost 8 o'clock. The Cork No. 3 section remained in position and the Free State convoy withdrew under fire. No one in the Republican party knew that Collins had been killed or that the convoy had suffered any casualty. It was only when Sean Galvin came to Bealnablath about 11 o'clock that they got their first report of his death.

6) Private John "Jock" McPeak

(*The account below comprises his interviewers direct quotes of McPeak; excepting words in [brackets], which represent indirect quotes.*)

I was awakened on Sunday morning (August 20th) in Portobello Barracks and told to get ready as we were going to Cork. We were given no instructions about who would be going with us. It was simply a case of "Get the armoured car and stand by." There should have been two gunners. I should have had someone else with me, but I hadn't. I was probably the only machine-gunner available at the time. The others being Irishmen may have had weekend passes to go home. It is not true that I, an ordinary gunner, could have used undue influence to have obtained the job of escort to the Commander-in-Chief.

As we left Portobello, General Collins was in the Lancia, immediately ahead of the Crossley tender, bearing the troops, and then the armoured car, which had two drivers but as I have said I was the only gunner. We stopped at various barracks on the way south. They had meals laid on for us and there was a drink for us too, but there was no serious drinking on that trip. On the way down to Cork and in the sorties out from Cork itself, the people all crowded out to see Collins, waving from the windows and from the roadside as the convoy passed.

He was a man you couldn't miss, a fine big man, whose uniform really looked well on him. I could see that he was extremely popular with all the people, as he was with the men in the column. It was a terrible tragedy that he was killed, because I really think that he had that kind of personality that would have brought the people together in the end. The people of Ireland must have been fed up with war.

[Michael Collins at no stage expressed any desire to travel in the armoured car.]

[On August 22, Collins "stood" all a drink at the public house at Sam's Cross, but there wasn't a lot of drinking.]

[It was approaching dusk when the convoy reached Béal na mBláth, the dispatch rider out front, the Crossley tender, the staff car, bearing Generals Collins and Dalton and the armoured car bringing up the rear. The reason the armoured car was at the rear] ...was probably fear of an ambush blocking a cross roads and the car might have been damaged running into it. Armoured vehicles at that time were at a premium, so we always sent a scout ahead and he could pass back any information of a possible ambush, as happened on this day. He was the first to see the block across the road.

The men in the Crossley tender could have cleared the obstruction in a couple of minutes. It was only a wagon and we could have gone straight through. But General Collins would not have it. It was he who ordered the convoy to stop.

Some shots were fired from the hill - just an odd shot at first, a few odd shots and I am convinced that it was a small ambush, involving only three or four men to begin with; perhaps they may have been joined by more as the engagement developed. There was only rifle fire coming from the hillside, no machine gun fire - and that is why I maintain we could easily have gone past.

I saw General Collins and General Dalton in the car, as I was standing in the turret with my head out the hatch when the firing started. But then I closed the hatch cover. The Generals had got out of their car and they must have gone up the left and behind the armoured car into the ditch and were returning the fire from there. I never saw them anymore after I closed the hatch. I couldn't see the men either. I was looking through my gun sights.

I had two belts of .303 ammunition, each containing 250 rounds and one box of 1000 rounds loose, which was to be used for replenishing the two belts when empty. This should have been the job of my number two gunner - but for some unknown reason he had been left behind in Cork. In his place I had two staff captains who had come inside the car when the evening began to get chilly. We, the two drivers and I had no objection to making them comfortable, although it was rather crowded in such a confined vehicle. When the action began I asked them to leave but they ignored me, and I had no authority to order them to leave. The number one driver like myself was probably afraid of the consequences if he were to order them to leave. They were not in his way - only in mine and after I had used one belt I asked them if they would help me by refilling this belt from the 1000 round box.

One did try but the other thought it was beneath his dignity to do things of that sort. The officer helping to refill the belt wasn't really able to do it properly. I demonstrated how it should be done, that each round should be absolutely even at the caps, you had to put them on a perfect edge, not one of them should be an eighth of an inch out. But, of course, this was what was happening. From then on there was nothing but stoppages, continuous stoppages. You had to clear the gun, you had to take the round out again. This meant very desultory fire.

I was in an impossible position after I had used up my second belt, and started on the one the officer had been trying to refill. But even if everything had gone perfectly, it would not have made a whole deal of difference because we didn't have a real target. I probably wasted the first belt by letting it go. I wanted to let the ambushers know that there was a machine gun: I wanted to make them keep their heads down.

I kept firing very short bursts, two or three rounds, between each stoppage until there came a lull in the fighting. I opened the hatch to get some cool air inside the turret which was stifling. I had no sooner opened it when a bullet struck the lug which fastens the cover from the inside and sheered it off.

This may have been the ricochet which Dr St John Gogarty was convinced caused Collins' death – or it could have been any one of the numerous bullets which hit the 'Slievenamon' and bounced off the armoured plating at all sorts of angles. To say that a stray or deliberate shot from the machine gun could have caused his death is absolute nonsense because the gun was pointed upward at the hillside from which the attack came, all through the engagement.

There were plenty of marks on the armoured car. It had been hit many times. There were little dents and the paint was knocked off in places. Coming at an angle – as the bullets were – the bullet that killed General Collins could have come off the car.

I suppose every man in a way felt more or less responsible that the Commander-in-Chief should have died while the rest of us escaped without a scratch – expeting the motor cycle outrider, Lieut. Smith, who was shot in the neck; evidently the wound was not too bad as he helped to carry Collins to the Crossley tender.

I didn't know at first that General Collins had been shot. They lifted him from where he fell round the wing of the armoured car. I didn't even know that until they told me. Because the hatch was closed again. I think it was one of the drivers who said "Collins has been hit." He didn't say he was dead at the time. Then the men helped to carry his body to the Crossley tender.

The doctor at the hospital to which Collins was taken maintained that it was a ricochet. The whole back of the head was gone. A bullet coming straight would have made a little hole the size of a pencil.

I must deny allegations that I was armed with a revolver. The number one machine gunner in the British army was always supplied with a revolver. This was standard practice – the idea being that in the event of his armoured car being captured he could put the machine out of action with the revolver or a mills bomb. Gunners, however, in the Free State Army in 1922 were not issued with revolvers.

[There] never was any suspicion, hint of neglect, or accusations of carelessness made against me during the period between that day in August, 1922 and the day in early December 1922, when I walked out, or rather drove out to the Republicans at Bandon taking the armoured car with me.

7) William McKenna

(Feehan's summary from interviews) It was generally rumored among members of the convoy that Collins was going south to try to bring the war to an end. Dalton knew this and had in his possession details of some mined roads and some blown bridges given to him (Dalton) on behalf of the anti-Treaty forces as a kind of an assurance of safe-conduct and goodwill. McKenna at the time also saw copies of an exchange of decoded radio messages between Collins in Portobello Barracks and Dalton in Cork concerning the program for a visit south and matters referring to conditions for a cease-fire.

As they rounded a long curve on the narrow road near Béal na mBláth they stopped suddenly when they saw an overturned dray cart and broken bottles barring the way. Lieutenant Smith had left his motorcycle and was close to the barricade. As they dismounted they came under fire, not heavy, but rapid, which lasted about two minutes. They divided into two sections one of which began to remove the barricade and the other returned the fire. When the shooting ceased they could hear firing at the Bandon end of the ambush site but could not see anything as the armoured car and touring car were around the bend. After a short while the firing there stopped and the two sections moved cautiously in that direction. By the time they got there Collins was dead. It was just dusk and McKenna did not see the wound. On the way back to Cork most members of the convoy showed signs of great distress, Commandant O'Connell weeping openly. At

Cork they drove to the Imperial Hotel where some officer took charge of the body and brought it to the British military hospital at Shanakiel.

Three days later, in Dublin, McKenna was present with Dr Oliver St John Gogarty, Desmond Fitzgerald, Moira Llewellyn Davies and some relatives of Collins, when Gogarty showed them the wounds. There was a large part of the flesh under the right ear blown away and Gogarty had fitted the cavity with a wax-like substance. Close to the left ear there was a small circular wound which seemed "bluish" in color. He has further stated that this wound was clearly visible when Collins was later lying in state. McKenna recollects Gogarty saying that Collins must have been shot at very close range.

8) Liam Deasy, anti-Treaty Commander, First Southern Division and Adjutant Tom Crofts

(Feehan's summary from interviews, combined with details included by Deasy in his own book on the Civil War.)

They spent the day of 22 August dealing with administrative matters at the temporary headquarters of the First Southern Division of which Deasy was Commander, at Sullivans of Gurranereagh, which was close on three miles from Béal na mBláth. At about 5PM or 5:30PM they left Gurranereach, walking, for Béal na mBláth. When they got to the village they turned out the Bandon road towards the ambush position which was about half a mile along this route. A short distance out they met Tom Hales and a number of other officers returning. Hales told them that he had called off the ambush and sent the protecting column home, leaving five men to remove the mine and cart. Deasy and Crofts returned to Béal na mBláth with Hales and the other officers. They went into the pub for a drink and something to eat. They were there about fifteen or twenty minutes when they heard the sound of firing coming from the ambush site. They immediately rushed out and ran along the old Bandon road which is parallel to the ambush road. They crossed a few fields and after about fifteen or twenty minutes came to high ground about 300-400 yards from the site. They could see some activity around the armoured car, although it was hazy and getting dark. They fired a few shots in that direction, but almost immediately the whole convoy moved off. They returned to Béal na mBláth and after a short while the five men who carried out the ambush joined them. They reported that there were no casualties on either side. The officers then started their postponed meeting at Murray's house at about 9:30PM. The meeting had just begun when a scout named Sean Galvin of

Crookstown rushed in and told them Collins had been killed. They were so stunned that they called off the meeting and dispersed.

9) Ambushers 1981

(Feehan's summary from interviews) All during that day it was freely rumored among them that the war would soon be over, and as one of them said, "We had no great mind to shoot anybody." ... They put an old dray cart across the road at the Béal na mBláth end of the position and a short distance further up, a mine. The mine was to be detonated from a position up a laneway which ran first west, and then south, parallel to the main road. About 6:30 or so it was decided to call off the ambush, as it was felt that the convoy would not return by that route. Two men were detailed to remove the cart off the road and also to defuse the mine. Three more were left behind to protect them just in case anything happened. Two of these men were at the southern side of the laneway, at a slight angle to where the monument is today. The other was about half way along the laneway at a position near two stone piers which are still to be seen. The two men detailed to clear the obstacles on the road first of all defused the mine and one of them proceeded up the laneway laden down with cables and plunger. The other man commenced to move the cart away. While he was engaged in this the men in the laneway saw the convoy coming. It was moving very slowly, they say, between 15 and 20 mph. There was a motorcyclist in front followed by a Crossley tender, in which all the men seemed to be standing up. Then came the touring car and then the armoured car. After some hesitation one of the men in the laneway fire two shots, primarily to warn the man who was clearing the barricade, who immediately took cover and ran back up the laneway towards his other companion. It has been said that these two shots were fired at the roof of the touring car, but this could not be correct since the cover was completely down. The members of the convoy jumped out and took cover behind a little ditch hardly two feet high and commenced firing. The IRA say that despite their small number they had the convoy at their mercy. They had excellent cover, they were firing down on them only a short distance away and they could have picked them off one by one without difficulty. But they did not seem to want to do this. Whatever firing they did was very half-hearted, they say, and only enough to give the body of officers in Béal na mBláth a chance to disperse.

The Free State party committed almost every military blunder they could. Instead of trying to hold down the IRA with covering fire while a section outflanked them, they simply ran up and down the road as if in a panic and needlessly exposed themselves. One section did attempt to move up the laneway, but the men near the piers had moved down and held them back, and even when these two men retreated the Free Staters did not exploit the advantage. After about fifteen minutes the IRA felt that the ambush had served its purpose and they retreated, three men up a small laneway to the north-west and the two other men up another small laneway to the west. These two men returned fire for about a minute and then made good their escape. These two men say that as they were firing at an angle any bullet that hit the armoured car would ricochet away from Collins

While the IRA do not deny the possibility of one of their bullets killing Collins, they say it would be one chance in a thousand since they were not aiming at anybody or anything in particular and were only holding the fort to give their officers a chance to hide. They say that the various published accounts by Free State eye-witnesses are teeming with inaccuracies and thoroughly unreliable. With regard to their fire power they say that while there were five of them there, only three of them had rifles - the other two had revolvers. They claim that Collins must have been killed either accidentally or deliberately by one of his own party.

APPENDIX 3

CONTRADICTIONS AND CORROBORATIONS CATALOGUED

I never believe more than 50% of any military report.
- Marshall Foch

The following is a summary of salient points of each eye-witness report which exists on record. Each statement is then cross-referenced with a list of points in which it is contradicted by other witnesses' versions; as well as a list of points in which it is corroborated by others. Each witness' section ends with notation as to whether they testified to anything which was not within their direct knowledge (such as hearsay, etc.); as well as any self-contradiction, or other glaringly dubious points.

In charting the various contradictions and corroborations below, this author has been considerably kinder than Feehan. I have passed over a few discrepancies in small details, which seem unimportant; and which may reasonably be attributed to the passage of time, confusion in the excitement, etc. However, other fine points are scrutinized, which may prove telling in the overall picture.

(The witnesses' actual reports, where available, are reproduced *verbatim* in Appendix 2.)

THE WITNESSES

1) Lieut. John Joseph Smith
2) Major General Emmett Dalton
3) Private M B Corry
4) Private John O'Connell
5) The ambushers 1964
6) Private John "Jock" McPeak
7) William McKenna
8) Liam Deasy and Tom Crofts
9) The ambushers 1981
10) Commdt Frank Friel
11) Matron Miss Eleanor Gordon
12) Dr Patrick Cagney
13) Albert Power

THEIR ACCOUNTS

1) *Lieut. John Joseph Smith, motorcycle scout*
First published: August 24, 1922 (two days after the ambush)
(The statement attributed to Lieut. Smith "was not written by himself, but given in the form of an interview to newspaper reporters." As such it may or may not faithfully record his statements.)

Lieut. Smith is reported to have said that:
> the first shots were fired at himself, a quarter mile ahead of the Leyland touring car, as soon as he came to the ambush site;

> he rode straight on about 300 yards and stopped at a dray cart which was blocking the road;

> he (Lieut. Smith) was wounded in the hand by the first shots;

> he dismounted and took cover in a ditch;

> Crossley tender came up to him, and he told them to take cover;

> they were under heavy fire while Commdt O'Connell directed the soldiers from the tender to form two parties;

> the soldiers from the tender then replied to the ambushers with rifles and the Lewis machine gun;

> the C-in-C ordered the touring car to stop;

> they could tell that the touring car and armoured car were also engaged because they could hear the firing up the road;

> the ambush site was spread out over about a quarter mile;

> the entire convoy was under heavy, continuous firing for a prolonged time, from both sides of the road;

> the convoy was attacked by 200 men (this appeared in one newspaper's version of his statement);

> they "picked off" some of the ambushers and "saw them fall";

> the battle lasted an hour;

> under heavy fire, he made his way to the touring car and found the C-in-C lying by the armoured car wounded, with Dalton and Commdt. O'Connell attending him and trying to bandage his head.

> Dalton called him (Lieut. Smith) and another (officer?) over to help move the C-in-C to the armoured car; while attempting to do so, he (Lieut. Smith) was hit in the neck;

> the others moved the C-in-C onto the armoured car, which moved down to the touring car

> the armoured car had to push-start the touring car;

> throughout this time, the armoured car kept up machine gun fire;

> the C-in-C's body was then moved into the Leyland touring car;

> he (Lieut. Smith) also rode in the touring car, in the front seat next to the driver, because he had to abandon his motorcycle.

Contradicted by other accounts:
Dalton contradicts Lieut Smith (cyclist) as follows:
x says that the touring car was the first hit, and by a burst of heavy fire (i.e. first shots would not have hit near the cyclist);

x refers to Lieut. Smith being wounded in the neck, much later, as "*our second casualty*" of the engagement (i.e. that Smith was *not* wounded in the hand before that);

x says that Smith helped move the C-in-C's body after being hit in the neck (i.e. it was Smith and not just "the others" who moved the body);

x says that the ambushers had "practically all" retreated by the time that Smith came up to them (i.e. if so, would the armoured car have kept up machine gun fire throughout this time?);

Corry (touring car driver) contradicts Lieut Smith as follows:
x a single shot rang out, and that was the first fire at the convoy (i.e. the cyclist was not under continuous fire as he first rode through the site, a quarter mile ahead of the touring car);

- x there was no further firing at the convoy until after the C-in-C ordered his car to stop and they all got out (i.e. the cyclist was not under continuous fire as he first rode through the site, a quarter mile ahead of the touring car);
- x the convoy came under fire only from the hill on the west side of the road (i.e. they were not under attack from both sides);
- x neither Cmmdt O'Connell nor Lieut. Smith were present either before, during or after Collins fell;
- x neither Cmmdt O'Connell nor Lieut. Smith helped to move Collins' body;
- x neither Cmmdt O'Connell nor Dalton attended the wounded Collins, nor tried to bandage his head;
- x there was no problem starting the touring car;

McPeak (armoured car driver) contradicts Lieut Smith (cyclist) as follows:
- x says Lieut Smith was wounded in the neck; (not in the hand);
- x says Collins was taken to hospital; (but not Smith);
- x says Smith "passed back" information to the convoy about the barricade, and about possible ambush; (Smith does not say that he did so);
- x says the first shots were fired from the hillside near the armoured car; (not at Smith, a quarter mile ahead of the armoured car);
- x reports just a few odd shots, from three or four men, on one side of the road only; (not heavy, prolonged fire, form a large body of men, on both sides of the road);
- x says Smith carried Collins' body;
- x says the C-in-C's body was carried to the Crossley tender; (not to the armoured car.)

McKenna contradicts Lieut Smith (cyclist) as follows:
- when the tender came up to him, the cyclist was standing near the cart which blocked the road; (i.e. cyclist was not on hands and knees in the ditch, seeking cover from fire, when the tender came up to him);
- only after they rounded the curve, saw the barrier and dismounted, did they come under fire (i.e. cyclist was not fired on before they reached him and did not drive through the ambush site under fire);
- first shots were fired a quarter mile ahead of the touring car, near the barricade at the northern end of the site (i.e. not at the cyclist, when he first reached the southern end of the site.)
- reported no injury to the motorcyclist (i.e. cyclist was not hit in the hand by the first shots);
- firing was "*not heavy, but rapid*" and "*lasted about two minutes.*" (i.e. they were not under machine gun fire, nor under heavy fire which lasted "*an hour*");
- all the soldiers from the Crossley tender moved back to the touring car after all firing had ceased (Smith says only he and Commdt Sean O'Connell went from the tender back to the touring car);
- says that Collins' body was taken to hospital, but not Lieut Smith (i.e. no medical attention was sought for wounds to Smith);

Deasy and Crofts contradict Lieut Smith (cyclist) as follows:
- there were only five anti-Treaty men at the site when the ambush took place (i.e. there was not a large body of troops, as Smith's account suggests, and certainly not "200" attackers, as one newspaper quoted him as saying);
- the convoy came under fire only from the hill on the west side of the road (i.e. it was not attacked from both sides of the road);
- although Deasy and Crofts were on the other side of the road, and fired a few shots, they got there when the ambush was over and the convoy began moving off "almost immediately" they arrived within sight;;
- the ambush lasted no more than 15 or 20 minutes (i.e. not "*an hour*");
- ambushers reported to them that there had been no casualties on either side (i.e. they did not see Collins or Smith wounded);

The ambushers 81 contradict Lieut Smith (cyclist) as follows:
x they say that the accounts published by the Free State witnesses prior to 1981 were "teeming with inaccuracies and thoroughly unreliable";

x the first firing was two warning shots, soon after the convoy came into sight (i.e. first shots would not have hit or neared the cyclist);

x the ambushers came under aggressive fire from the convoy following just two warning shots (i.e. the convoy did not have fire "opened on them" immediately upon arriving at the site);

x the convoy came under fire only from the hill on the west side of the road (i.e. it was not attacked from both sides of the road);

x The convoy came under no intense, heavy, or prolonged fire such as described by Smith;

x The ambushers' good cover and advantageous position on high ground was such that, had they made any very determined effort to hit the Free State men, they would easily have effected many casualties; and may even have wiped them out (i.e. there was no heavy, aggressive fire from ambushers such as Smith describes);

x The ambush lasted about 15 minutes (i.e. not an hour);

x there were no anti-Treaty casualties (i.e. Smith did not "pick them off" nor "see them fall");

x ambushers reported no casualties on either side (i.e. they did not see Collins wounded).

All other relevant accounts contradict Lieut Smith (cyclist) as follows:
x there were no anti-Treaty casualties;

x the ambush lasted between ten and twenty minutes (i.e. not one hour);

x the ambushers were a small band; definitely not 200 men;

x the ambushers were assembled on the hill to the convoy's left (i.e. not on both sides of the road.)

Lieut Smith's points corroborated by some other accounts:

* the ambush site was flanked by steep hills on both sides of the road; corroborated by:

    - Dalton
    - Corry
    - McPeak
    - Deasy
    - McKenna
    - Ambushers 81

* The Crossley tender stopped at the barricade, the soldiers in it dismounted, and formed two groups, one to move the obstacle, and the other to return fire; corroborated by:

    - McKenna

* The soldiers in the Crossley tender came under heavy fire; corroborated by:

    - Private J O'Connell

* The convoy was under heavy, prolonged fire; corroborated by:

    - Dalton
    - Corry

* The soldiers at the Crossley tender exchanged fire with the ambushers; corroborated by:

    - Dalton
    - Corry
    - Priv J O'Connell
    - McKenna

* The soldiers from the tender answered the ambushers' fire with rifles and a Lewis machine gun; corroborated by:

    - Dalton
    - McKenna
    - Deasy

* Members of the convoy took cover behind a small bank or ditch; corroborated by:

    - Smith
    - Dalton
    - Corry
    - Ambushers 81

* The C-in-C ordered the touring car to stop; corroborated by:

    - Dalton
    - Corry
    - McPeak

* There was firing in the area of the touring car and armoured car; corroborated by:

    - Dalton
    - Corry
    - McPeak
    - McKenna
    - J O'Connell

* The armoured car's machine gun bombarded the ambushers continuously; corroborated by:

    - Dalton
    - McPeak
    - Deasy and Crofts
    - Ambushers 81

* From the Crossley tender, they could only hear what was happening at the touring car and armoured car (but could not see them): corroborated by

    - McKenna;
    - Dalton

* the ambush site was spread out over about a quarter mile; corroborated by:

- the ambushers 81

* Dalton and Commdt. O'Connell were attending Collins, who lay on the ground wounded, and were attempting to bandage his head; corroborated by:

    - Dalton

* Smith was wounded in the neck while attempting to help carry the body; corroborated by:

    - Dalton
    - McPeak

* "There was activity around the armoured car" just before the convoy left the ambush site; corroborated by:

    - Dalton
    - McPeak
    - Deasy and Crofts

Lieut Smith's points corroborated by all other relevant accounts:
* an old dray cart blocked the road, causing the convoy to stop;

* All firing ceased when Collins died;

* dusk was approaching and it was beginning to get dark as the ambush concluded;

Lieut Smith's points included which were *not* within the witness' direct personal knowledge
? Smith says that the C-in-C ordered the car to stop. This concurs with Dalton's statement; but since this witness was by his own account at least 100 yards away, he could not have personally overheard any such order. Therefore this must be hearsay.

Lieut Smith's points of question / self-contradiction
? Smith says that firing began as soon as he reached the scene, and that he then cycled through the ambush site, until stopped by the barricade. Since Smith led the convoy, that would place the touring

321

car and armoured car a quarter mile away from the ambush site when the firing started. This suggests that, well away from the site when the shooting began, they then drove on a quarter mile, expressly placing themselves under fire.

? Although Smith says that he handled Collins' body, he says nothing about the nature of the C-in-C's wounds. By contrast, all others, who claim to have been nearby, comment on the nature and location of his wound(s). This seems significant, as other accounts contradict him in this, saying he did not handle the body, and placing him nowhere near the wounded C-in-C.

2) *Major General Emmett Dalton*
First published: August 22, 1923
(Dalton's statement was published on the first anniversary of the ambush, in the Freemen's Journal newspaper. It is alleged that he also submitted an official report for the Provisional Government; and that this is the version quoted by Pearas Beaslaí's biography of the C-in -C.)

Dalton's statement says that:
> the motorcyclist was about 50 yards in front of the Crossley tender, the touring car about 50 yards behind that, followed by the armoured car;

> at the ambush site the road was flat, skirted by a two foot earth bank on the left; there were hills on both sides, a stream on the left, and halfway up the hill on the left another road ran parallel, screened from view by a wall, trees and bushes;

> the first shots were "*a heavy fusillade of machine-gun fire*" which shattered the windscreen of the Leyland touring car (in which he rode with the C-in-C);

> he ordered the driver to "*Drive like hell!*" But Collins countermanded, "*Stop! Jump out and we'll fight them*";

> they took cover behind a two-foot high bank or ditch;

> they were under continuous heavy fire until just after Collins fell;

> the armoured car bombarded the ambushers' positions with machine gun fire;

> he could hear rifle and machine gun fire, indicating that the soldiers in the Crossley tender were engaged "*down the road and around the bend*";
> they remained exchanging heavy fire for about twenty minutes;
> Collins then took cover behind the armoured car;
> Collins then ran fifteen yards back up the road (in the direction of Bandon,) assumed a prone position and commenced firing on ambushers who were retreating;
> Commdt. O'Connell came running, under fire, round the bend from the Crossley tender and reported that they had cleared the obstacle and that the ambushers there had retreated; Commdt O'Connell then asked "*Where's the Big Fella?*"
> he (Dalton) heard a faint cry from Collins, saying that he was hit; and rushing over, he and O'Connell found him lying on the ground across his rifle, with a gaping wound at the base of his skull behind the right ear, and seemingly near to death;
> ambushers' fire then intensified, and he (Dalton) intermittently returned fire while O'Connell dragged the C-in-C behind the armoured car;
> he (Dalton) was bandaging the C-in-C's wound when Collins died, while bullets hit the ground around them;
> by then the ambushers had practically all retreated;
> the motorcyclist Lieut. Smith then came up to them and was at that point hit by a gunshot in the neck; but still assisted them to place the C-in-C's body on the back of the armoured car.
> Collins' body was taken to Bon Secours hospital by Dr. Leo Ahern;
> denies that there was more than one wound.

Contradicted by other accounts:
Lieut Smith contradicts Dalton as follows:
x says that he (Smith, the cyclist) was the first vehicle to be fired upon, and the first to be hit (i.e. not the touring car, a quarter mile behind him);
x although Smith maintains that the convoy was under prolonged, heavy fire, he never mentions any machine gun fire from the ambushers;

- x says that the engagement lasted one hour (i.e. not 20 minutes);
- x says that "the others" moved the body (i.e. he (Smith) did not assist moving the body after being wounded in the neck);
- x says that after Collins had died, and while they moved his body and push-started the touring car, the armoured car kept up its bombardment of machine gun fire (Dalton says the ambushers had retreated by the time Collins died);

Corry contradicts Dalton as follows:
- x "*a single shot rang out*" (i.e. there was no "*fusillade of machine gun fire*" sweeping the road before and behind them);
- x although, as a driver, Corry's account includes particular detail of the touring car's make and features, he does not report any damage to it from gunfire (i.e. the windscreen was not shattered by machine gun fire);
- x reports no orders from Dalton; only that the C-in-C said to "*Stop*";
- x there was no further firing at the convoy until after the C-in-C ordered his car to stop and they all got out (i.e. as they were under no fire, they would not have "*leaped from the car and took what cover we could*");
- x after coming under heavy fire, all the occupants of the touring car walked back up the road toward the armoured car, about 50 yards; only then did they take cover behind a ditch;
- x when Dalton called to the armoured car gunner about having ceased firing, the gunner replied that the machine gun was jammed (Dalton describes the armoured car's machine gun firing, but does not say it jammed);
- x the C-in-C had a large wound near the left ear lobe (i.e. not behind the right ear);
- x neither Cmmdt O'Connell nor Lieut. Smith were present either before, during or after Collins fell;
- x neither Cmmdt O'Connell nor Dalton attended the wounded Collins, nor tried to bandage his head, nor said prayers;

- x attributes to Dalton only the terse statement "*The General's finished.*" (i.e. contradicts Dalton's account of his own frame of mind and demeanor);
- x says firing ceased when Collins died (i.e. after the C-in-C's death, Dalton did not sit by the body in prayer while bullets "*ripped the ground*" around him);
- x says that he himself helped Dalton move the C-in-C's body (i.e. it was not Lieut. Smith nor Commandant S. O'Connell who carried the body);
- x Reports no casualties other than Collins (i.e. no injury to Lieut Smith);

Priv John O'Connell contradicts Dalton as follows:
- x says that the first shots were heavy machine gun fire at the Crossley tender, at the forward end of the convoy near the barricade;
- x no one could get near Collins' body for ten minutes after he fell, due to heavy fire (i.e. he did not die in Dalton's arms);
- x there was a large wound near his left ear (i.e. not near the right ear);

McPeak contradicts Dalton as follows:
- x says the first fire at the convoy was "*just a few odd shots*," and only rifle fire; (not a "*fierce fusillade*" of machine gun fire, which swept the road and shattered the windscreen);
- x says the armoured car's machine gun jammed; (machine gun could not keep up bombardment of the ambushers' positions throughout the engagement);
- x indicates that fire from the ambushers was not heavy or prolonged; (the convoy was not under heavy fire for twenty minutes);
- x says Smith carried the body to the Crossley tender; (not to the armoured car);
- x says Collins' body taken to Shanakiel Hospital; (not to Bon Secours.)

McKenna contradicts Dalton as follows:
- x first shots were fired a quarter mile ahead of the touring car, near the barricade (i.e. not near Dalton.)

- x fire from ambushers was not heavy and was of short duration. (i.e. not heavy fire, not machine gun fire, and not for 20 minutes or more);
- x all the soldiers from the Crossley tender moved back to the touring car after all firing had ceased (Dalton says only Commdt O'Connell came up to him from the tender);
- x in addition to the large wound under his right ear, and what seemed to be an entry wound on his forehead, there was a small wound close to the left ear;
- x says that the C-in-C's body went to hospital, but not Lieut Smith (i.e. recounts no attempt to seek medical attention for any wounds to Smith);

Deasy and Crofts contradict Dalton as follows:
- x ambushers reported to them that there had been no casualties on either side (i.e. they did not see Collins or Smith wounded);

The ambushers 81 contradict Dalton as follows:
- x they say that the accounts published by the Free State witnesses prior to 1981 were "*teeming with inaccuracies and thoroughly unreliable*";
- x the first shots fired were two warning shots, fired by just one sentry (i.e. there was no "*fierce fusillade of machine gun fire*" around the touring car);
- x the ambushers came under aggressive fire from the convoy following just two warning shots (i.e. convoy was not the first to come under fire);
- x the ambushers had no machine guns (i.e. the convoy did not come under machine gun fire);
- x the convoy came under no intense, heavy, or prolonged fire such as described by Dalton;
- x the ambushers' good cover and advantageous position on high ground was such that, had they made any very determined effort to hit the Free State men, they would easily have effected many more casualties; and may even have wiped them out. (i.e. had their fire been aggressive and prolonged as described, Collins would not have been the only fatality);

- x after about 15 minutes, all the ambushers retreated (i.e. there was no "sniping" nor re-intensification of fire after that time);
- x ambushers reported that there had been no casualties on either side (i.e. they did not see Collins wounded);

Cmmdt. Frank Friel contradicts Dalton as follows:
- x Dalton ordered him to take the body to the British military hospital at Shanakiel, and he did so; (i.e. the body was not taken to Bon Secours);
- x there was an entry wound on his forehead as well as a large exit wound at the back of the head; (Dalton denied that there was more than one wound);
- x says that Collins' body was sent to hospital, but not Lieut Smith (i.e. no medical attention was sought for wounds to Smith);

Miss Eleanor Gordon contradicts Dalton as follows:
- x Collins' body was brought to her at Shanakiel hospital by a military escort (i.e. not to Bon Secours by a doctor);
- x there was an entry wound on his forehead as well as a large exit wound at the back of the head; there was also evidence of a wound in his back;(Dalton denied that there was more than one wound);
- x says that Collins' body was sent to hospital, but no other casualties from the convoy (i.e. no medical attention was sought for any wounds to Smith);

Dr Patrick Cagney contradicts Dalton as follows:
- x there was an entry wound as well as an exit wound.

Mr. Albert Power contradicts Dalton as follows:
- x there was an entry wound as well as an exit wound.

All relevant accounts contradict Dalton as follows:
- x No one else reports the words he attributes to himself and to Collins.

Dalton's points corroborated by some other accounts:

* The motorcyclist was followed by the Crossley tender, then the touring car, then the armoured car; corroborated by:

    - McPeak
    - Ambushers 81

* At the ambush site the road was flanked by hills on both sides; corroborated by:

    - Smith
    - Corry
    - McPeak
    - Deasy
    - McKenna
    - Ambushers 81

* Halfway up the hill, on the left, another road ran parallel, screened from view by trees and bushes; corroborated by:

    - Ambushers 81

* Collins ordered the touring car to stop; corroborated by:

    - Corry
    - Lieut Smith
    - McPeak

* The convoy came under heavy machine gun fire; corroborated by:

    - Priv J O'Connell

* The convoy was under prolonged, heavy, continuous fire; corroborated by:

    - Lieut Smith
    - Corry
    - J O'Connell

* The Vickers gun on the armoured car continuously bombarded the ambushers with machine gun fire; corroborated by:
  - Smith
  - McPeak
  - Deasy
  - Ambushers 81

* Members of the convoy took cover behind a ditch or mud bank about two feet high and commenced firing; corroborated by:
  - Lieut Smith
  - Corry
  - Ambushers 81

* Collins took cover behind the armoured car; corroborated by:
  - McPeak

* From the touring car, they could only hear what was happening at the Crossley tender (but could not see them): corroborated by:
  - Lieut Smith;
  - McKenna;

* The men in the Crossley tender exchanged fire with the ambushers at the other end of the convoy; corroborated by:
  - Lieut Smith
  - Priv J O'Connell
  - McKenna

* There was rifle and machine gun fire coming from the forward end of the convoy, around the bend from where Dalton was;
  - McKenna;
  - Deasy;

* Collins had been firing a rifle from a prone position when he was hit; corroborated by:

- Corry

* The fighting went on for 15 or 20 minutes; corroborated by:
  - Deasy and Crofts;
  - Ambushers 81;

* The ambushers retreated after about 15 minutes; corroborated by:
  - Ambushers 81;

* Commdt O'Connell and Dalton attended the wounded Collins as he lay next to the armoured car, and attempted to bandage him; corroborated by:
  - Lieut Smith;

* Lieut Smith came up to them and began to assist them to carry the body; corroborated by:
  - Lieut Smith;

* Lieut Smith was wounded in the neck while trying to help move the body; corroborated by:
  - Lieut Smith;

* Lieut Smith helped carry the C-in-C's body; corroborated by:
  - McPeak

* There was "activity around the armoured car" just before the convoy left; corroborated by:
  - Deasy and Crofts;

Dalton's points corroborated by all other relevant accounts:
* the C-in-C suffered a large head-wound, behind the ear;
* All firing ceased when Collins died;

* dusk was approaching and it was beginning to get dark as the ambush concluded;

Dalton's points of question / self-contradiction
? Dalton claims to have ordered the driver to move on. However, with the tender of soldiers and barricade blocking the road ahead, it would have been impossible to drive on.

? Says that the ambushers had left their positions and were retreating; and that Cmmdt O'Connell reported that ambushers near the Crossley tender had already retreated. If so, how could O'Connell have been "under fire" at that point?

? Likewise says that Lieut. Smith was hit after the ambushers had retreated.

? Says that the C-in-C's body was first placed behind the armoured car; then that it was placed on the back of the armoured car; that after this it was carried around the bend to cover near the armoured car; then that it was placed in the touring car.

Dalton's points included which were *not* within the witness' direct personal knowledge
None

3) *Private Michael B Corry (driver of the touring car)*
First published: 1958 (in "*Michael Collins*" by Rex Taylor)
(Said to have "*circulated privately for many years*" before that. How it was recorded, whether written by himself, or by an interviewer, etc. is not known.)

Private Corry's account says that:
> he and others in the convoy "*were aware of*" the presence of anti-Treaty flying column(s) at various points throughout their journey through Cork, but encountered no hostilities;

> there were three Crossley tenders in the convoy: two with ten soldiers in each one, and a third with "*ropes, saws, picks, food etc. for emergency use*";

> two other men observed the time of their departure from Bandon was 8PM (GMT)

> they rounded a sharp curve onto a stretch of straight road;

> a single shot then "*rang out*";

> the C-in-C commanded "*Stop*" and was immediately obeyed;

> there was no obstruction on the road in front of the car;

> after they got out of the car, they came under heavy fire, but no one was hit;

> the four occupants of the Leyland touring car (himself, co-driver Quinn, Dalton and Collins) then walked back about 50 yards;

> they took cover at a bank or ditch two feet high, under heavy fire;

> behind them and in front of them was steep hillside;

> [as they faced the hill to the west of the road] firing came from directly in front only;

> on their extreme right the men from the Crossley tender were returning fire;

> on their extreme left the road was clear;

> Dalton called out to the armoured car gunner, when he observed that the Vickers gun was not firing;

> the gunner replied that the gun was jammed;

> about 6 feet from him, the C-in-C was firing from a prone position;

> the C-in-C then stood up and, after firing several rounds, fell on the roadside with a gaping head wound;

> the wound extended from "*near the left ear lobe*" to the "*upper section of the skull*";

> there was also a "*tear in the front of the forehead and a hole ripped in the front of his cap close to the badge*";

> Dalton then said to him, "*The General's finished*";

> Dalton and he placed the body across the Leyland touring car;

> as Collins died, the firing ceased.

Contradicted by other accounts:
Lieut Smith contradicts Corry as follows:
- x says that he (Smith, the cyclist) was the first vehicle to be fired upon, and the first to be hit (i.e. not the touring car, a quarter mile behind him);
- x the convoy immediately came under continuous fire (i.e. not "*a single shot*");
- x says that they were under continuous, heavy fire from both sides of the road (i.e. fire did not come from "*directly in front only*");
- x says that he (Lieut. Smith) began to help move the C-in-C's body, and was wounded in the neck in the attempt (Corry says that it was himself, and not Smith, who helped move the body);
- x says that the armoured car kept up machine gun fire at the ambushers' positions while Collins body was moved into the car (i.e. Vickers gun was not jammed);

Dalton contradicts Corry as follows:
- x says that the touring car was first hit by a burst of heavy machine gun fire (i.e. there was no "*single shot*" that "*rang out*");
- x says he (Dalton) first ordered driver to "*Drive like hell*" but that Collins countermanded him and ordered them to "*Jump out and we'll fight them.*" (Corry says only the C-in-C gave an order, which was simply "*Stop*");
- x the C-in-C's wound was behind the right ear (i.e. not behind the left ear);
- x describes his own (Dalton's) emotional state as deeply moved and chagrined by Collins' fate (i.e. not tersely announcing "*The General's finished*");
- x describes his own (Dalton's) actions as kneeling beside the C-in-C, applying bandages and saying prayers (i.e. did not follow that terse statement by simply moving the body onto the car);

- x says they first placed the body on the armoured car (i.e. not onto the touring car);
- x says that Lieut Smith helped them move the body (i.e. it was not Dalton and Corry alone who carried the body);
- x says that Lieut Smith was shot in the neck while they moved the body (Corry does not place Smith anywhere near them, and reports Collins as the only casualty);

Priv J O'Connell contradicts Corry as follows:
- x says that the first shots were heavy machine gun fire at the Crossley tender, at the forward end of the convoy near the barricade;

McPeak contradicts Corry as follows;
- x says that Lieut Smith carried Collins' body; (not Corry);
- x says that they carried his body to the Crossley tender; (not to the touring car);

McKenna contradicts Corry as follows:
- x first shots were fired a quarter mile ahead of the touring car, near the barricade;
- x Fire from ambushers was not heavy and was of short duration. (i.e. not heavy fire, and not for 20 minutes or more);
- x all the soldiers from the Crossley tender moved back to the touring car after all firing had ceased (Corry reports no one coming to them from the tender);

Deasy and Crofts contradict Corry as follows:
- x ambushers reported to them that there had been no casualties on either side (i.e. they did not see Collins wounded);

The ambushers 81 contradict Corry as follows:
- x they say that the accounts published by the Free State witnesses prior to 1981 were "*teeming with inaccuracies and thoroughly unreliable*";

x the motorcyclist was followed by one Crossley tender, after which came a touring car and then an armoured car (i.e. there was one tender, not three);

x the ambushers came under aggressive fire from the escort, following just two warning shots (i.e. convoy was not the first to come under fire);

x fire from the ambushers was not heavy;

x members of the convoy "*ran up and down the road*" (i.e. everyone in the touring car did not walk "*50 yards up the road*");

x ambushers reported that there had been no casualties on either side (i.e. they did not see Collins wounded);

All other relevant accounts contradict Corry as follows:
x there was only one Crossley tender (not three);

Corry's points corroborated by other some accounts:
* Anti-Treaty units in West Cork that day appeared to allow the convoy to pass unmolested; corroborated by:

    - McKenna (i.e. McKenna's account of a safe conduct, provided to the C-in-C, for peace negotiations)
    - Ambushers 81 (i.e. rumours of peace talks in progress current among ambushers);

    - Deasy (i.e. peace negotiations under discussion among anti-Treaty officers);

* At the ambush site the road was flanked by hills on both sides; corroborated by:

    - Smith
    - Dalton
    - McPeak
    - Deasy
    - McKenna
    - Ambushers 81

* A single warning shot "rang out"; corroborated by:

    - McPeak
    - Ambushers 81

* The C-in-C ordered the touring car to stop; corroborated by:

    - Dalton
    - Smith
    - McPeak

* The touring car came under fire only from the west side of the road; corroborated by:

    - McPeak
    - Deasy and Crofts
    - Ambushers 81

* Members of the convoy took cover behind a small bank or ditch; corroborated by:

    - Dalton
    - Smith
    - Ambushers 81

* There was firing at the rear end of the convoy near the touring car; corroborated by:

    - McKenna

* The men in the Crossley tender exchanged fire with ambushers at the forward end of the ambush site; corroborated by:

    - Dalton
    - Lieut Smith
    - Priv J O'Connell
    - McKenna

* The ambushers were a small party of only about four men; corroborated by:

- McPeak

  - Deasy and Crofts
  - Ambushers 81

* There was no machine gun fire from the ambushers; corroborated by:

  - McPeak
  - Ambushers 81
  - Deasy

* There was a problem with the Vickers gun in the armoured car; corroborated by:

  - McPeak
  - Priv J O'Connell

* Collins stood up, and then fell wounded; corroborated by:

  - Priv J O'Connell

* There was a wound near the left ear; corroborated by:

  - Priv J O'Connell
  - McKenna

* There was a wound in the forehead as well as near the ear; corroborated by:

  - Commdt. Frank Friel
  - Miss Eleanor Gordon
  - Dr Patrick Cagney
  - Albert Power

Corry's points corroborated by all other relevant accounts:
* the C-in-C suffered a large head-wound, behind the ear;
* all firing ceased when Collins died;
* dusk was approaching and it was beginning to get dark as the ambush concluded;

Corry's points of question / self-contradiction
? It has already been noted above that, by all accounts, there was one Crossley tender and not three, as in Corry's report. It seems rather a remarkable error to make: Corry being a driver, and vehicle specialist; and he goes into such detail about the contents of each one.

Corry's points included which were *not* within the witness' direct personal knowledge
None

4) *Private John O'Connell* [262]
First published: 1958 (in "*Michael Collins*" by Rex Taylor)

This account provided to Rex Taylor by letter, in response to newspaper articles by Taylor about Collins. Claims to have joined the convoy in Mallow, as a guide for the road to Cork.

According to Private O'Connell's account:

x the Leyland touring car carrying the C-in-C was at the head of the convoy, just behind the motorcyclist and in front of the Crossley tender;

x they travelled from Cork to Bandon "*via Skibbereen*";

x they saw an old dray cart blocking the road, and came under heavy machine gun fire;

x They got out of the tender and returned fire.

x The gun in the armoured car ceased firing because two belts fell off.

x There was a lull in the firing, and Collins stood up, looked around and started to reload his rifle.

x There was a single shot and Collins fell.

x On account of the firing it was almost ten minutes before anyone could get near his body.

x There was a ghastly wound near his left ear.

x On the return trip the armoured car and the touring car had to be abandoned.

Contradicted by other accounts:

Lieut Smith contradicts O'Connell as follows:
x says the armoured car's Vickers machine gun kept firing after the C-in-C was dead, while they moved his body and push-started the touring car (i.e. the Vickers gun was not jammed and had not ceased firing);

Dalton contradicts J O'Connell as follows:
x the motorcyclist was followed by a Crossley tender, after which came a touring car and then an armoured car (i.e. the touring car was not at the front near the cyclist);

x says that the touring car was the first hit, and by a burst of heavy fire (i.e. Crossley tender not the first to come under fire);

x says the Vickers gun kept up continuous fire on the ambushers (i.e. had not ceased firing);

x no ten minute delay before reaching the wounded C-in-C;

Corry contradicts J O'Connell as follows:
x first fire was "a single shot" (i.e. not heavy machine gun fire);

McKenna contradicts J O'Connell as follows:
x the Crossley tender came under fire only after they had stopped and the soldiers began to dismount (i.e. not before they got out);

x there was no machine gun fire from the ambushers;

x they came under rapid but not heavy fire;

x soldiers from the Crossley tender (such has McKenna and J O'Connell) were separated from the C-in-C by sight until the ambush was over and Collins already dead (i.e. J O'Connell would have had no direct knowledge of how Collins fell);

x soldiers from the tender (such has McKenna and J O'Connell) had no knowledge of any delay between the time Collins fell and when others reached his body;

Deasy and Crofts contradict J O'Connell as follows:

- x the ambushers had no machine guns;
- x ambushers reported to them that there had been no casualties on either side (i.e. they did not see Collins wounded);
- x the ambushers had been under "*withering fire*" from the armoured car's Vickers machine gun (i.e. there was no problem with Vickers gun);

Ambushers 81 contradict J O'Connell as follows:
- x they say that the accounts published by the Free State witnesses prior to 1981 were "*teeming with inaccuracies and thoroughly unreliable*";
- x the motorcyclist was followed by a Crossley tender, after which came a touring car and then an armoured car (i.e. the touring car was not at the front near the cyclist);
- x the first firing was two warning shots (i.e. not heavy machine gun fire);
- x the ambushers came under aggressive fire from the escort following their two warning shots (i.e. convoy was not the first to come under fire);
- x the ambushers had three rifles and two revolvers (i.e. they had no machine guns);
- x ambushers reported no casualties on either side (i.e. they did not see Collins wounded);

All relevant accounts contradict J O'Connell as follows:
- x The Leyland touring car carrying the C-in-C was at the *end* of the convoy, just before the armoured car, which brought up the rear (i.e. touring car was not at the front near the cyclist);
- x no other account which refers to the armoured car's machine gun reports anything about belts falling off;

J O'Connell's points corroborated by some other accounts:
- * The convoy came under heavy machine-gun fire; corroborated by:
    - Dalton

* The Crossley tender stopped at the barricade and the men got out; corroborated by:

    - Lieut Smith;
    - McKenna;

* The men in the Crossley tender exchanged fire with ambushers at the forward end of the ambush site; corroborated by:

    - Dalton;
    - Lieut Smith;
    - Corry;
    - McKenna;

* There was a problem with the Vickers gun in the armoured car; corroborated by:

    - Corry
    - McPeak

* Collins at one point was firing his rifle from a prone or kneeling position; corroborated by:

    - Dalton;

* Collins stood up, and then fell wounded; corroborated by:

    - Corry

* The Leyland touring car was abandoned on their way back to Cork City;

    - Lieut Smith;

J O'Connell's points corroborated by all other relevant accounts:
* the convoy encountered an old dray cart which formed a barricade, blocking the road ahead;

* the C-in-C suffered a large head-wound near the ear;

* dusk was approaching and it was beginning to get dark as the ambush concluded;

J O'Connell's points of question / self-contradiction
? the route from Cork to Bandon does not pass near Skibbereen, which is 30 miles in the opposite direction;

? if there was a "*lull in the firing*" and then only "*a single shot*" when the C-in-C fell, how could it have also been impossible to reach the body for ten minutes due to heavy fire?

J O'Connell's points which were *not* within the witness' direct personal knowledge:
As one of the soldiers in the Crossley tender:

? he was not near enough to the armoured car to know anything first-hand about what happened with the Vickers gun inside it during the ambush;

? he was not by anyone's report, near enough to see Collins shot, nor does he claim that he was; therefore his information on how the C-in-C fell, or what happened either directly before or after, can be, at best, no more than hearsay.

5) *The ambushers 1964*
First published: 1964
(As detailed in its first paragraph (see preceding Appendix) this statement was composed by a meeting of survivors of the ambush, which took place 15 February 1964. Those present were: Liam Deasy, Tom Kelleher, Jim Hurley, Dan Holland, Pete Kearney, Tom Crofts; with Florence O'Donoghue of the Neutral IRA acting as secretary / recorder.)

This account says:
> Denis Long was on sentry duty at Béal na mBláth Cross for the night of 21-22 August;

>Tom Crofts spent the night of 21-22 August at Bill Murray's farmhouse near Béal na mBláth; Con Lucy spent that night at Jehr Long's pub; Liam Deasy and DeValera spent that night at Gurranereagh;

> the anti-Treaty officers first learned of Collins' presence in the area on the morning of 22 August, when it was reported to them by Denis Long;

>there was no order to kill Collins;

> Deasy and DeValera arrived at Béal na mBláth on the morning of 22 August, in company with Sean Hyde;

> DeValera continued on, "apparently to Ballyvourney"

> A decision was taken "on Divisional initiative" to lay an ambush 400 yards south of the cross, on the assumption it would probably return later in the day by the same route;

> "The ambush was decided on as part of the general policy of attacking Free State convoy..."

> when four 3rd Brigade officers arrived, the ambush was in preparation;

> The main ambush party numbered 20-25 men;

> The main ambush party included Liam Deasy, Tom Kelleher, Jim Hurley, Pete Kearney, Dan Holland, Tom Hales, Tom Crofts, Con Lucey, Sean Culhane, John Lordan, Bill Desmond, Dan Corcoran, C O'Donoghue, John O'Callaghan, Sonny O'Neill, Paddy Walsh, Sonny Donovan, Jim Crowley, Taddy O'Sullivan, Jerh Mahony;

> a mine was laid and a mineral water lorry with one wheel removed was set up as a road block;

> a farm butt was also placed across the entrance to the laneway which ran parallel to the road ;

> this ambush party remained in position during the day without any action taking place;

> In the afternoon a message was received from Bandon that Collins was there;

> It was then "considered unlikely that the convoy would return";

> the decision was made "probably by Deasy" to call off the ambush;

> when the main ambush party evacuated the position, a Cork No. 3 Brigade section remained to cover the withdrawal and clear the road;

> this group consisted of Tom Hales, Jim Hurley, Dan Holland, Tom Kelleher, Sonny O'Neill, Paddy Walsh, John O'Callaghan, Sonny Donovan, Bill Desmond and Dan Corcoran;

> they had left cover and were clearing the road when they heard the noise of a motorbike and lorries coming from the south;

> they thought that others of their party, who were walking down the road toward Long's pub, in a dangerously exposed position, would not be able to reach cover before the convoy overtook them;

> seven or eight of the Cork No. 3 section took up makeshift positions on the laneway and opened fire on the oncoming convoy;

> Jim Hurley fired at the motorcyclist and missed;

> Tom Kelleher fired at the following vehicle;

> the convoy stopped and opened fire;

> the ambushers had no machine guns, only rifles and revolvers;

>two machine guns in the convoy "raked" the ambushers' positions;

> the ambushers were not able to get off an aimed shot;

> the action lasted between 20 and 30 minutes;

> before it ended, it was getting dark enough to see flashes from the gunfire;

>it was almost 8 PM when the firing stopped;

> the Cork No. 3 section remained in position;

> the convoy withdrew under fire;

> no one in the ambush party knew of any Free State casualties;

> the ambushers learned of Collins' death only at 11PM that night, when the news was brought by Sean Galvin.

Contradicted by other accounts:
Lieut Smith contradicts the ambushers 64 as follows:
x says he was hit in the hand by the first shots (i.e. firing at him did not miss);

x reports wound to his neck (ambushers saw no casualties);

x reports hitting ambushers and seeing them fall (ambushers reported no casualties);

x says action lasted an hour (i.e. not 20 minutes)

x saw Collins wounded (ambushers saw no casualties);

Dalton contradicts the ambushers 64 as follows:
x   says that the touring car was the first to be hit, by a burst of heavy machine gun fire (i.e. ambushers 64 say they had no machine guns);

x   says that the ambushers "practically all retreated" soon after Collins was hit (i.e. ambushers did not remain in position, and the convoy did not withdraw under fire);

x   reports wounds to Lieut Smith and to the C-in-C (ambushers 64 saw no casualties);

Priv Corry contradicts the ambushers 64 as follows:
x   says convoy came under heavy fire only after they stopped and got out (i.e. ambushers 64 say they "opened fire" on the "oncoming convoy");

x   says that ambushers' firing ceased as Collins died (i.e. the convoy did not withdraw under fire);

x   saw Collins wounded (ambushers 64 saw no casualties);

Priv J O'Connell contradicts ambushers 64 as follows:
x   says that the convoy came under heavy machine gun fire from the ambushers (ambushers 64 say they had only rifles and revolvers);

x   saw Collins wounded (ambushers 64 saw no casualties);

McKenna contradicts the ambushers 64 as follows:
x   says the tender was fired on only after they stopped and were getting out (i.e. not while "oncoming");

x   says all firing over when men from the tender moved back to the touring car (i.e. convoy did not withdraw under fire.)

x   says Collins was dead when the men from the tender reached him (ambushers 64 saw no casualties);

Deasy and Crofts contradict the ambushers 64 as follows:
x   say that Deasy returned to Béal na mBláth around 7PM, from Gurranereagh, where he'd spent the day (i.e. he did not form part of the main ambush party during the afternoon);

x   say that Tom Hales called off the ambush (i.e. not Deasy);

x say that Tom Hales and other officers were walking away from the ambush site around 7PM (i.e. Hales did not remain on site at the time of the action);

x say that Hales left just five men behind to remove the mine and roadblock, and provide cover (i.e. not ten men);

x say there were five anti-Treaty men at the site when the ambush took place (i.e. not ten, six or seven);

Ambushers 81 contradict ambushers 64 as follows:

x there were five anti-Treaty men at the site when the ambush took place (i.e. not ten, six or seven);

x the ambushers fire was half-hearted and not aimed (ambushers 64 say J Hurley aimed a shot at the cyclist, and T Kelleher at the vehicle following it);

x all five ambushers retreated under fire "after about fifteen minutes" (i.e. they did not remain in position, and the convoy did not withdraw under fire);

Ambushers 64 points corroborated by some other accounts:

* There was no order to kill Collins; corroborated by:

    - Deasy and Crofts (i.e. ambush general policy on incursions into rebel territory);
    - Ambushers 81 (i.e. ambushers on site discussed peace moves under way, expected hostilities soon to end, and not focussed to eliminate any particular target);

* Deasy and DeValera arrived at Béal na mBláth together on the morning of 22 August ; corroborated by:

    - Deasy and Crofts

* The ambush was laid due to "general policy" of attacking Free State convoys in rebel territory; corroborated by:

    - Deasy and Crofts

* A mine was laid and a cart set up as a roadblock ; corroborated by:

    - Ambushers 81

* The ambushers position was in a parallel laneway west of the main road; corroborated by:

    - Dalton
    - Ambushers 81

* It was decided that the convoy was unlikely to return via Béal na mBláth; corroborated by:

    - Deasy and Crofts;

* It was then decided late in the afternoon to call off the ambush; corroborated by:

    - Deasy and Crofts
    - Ambushers 81

* When the main ambush party dispersed, a small section remained behind to cover the withdrawal and clear the road; corroborated by:

    - Deasy and Crofts
    - Ambushers 81

* When the small section remaining realized the convoy was coming, they were concerned about members of the party still walking down

    the road, whom the convoy might overtake unless held back by some action; corroborated by:

    - Deasy and Crofts (i.e. party of officers was walking down the road shortly before the ambush began);
    - Ambushers 81 (i.e. fire intended chiefly to give warning and cover to anti-Treaty officers in Béal na mBláth)

* There were six or seven ambushers; corroborated by:

    - McPeak (i.e. ambushers were a small party, perhaps five);

- Deasy and Crofts (i.e. T Hales and others had left just before);
- Ambushers 81 (give their number as five, perhaps leaving out T Foley, who was under age and unarmed.)

* Jim Hurley fired at the cyclist and missed, Tom Kelleher fired at the vehicle following it; corroborated by:

  - Corry ("a single shot rang out")
  - Smith (says he was the first fired on)
  - McPeak ("just a few odd shots")
  - McKenna (reported no wound to cyclist)
  - Ambushers 81 (say that initially just two shots were fired)

* The ambushers had no machine guns; corroborated by:

  - McPeak
  - Ambushers 81

* The convoy bombarded the ambushers with machine gun fire ; corroborated by:

  - Smith
  - Dalton
  - Corry
  - J O'Connell
  - McPeak
  - McKenna
  - Deasy and Crofts
  - Ambushers 81

* The ambushers were not able to get off an aimed shot; corroborated by:

  - Ambushers 81

* The ambush lasted between 20 and 30 minutes; corroborated by:

  - Dalton
  - Ambushers 81

* The ambushers did not see any casualties, and did not of Collins' death until the news was reported to them later that night ; corroborated by:
  - Deasy and Crofts
  - Ambushers 81

Ambushers 64 points corroborated by all other relevant accounts:
* the convoy encountered an old dray cart, blocking the road;
* The convoy stopped and returned fire
* dusk was approaching and it was beginning to get dark as the ambush concluded;

Ambushers 64 points of question / self-contradiction
? They say that conditions did not enable the ambushers to get off an aimed shot. Yet also report that J Hurley fired at the cyclist, and T Kelleher at the vehicle following it.

? They say that 10 men remained after the main ambush party dispersed, to cover withdrawal and clear the road. Although they do not say that any more men left between then and the ambush, they then say only 6 or 7 took part in the ambush.

Ambushers 64 points which were *not* within the witness' direct personal knowledge:
? Conflicting reports as to where DeValera went on leaving them.

6) *Private John "Jock" McPeak armoured car gunner*
First published: 1971
(A member of the C-in-C's convoy, Jock McPeak was the machine-gunner who manned the Vickers water-cooled machine gun in the turret of the armoured car. He was interviewed at length for a series of articles by Ray Smith and Jim Nicoll, which appeared in The Irish Independent newspaper, May 18 – 21, 1971. These are McPeak's statements, by direct and indirect quotation, from said newspaper articles.)

McPeak said that:
> He first heard of the convoy trip on the morning of August 20, shortly before leaving Portobello Barracks, Dublin, at 6AM.

> He received no instructions as to who would be in the convoy.

> He was initially told nothing but just *"Get the armoured car and stand by."*

> He had no second gunner, but did have a driver and co-driver.

> Calls the touring car a Lancia.

> Places the touring car at the head of the convoy, in front of the Crossley tender, upon leaving Portobello Barracks.

> There was no serious drinking by members of the convoy during the trip, of a nature to interfere with their duties.

> Lieut Smith, the motorcycle scout, was first to see the roadblock.

> Lieut Smith *"passed back information of a possible ambush."*

> Men in the tender could easily have cleared the obstacle in a couple of minutes, and then *"we could have gone straight through."*

> Said Collins *"would not have it…he who ordered the convoy to stop."*

> Said it was "silly" and unnecessary to stand and fight, as they could have easily gone around the barrier in the road.

> There were *"just a few odd shots at first"* from the ambushers.

> He believed that the attackers were a small party, of only three or four men.

> There was no machine gun fire from the ambushers, only rifle fire.

> When the ambush began, he (McPeak) was riding standing up in the turret, with his head outside the hatch.

> He could then clearly see the C-in-C and Dalton sitting in the touring car, just in front of him.

> When firing began, he closed the hatch cover.

> *"I never saw them anymore after I closed the hatch."*

> The entire convoy likewise was virtually invisible to him for the rest of the engagement, during which he looked only straight through his narrow sights, at the hill to the left of the armoured car, where the ambushers were.

> He had two belts of .303 ammunition, with 250 rounds each; plus a box of 1000 rounds loose (for re-filling the belts.)

> It would normally be the second gunner's job to re-fill the belts with ammunition.
> *"But for some unknown reason he [the armoured car's second gunner] was left behind in Cork [City]"*
> He emptied two belts (500 rounds); to *"let [them] know there was a machine gun"* and to *"make them keep their heads down."*
> When the ambush began, two "staff captains" were riding inside the armoured car as passengers.
> When the shooting began, he asked them to get out of the armoured car.
> They ignored this request.
> He then asked the two captains to assist him by refilling the ammunition belts for the Vickers gun; and spent some time explaining and demonstrating how to do this.
> One captain did refill the belts, but didn't do it properly.
> This caused the Vickers gun to jam and fire only sporadically for the rest of the engagement.
> He opened the hatch to let in some cool air, and a shot sheared off a bolt of the hatch.
> The Vickers gun was pointed up at the one hillside to the west, throughout the engagement.

> He didn't know that Collins had been hit, until his driver told him; and then did not know that the wound was fatal.
> Lieut Smith carried the C-in-C's body.
> *"They lifted him from where he fell around the wing of the armoured car."*

> Collins was taken to Shanakiel Hospital.
> The armoured car's outer surface showed *"plenty of"* visible marks where it had been hit by gunfire.
> The doctor at the hospital to which Collins was taken *"maintained"* that he had been killed by a ricochet.

> Quoted Dr Gogarty as saying Collins was hit by ricochet.

> There was *"never was any suspicion, hint of neglect, or accusations of carelessness made against me during the period between that day in August1922, and the day in early December 1922"* when he deserted and stole the armoured car which had been used in Collins' fatal convoy.

Contradicted by other accounts:
Lieut Smith contradicts McPeak as follows;
- x says that he (Lieut Smith) was wounded first in the hand, then in the neck; (not just in the neck);
- x never says that he (Smith) ever *"passed back"* any information whatever to anyone in the convoy about either the barricade, or about possible ambush;
- x reports heavy, prolonged fire, from a large body of men, on both sides of the road; (not just a few odd shots, from three or four men, on one side of the road only);
- x says he (Smith) did not carry Collins' body;
- x says the C-in-C's body was carried to the armoured car; (not to the Crossley tender.)

Dalton contradicts McPeak as follows;
- x says the first fire at the convoy was a *"fierce fusillade"* of machine gun fire, which swept the road and shattered the windscreen; (not just a few odd shots, not rifle fire only);
- x says the armoured car's machine gun bombarded the ambushers' positions throughout the engagement; (i.e. armoured car's machine gun did not malfunction);
- x says that, for about twenty minutes, the convoy remained under heavy fire; (not just a few odd shots);
- x says Smith carried the body to the armoured car; (not to the Crossley tender);
- x says Collins' body was taken to Bon Secours hospital; (not to Shanakiel Hospital.)

Corry contradicts McPeak as follows;

x says that he (Corry) and Dalton carried Collins' body; (not Smith);

x says that they carried his body to the touring car; (not to the Crossley tender);

Priv J O'Connell contradicts McPeak as follows;

x says the touring car was at the head of the convoy, just behind the cyclist and in front of the Crossley tender; (not at the rear, just before the armoured car.)

McKenna contradicts McPeak as follows;

x names several persons as being present with him (McKenna) to hear Dr Gogarty's comments on the C-in-Cs wounds; (does not name McPeak as being there);

x heard Dr Gogarty say that Collins must have been shot at very close range; (not that he was killed by a ricochet);

McPeak's points corroborated by some other accounts:

* At the ambush site, the road was flanked by steep hills on both sides; corroborated by:

    - Dalton
    - Smith
    - Corry
    - Deasy
    - McKenna
    - Ambushers 81

* As the convoy approached the ambush site, the motorcyclist was followed by the Crossley tender, then the touring car, then the armoured car; corroborated by:

    - Dalton
    - Ambushers 81

* There was a warning shot; corroborated by:

    - Corry

- Ambushers 81

* The first fire at the convoy was only a few odd shots; corroborated by:

    - Corry
    - McKenna
    - Ambushers 81

* The C-in-C ordered the car to stop; corroborated by:

    - Dalton
    - Corry

* The convoy was fired on only after it stopped; corroborated by:

    - McKenna

* The convoy came under fire only from the west side of the road; corroborated by:

    - Corry
    - Deasy and Crofts
    - Ambushers 81

* The ambushers were a small party of only about four men; corroborated by:

    - Corry
    - Deasy and Crofts
    - Ambushers 81

* Fire from the ambushers was not intense, heavy or prolonged ; corroborated by:

    - McKenna
    - Deasy
    - Ambushers 81

* There was no machine gun fire from the ambushers ; corroborated by:

    - Corry

- McKenna
- Ambushers 81

* Collins took cover behind the armoured car ; corroborated by:

    - Dalton

* The armoured car's machine gun bombarded the ambushers continuously; corroborated by:

    - Dalton
    - Smith
    - Deasy
    - Ambushers 81

* The armoured car's machine gun malfunctioned, so that it could not fire continuously; corroborated by:

    - Corry
    - J O'Connell

* Lieut Smith carried the C-in-C's body; corroborated by:

    - Dalton

    * Lieut Smith was wounded in the neck; corroborated by:
    - Dalton
    - Smith

* "There was activity around the armoured car" just before the convoy left the ambush site; corroborated by:

    - Dalton
    - Smith
    - Deasy and Crofts
    - Ambushers 81

* The C-in-C's body was taken to Shanakiel Hospital; corroborated by:

    - McKenna

- Frank Friel
- Miss Gordon
- Dr Cagney

McPeak's points corroborated by all relevant accounts:
* the convoy encountered a barricade, blocking the road ahead;
* at the time of the ambush, dusk was approaching;

McPeak's points which were not within the witness' direct personal knowledge:
? Repeatedly insists how easily the convoy could have passed around the barricade which, according to his own account, *he never saw*.

? By his own account, never saw Collins after he closed the hatch at the first shots; so could not have seen who carried him.

? Reports a hospital doctor's medical assessment of Collins' wounds, but never claims that he (McPeak) was ever at the hospital.

? Likewise does not claim to have been present to hear any report by Dr Gogarty concerning the wounds.

McPeak's points of question / self-contradiction
? Says there was no second gunner in the armoured car when it left Dublin; later says that his second gunner was left behind in Cork City. Others report him commenting on a second gunner who joined the convoy at Cork City.

? Never specifies what *"information of a possible ambush"* Lieut Smith *"passed back,"* when, or to whom. While his other statements indicate that he remained inside the armoured car throughout the engagement, and had no conversation with anyone outside it.

7) *William McKenna*
First published: 1981
(Bill McKenna was a very young Volunteer, about 17 years old in 1922. Before the ambush, he acted as a courier, delivering urgent messages of the most sensitive nature, wherever Collins happened to be. This placed

McKenna in a position of the highest trust, at the innermost circle of his usual Dublin bodyguard.

For his 1981 book, Feehan interviewed him, as one of the last survivors of the C-in-C's escort. McKenna had been a member of the detachment of soldiers who travelled in the Crossley tender.)

McKenna reported that:

> during the journey, it was generally rumoured among the soldiers of the convoy that Collins' purpose on this trip was to negotiate an end to the Civil War;

> Dalton was aware of this purpose, and had been in communication with the C-in-C about it from Cork City,

> McKenna saw copies of decoded messages from Dalton to the C-in-C which included proposed terms for a cease-fire; as well as Collins' reply, that the anti-Treaty side should provide details of their damage to bridges, roads, etc.

> Dalton had in his possession such a list of blown bridges and mined roads *"which had been given to him on behalf of the anti-Treaty forces as a kind of assurance of safe-conduct and goodwill"*;

> coming into Béal na mBláth, they rounded a long curve, and stopped suddenly when they saw an overturned dray cart and broken bottles barring the way;

> Lieutenant Smith had left his motorcycle and was near the cart;

> the first shots were fired as the soldiers dismounted from the Crossley tender;

> fire from the ambushers was *"not heavy, but rapid"* and lasted about two minutes;

> they divided into two sections: one of which began to remove the barricade and the other to return fire;

> when the shooting stopped near the barricade, they could hear firing at the Bandon end of the ambush site but could not see the armoured car or touring car, because of the bend in the road;

> "*after a short while*" firing stopped, and the soldiers from the tender "*moved cautiously*" back toward the C-in-C's car;

> by the time they got to the touring car, the C-in-C was dead;

> it was getting dark and McKenna did not then see the wound;

> there was great emotional distress among the convoy members on the rest of the journey and Cmmdt. O'Connell (commander of the Crossley tender) wept openly;

> at the Imperial Hotel in Cork City "some officer" took the body and delivered it to the British military hospital at Shanakiel;

> three days later, in Dublin, McKenna was present when Dr Oliver St John Gogarty showed the wounds to Desmond Fitzgerald, Moya Llewellyn Davies and some relatives of Collins;

> a large portion of flesh under the right ear had been blown away and Gogarty had filled in the cavity with a wax-like substance;

> close to the left ear there was a small circular wound which seemed "bluish" in color;

> this "bluish" wound was clearly visible when the C-in-C was later lying in state;

> he heard Dr. Gogarty say at this time that Collins must have been shot at very close range;

> he and most of his fellow soldiers in the tender felt sure that Collins was *not* shot by the ambushers.

Contradicted by other accounts:
Lieut Smith contradicts McKenna as follows:

x says that the first shots were fired at himself (Lieut Smith) immediately upon reaching the ambush site, before he dismounted from his motorcycle (i.e. first shots were not after he had dismounted and the Crossley tender had come up to him);

x says that he (Lieut Smith) was taking cover in a ditch when the Crossley tender came up to him at the barricade (i.e. he was not standing next to the barricade);

x says that they were under prolonged, heavy fire around the tender (i.e. lasted more than two minutes);

x says that only he (Smith) went back to the touring car (i.e. the soldiers from the Crossley tender did not move back there);

x says that the ambush lasted an hour (i.e. did not end just "*a short while*" after two minutes of firing ceased.)

Dalton contradicts McKenna as follows:
x says that the touring car was the first hit, and by a burst of heavy fire (i.e. not the Crossley tender);

x says convoy was under heavy, continuous fire, including machine gun fire, from the ambushers, for a prolonged time, until just after Collins fell; (McKenna says fire was not heavy and was of short duration);

x says the first shots were machine gun fire, at the touring car (i.e. not at the Crossley tender, 50 yards ahead of the touring car);

x Dalton says only Commdt O'Connell came up to him from the tender (i.e. all the soldiers from the Crossley tender did not move back to the touring car);

Priv J O'Connell contradicts McKenna as follows:
x The Crossley tender came under fire as soon as they saw the dray cart blocking the road (i.e. not after dismounting);

x They immediately experienced heavy machine gun fire (McKenna says fire was "*not heavy*" and does not indicate machine gun);

McPeak contradicts McKenna as follows;
- x Gives a different account of Dr Gogarty's assessment of Collins' wounds; (McKenna does not include McPeak among those he reports as present to hear Dr Gogarty's comments);

- x Says that Dr Gogarty attributed Collins' wounds to ricochet; (not to fire at very close range.)

The ambushers 81 contradict McKenna as follows:
- x the ambushers came under aggressive fire from the convoy following just two warning shot (i.e. convoy was not the first to come under fire);

- x ambushers reported no casualties on either side (i.e. they did not see Collins wounded);

McKenna's points corroborated by some other accounts:
* Discussion about peace talks in progress was current on both sides in West Cork that day; corroborated by:
  - Ambushers 81 (i.e. rumours of peace talks in progress current among ambushers);
  - Deasy (i.e. ending the war under discussion among anti-Treaty officers);

* Collins was travelling under safe conduct agreements from anti-Treaty representatives; corroborated by:
  - Corry (i.e. Corry's statement anti-Treaty columns were nearby throughout the journey, but did not interfere with the convoy)

* At the ambush site, the road was flanked by hills on both sides; corroborated by:
  - Dalton
  - Smith
  - Corry
  - McPeak
  - Deasy
  - Ambushers 81

* Crossley tender stopped at the barricade and the soldiers dismounted; corroborated by:
    - Smith
    - Priv J O'Connell

* The convoy was fired on only after it stopped; corroborated by:
    - McPeak

* The men from the Crossley tender formed two groups, one to move the obstacle, and the other to return fire; corroborated by:
    - Smith

* The men from the Crossley tender exchanged fire with the ambushers; corroborated by:
    - Smith;
    - Dalton
    - Private O'Connell
    - Corry

* The fire from the ambushers was not heavy and was of short duration; corroborated by:
    - McPeak
    - Deasy and Crofts
    - Ambushers 81;

* There was no machine-gun fire from the ambushers; corroborated by:
    - McPeak
    - Ambushers 81
    - Deasy

* From the Crossley tender, they could only hear what was happening at the touring car and armoured car (but could not see them): corroborated by
    - Smith;
    - Dalton

* There was firing in the area of the touring car; corroborated by:
    - Smith;
    - Dalton;
    - Corry

- J O'Connell
  - McPeak

* When the C-in-C was dead, the ambushers had retreated; corroborated by:
  - Dalton

* Collins was *not* shot by the ambushers; corroborated by:
  - Ambushers 81

* The C-in-C's body was taken to Shanakiel Hospital; corroborated by:
  - McPeak
  - Frank Friel
  - Miss Gordon
  - Dr Cagney

McKenna's points corroborated by all other relevant accounts:
* a cart blocked the road, causing the convoy vehicles to stop;

* the C-in-C suffered a large head-wound, behind the ear;

* The fighting came to an end as Collins died;

* dusk was approaching and it was beginning to get dark as the ambush concluded;

McKenna's points which were *not* within the witness' direct personal knowledge
None

8) *Liam Deasy and Tom Crofts*
First published: 1981
(Deasy was anti-Treaty Commander of the First Southern Division and Tom Crofts was his Divisional Adjutant. Feehan included a summary of their statements together in his book. Deasy's own book "*Brother Against Brother*" appeared shortly afterward, reiterating and expanding this version.)

Deasy and Crofts say that:

> about 7PM they were walking from Béal na mBláth village out the Bandon road toward the ambush site when they met Tom Hales (the Brigade Commandant) coming away from it;

> Hales said to them that he'd called off the ambush and sent the men home, because the convoy was unlikely to return by the same route as it had passed that morning; [261]

> Hales said he'd left just five men behind: one Battalion Engineer to remove the mine, and four others to provide him protection;

> with Hales and several other officers who had been waiting in ambush, they (Deasy and Crofts) returned to Long's pub in Béal na mBláth village for something to eat;

> they were in the pub between 10 and 20 minutes when they heard gunfire from the direction of the ambush site;

> they rushed out and ran along the old Bandon road, which is parallel to the road the convoy had taken;

> it took them about 15 or 20 minutes to cross the fields to high ground about 300-400 yards from the convoy;

> it was dark and hazy, and they could see very little besides the tender and the turret of the armoured car;

> they saw some activity around the armoured car;

> they fired a few shots in that direction;

> convoy moved off "*almost immediately*" they came in sight of it;

> they returned to Béal na mBláth village, and were shortly joined by the ambush party;

---

261 It is standard military practice, when moving through hostile territory, never to return by the same route as one came by.

> the ambushers reported *no casualties on either side;*

> the ambushers reported that they had been under "*withering fire*" from the machine gun in the armoured car;

> the officers' meeting, which had been postponed, got under way about 9:30PM;

> the meeting had just begun when Sean Galvin of Crookstown rushed in and told them that Michael Collins had been shot dead in the ambush;

> Galvin also reported that the convoy had taken Collins' body to Cork City via Crookstown, Cloughduv and Kileeny;

> the meeting was immediately adjourned;

> many of those present, who had been Collins' personal friends, grieved for his loss.

Contradicted by other accounts:
Lieut Smith contradicts Deasy & Crofts as follows:

x says that the convoy was under prolonged, heavy fire from both sides of the road, throughout the ambush (i.e. from the east side of the road, as well as the west, not just "a few shots", and not only moments before the convoy moved off);

x indicates that the convoy engaged in a major battle with a large body, comparable in numbers to the 25 soldiers in the convoy (i.e. not just five men);

x says that the convoy men shot some of the ambushers and saw them fall (i.e. no lack of anti-Treaty casualties);

x reports Collins was wounded (i.e. no lack of Free State casualties);

x says the battle lasted an hour (i.e. it was not over within 15 or 20 minutes);

Priv J O'Connell contradicts Deasy & Crofts as follows:
x saw Collins wounded (Deasy & Crofts say their men reported no casualties on either side);

McKenna contradicts Deasy & Crofts as follows:
x says the C-in-C was dead when they reached the touring car's end of the convoy (Deasy & Crofts say their men reported no casualties on either side);

Deasy and Crofts' points corroborated by some other accounts:
* Deasy [262] states that there were a number of meetings of anti-Treaty officers, on 21 and 22 August, regarding ending the war; corroborated by:
    - McKenna (i.e. McKenna's account of peace negotiations under discussion)
    - Corry (i.e. Corry's statement that anti-Treaty columns were nearby throughout the journey, but did not interfere with the convoy)
    - Ambushers 81 (i.e. rumours of peace talks in progress current among ambushers);

* At about 6:30PM the ambush was called off and most of the anti-Treaty men dispersed; corroborated by:
    - Ambushers 81

* Five men then remained of the ambushing party; corroborated by:
    - McPeak (i.e. McPeak's account tallies with Deasy & Crofts' number of attackers)
    - McKenna (i.e. McKenna's account tallies with Deasy & Crofts' number of attackers)
    - Ambushers 81

* At the ambush site, the road was flanked by hills on both sides; corroborated by:
    - Smith
    - Corry
    - McPeak

---

262 In Deasy's separate memoire "*Brother Against Brother*"

- McKenna
- Ambushers 81

* The ambushers were on the west side of the road only; corroborated by:
    - Corry
    - McPeak

* Fire from ambushers was not intense, heavy or prolonged; corroborated by:
    - McPeak
    - McKenna (i.e. McKenna tallies with numbers and weaponry given by Deasy & Crofts)
    - Ambushers 81

* There was rifle and machine gun fire from the convoy; corroborated by:
    - Smith
    - Dalton
    - McKenna

* The armoured car bombarded the ambushers with machine gun fire; corroborated by:
    - Smith
    - Dalton
    - Priv J O'Connell
    - McPeak

* The ambush lasted between 15 and 20 minutes; corroborated by:
    - Dalton
    - McKenna
    - Ambushers 81

* There was "*activity around the armoured car*" just before the convoy left; corroborated by:
    - Smith
    - Dalton
    - McPeak
    - Ambushers 81;

* The ambushers believed that they had incurred no casualties on either side, and did not believe that they had shot Collins; corroborated by:

- Ambushers 81

Deasy and Crofts' points corroborated by all other relevant accounts:
* an old dray cart blocked the road, causing the convoy vehicles to stop;

* dusk was approaching and it was beginning to get dark as the ambush concluded;

Deasy and Crofts' points which were *not* within their direct personal knowledge
None

9) *The ambushers 1981*
First published: 1981
(Feehan interviewed "*all known survivors*" from the ambush party "*except John Callaghan,*" and summarized their accounts collectively. The points below are taken from that version. It seems the men cooperated with him initially on condition that their names not be published; for they were not identified by Feehan until his 6th edition.

A detailed list of those responsibly alleged to have taken part, are shown in the chapter *"What does the eye-witness testimony tell us?"* (under the sub-headings *"The Anti-Treaty Men's Accounts" "Who were they?"* Debate regarding their identity is unlikely to be settled here.)

This account says:

> throughout the day, as they waited in ambush, it was freely rumoured among them that the war would soon be over;

> therefore they were not in any very belligerent mood, and did not feel set upon any particular determination to shoot anyone;

- they put an old dray cart across the road at the Béal na mBláth end of the position and a short distance further up, a mine;

- the mine was to be detonated from up a laneway which ran off the main road west, and then south, parallel to the main road;

- at about 6:30 it was decided to call off the ambush, because the convoy was unlikely to return by that route;

- two men were detailed to remove the cart off the road and also to defuse the mine; three others stayed to protect them "*just in case anything happened*";

- three of the men had rifles; the other two had revolvers; they had no machine guns;

- two of these [three men standing guard] were southward down the laneway, at a slight angle to where the monument is today; the other one was on the laneway about half way between the other sentries and the engineers' party, near two stone piers;

- two men clearing the road first defused the mine;

- one of them went up the laneway with the cables and plunger;

- the other one started to move the cart out of the road;

- while he was doing so, the sentries saw the convoy coming;

- the convoy was moving very slowly, between 15 and 20mph;

- there was a motorcyclist in front, followed by a Crossley tender, in which there were men standing up; then came the touring car and then the armoured car;

- after some hesitation, one of the sentries fired two shots, to warn their men clearing the road to take cover;

- accordingly, the men clearing the road ran up the laneway;

> members of the convoy jumped out and took cover behind a little ditch about two feet high and started firing;

> with their elevated position and good cover, the convoy was at their mercy, and they could easily have "*picked them off*";

> ambushers' fire was half-hearted, not aimed at particular targets;

> their fire was intended chiefly to delay the convoy, give warning and cover to officers walking toward Béal na mBláth Cross;

> the Free State party adhered to no strategy, but simply ran up and down the road needlessly exposing themselves;

> after about 15 minutes the ambushers retreated from the position, three up a lane running off to the northwest, and the other two up another lane running west;

> they do not deny the possibility that one of their bullets might have killed Collins, but it would be one chance in a thousand, as they were not aiming at anyone or anything;

> the published accounts attributed to the Free State party before 1981 are "*teeming with inaccuracies and thoroughly unreliable*";

> Collins must have been killed either accidentally or deliberately by one of his own party.

Contradicted by other accounts:
Lieut Smith contradicts the ambushers 81 as follows:
    x gives the impression that the convoy was attacked by a substantial body of men, of comparable numbers (i.e. not by just five men);

    x says that the convoy was attacked from both sides of the road (i.e. not from the left (west) side only);

    x says that he was wounded in the hand and neck (ambushers 81 reported no casualties on either side);

- x says that the convoy was under heavy fire for a prolonged period (i.e. not "*half-hearted*" firing for fifteen minutes);

- x says that he saw several ambushers fall, hit by gunfire (ambushers 81 reported no casualties);

- x saw Collins wounded (ambushers 81 saw no casualties on either side);

- x says that the ambush lasted one hour (i.e. not 15 minutes);

Dalton contradicts the ambushers 81 as follows:
- x the first shots were a burst of heavy machine gun fire from the ambushers (i.e. no single warning shots);

- x says that the convoy was under heavy fire before returning any fire (i.e. convoy did not start firing after isolated warning shots from ambushers);

- x says that the convoy was under heavy fire for a prolonged period (i.e. not "*half-hearted*" firing);

- x reported Collins wounded, and also Lieut Smith (ambushers 81 reported no casualties on either side);

Priv Corry contradicts the ambushers 81 as follows:
- x says there were three Crossley tenders in the convoy (not just one):

- x says the first shots were heavy machine gun fire from the ambushers (i.e. not warning shots);

- x says the occupants of the touring car got out and walked 50 yards up the road (i.e. did not "*run up and down the road*");

- x saw Collins wounded (ambushers 81 did not see any Free State casualties);

Priv J O'Connell contradicts the ambushers 81 as follows:
x the touring car was at the head of the convoy, following the cyclist, in front of the Crossley tender (i.e. not at the rear, just before the armoured car);

x the convoy came under heavy machine gun fire from the ambushers (ambushers 81 say they had only rifles and revolvers);

x saw Collins wounded (ambushers 81 did not see Collins wounded);

McKenna contradicts the ambushers 81 as follows:
x the Crossley tender came under fire as the soldiers dismounted (i.e. there were no warning shots);

x after coming under fire, soldiers in the Crossley tender replied (i.e. they did not commence aggressive firing, in response to warning shots from ambushers);

x the soldiers from the Crossley tender "*moved cautiously*" up the road (i.e. they did not "*run up and down the road*");

x Collins was dead when the soldiers from the tender reached him (ambushers 81 did not see Collins wounded);

The ambushers 81 points corroborated by some other accounts:
* Rumours of peace talks in progress were current on both sides in West Cork that day; corroborated by:
    - McKenna (i.e. McKenna's account of peace negotiations under discussion)
    - Corry (i.e. Corry's statement that anti-Treaty columns were nearby throughout the journey, but did not interfere with the convoy)
    - Deasy (i.e. ending the war under discussion among anti-Treaty officers);

* The ambush was called off and the column sent home about 6:30 PM; corroborated by:
    - Deasy and Crofts

* At the ambush site, the road was flanked by steep hills on both sides; corroborated by:
    - Smith
    - Dalton
    - Corry
    - McPeak
    - Deasy
    - McKenna

* Halfway up the hill on the left another road ran parallel, screened from view by trees and bushes; corroborated by:
    - Dalton

* Ambushers were on the west side of the road only; corroborated by:
    - Corry
    - Deasy and Crofts

* There were just five ambushers left at the site, when the convoy arrived; corroborated by:
    - Deasy and Crofts
    - McKenna (his account of fire agrees with numbers given by the ambushers)
    - McPeak

* The motorcyclist was followed by the Crossley tender, then the touring car, then the armoured car; corroborated by:
    - Dalton
    - McPeak

* The ambushers fired warning shot(s); corroborated by:
    - Corry
    - McPeak

* Members of the convoy took cover behind a small bank or ditch and began firing; corroborated by:
    - Lieut Smith
    - Dalton
    - Corry

* The ambush site was spread out over about a quarter mile; corroborated by:
    - Lieut Smith

* The ambushers' fire was not heavy, intense or prolonged; corroborated by:
    - McKenna
    - Deasy

* There was no machine gun fire from the ambushers; corroborated by:
    - Corry
    - McPeak
    - McKenna

* The armoured car's machine gun bombarded the ambushers continuously; corroborated by:
    - Smith
    - Dalton
    - Deasy
    - McPeak

* Members of the convoy "*ran up and down the road*"; corroborated by:
    - Dalton

* Ambush lasted about 15 or 20 minutes; corroborated by:
    - Dalton
    - McKenna
    - Deasy and Crofts

* There was "*activity around the armoured car*" just before the convoy left; corroborated by:
    - Deasy and Crofts;

* Ambushers reported no casualties on either side; corroborated by:
    - Deasy and Crofts

* Collins was not shot by the ambushers; corroborated by:
    - McKenna

The ambushers 81 points corroborated by all other relevant accounts:

* an old dray cart blocked the road, causing the convoy to stop;

The ambushers 81 points which were *not* within their direct personal knowledge
The ambushers 81 assertion that Collins must have been shot by one of his own party may be considered conjecture. However, their conviction that they themselves inflicted no fatalities is within their own observation, to at least some extent.

10) *Commandant Frank Friel*
First published: 1981
(A Free State Army officer at the Imperial Hotel on the night of August 22-23. His testimony was published by Feehan; and he had apparently spoken publicly on these points as early as 1968, when Dalton made reference to Friel's contradiction of his (Dalton's) version of events.)

Cmmdt Friel reported that:

> at the Imperial Hotel, he was ordered by Dalton to take the body to the British Military Hospital at Shanakiel;

> at Shanakiel, he assisted Matron Miss Eleanor Gordon to wash Collins' face and bandage the head;

> there was an entry wound on the hair-line as well as the exit wound at the back of the head;

> he had experience with war injuries, and believed that the wound he saw could not have been made by a .303 rifle;

> it seemed to him more likely that the entry and exit wounds were made by a Mauser revolver bullet.

Cmmdt Friel Contradicted by other accounts:
Dalton contradicts Cmmdt Friel as follows:
x   says that the C-in-C's remains were taken to Bon Secours hospital (i.e. were not taken to Shanakiel);

Cmmdt Friel's points corroborated by other accounts:

* Collins' body was taken to the British military hospital at Shanakiel corroborated by:
  - McPeak
  - McKenna
  - Miss Eleanor Gordon
  - Dr Patrick Cagney

Cmmdt Friel's points included which were *not* within the witness' direct personal knowledge:
None

11) *Matron Miss Eleanor Gordon, Shanakiel Hospital*
First published 1981
(Miss Gordon was the matron at Shanakiel Hospital. She had been a military nurse in the First World War, and had considerable experience with gunshot wounds. Her testimony was published by J Feehan.)

Miss Gordon reported that:

> Collin's remains were brought to Shanakiel Hospital;

> the body was brought there by a military escort, not by a doctor;

> the military escort demanded at gunpoint that she handle Collins' body; although such duties were usually never performed by the matron, but by the nurse on duty;

> the military escort then disconnected telephone communications with the outside and forbade anyone to leave the hospital;

> assisted by Cmmdt. Frank Friel, she washed Collins' face and bandaged the head.

> there was an entry wound on the hair-line as well as an exit wound at the back of his head;

> there was a singed hole on the back of his tunic like a bullet hole.

Miss Gordon contradicted by other accounts:

Dalton contradicts MIss Gordon as follows:
- x says that the C-in-C's remains were taken to Bon Secours hospital (i.e. were not taken to British military hospital at Shanakiel);

- x maintains that there was only one wound.

Miss Gordon's points corroborated by other accounts:
* Collins' body was taken to the British military hospital at Shanakiel corroborated by:
    - McPeak
    - McKenna
    - Dr Patrick Cagney
    - F Friel

* Miss Gordon washed and bandaged the body at Shanakiel corroborated by:
    - F Friel

* There was an entry wound at the hair-line and exit wound corroborated by:
    - Corry
    - McKenna
    - Cmmdt Friel
    - Dr Patrick Cagney
    - Dr Oliver St John Gogarty
    - Albert Power

Miss Gordon's points included which were *not* within the witness' direct personal knowledge:
None

12) *Dr Patrick Cagney*
(Dr Cagney examined Collins' body at Shanakiel, after the Matron. He had been a surgeon in the British army during the war and had a wide knowledge of gunshot wounds. Dr Cagney has been quoted in a number of books about Collins. Feehan seems to have provided the most complete published version of Dr Cagney's testimony, with the first appearance of his book in 1981.)

Dr Cagney reported that:

> He examined the C-in-C's remains at Shanakiel Hospital; and

> there was an entry wound as well as a large exit wound

> *Dr Cagney contradicted by some other accounts:*
> **Dalton contradicts Dr Cagney as follows:**
> x   says that the C-in-C's remains were taken to Bon Secours hospital (i.e. were not taken to British military hospital at Shanakiel);
>
> x   maintains that there was only one wound.
>
> *Dr Cagney's points corroborated by other accounts:*
* Collins' body was taken to Shanakiel; corroborated by:
   - McPeak
   - McKenna
   - F Friel
   - Miss Eleanor Gordon

* There was an entry wound and exit wound corroborated by:
   - Corry
   - McKenna
   - Cmmdt Friel_
   - Miss Eleanor Gordon

   Dr Cagney's points included which were *not* within the witness' direct personal knowledge:
   None

13) *Albert Power*
(Sculptor who made Collins' death mask. His testimony reported by Feehan in 1981.)

Mr. Power reported that:

> there was an entry wound as well as an exit wound

377

<u>Mr Power contradicted by other accounts:</u>
Dalton contradicts Mr Power as follows:
x maintains that there was only one wound.

<u>Mr Power's points corroborated by other accounts:</u>
* There was an entry wound and exit wound corroborated by:
    - Corry
    - McKenna
    - Cmmdt Friel
    - Miss Eleanor Gordon

Mr Power's points included which were *not* within the witness' direct personal knowledge:
None

Appendix 4

Peace Terms Connected to the C-in-C's Journey

A) On 18 August 1922, Major General Emmett Dalton communicated by radio from Cork with Commander-in-Chief Michael Collins at Portobello Barracks, Dublin the following terms for a cease-fire. These terms had been handed to Dalton by prominent neutral citizens in Cork.

    1) A week's truce to be immediately arranged on the basis of the existing military position;

    2) During the interval facilities to be afforded to Republican military and political leaders to hold a meeting to discuss the making of peace on the following basis:

        a) Republican opposition to the government and parliament to be on constitutional lines.

        b) Members of the Republican forces who desire to return to civil life will be allowed to return to their occupations without molestation or penalisation.

        c) Members of the Republican forces who wish to join the National Army will be received therein with due recognition of rank and service.

        d) Arms and munitions in possession of Republican forces will be handed over to a committee to be mutually agreed upon.

        e) There will be a general amnesty for all political prisoners.

B) Collins radioed the following reply from Portobello Barracks at 10:50 AM on the morning of 19 August 1922:

"(To be ciphered on Sunday's second word)

Wireless dispatch received. Will you say by cipher who the prominent citizens responsible for the offer are. Have the Irregular leaders, political and military agreed to the offer and is it made on their behalf?

Government offer published in the press 5th June and conveyed to the Peoples Rights Association, Cork stands. For your guidance the terms are:

First: Transfer into the National Army of all war materials.

Second: Restoration, without exception, of all seized property and money.

Third: Particulars be furnished of bridges, railways, roads which are or have been mined or rendered otherwise unsafe.

Commander-in-Chief"

(These two messages would seem to constitute A) what the anti-Treaty side wanted and B) what the Provisional Government sought in return. Note the C-in-C's question: to confirm that the offer was genuine, from precisely what source; and did it authentically represent the anti-Treaty side.)

Appendix 5
People's Rights Association:
Mediation between the Provisional Government and Anti-Treaty Forces

On 17 July 1922, a meeting was convened under the leadership of Frank Daly, Chairman of Cork Harbour Commissioners. The purpose was to organize neutral civil bodies, to take action toward ending the Civil War. Representatives of Cork City and County public bodies, as well as commercial and labour organizations attended. They constituted themselves a People's Rights Association.

This organization went on to undertake "*one of the earliest efforts*" [263] to secure a negotiated end to the war. Following are excerpts from that effort.

1) Excerpts from resolutions 17 July 1922:

   [We are] not satisfied that such a disastrous fratricidal strife is unavoidable. ...
   [We appeal] to those who fought so nobly for freedom to consider whether we are drifting towards the greatest calamity in Irish history.

   a) The Dáil should assemble in Cork, if unable to meet in Dublin;
   b) appeal to both sides to guarantee safe conduct for all TDs;
   c) call for an immediate cessation of hostilities;
   d) call on Dáil Eireann, (as the only authority recognized by both sides) to immediately exercise its authority and order a cessation of military action

2) Copies of resolutions by were sent to Liam Lynch.
   A memorandum in reply, received 18 July, included the following statements:

   We shall be pleased that second Dáil should meet at once in either Cork or Dublin. We shall guarantee safe conduct to all members attending this meeting, and if necessary we shall provide an escort for them.

---

263 F O'Donoghue

> *[The Army Executive's position is a defensive one, against] unconstitutional and illegal attack ordered by a group of individuals who are usurping Government and acting as a military dictatorship.*

3) Meeting 28 July 1922 between Frank Daly, Professor O'Rahilly (President of University College, Cork) and Liam Lynch at Fermoy Barracks.

   Daly and Prof O'Rahilly posed two questions to Lynch:
   a) Would he agree to cease hostilities if the other side did; and
   b) Would he recognize the authority of the second Dáil?

   Lynch's answer of 29 July:

   > *In answer to your queries last evening I wish to inform you that when the Provisional Government cease their attack on us, defensive action on our part can cease.*

   > *If the second Dáil, which is the Government of the Republic, or any other elected assembly carry on such Government I see no difficulty as to the allegiance of Army.*

4) On August 1, People's Rights Association sent Lynch's reply to Michael Collins, and added these questions:

   a) Do you agree to arrange such a cessation of hostilities as General Liam Lynch intimates he is prepared to accept?

   b) Do you agree to call forthwith a meeting of the second Dáil to be followed by a meeting of the third Dáil, as previously arranged, and to allow the Sovereign Assembly of the people to decide on the necessity or policy of a bitter and prolonged Civil War?

   This message was delivered by Mr TP Dowdall and Fr Tom Duggan. Collins' reply of August 4 included the following:

   > *So far as the Army is concerned I am merely obeying the orders of my Government and all the general staff and soldiers of the Army are merely carrying out the instructions given in accordance with such orders.*[264]

> *This Government has made it fully clear that its desire is to secure obedience to proper authority. ... When the irregulars - leaders and men - see fit to obey the wishes of the people, as expressed through their elected representatives, when they will give up their arms and cease their depredations on the persons and property of Irish citizens, there will be no longer need for hostilities.*
>
> *The choice is definitely between the return of the British, and the irregulars sending in their arms to the People's Government, to be held in trust for the people.*

5) Arthur Griffith, as acting Chairman of the Provisional Government, sent the following replies to the two questions posed by the People's Rights Association:

> a) *The irregulars actions are wrongly described as defensive. The existence of an armed body which claims independent authority and commits outrages on persons and property cannot be tolerated.*
>
> b) *The functions of the Second Dáil came to an end on June 30th. The meeting which was to have taken place on that date would have been purely formal for the purpose of bringing its business to a conclusion. The Sovereign assembly of Ireland is now the Parliament elected in June last whose authority the irregulars have flouted.*

---

264 By this date, Collins had "temporarily" doffed his title as "Chairman of the Cabinet" and been designated "Commander-in-Chief" of the armed forces.

Appendix 6

The Myths

In the absence of any public inquest, the story of Michael Collins' end, as we know it, is largely not much more than a folk tale. A number of myths have taken on a powerful life of their own; often tolerated and even disseminated by official sources.

Mythology can have two potential functions: to illuminate the facts, or to obscure them. The popular misconceptions listed below have in no way increased our understanding of the events; but have, almost without exception, served exclusively to mislead the public about what really happened.

The origins of these myths are discussed below, each in its own section. Most are easily traceable to sources by no means entirely objective or disinterested; when not to actual political opponents of the man whose death they seem to trivialize.

> Myth 1: That there is any "official story"; that we know what happened.
>
> Myth 2: The anti-Treaty side did it.
>
> Myth 3: *"No, stop and we'll fight them."*
>
> Myth 4: Collins died because "careless of personal danger"
>
> Myth 5: Collins died because "inexperienced in live combat"
>
> Myth 6: Collins was merely one of several ambitious men of the time, only less successful than others.
>
> Myth 7: He was "not assassinated." It was an "accident of war."
>
> Myth 8: Collins' War of Independence strategy may be described as a "killing spree"
>
> Myth 9: Collins was invincible; his judgement was infallible
>
> Myth 10: Collins was "ruthless"

Myth 11: It's too late now for an inquest / investigation / solution to the case

DEBUNKING THE MYTHS

Myth 1: That there is any "official story"
Origin: Anecdote, folklore, irresponsible commentators
Translation: "No investigation necessary."

That there never has been any official, public inquiry into the death of Michael Collins, is a glaring omission which cannot be excused in any modern democracy.

We haven't even the basic dignity of an official story to pull to pieces. We have only the illusion of one. Unexamined anecdote, conflicting testimony and rumour have been allowed to stand in its place. *There is no official story.*

> *As matters stand there is no real evidence to show what caused his death, and we can only presume it was caused by gunshot . ... There is no evidence to show [Collins] didn't die of heart attack, or that he was not poisoned and that the wounds were not inflicted afterward.* [265]

The eye-witness reports are highly contradictory. None of those present were ever formally questioned by the authorities. There is no autopsy report that we can read. All we know for certain is that shots were exchanged at Béal na mBláth, and only Collins died.

Yet inquests were held in the death of Cathal Brugha, Harry Boland, Sean Hales, Liam Lynch "and a *host of others who died from gunshot wounds ... Contemporary newspapers show inquests in the deaths of soldiers as well as officers killed in action were commonplace.*" [266] The authorities' failure to convene any such examination in Collins' death is more than a regrettable oversight.

---

265 J Feehan

266 Ibid. Coogan seems to err in asserting that no inquests were held in deaths which occurred during "*military action.*"

Myth 2: The anti-Treaty side did it
Origin: Popular assumption, based on contemporary press reports
Translation: "Case closed."

The assumption that the anti-Treaty soldiers shot Collins is no more than that. As such, it is directly attributable to the lack of any professional investigation.

As set forth in the body of this book, allegations that he was shot by someone other than the ambushers is not a far-fetched theory, but originates with corroborated eye-witness testimony.

Myth 3: "No, stop and we'll fight them."
Origin: Dalton
Translation: "Dalton was not to blame." "Collins (i.e. the victim) was to blame."

How many discussions of the events at Béal na mBláth turn on references to these words, as attributed to the C-in-C? How many of the journalists, politicians and others who've quoted this famous line have any idea of its provenance?

Like so much conventional wisdom about Béal na mBláth, this anecdote originates in the account given by one single witness only. It is the version of events given by Dalton. Significantly, *it is the version which most seems to excuse Dalton's failure, as chief body guard, to keep his priceless charge alive.* It is not corroborated by any other source.

This should be enough to restrain prominent commentators from quoting it as gospel. However, there are a number of other factors which raise serious doubts as to the likelihood that the C-in-C ever spoke those words.

Myth 4: "Careless of personal danger"

Origin: Folklore, well-meaning biographers
Translation: "Collins (i.e. the victim) was to blame."

> *Where courage and judgement are equally required, I would rather send in a clever coward, than a stupid hero.*
> *- Michael Collins, 1922* [267]

No one survives the kind of attention which the British secret service focussed on Michael Collins by mere "luck." In the course of several years on their "most wanted" list, he survived continuous, organized, sophisticated efforts, by the world's most formidable imperialist war machine, to infiltrate his organization, capture and/or kill him.

Running an army entirely dependent on volunteers and constantly recruiting them, he was particularly exposed to such assailants. A number of operatives did join the movement, distinguish themselves, and managed to penetrate quite near him. Expressing a keen desire to meet Collins, some were ultimately exposed and executed.

This was sending a very clear message indeed: trying too hard to find Collins was a short way to end in a ditch with a hole in the head. Then there are the many eye-witness reports, scattered throughout his life in Dublin, of his stunning skill in swiftly dispatching the occasional lone armed attacker, with his bare hands and championship wrestling skills.

These were dangerous times. The Irish were playing for high stakes, and had their eyes on the prize: the golden ring of national freedom, which had eluded their forebears for centuries. The struggle required great physical courage in its combatants, and a willingness to take risks.

No one in Collins' position could have survived the War of Independence, had he been "careless of personal danger."

Myth 5: "Inexperienced in live combat"
Origin: Dalton, political adversaries among anti-Treaty leaders
Translation: "Collins was incompetent." "Collins was no real hero." "Collins (i.e. the victim) was to blame."

This particularly false and vicious slander had its origins among Collins' avowed opponents, at the time of the Dáil debates on the Treaty. This in itself, places the question in the context of precisely the political

---

[267] H Talbot

conflict which culminated in his assassination. It thus cannot be separated from efforts at *character assassination* which immediately preceded, and then later, attempted to excuse his death (a common feature of political murder everywhere.)

This misrepresentation is in no way improved by its association with Emmet Dalton, nor vice versa. The ranking officer under Collins responsible for the C-in-C's safety that day, his testimony is consistently and suspiciously self-exonerating. Common sense likewise belies his "expert opinion" on the military prowess of "*the man who won the war.*" In his early twenties at the time, his insinuation is that, of course, his own military experience was vastly superior to that of the man who had orchestrated the defeat of the most sophisticated imperialists in the world. If so, it's remarkable that Ireland did not seem to make much progress under Dalton's leadership, once that supposedly less-competent superior was removed from the scene. How's the body-guard business going, General?

The contention that Collins was inexperienced in live combat is entirely contradicted by eye witness testimony, from a wide range of participants in the War of Independence. On the contrary, the evidence is overwhelming that he planned, personally commanded, carried out and survived more such actions than can ever be known: due to the clandestine nature of the armed struggle 1919 - 1921, and other factors which made public statements or written records far less available to historians than under normal circumstances.

Even those who later bore arms against him during the Civil War have left vivid accounts of Collins' hands-on leadership under fire, in countless daring raids and ambushes.

> *Collins was apt to come up suddenly behind someone in the street and invite him to join him immediately in blowing up a barracks. . .. they never knew when he might be serious.* [268]

> *Collins got word that Lord French would be passing through College Street a little later and he got himself a gun, rounded up anyone who happened to be nearby, and set off to lead an ambush.* [269]

> *A friend rushed in to Devlin's to tell him that Mulcahy and Diarmuid O'Hegarty were trapped by police at a meeting in Parnell Square.*

---

268 T P Coogan
269 Patrick Daly memoir, Mulcahy papers, UCD

> "I'll get Tobin and some of the boys and we won't be long getting them away," was Collins' reaction. Then he ran upstairs, whistling, to get his gun, and he and the friend headed up the square without waiting for Tobin. ... "Can ye bloody children not look after yourselves yet?" was his salutation. [270]
>
> ... A car in which Collins [was] travelling back from Naas [was] attacked in a Dublin street. ... A bullet ... narrowly missed Collins. Drawing a revolver he replied to the fire and, jumping from the car, caught the assailant in a doorway and held him prisoner.[271] [Collins' letter to Kitty about this incident states:] "It was immediately after our return that the shooting took place. I think they must have meant to capture me only. They were great optimists. God help them, but they are carrying things a bit too far."

Above we read several of his blasé references to such battles, often touched with humor. This was neither the speech nor the actions of a man "*inexperienced in live combat.*" As Scott put it: *One must become accustomed to danger, ere one can dally with her, as with a mistress.*

Surprisingly, Feehan accepted and reiterated this concept (that the C-in-C was not experienced in battle); and cannot be dismissed as wishing to do Collins any less than justice. Neither was he unacquainted with the War of Independence in general. On the contrary, his original research made a significant contribution to our records of the period. He had excellent access to many whose experience ought to have enabled them to enlighten him. This might be due to agreed prohibitions, which inhibited veterans from uncovering details, some of which became public only in the 1990s.

It is notable that, when this issue was raised during the Treaty debates, neither Collins nor his fellow members, many of whom had accompanied him on such raids and ambushes, attempted to answer with any listing of precise actions in which he had taken part. Arthur Griffith's famous, unanswerable reply, "*This is the man who won the war,*" was interestingly preceded by the non-committal preface "*However that may be ...* " From all this, it would seem that there were particular reasons for this reticence, well known to the participants.

---

270   Frank O'Connor and Mulcahy papers, UCD

271   L O'Broin

This is hardly surprising, given the clandestine nature of the war. In the unsettled state of the country, any publication of details about the underground forces' personnel, numbers, operations, precise past whereabouts, etc., would have been a highly sensitive issue, even a matter of national security. The possibility that war with Britain might break out anew was ever-present as said debate raged. The large number of secretive attacks on individual British operatives which had formed part of the war, the danger of reprisals ... Consider the volatility, at this writing, of similar details in connection with armed conflict in Ulster (1970s - 1990s). Any realistic examination suggests abundant reasons why the exact role of an individual who had been active in the war would not be open to public discussion in 1921. The more active and responsible, the greater the danger inherent in such revelations.

In view of Michael Collins' ultimate fate, and that of his best and brightest, such threat to those "*who won the war*" was certainly very real and present indeed.

Myth 6: Collins merely one of several ambitious men of the time
Origin: DeValera apologists
Translation: "Collins' death didn't matter. Nothing would have been better had he lived." "Collins just wasn't as successful as others. Collins was a loser."

> If Mr. DeValera can by reason and argument induce the people of Ireland to entrust the Nation's fortunes to him and his party ... in that event the duty of the Army, no matter what were their individual views, would be to support Mr. DeValera's government, and I would exhort the people to support that government, as a government, even if I were in political opposition ... [272]

Progressive campaigning often turns on convincing people that (1) change is possible and (2) their candidate / party is different from the establishment, and will make change happen.

For the same reason, these two principles are often targeted by entrenched political establishments. It becomes, in a sense, their job (if they want to keep their jobs) to convince the public that change is *not* going to happen. It is in their interests to encourage a general disbelief that *any*

---

[272] M Collins (see Appendix 7)

politician is going to be different. A general hopelessness that anything can change, is advantageous to the status quo.

Such inertia keeps people away from the polls: they don't bother to vote. This is good for entrenched establishments. The fewer people vote, the more likely that the usual suspects will keep their seats. Large voter turn-outs are generally good news for progressives, bad news for conservatives. When the public perceives a chance for positive improvements, when a candidate stands out as offering something genuinely valuable and innovative; when the public imagination is fired: then they stand up to be counted. It is therefore definitely in the interests of some political elements to discourage this sort of thing.

Government by assassination is the most extreme form of that strategy. It is one very destructive and dangerous way to make sure that *there will be only one kind of candidate*.

Obviously, if this were a mere question of struggle between two equally selfish and unethical men, it is *not* Michael Collins who would have been assassinated. If he could wipe out virtually the entire British secret service in Dublin in one day, there was no one in Ireland likely to outdo him in that department.

> *... while it was perfectly justifiable for any body of Irishmen, no matter how small, to rise up and make a stand against their country's enemy, it is not justifiable for a minority to oppose the wishes of the majority of their own countrymen, except by constitutional means.* [273]

Collins never said it was *"necessary to shoot men like"* Liam Lynch or Rory O'Connor [274] Nor did he ever call on the public to wade through the blood of anti-Treaty leaders. He *never* advocated firing on comrades as a solution to the Dáil / Army split. On the contrary, he resisted doing so longer than anyone else in a comparably responsible position (although no one's position at the time can really be compared with his.)

As explored in this volume, the solution he consistently sought was a just and amicable reunification of all factions. The analysis he repeatedly emphasized was the danger of dividing the country's strength, in the presence of their traditional foe, at this volatile juncture. History has justified him.

---

[273] Ibid.
[274] In direct contrast to Liam Lynch's notorious editorial comment on the C-in-C's demise.

As Collins clearly declared, while he had no problem with assassination as a weapon of war against a violent foreign occupation force, he did *not* believe in it as a form of government. That, apparently, is how he differed from his opponents. Tragically for us, he paid the supreme price for that difference.

Myth 7: "Not assassinated: 'accident' of war"
Origin: M Ryan, DeValera apologists
Translation: "DeValera is not to blame (because no one is to blame.)"

> *"Nothing accidental ever happens in politics."*
> - Franklin D. Roosevelt

This myth is unsurprisingly favoured in quarters most liable to be charged as perpetrators in Collins' death. The "accident" theory of course means there is no crime. No crime, no perpetrator. Also no meaning, no ramifications. It's fantastically convenient for all those whose interest lies in minimizing discussion of Collins' end.

This is not to say that it shouldn't be considered by responsible, disinterested researchers. It is one of the possible explanations carefully examined by Feehan. That study was certainly called for at the time, and history is well served by his excellent treatment. However, at this juncture, there are reasons for classifying the "accident" theory as a myth.

> *No doubt this theory made a lot of people happy. They were all blameless and nobody was really responsible for the death of Michael Collins!* [275]

The first rule of thumb in investigating political assassination is: there is never anything "accidental" about the sudden death of a leader of Collins' stature, in the midst of fulfilling such a pivotal role and at such a critical moment in his people's struggle. The nature of the situation so defines such a demise as automatically "suspicious," as to render the odds astronomically against there being anything merely accidental about it. This is true for reasons which all such leaders share with Collins. The particulars in his story may highlight the general in theirs.

---

275 J Feehan

One could also point out the several acute assassination attempts aimed very accurately at himself in the weeks preceding Béal na mBláth, which were witnessed by a number of friends. On several such occasions, while horrified companions looked on helpless, Collins, disabled and disarmed gun-wielding assailants, with the blasé efficiency with which one might swat a harassing fly. There are a number of such accounts, from bystanders who happened to be in his company walking down the street, getting in or out of a car, attending a dinner party, etc., in the weeks preceding his assassination. No one who reads these accounts can escape the impression that there was a campaign to eliminate him under way; clearly supported by intimate and timely knowledge of his daily schedule.

In addition to all that, of twenty-five soldiers present, Collins was the one and only fatality; none of the witnesses' statements match up; the army and government, of which he was the leading member, entirely omitted to inquire into his death in any way.

All of these suspicious factors could not come together "accidentally". At this writing, an "accidental" theory can only be maintained by so wilfully ignoring these factors, as to suggest an interested agenda.

Feehan, in his study of the "accident" theory, picked apart the various contentions on this, and reduced the evidence to two possibilities which he concluded could have happened: that Collins was accidentally hit, either by a member of his own party, or by a stray shot from the ambushers. As noted above, the anti-Treaty men themselves admitted that the latter was not impossible. But they severely doubted it. And they were there! [276] This then, is the best that can be said for the "accident theory".

Ultimately, even if Collins' end could be called merely one lamentable result of the Civil War, it is offered that the one and only real purpose of that war (by its true authors) was to eliminate Collins, his closest associates and his organization.

> *It was a most savage, hateful and cruel war which cost the country the lives of virtually all its outstanding leaders.* [277]

---

276 It is interesting to note that, in any publication about this historical period, which includes both eye witness reports and analysis by historians, it's often easy to tell the two apart by virtue of one distinguishing trait: only those who were _not_ there at the time are _sure_ what happened!

277 J Feehan

What the British were unable to achieve, only the Civil War accomplished for them: the division into warring factions of the armed forces who had defeated them; the elimination of Collins and other key military leaders; the execution of many of Ireland's best fighting men and heroes of the War of the Independence; the decimation of Ireland's unity, economy and general development as an emerging nation; and of course, the cementing of partition. Collins saw this coming a long way off, at the very first British overtures:

> *This talk about Dominion Home Rule is not prompted by England with a view to granting it to us, but merely with a view to getting rid of the Republican movement.*[278]

In short, it assured a politically, economically and militarily neutralized Ireland: the only kind of republic the British establishment meant to live with.

As discussed in Part 2, the meaning and nature of his demise must be scrutinized in full context of the big picture: including what preceded it, how it happened, as well as the dénouement which followed.

Myth 8: Collins' War of Independence strategy may be described as a "killing spree"

Origin: Sensationalist "pop" history
Translation: "Collins' assassins no worse than himself." "His assassination was excusable." "Collins' death didn't matter. Nothing would have been better had he lived."
"Collins (i.e. the victim) was to blame."

The operations and tactics of Ireland's secret revolutionary army, under Collins during the War of Independence, have sometimes been not only mythologized but also sensationalized. Treatments of the period have appeared, whose distortions and inaccuracies have gone beyond opportunistic profiteering; to an extent which demonstrates a political agenda to discredit Collins, his comrades, if not the Irish nation in general.

A recent literary "pop history" production, characterized Collins' "Squad" as engaging in what that author sensationally dubbed a "killing spree". The word "spree" in association with the word "killing" produces a

---

278 Michael Collins, newspaper interview, August 1921

sick concept. "Spree" meaning something undertaken for fun, out of an intrinsic drive which is fundamentally pleasurable in nature. The dictionary defines it as "*indulgence of a wish or craving, [such as a shopping spree, eating spree or drinking spree.]*" Such insulting characterization of the armed struggle for Irish independence as a binge of self-indulgence is too wildly inaccurate to be merely shameful sloppiness in any work pretending to recount history. It is a fraudulent misrepresentation: that is, made while knowing it to be false.

> *Every construction with a design and an end announces an artisan.* - Voltaire

Indeed, looking over the prominent names and organizations [279] connected to the publication in question, one scratches one's head in wonder: why bother? Why would people like this go to so much trouble to mount such rubbish? To step so far out of the way to assert and support a falsehood, announces a purpose in doing so. What purpose could this falsehood serve? What could be the motive here?

To characterize Collins and his unit(s) as irresponsible homicidal maniacs (as such language does) is *to justify and excuse his murder; which thereby diminishes public interest in the unanswered questions surrounding his death.* It could be proposed with reason, that the appearance of such smears expresses a fear you can smell: a fear in powerful quarters that new public sympathy and interest in his story might result in new investigations.

The executions carried out by Collins' "Squad" were carefully chosen and subject to Dáil approval, on evidence beyond reasonable doubt. Their targets were primarily the British secret service and informers: those most directly active in hunting down and killing Irish volunteers and their leaders. In publicly acknowledging these actions against those "*seeking victims for execution,*" Collins said, "*My conscience is clear*," and pointed out that this was completely within the rights of any wartime national defense.

The provisional government went to a great deal more trouble in these matters, than did some British forces in Ireland at the time, who simply shot anyone in sight, when they cared to; having been authorized by British government to do just that. The Irish side in that war can justly be

---

[279] The title and authors of the work described shall not be honored with any mention here. This type of flippant approach to Collins' story is one which rears its ugly head periodically; ever since the cynical personal smears which soiled anti-Treaty publications during the Civil War.

said to have outdone any other army in striving to preserve even in wartime the democratic values of due process; and to avoid the "*dishonour*" of "*cruelty, inhumanity or rapine.*"

In the question of reasons why a particular person was targeted, the testimony of Squad members themselves may not always be the most informative. The men who carried out the orders were not informed of the reasons for any given "job". Surviving members, decades after the fact, could hardly provide more than conjecture. Suggestions that anyone was intentionally executed for nothing more than harmless ties of association is entirely refuted by Dáil records of the time.

Myth 9: Collins was invincible / his judgement infallible
Origin: Folklore, well-meaning eulogists
Translation: "Collins couldn't have made such a mistake."
"So it must have been drink, or death wish, or (wildly improbable etc's.)"
*   "Collins (i.e. the victim) was to blame."*

It is the idea, conscious or unconscious, of Collins' fabled invincibility which has skewed the judgement of many well-meaning biographers. It is one of the factors which causes Béal na mBláth to distort our vision, an insoluble puzzle. A veritable koan of history, it has reduced otherwise competent researchers to gossip or imagination for the answer: because reason fails.

Another function of myth is to inspire. This was one of his many gifts as a leader: he had *"the stuff that dreams are made of."* One of his techniques was his keen sense of the dramatic. In his strictly pragmatic campaign, his famous flair for the theatrical was frequently used to great effect. His talent for playing to the audience, in a way that inspired confidence and fired the imagination was legendary. As noted in the biographical sketch above, this talent was supported by theatrical studies during his youth in London.

This was the positive flip side of his psychological warfare campaign: not only did he show great skill in destroying the enemy's confidence, but also in building up that of his own people, into a positive steam-engine force; which ultimately swept all before it.

> *He exuded an aura of confidence that inspired both men and women ... His presence made them feel safe, strong and fearless, and enabled them to undertake the most dangerous of missions ...* [280]

This was in the context of a long folkloric tradition, which he thoroughly understood. Throughout centuries of Irish struggle against foreign occupation, from Robin Hood-esque highwaymen like Liam Crotty or Sam Wallace [281] to great leaders like Red Hugh O'Donnell, folk heroes made effective use of the theatrical and psychological, to inspire friends and deflate opponents.

Collins knew that the Irish love a hero, and needed a hero. He gave them one: in his daring, mind-boggling escape from the Mansion House raid; immediately followed by his appearance at a public meeting in immaculate dress uniform; in his athletic feats as a wrestler; in the Bloody Sunday executions (a stunning tactical and psychological blow from which the British administration never recovered.)

Small Native American war parties had a trick of rattling distant bushes, in order to awe their opponents with the illusion that they were up against a massive host. Collins and his comrades likewise practiced much sleight-of-hand to strike terror in their adversaries, by creating exaggerated illusions about the outnumbered and out-gunned republican forces in Ireland. One of these was the myth of Collins' invincibility. In 1921, he spoke candidly about this psychological strategy:

> *For several years (rightly or wrongly made no difference) the English had held me to be the one man most necessary to capture because they held me to be the one man responsible for the smashing of their secret service organization and for their failure to terrorize the Irish people with their Black and Tans ... the important fact was that in England as in Ireland, the Michael Collins legend existed. It pictured me as a mysterious active menace, elusive, unknown, unaccountable, ... Bring me into the spotlight of a London conference and quickly will be discovered the common clay of which I am made. The glamour of the legendary figure will be gone.*[282]

---

280   C Osborne

281   The village nearest Collins' birthplace, Sam's Cross, was named after this famous outlaw.

282   Michael Collins to Hayden Talbot, 1921

If this is a "good myth", it has nonetheless hampered the search for truth at Béal na mBláth. Collins was able to carry out so many amazing feats, which have become the stuff of legend, because he was the spearhead of an entire people united. Although a brilliantly talented man, he was far from infallible, and well aware of it himself.

This was particularly true in his renowned impenetrability to British operatives. He and his men were remarkably keen and sharp, of course. But when they wanted to be really sure about a new prospect, they took him to have lunch with a certain little old lady. They'd have to pass the test of being "vetted" by Mrs. O'Donovan. If she didn't like them, they were out. Much of the movement's "invincibility" was due to the support of ordinary citizens like this. [283]

In the case of the assassination of Malcolm X, once he had been made famous as the leader of a movement with so many powerful enemies, all the leaders of that movement had to do to assure his death was ... do *nothing*. It was as a spokesman for many that Malcolm X had the power and security to speak out and live on. Once denuded of the movement's security machine, he was a sitting duck.

In the upheaval which led up to Béal na mBláth, Collins lost a large part of his organization. The unity and trust which ran the movement was broken up on a large scale. He no longer operated in secret, surrounded only by tried and true comrades. He was taken out of the element in which he had thrived and proved victorious, and robbed of many close and valuable allies. He was painfully aware that he had to fear not only a foreign adversary, but even people in his own circle: former colleagues, who might now be enemies.

This was key in the events which led to his death.

Myth 10: Collins was "ruthless"

Origin: Contemporaries, well-meaning eulogists, biographers
Translation: "Collins' assassins no worse than himself." "His assassination was excusable." "Collins' death didn't matter. Nothing would have been better had he lived."
"Collins (i.e. the victim) was to blame."

---

[283] "*This factor deserves far more attention in evaluations of the extraordinary ability of the IRA to resist vastly superior British power. It might even be argued that the overwhelming British superiority in manpower was partly countered by Irish superiority in woman power.*" - J J Lee. For details on this aspect, see *No Ordinary Woman: Women in the Revolutionary Era 1900 - 1923,* by Sinead McCoole

"Ruthless" is this writer's candidate for the world's most misapplied word with regard to Collins. It was used, admittedly, by some of his own associates in describing one aspect of his approach to the war.

However, these friends of his spoke off the cuff. Although perfectly literate, they were not language experts. More qualified wordsmiths, who otherwise demonstrate a fine understanding of their subject, have erred in recycling it. To be precise, "ruth" means pity, compunction, compassion. To be ruthless is to be utterly without compassion or sympathy. There was nothing further from Collins' personality.

At the very time that some of his opponents were baying literally for rivers of his blood, Collins brushed off bullets he dodged in Dublin with the words, "*They were great optimists. God help them, but they are carrying things a bit too far.*" This was typical of his private conversation regarding his erstwhile comrades in the anti-Treaty ranks.

Let us examine the use of this word and its context here. Most people, even the most apolitical, feel at least some sense of indebtedness and respect to those who play a role in the defence of their country, at the risk of their own lives. Would we usually designate a common foot soldier "ruthless", because s/he carried a weapon, and used it in national defence? Would we use that term to describe captains or generals, who provided the vital leadership necessary to the success of such defence?

What we know of Michael Collins, and of the organization of volunteers which he commanded, places them in a class quite by themselves. Any modern army or commander on record would have to be called, more accurately, "ruthless" by comparison.

The War of Independence Volunteers (unlike the nice, non-"ruthless" British Army) did not have the benefit of a formal, government-sponsored military establishment, which could recruit at the Post Office and drill in the town square. They did not have an abundance of professional officers, or a culture of full-time military discipline.

They were farmers and shop assistants, who trained in secret, in their spare time. In place of their opponents' massive budget and orthodox hierarchy, their discipline depended largely on simple beliefs, deeply held. They believed in what they were doing. They were not mercenaries serving an empire, but plain men defending their homes.

They were not highly-trained human killing machines. Killing, contrary to the mythology of "action adventure entertainment", is an unpleasant business. Thankfully, it does not come easily to those not drummed into a desensitized state, by sophisticated military indoctrination programs.

For clerks and schoolteachers and repairmen, it was a lot to ask. For people raised in a staunchly religious culture, as in Ireland then, it might not be undertaken without grave doubts. For anyone imbued with a Celtic sense of spiritual reality, such a relationship to the dead was not one to be entered into lightly.

"*The priests tell them it's no sin to kill a policeman,*" complained an RIC constable. The Irish Volunteers, not unlike insurgents such as the Sandinistas of Central America, were held together by deep religious belief in connection with their cause. Combatants of the Squad and Active Service Units often fortified their courage before actions with prayer. By and large, they did not like to go into battle without taking the sacraments beforehand.

Whenever practical, their targets were given a moment to address their deity, at the hour of death. In this same spirit, the notorious Squad itself maintained a kind of shrine for the very agents whom they had executed. A hat, a watch chain, a photo ... personal items of this kind were enshrined in a cellar gallery, as a respectful memorial to opponents who had lost their lives at their hands.

Collins considerably endangered himself by his care in this spirit. When one office of his was suddenly raided, he was obliged to escape without a letter to loved ones which had been in the pocket of one of the Squad's victims when he died. He had taken it to his office, along with some other of the man's personal effects, in order to mail them to the family in England. Had he been searched with these items on his person, it would have meant his certain death.

To 21st century readers, some of this may sound like either religious fanaticism or nonsense. But perhaps they live in a more "ruthless" world. It would not be laughed at in Ireland, either then or now. There are no atheists in foxholes. But most military establishments would not care to encourage in their troops either much religious compunction or humane compassion toward "the enemy".

Tenacious? Terribly. Efficient? Exhaustively. Decisive? Devastatingly. Perhaps there is a word for what he was. But "ruthless" is *not* one of them.

Myth 11: It's too late now to solve the case
Origin: Well-meaning biographers

Translation: "Do not investigate."

> *No man can set a boundary to the progress of a nation.*
> *- Charles Stewart Parnell*

"It's too late now" ... "We'll never know" ... "unsolvable" ... These are all positions which benefit the perpetrators.

How can we talk about having an effect on perpetrators, after all those concerned have long gone to their graves? We can, when the perpetrator is not only an individual who pulled a trigger, but an institution. An institution which doesn't go away, and which affects our lives every day: imperialism. It has been shown that such institutions will go to great lengths indeed to keep the coldest case a mystery: when to penetrate it might expose the tricks of their trade.

It may also be said that on the question of Irish independence, there is no such thing as a "dead issue." This could apply to any key question of national history anywhere; especially because history repeats itself. For Ireland, the struggle for self-determination has been a permanent feature of national life for a thousand years; and shows no promise of going away soon.

The issues of the War of Independence and Civil War are far from entirely resolved at this writing. It is no coincidence that, for seventy-five years after his death, key institutions demonstrated a heavy investment in stifling discussion of Michael Collins, and strangled public access to information about that period. This "less said about it the better" attitude has not evaporated from powerful quarters. It does them no honor.

This in itself strongly suggests several things: a) there is "something there" which remains hidden; b) that the "something" hidden is well known in some quarters (or why would they be keen to conceal it?) c) that the exposure of this "something" would have unwelcome consequences for some parties; d) it is therefore not a "dead issue." e) Likewise, there must be considerable danger of its discovery: if it couldn't possibly be discovered, why discourage examination? f) On the contrary, all of this would seem to announce that, if someone looks carefully, they will find "something." That is, if there is a careful, competent, unbiased examination of the existing evidence.

Characteristically, such elements advertise what they most endeavor to conceal, and prove what they strive to deny: that we have access to all the information we need to learn a great deal more about precisely what happened to Michael Collins, and perhaps even something about who was responsible.

Is the distance of time always a disadvantage? *Au contraire*, particularly in cases of political assassination, perspective can often reveal much that is obscure at the time. Political reality can be a highly perishable item. It goes out of date faster than a popular song or a fashion of clothes. For this reason, many of history's mysteries have been cleared up, but only generations, even centuries after the fact.

History is our collective memory: our national identity. No one can set a boundary to our understanding of who we are and where we have been.

APPENDIX 7
"FREE STATE OR CHAOS"
(A tract by Michael Collins for the Pact Elections)

Discussions of Collins' death frequently turn on questions about his politics: his principles and plans for the pivotal role played in the new, independent Irish state. However, his own writings, which provide answers to those questions, are often less available than disinformation, rumour and insinuations by detractors.

It therefore seems important to include here a reprint of the following tract: which sets forth Collins' views and proposals, during the political upheaval which precipitated his assassination.

The text was transcribed and excerpted from his speech at Waterford on 26 March 1922.

The Treaty and the establishment of the Free State mean peace, freedom and security. The alternative is chaos, disunion and anarchy.

If it is your will the Free State will be established. We shall have complete control. Our country will be our own. We shall have our own Army. We can build a Mercantile Marine. We shall have control of every public department. We can promote trade internal and external. We shall be free to deal with unemployment. To get the land into the hands of our people to cultivate. To deal with housing. To have our education under our own control.

What do our Opponents offer you? What *have* they to offer you?

Up to the time of the evacuation their policy was represented by an unsigned document fashioned on the lines of the Treaty. Most of the Clauses were identical with the Articles of the Treaty. On behalf of the Irish People they voluntarily agreed to the British occupation of the six Ports, to the same arrangements in regard to NE Ulster, to similar adjustments of the financial arrangements between the two countries.

But the Policy has now been changed. With the departure of the enemy secured by the Treaty, Mr. DeValera and his followers have grown bolder. We hear no more about Document 2. "The Republic" which was surrendered by Mr. DeValera in July is restored as the policy of Mr. DeValera and his followers in February and March.

You know our policy and you know our programme. It may not be perfect, but it is straightforward.

If you prefer Mr. DeValera's Policy which he tells you is now a republic, can he give it to you? He was unable to secure it for you last July, and he surrendered it in favor of what is known as Document 2 or 3. He is no more able to get you a republic now, than he was able last July, unless we are able to do now what we failed to do last July.

Unless we are prepared and are able to beat out of Ireland the British forces which would be sent there if we attempted to set up a republic, and unless we are prepared, and are able, to beat those in NE Ulster who do not share our national views supported as they would be by British forces, unless we can do these things the realization of the full republican ideal for all Ireland is at present impossible.

Policies are useless unless they can be carried out.

Mr DeValera can give you something. He can perpetuate disunion, he can give you the loss of all that you have won - he can give you anarchy - full measure of that anarchy of which his tactics have already given you an unpleasant sample. We are already hearing less about his policy and more about his threats. Threats against you, the people of Ireland. Such freedom as we have won was beyond our wildest dreams six years ago. We did not dream that by means of one struggle we should have reached up to so high a step on the ladder of freedom.

Will you take that freedom? If we are wise we will take it, and will thank God for it, and will reap the rich fruits, we can gather under it: prosperity, spiritual freedom, power to become again the distinctive Irish people of the Irish nation; to speak our own language, to grow rich again in our own Gaelic culture.

Mr. DeValera said at a meeting at Ennis that we ought not to be afraid to face each other in argument and to abide by whatever the result was. The Irish people might be excused if they said it was not now time for argument - that it is time for work.

And their arguments having failed to win the people to their changing and impracticable policies, a Black and Tan campaign, and worse, is taking their place. They are becoming violent - a way with weak people when beaten in argument. A little of their own pepper has got into their own throats.

Where reason has failed to convince the Irish people, pepper and revolver shots, incitements and threats will not avail.

"Use your free choice," said Mr DeValera at Ennis. "Vote for a republic." What is his idea of a free choice? To allow his supporters to fire revolver shots lower and lower over the heads of large crowds in which there are women and children, hoping for a stampede, indifferent to the danger to those women and children, as long as the people can be prevented from hearing what the supporters of the Treaty have to tell them.

To resort to every manoeuvre to delay giving the people the opportunity to exercise their free choice at an election.

To prepare intimidation in advance for the election when it does come.

To look on in silence while his former Minister of Defence incites to mutiny in the army.

To look on in silence while his former Minister of Home Affairs puts difficulties in the way of establishing an efficient police force to deal with crime and to protect our people; and to make threats of violence against the force when it is established.

Is the Irish nation to be dragged with them down these slippery slopes?

They failed in Dáil Éireann to defeat the Treaty. And they said "there is a constitutional way of resolving our differences" - "we will accept no verdict except that of the people."

But the people are already silently giving their verdict, and Mr DeValera is not pleased with it. And so we hear no more of constitutional ways; we begin to see instead the ways of violence.

The people of Ireland are now to be intimidated and terrorised. The country is threatened with Civil War. "If the Treaty was accepted," said Mr DeValera at Carrick-on-Suir, "the Irish people instead of fighting foreign soldiers would have to fight the Irish soldiers of an Irish government set up by Irishmen."

And lest you should think I am scoring off Mr DeValera for a mere party advantage, I want to put the position to you as clearly as I can in this way: Statements were made in certain papers with regard to his speeches, and he published an explanation. In my opinion that explanation does not make his position any clearer. He states it was to future generations he was referring when he spoke of "civil war" and "wading through Irish blood" in order to get Irish freedom. No one can speak for the next generation, and no one can tie the hands of the next generation.

He does not make it clear which of the two possible interpretations of his speeches he wishes the public to accept.

That:
(1) Thinking in the language of mutiny for the next generation he pictures the Irish Volunteers of the future - Does he mean the army of the Irish nation - refusing to obey the will of the People as voiced in the nation's parliament and "wading through Irish blood,"

or

(2) That the way to independence is forever barred because it could only be achieved through civil war, and civil war is impossible.

He says his remarks were in answer to the statement made that the Treaty was "freedom to achieve freedom." That was my statement, and I do not shrink from it. Nobody knows better than Mr DeValera that the Treaty gives freedom to achieve freedom. He is already using the freedom won to shout for a republic.

Since he has asked for your suffrages and claims to stand for independence under a republican form of government, which he suggests can only be achieved by civil war, then he must be in favor of civil war. He cannot have it both ways. If Mr DeValera can by reason and argument induce the people of Ireland to entrust the nation's fortunes to him and his party, to carry out on behalf of the Irish nation whatever is his policy, there is still no need for civil war.

What Mr DeValera would do in that event I don't know. Let us assume he would establish a republic, the country having been evacuated of British troops by means of the Treaty.

In that event the duty of the army, no matter what were their individual views, would be to support Mr DeValera's government, and I would exhort the people to support that government, as a government, even if I were in political opposition; and the army and the civil authorities should obey that government, no matter what its political creed may be.

If the people by a majority decide in favor of our opponents, although I believe that decision would be a fatal and disastrous decision, yet it would have been made, and I for one would still stand in with the people in whatever conditions arose as a result of that decision. Mr DeValera must know, and it is his duty as their leader to enlighten any of his inexperienced followers who do not know, that while it was perfectly justifiable for anybody of Irishmen, no matter how small, to rise up and make a stand against their country's enemy, it is not justifiable for a minority to oppose the wishes of the majority of their own countrymen, except by constitutional means.

And to the soldiers of the nation, while they may hold their individual political views, there is only one course, - obedience to the constituted authority. Unless this is driven home to the minds of the people, there is no future before the Irish nation, except anarchy, chaos and ultimate destruction.

Whatever Mr DeValera's meaning, the effect of his language is mischievous. A leader must not be unmindful of the implications of his words, especially when speaking to people just emerging from a great national struggle with their outlook and their emotions not in a normal state. If Mr DeValera really wishes to convince the public that he did not mean to indulge in violent threats and in the language of incitement, and wants to wipe out the impression caused by his speeches, he must take instant action. His explanation as published will not do. He must press home the foregoing truths to all his supporters, and he must publicly dissociate himself from the utterances of the former Ministers of Defence and Home Affairs, and from such mutinous views as those expressed by Commandant Roderick O'Connor.

We would not be hearing those blood and thunder speeches, we would not be seeing the revolver, if argument could have prevailed. Our age-long enemy when "constitutional ways" failed, also used the revolver to try and suppress us, and threats to frighten us into submission to his will - to exercise our "free choice" in the way he wished.

Is peace never to be allowed to our poor people?

But the Irish people were not intimidated by the threats or by the tanks and machine guns of the old enemy. Neither will they be intimidated by the threats and feeble weapons in the hands of the new enemies of the Irish nation.

Our opponents are keeping passions alive, directing them from their legitimate use against the enemy who was standing in the way of our freedom - directing them now that the enemy has gone, for illegitimate use against the people of their own nation to deprive them of that freedom.

And I say, deliberately, that in doing so Mr DeValera and his followers are proving themselves to be the greatest enemies that Ireland has ever had.

Mr DeValera told you on St Patrick's Day that it was the saddest one he had spent in five years, and I can well believe it. Is his conscience troubling him? Does he see in his mind's eye those terrible doings in Belfast? Dream of the worse things that may yet happen? See our poor Catholic and nationalist countrymen at the mercy of a relentless majority; who, taking advantage of our weakness from disunion, are making a last desperate effort to keep the British forces in Ireland, and to get them to return in order to maintain their ascendancy.

Up in the northeast three months ago they were in a chastened mood. There was nothing left for them but to mend their ways. To consider, how they could join in without too great an appearance of surrender - with the rest of their countrymen. No other alternative was left to them.

But they have received new allies where they least expected them! The "North" and the "South" have at last joined together. The wreckers are united. It is an unholy brotherhood.

Had Mr DeValera any better scheme for unity than the proposals of the Treaty? Does he remember the clauses of his abandoned Document No. 2? How does he intend to bring them in, if he could achieve what he says is his policy, the establishment of a republic? And, if not, how could he deal with the situation?

If we were presenting a united front to England and to northeast Ulster, I defy anyone to deny that at this moment we would not be seeing the northeast Ulster "parliament" legalizing tyranny, instituting flogging, establishing for our helpless fellow countrymen up there the very reign of terror, under the very same so-called Law and Order Act, from which we have just emerged.

We can yet stop that horror if we will close our ranks and can speak to England and the northeast as one people. Is there any use in asking our opponents to think of Ireland, of what she may become, free and splendid, or once more tortured and degraded; to forget himself, his party, to give language a rest for a little; to think of the facts which principles and ideals stand for.

BIBLIOGRAPHY

Bíaslaí, Píaras	*Michael Collins and the Making of a New Ireland* Phoenix Publishing Co, Dublin 1926
Childers, Erskine	*The Riddle of the Sands* London, Smith Elder 1903
Collins, Michael	*Free State or Chaos* Dublin 1922
Collins, Michael	*The Path to Freedom* Cork, Mercier 1968
Colum, Padraig	*Arthur Griffith* Dublin, Browne and Nolan c1959
Coogan, Tim Pat	*Michael Collins* London, Arrow Books 1991
Deasy, Liam	*Brother Against Brother* Dublin, Mercier 1982
Doherty, Gabriel & Keogh, Dermot (contributors & editors)	*Michael Collins and the Making of the Irish State* Cork, Mercier Press 1998
Fanning, Ronan	"Michael Collins: an Overview", *Michael Collins and the Making of the Irish State* (Doherty & Keogh, editors) p202
Feehan, John	*The Shooting of Michael Collins: Murder or Accident?* Cork, Mercier Press, 1981
Feeney, Brian	*Sinn Fein: a Hundred Turbulent Years* Dublin, O'Brien Press Ltd. 2002
Fitzpatrick, David	*Harry Boland's Irish Revolution* Cork, Cork University Press, 2003
Forester, Margery	*The Lost Leader* London, Sidgwick & Jackson 1971
Gearty, Margot	"The Granard Connection", from *Michael Collins and the Making of the Irish State* (Doherty & Keogh, editors) p38
Lee, J J	"The Challenge of a Collins Biography", *Michael Collins and the Making of the Irish State* (Doherty & Keogh, editors) p19

Neligan, David	*The Spy in the Castle* London; Prendeville Publishing Ltd. 1999
O'Bróin, Leon	*In Great Haste: the letters of Michael Collins and Kitty Kiernan* Dublin, Gill & Macmillan 1983
O'Connor, Frank	*The Big Fellow* London, T Nelson & Sons, 1937
O'Donoghue, Florence and Josephine	*Florence and Josephine O'Donoghue's War of Independence* Dublin, Irish Academic Press, 2006
O'Donoghue, Florence	*No Other Law* Dublin, Irish Press 1954
Osborne, Chrissy	*Michael Collins Himself* Cork, Mercier 2003
Osborne, Chrissy	*Michael Collins : a life in pictures* Cork, Mercier 2007
Phillips, Alison	*The Revolution in Ireland 1906-1923* New York: Longmans, Green 1923
Phoenix, Eamonn	"Michael Collins - The Northern Question 1916-22", *Michael Collins and the Making of the Irish State* (Doherty & Keogh, editors) p92
Ryan, Meda	*The Day Michael Collins Was Shot* Dublin, Poolbeg Press, 1979
Shirer, William	*The Rise and Fall of the Third Reich* London, Secker & Warburg 1960
Collins, Michael (Talbot, Hayden, Ed.)	*Michael Collins' Own Story* London, Hutchinson & Co, 1923
Collins, Michael (Costello, Francis J, Ed.)	*Michael Collins In His Own Words* Dublin, Gill & Macmillan 1997
Taylor, Rex	*Michael Collins* London, Hutchinson 1958
Taylor, Rex	*Assassination: the death of Sir Henry Wilson and the tragedy of Ireland* London, Hutchinson 1961

Turi, John	*England's Greatest Spy: Eamonn DeValera* London, Stacey International 2009
Younger, Calton	*Arthur Griffith* Dublin, Gill & Macmillan, 1981
Yeates, Padraig	*Michael Collins an illustrated life* Dublin, Tomar Publishing 1989

Printed in Great Britain
by Amazon.co.uk, Ltd.,
Marston Gate.